CONTEMPORARY
Black
Biography

ISSN-1058-1316

CONTEMPORARY

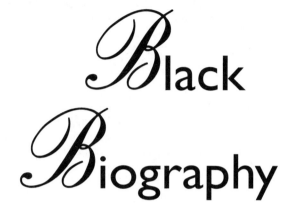

Black

Biography

Profiles from the International Black Community

Volume 31

Ashyia N. Henderson, Editor

GALE GROUP
™
THOMSON LEARNING

Detroit • New York • San Diego • San Francisco
Boston • New Haven, Conn. • Waterville, Maine
London • Munich

STAFF

Ashyia N. Henderson, *Editor*

Rebecca Parks, Jennifer M. York, *Contributing Editor*

Shelly Dickey, *Managing Editor, Multicultural Department*

Maria Franklin, *Permissions Manager*

Margaret Chamberlain, *Permissions Specialist*

Dorothy Maki, *Manufacturing Manager*

Stacy Melson, *Buyer*

Gary Leach, *Composition specialist*

Nataliya Mikheyeva, *Programmer/Analyst*

Barbara Yarrow, *Manager, Imaging and Multimedia Content*

Robyn V. Young, *Project Manager, Imaging and Multimedia Content*

Leitha Etheridge-Sims, Mary Grimes, David G. Oblender, *Image Cataloguers*

Randy Bassett, *Imaging Supervisor*

Robert Duncan, *Sr. Imaging Specialist*

Dan Newell, *Imaging Specialist*

ISBN 0–7876–5282–2

ISSN 1058–1316

10 9 8 7 6 5 4 3 2 1

Contemporary Black Biography
Advisory Board

Contents

Introduction

Contemporary Black Biography provides informative biographical profiles of the important and influential persons of African heritage who form the international black community: men and women who have changed today's world and are shaping tomorrow's. *Contemporary Black Biography* covers persons of various nationalities in a wide variety of fields, including architecture, art, business, dance, education, fashion, film, industry, journalism, law, literature, medicine, music, politics and government, publishing, religion, science and technology, social issues, sports, television, theater, and others. In addition to in-depth coverage of names found in today's headlines, *Contemporary Black Biography* provides coverage of selected individuals from earlier in this century whose influence continues to impact on contemporary life. *Contemporary Black Biography* also provides coverage of important and influential persons who are not yet household names and are therefore likely to be ignored by other biographical reference series. Each volume also includes listee updates on names previously appearing in CBB.

Designed for Quick Research and Interesting Reading

- *Attractive page design* incorporates textual subheads, making it easy to find the information you're looking for.

- *Easy-to-locate data sections* provide quick access to vital personal statistics, career informa-tion, major awards, and mailing addresses, when available.

- *Informative biographical essays* trace the subject's personal and professional life with the kind of in-depth analysis you need.

- *To further enhance your appreciation* of the subject, most entries include photographic portraits.

- *Sources for additional information* direct the user to selected books, magazines, and news-papers where more information on the individuals can be obtained.

Helpful Indexes Make It Easy to Find the Information You Need

Contemporary Black Biography includes cumulative Nationality, Occupation, Subject, and Name indexes that make it easy to locate entries in a variety of useful ways.

Available in Electronic Formats

Diskette/Magnetic Tape. *Contemporary Black Biography* is available for licensing on magnetic tape or diskette in a fielded format. Either the complete database or a custom selection of entries may be ordered. The database is available for internal data processing and nonpublishing purposes only. For more information, call (800) 877-GALE. **Online.** *Contemporary Black Biography* is available online through Mead Data Central's NEXIS Service in the NEXIS, PEOPLE and SPORTS Libraries in the GALBIO file.

Disclaimer

Contemporary Black Biography uses and lists websites as Sources and these websites may be obsolete.

We Welcome Your Suggestions

The editors welcome your comments and suggestions for enhancing and improving *Contemporary Black Biography*. If you would like to suggest persons for inclusion in the series, please submit these names to the editors. Mail comments or suggestions to:

The Editor
Contemporary Black Biography
Gale Group
27500 Drake Rd.
Farmington Hills, MI 48331–3535
Phone: (800) 347–4253

Photo Credits

PHOTOGRAPHS AND ILLUSTRATIONS APPEARING IN *CONTEMPORARY BLACK BIOGRAPHY*, **VOLUME 31, WERE RECEIVED FROM THE FOLLOWING SOURCES:**

Osceola Macarthy Adams

1890-1983

Actress, stage director

By the beginning of the twenty-first century, such African-American actors and actresses as Sidney Poitier, Ossie Davis, and Ruby Dee were thought of as pioneers who helped black performers break into the field of dramatic arts. Even before these famous names, however, came a generation of African-American theatrical figures whose efforts have been mostly shrouded in obscurity. Among them was Osceola Macarthy Adams, who worked under the stage name Osceola Archer. Her career stretched from the 1930s to the 1970s, and she taught or inspired, in addition to the three performers mentioned above, an entire generation of black dramatic talent.

Of tri-racial ancestry (black, white, and Native American), Osceola Marie Macarthy was born in Albany, Georgia, on June 13, 1890. The daughter of a life insurance executive, she benefitted from some of the best educational opportunities available to a Southern black woman of the time: after attending schools in Albany, she enrolled at the private Fisk University Preparatory School in Nashville and then at Howard University in Washington, D.C. She studied ancient Greek and philosophy. Her philosophy professor was Alain Locke, the influential editor of *The New Negro*. Macarthy and 21 other How-

ard students founded the Delta Sigma Theta sorority, an organization primarily devoted to community service. By the time of her death in 1983 there were 713 chapters of the sorority around the country.

Supported Husband's Medical Studies

Acting held an attraction for Macarthy from the start, and in the spring of her senior year, 1913, Adams made her stage debut at Howard in a student production. After graduating from Howard, Macarthy in 1915 married Numa P. G. Adams, who later became the first dean of Howard's medical school. At the time, however, Adams was still some time away from obtaining his own medical degree; the family moved to Chicago, and, facing considerable racial discrimination along the way, Adams completed his medical studies in 1929. While raising a young son, Osceola Adams helped to support her husband by working as a clothing designer at the J. Reinhardt firm in Chicago.

Perhaps grateful for the support and perhaps having premonitions of his own death that came in 1940, Dr. Numa Adams encouraged his wife to resume her dramatic studies. She enrolled at New York University,

At a Glance . . .

Born in Albany, GA, on June 13, 1890; died in New York, November 20, 1983; daughter of a life insurance executive; married Numa P.G. Adams, a physician and later dean of the Howard University Medical School; one son, Charles. *Education:* Fisk University Preparatory School, diploma; Howard University, B.A., 1913; New York University, M.A., 1936.

Career: Actress and director. Made stage debut in student production at Howard, 1913; worked as clothing designer in Chicago, 1920s, while her husband completed medical studies; made professional debut in summer theater, Putney, VT, 1934; adopted stage name Osceola Archer, 1930s; taught dramatic arts at Bennett College, NC, late 1930s; resident director, Putnam County (NY) Playhouse, 1946–56; top-level stage appearances, 1950s-1960s, including New York Shakespeare Festival production of Shakespeare's *Romeo and Juliet;* made television commercials, 1970s.

Member: American Negro Theater company, 1940–49; executive committee, Stage Door Canteen during World War II.

finishing an M.A. degree in 1936, and also taking acting and playwriting classes in hands-on theatrical organizations. In the summer theater season of 1934 she made her professional stage debut in the resort town of Putney, Vermont, playing a factory worker in a production called *Strange House;* that fall, she appeared on Broadway as a well-educated maid in Elmer Rice's play, *Between Two Worlds.* It was in the 1930s that she adopted the professional name of Osceola Archer.

After receiving her degree Adams taught dramatic arts for a time at Bennett College in North Carolina, and she taught on and off for much of the rest of her life. But, difficult as it was for blacks to find theatrical work of any kind, much less roles that broke away from established stereotypes, she nevertheless gravitated strongly to the stage. In 1940 she appeared in a touring production of Eugene O'Neill's *The Emperor Jones,* one of the few works by a white playwright of the time to feature multi-dimensional African-American characters. While on tour, Adams heard about her husband's death.

Directed Plays

At the pioneering American Negro Theater (ANT), a New York group that was among the first on-going

attempt to present black theatrical talent to the public, Adams added another facet to her repertoire of abilities: she directed several plays during her association with the group, which lasted from 1944 to 1948. Among them was a production of Thornton Wilder's *Our Town* in 1944; another was the comedy *On Strivers' Row* in 1946, whose touring cast included a then-unknown entertainer named Harold Belafonte (who within the decade would rocket to popularity as Harry Belafonte).

During her acting career Adams suffered discrimination in various forms. Light-skinned, she sometimes disguised herself as white to attend plays at the National Theater in segregated Washington during her days at Howard University. According to a *New York Times* interview, she sometimes lost roles because she was told, in her own words, "You're not Negroid enough, you're too light, you will photograph too white, your speech is too perfect." Through much of her career Adams worked to combat discrimination as a member of the Actors' Equity labor union and serving on the organization's Committee for Minority Affairs. As a result of an Actors' Equity boycott, the National Theater eventually reversed its whites-only admissions policy.

Despite the problems she encountered, Adams found increasing success in the 1940s and 1950s. She won friends in the industry as a member of the executive committee of the Stage Door Canteen, a New York eatery that entertained U.S. military personnel during World War II, and in 1946 she became resident director at the Putnam County Playhouse outside New York. Her ten-year tenure there gave her a measure of stability that permitted her to explore roles with greater depth and variety than she had previously attempted.

The 1950s and 1960s saw Adams grace the stages where some of the top dramatic productions in the United States were being presented. Twice she appeared in Arthur Miller's *The Crucible,* a play whose chilling portrayal of the Salem witchcraft trials in colonial America served as an indictment of 1950s anti-Communist hysteria and of the country's general closed-mindedness and bent toward irrational stereotyping. In 1960 she appeared in a New York Shakespeare Festival production of *Romeo and Juliet,* joining the company for a national tour of high schools and colleges the following year, and in 1963 she appeared at the same National Theater in Washington where she had worn disguises to attend plays as a student.

Adams appeared in the film *An Affair of the Skin* in 1963 and spoke out in later life about how cinematic opportunities had been denied her because of her race. In 1978 Delta Sigma Theta named its award for achievement in the arts, the Osceola, after her. She was active in her profession well past the usual retirement age and made television commercials into the late 1970s. Osceola Adams died in New York on November 20, 1983, at the age of 93.

Selected performances

The Emperor Jones, 1935 (with Paul Robeson)
Our Town, American Negro Theater, 1944 (director)
On Strivers' Row, American Negro Theater, 1946 (director)
The Crucible, 1953.
Romeo and Juliet, New York Shakespeare Festival, 1960.
Appeared in film *An Affair of the Skin,* 1963.

Sources

Books

Hine, Darlene Clark, *Black Women in America: An Historical Encyclopedia,* Carlson Publishing, 1993.
Mapp, Edward, *Directory of Blacks in the Performing Arts,* Scarecrow Press, 1990.
Mitchell, Loften, *Black Drama,* Hawthorn Books, 1967.
Notable Names in the American Theatre, James T. White and Co., 1976.

Periodicals

New York Times, August 27, 1968, p. 83; November 24, 1983, p. B16.
Washington Post, November 25, 1983, p. B6.

—James M. Manheim

Theodore M. Berry

1905-2000

Lawyer, Mayor, Civil Rights Activist

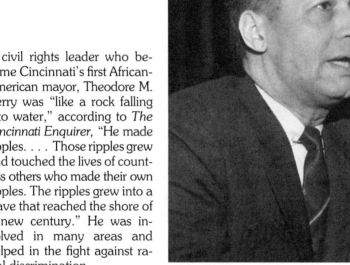

A civil rights leader who became Cincinnati's first African-American mayor, Theodore M. Berry was "like a rock falling into water," according to *The Cincinnati Enquirer,* "He made ripples. . . . Those ripples grew and touched the lives of countless others who made their own ripples. The ripples grew into a wave that reached the shore of a new century." He was involved in many areas and helped in the fight against racial discrimination.

Berry was born on November 8, 1905 in Maysville, Kentucky, the illegitimate son of a deaf-mute housekeeper, according to the *Center for Voting and Democracy* web site. The family moved to Cincinnati rather early in Berry's life, and as a child there Berry did many odd jobs to help support his family, including shoe shining, coal shoveling, laundry delivering, book shelving at the local library, and newspaper selling. He was forced, as a young child, to speak with very careful diction so that his mother could read his lips. This habit helped him later on as he became a famous public speaker, in and out of court. He was valedictorian of his 1924 high school class—Woodward High School—but according to *The Cincinnati Enquirer,* he was forbidden to walk next to his white classmates, and was instead forced to walk alone. Even this small honor didn't come

easily. According to *Horizons* online magazine, "[h]e had to win a speech writing competition. Which he did. When the administration realized the winner was black, however, they disqualified him and requested new entries. . . . Keenly aware of what was happening, Berry wrote under a pseudonym the second time. And won once again." The pseudonym he used was "Thomas Playfair," a rather apt name for a man unfairly treated. After high school he attended the University of Cincinnati where he obtained first an AB in 1928, and then an LLD in 1931. He paid for his education by working at the Newport steel mills.

Right from the start Berry was interested in helping people suffering from racial prejudices. His first professional job was as a county prosecutor. He opened his own law office with help from Charles Taft, a Cincinnati Charterite and son of former U. S. President William H. Taft. He worked at the Cincinnati Branch of the NAACP from 1932 to 1946. In 1937 he was admitted to the United States Supreme Court Bar.

Berry had a brief stint in Washington in 1942, working with black soldiers who were suffering from poor morale. The armed services were still segregated in 1942 when he was working with them, and Berry wanted to change that. After a short time, though, Berry saw that things were not going to change anytime soon, and he went back to Cincinnati. "They wanted to play games with words without making any real fundamental changes," he is quoted as saying in the *Center for Voting and Democracy* web site, "After nine months, I resigned and returned to Cincinnati."

In 1945 Thurgood Marshall, then national legal counsel of the NAACP, approached Berry to represent three Army Air Force officers from the Tuskegee Airmen unit. The three men were facing a court martial because they protested the segregation of the officers' club at Freeman Field in Seymour, Indiana. It was an important case in the eventual desegregation of the armed forces, and

Berry managed to win acquittals for two of the men. In 1995, the Air Force officially vindicated all men and gave a pardon to the one who had been convicted. And in 1996 the Tuskegee Airmen gave an official thank you to the man who had defended them 50 years before.

Berry ran for the Cincinnati City Council in 1947, but lost. He was elected to the Council in 1949, however, and was elected as vice mayor in 1955. It was believed that he was the most likely choice of mayor in the 1957 election but because of a change in the voting method, he came in 14 out of 18 contestants. There were whispers of racial prejudice because the new voting structure gave little weight to the black vote, but this situation did not stop Theodore Berry. The following year Berry created Cincinnati's first Community Action Commission, which caught the attention of Washington, D.C. When the president asked him, Berry left the Cincinnati City Council and went back to Washington in 1964, this time to serve as a high official in President Lyndon B. Johnson's war on poverty. In 1965 President Johnson appointed him head of the Community Action Programs in the Office of Economic Opportunity (OEO), which included the initiation of such programs as Head Start, Jobs Corps, and Legal Services.

In 1970 when Richard M. Nixon was elected president, Berry returned to the Cincinnati City Council, and two years later, on December 1, 1972, he was finally elected mayor. *The Cincinnati Enquirer* said of the event, "[t]he moment that came in December 1972 was an important piece of political symbolism, marred only by the fact that it should have come 15 years earlier." It was seen as the triumphant pinnacle of Berry's career. He served in this position for four years.

Declining health eventually removed Berry from the public eye but not from its heart. In the year 2000 Berry died in the Lodge Care Center nursing home in Loveland, Ohio, just outside of Cincinnati, according to *Jet*. *The Cincinnati Post* made a note on October 23rd that Theodore Berry was being honored with flags at half-staff for 30 days. This honor is usually reserved for the president, but it seems apt that a man who fought for so long for racial equality should so be honored. To show that Cincinnati has not forgotten the man who loved and did so much for it, the Theodore M. Berry Head Start Children and Family Learning Center is slated to open in late 2001. Also in honor of the late mayor is a proposed riverfront park to be named for Berry, an honor for a man who Mayor Charlie Luken told *The Cincinnati Enquirer* was "one of the greatest Cincinnatians of all time. A kind man, an intelligent man. A true statesman in every respect. He led our city to a better place in the area of civil rights."

Sources

Periodicals

The Cincinnati Enquirer, October 16, 2000; October 19, 2000.

The Cincinnati Post, January 15, 1996; May 24, 1996; June 20, 1997, p. 16A; July 2, 1997, p. 10A; May 28, 1996; April 25, 1997; June 10, 1997; June 13, 1997; October 23, 2000.

Dayton Daily News, October 27, 2000.

Jet, November 6, 2000.

Los Angeles Times, October 20, 2000, p. B7.

New York Times, October 17, 2000, p. B12.

Online

http://www.fairvote.org/pr/berry.thm.

http://www.horizons.uc.edu/ JustCommunityMay2000/LegendsStruggles.htm.

—Catherine Donaldson

Kurtis Blow

1959-

Rapper

Considered by some the "King of Rap," Kurtis Blow is at the very least one of the genre's leading pioneers. For many years rap's best-selling solo artist, Blow was the first rap artist to release a major-label single, 1979's "The Breaks," and the first rapper to sell over a million copies. Blow's profile dropped in the late 1980s and the hardcore hip-hop sound began to take over. Inspired by his role in the rap film *Krush Groove,* he then sought to test his mettle as an actor. Blow's career was revived somewhat in the 1990s as interest grew in the "old-school" rap of his heyday. He hosted a radio show called "The Old-School Show," and organized a concert tour of some of rap's pioneers called "The Old-School Reunion Tour."

Born Kurt Walker on August 9, 1959, in New York City's Harlem borough, Blow enrolled in the City College of New York in 1976, where he studied vocal performance. He became program director of the college's radio station, and started hanging out with friends and City College fellows who would become rap legends. His circle in those days included Grandmaster Flash, Mele Mel, and future rap producer and co-founder of the Def Jam record label, Russell Simmons, among others.

Rap's First Major Label Artist

As early as 1976, Blow was rapping in Harlem clubs, including Small's Paradise and Charles Gallery. Blow borrowed heavily from his inspirations, including Cool DJ Herc, a Jamaican who has been described, according to the *Los Angeles Times,* as the "Godfather of Hip-Hop," and "blatantly copping rhymed lines from an originator of rap, Deejay Hollywood (Anthony Halloway)," according to the *Rolling Stone Encyclopedia of Rock & Roll.* Blow began his career with Russell Simmons as his manager and Simmons's younger brother, Joey—who would become Run of Run-DMC—on the turntables.

In 1979 Blow recorded the single "Christmas Rapping," which was co-written by *Billboard* columnist Rocky Ford. The song became an underground hit, and attracted the interest of the Mercury record label. Blow was the first rap artist to sign to a major label and released "The Breaks," from his forthcoming debut album, 1980's *Kurtis Blow.* "The Breaks" made it to Number four on *Billboard's* R&B chart and was certified gold for sales over a million. The single brought Blow up from the underground and placed him at the forefront of commercially successful rap.

At a Glance . . .

Born Kurt Walker on August 9, 1959, in Harlem, NY; married; children: three sons. *Education*: City College of New York, studied vocal performance, 1976.

Career: Worked as a club DJ in Harlem, began rapping, c. 1976; changed his stage name from Kool DJ Kurt to Kurtis Blow; released hit holiday single "Holiday Rapping," 1979; signed a record contract with Mercury Records, becoming first rap artist to cut records for a major label; released single "The Breaks," 1979; released first LP, *Kurtis Blow*, 1980; toured United States and Europe with Davey D, 1980–81; *Deuce*, 1981; *Party Time?*, 1983; appeared in the film *Krush Groove*, 1983; *Ego Trip*, 1984; appeared in commercials for Sprite, 1986; organized all-star King Dream Chorus and Holiday Crew to record the Martin Luther King tribute, "King Holiday"; *Kingdom Blow*, 1986; recorded anti-drug song, "Ya Gotta Say No," 1987; wrote rap segments for the soap opera *One Life to Live*, 1991–92; hosted radio program "The Old School Show" on KPWR-FM, 1995; organized "Old-School Reunion Tour," featuring rappers Grandmaster Flash, Whodini, Sugarhill Gang, and Kool Moe Dee, 1999.

Awards: Named Producer of the Year in New York for his work with Sweet G, Dr. Jekyll and Mr. Hyde, and the Fearless Four, 1983–85.

Addresses: c/o Allied Artists Entertainment Group, 1801 Avenue of the Stars, suite 600, Los Angeles, CA, 10067.

As the 1980s wore on, Blow's career began to wane. Rap was becoming increasingly harder-edged and began to outgrow its innocence. Blow's 1983 five-song EP, *Party Time?*, deserved more attention than it got, according to critic Ron Wynn in the *All Music Guide*, but failed to make waves beyond peaking at Number 67 on the UK charts. 1984's *Ego Trip* produced the novelty single, "Basketball," which made it to Number 71 in the United States, but failed to win critics' favor.

Though his own star was fading, Blow increasingly became known for his talents as a producer, guiding the sounds of such acts as Sweet G, Dr. Jekyll and Mr. Hyde, and the Fearless Four. He was named Producer of the Year in New York for three consecutive years, 1983–85. In 1985, Blow appeared on a single by René & Angela called "Save Your Love (For Number One)," and on the Artists United Against Apartheid single, "Sun City." Though it produced what would be his last, albeit lukewarm, hit, "I'm Chillin'," Blow's 1986 album, *Kingdom Blow*, was a "commercial and critical flop," according to

a review found on *RollingStone.com*, as was 1988's *Back by Popular Demand*. In 1987 Blow wrote and recorded the anti-drug rap "Ya Gotta Say No" with funding from President Ronald Reagan's "War on Drugs" campaign.

On Screen in Krush Groove

Blow made an appearance on the big screen in 1985's hip-hop drama, *Krush Groove*. The story is based on the life of Russell Simmons, and stars pop artist Sheila E., Run-DMC, The Fat Boys, Dr. Jekyll and Mr. Hyde, and Blow. In the movie, Run-DMC has a hit record on their hands, but no money to press copies of it. The fictitious young record producer, Russell Walker, played by Blair Underwood, borrows money from a shady character while attempting to woo Sheila E. Though it won only lukewarm reviews, the film has become something of a cult classic—a visual piece of rap history. Blow has also appeared on the small screen on the soap opera *One Life to Live*, and wrote some rap segments for the show in the early 1990s.

After the moderate success of *Krush Groove*, Blow moved to Woodland Hills, California with his wife and three sons to pursue an acting career in Hollywood. His acting career didn't take off beyond an appearance in a Sprite ad, but Blow found himself back on the radio airwaves. As a weekend DJ and Sunday host of "The Old-School Show" on Los Angeles' KPWR-FM, Blow revisited the music of rap's early days and played the soul, funk, and R&B standards that inspired rap's pioneers. A renewed interest in "old-school" music in general had breathed a little life into Blow's waning career. When Blow started hearing some of his old hits on the radio, he saw it as an opportunity for a comeback. A variety of guests made appearances on the weekly four-hour show, including pop singer Jody Watley, rappers Tone-Loc and Ice-T, and Blow's old pals Run-DMC.

The Old-School Revival

Blow's radio show evolved into 1999's "Old-School Reunion Tour," featuring rappers Grandmaster Flash, Whodini, Sugarhill Gang, and Kool Moe Dee. The tour played dates across the United States, but "What could have been an enjoyable evening of old-school hip-hop," wrote Soren Baker in the *Los Angeles Times*, ". . . turned into a showcase for a group of narcissistic artists who seemed more concerned with celebrating themselves than their music's achievements." The aging rappers appeared to be moving a little slow, Baker noted. She did add, however, that Blow's performance—backed by the

New York City Breakers break-dancing crew—was the "most enjoyable" of the show.

While Blow respected the work today's hard-core rappers have done to succeed, he lamented that rap and hip-hop have evolved into such a negative stereotype. "I have mixed feelings," he told Crowe in the *Los Angeles Times.* "I hate it because you work so hard . . . to build something positive . . . and it turns out to be negative. And that's not cool." While commercially successful rappers like Eminem, Snoop Dogg, and the late Tupac Shakur's rhymes are peppered with expletives and other controversial lyrics, Blow never even so much as uttered a single curse word on any of his releases. The rapper himself believed that his cleaner, more philosophical rhymes were the reason his career took a downturn. Blow told the *Los Angeles Times,* "The sacrifice was I didn't sell a lot of records [after his initial success], because a lot of people thought my stuff was corny."

Selected discography

Kurtis Blow, Mercury, 1980.
Deuce, Mercury, 1981.
Tough, Mercury, 1982.
Ego Trip, Mercury, 1984.
Rapper in Town, Mercury, 1984.
America, Mercury, 1985.
Kingdom Blow, Mercury, 1986.
The Breaks, Mercury, 1986
Back by Popular Demand, Mercury, 1988.
The Best of Kurtis Blow, Mercury, 1994.
Only the Strong Survive, Mercury.

Sources

Books

Erlewine, Michael, editor, *All Music Guide,* Miller Freeman Books, 1997.
Larkin, Colin, editor, *Encyclopedia of Popular Music,* Muze UK Ltd., 1998.
Pareles, Jon, and Romanowski, Patricia, editors, *Rolling Stone Encyclopedia of Rock & Roll,* Rolling Stone Press, 1983.
Rees, Dafydd, and Crampton, Luke, *Encyclopedia of Rock Stars,* DK Publishing, 1996.

Periodicals

Entertainment Weekly, February 21, 1992, p. 52.
Los Angeles Times, September 24, 1995, p. 76; September 14, 1999, p. 2.
Time, November 18, 1985, p. 94.
Washington Post, January 4, 1987, p. G3.

Online

AMG All Music Guide, http://www.allmusic.com (July 10, 2001).
Internet Movie Database, http://www.imdb.com (August 21, 2001).
Rolling Stone, http://www.rollingstone.com (August 3, 2001).

—Brenna Sanchez

Elton Brand

1979-

Professional basketball player

Named the National Basketball Association's Co-Rookie of the Year in 2000, Elton Brand was one of professional basketball's most promising young players at the dawn of the new century. But he was more than that: at the tender age of 21, he had become something of a team leader for the rebuilding Chicago Bulls. Basketball observers noted his ability and his devotion to hard work, but they also sensed a quality sometimes lacking at the top level of professional sports and especially surprising in a player who had skipped the last two years of his college career—maturity. "He's very mature for his age," Bulls guard B. J. Armstrong told *Sports Illustrated*. "He's like a 40-year-old man trapped inside the body of a 20-year-old."

Many observers have wondered about the source of Brand's almost supernatural calm in pressure-packed and often frustrating situations, but he and his family point to religion. Elton Brand was born north of New York City in Peekskill, New York, on March 11, 1979. Raised by his single mother Daisy Brand (and given his first name by his nine-years-older half-brother Artie), he grew up in an environment in which importance was placed on church attendance. "Going to church has had a peaceful effect on me," Brand told the *New York*

Times. "I just don't seem to get upset. When I do, I usually keep it inside of me and use it when I'm playing."

Growing up in Peekskill's Dunbar Heights Housing Complex, Brand lacked positive role models. "Living in an apartment complex like I do, a lot of the people smoke weed, but they don't approach me with that because they know I'm on a mission," he told the *Times*. "Even though we live in an environment that says you don't have much money and you're not going anywhere," his mother added, "Elton always saw himself as being somebody."

Mother Focused Him on Basketball

Brand took up basketball at age 10. With his massive frame—he weighed close to 250 pounds as a junior at Peekskill High School—he could easily have chosen to become a football player or divided his time and energy between the two sports. But his mother recognized where his true passion lay. "He wanted to play football and I wouldn't let him," she told the *New York Times*. "He wakes up basketball and he sleeps it. He pursues it. It is him."

At a Glance . . .

Born March 11, 1979, in Peekskill, New York; raised by mother, Daisy Brand. *Education:* Peekskill High School, diploma, 1997; attended Duke University, Durham, NC.

Career: Professional basketball player. High school standout heavily recruited by top national college basketball programs; led Duke team to NCAA finals as sophomore, 1999; became No. 1 pick in 1999 pro draft; signed to Chicago Bulls; traded to Los Angeles Clippers, 2001.

Awards: Atlantic Coast Conference Player of the Year and AP All-America selection, 1999; shared Rookie of the Year award with Steve Francis, 2000.

Addresses: *Team office*—Los Angeles Clippers, 1111 S. Figueroa St., Suite 1100, Los Angeles, CA 90015.

Despite his devotion to basketball, though, Brand never neglected his academic studies. While academic eligibility is sometimes a problem for phenomenal young basketball players, Brand's admission to highly competitive Duke University was never in doubt. During his high school junior year, Brand took honors or advanced-placement courses in English, chemistry, and American history, topping those off with doses of trigonometry and third-year Spanish. As a senior he ranked sixteenth academically in a class of 160. "Elton's an all-around, terrific kid," Peekskill guidance counselor Eleanor Frank Frey told the *Times.* "He's caring, kind, considerate and respectful. He doesn't have an attitude of superiority, and he could very well have that. He's a male mentor for freshman students."

Played in AAU League

On the court Brand was sensational, attracting visits from coaches of powerhouse basketball programs from all over the country. He led the Peekskill High team to two state championships, averaging nearly 26 points per game over his high school career. Brand was named a McDonald's All-American in his senior year and also played for the powerful Riverside Church (Manhattan, New York City) team in the off-season Amateur Athletic Union (AAU).

Over his two years at Duke, Brand seemed on his way to shattering school records. As a freshman, despite missing 15 games with a broken foot, he was named to the all-Atlantic Coast Conference freshman team and played a key role in Duke's advance to the quarterfinals of the National Collegiate Athletic Association's postseason

championship tournament, "Elite Eight." As a sophomore he averaged 17.7 points and 9.8 rebounds per game, won ACC Player of the Year, several national player-of-the-year awards, and led Duke to the national finals.

Despite his stated intentions to finish college, Brand left Duke after his sophomore year, becoming the first player ever under Duke coach Mike Krzyzewski to jump to the pros. The reason was simply that physically, technically, and emotionally, Brand was ready for the NBA. Of course, some expected Brand to encounter the same rude awakening faced by other college stars as they collide for the first time with courts full of players whose abilities are equal to their own. Adding to the challenge was a new set of technical skills to be learned: at 6' 8" Brand had played the position of center through high school and college, but in the pros, where seven-footers are common, he could no longer dominate the basket area through sheer size. He became a "power forward"—a forward who often drives to the basket and actively competes for rebounds on defense.

Named Rookie of the Year

Brand was the number one pick in the NBA draft of June of 1999. He was selected by the Chicago Bulls, a team that had struggled since the retirement of superstar Michael Jordan and other key players in the 1990s. Brand quickly adapted to the challenges he faced and emerged as a calming and unifying influence on the fresh group of Bulls players. He seemed unfazed by the big players he faced, barely breaking stride from his Duke totals as he averaged 20.1 points and 10 rebounds per game in his first year. His only frustrations came as a result of the Bulls' losing record—he had come out on the losing end of very few basketball games before coming to Chicago. In May of 2000, Brand shared NBA Rookie of the Year honors with Houston Rockets guard Steve Francis.

Through much of the 2000–2001 season Brand was hailed as the linchpin of a possible new Chicago dynasty, as a potential successor to Michael Jordan himself. Brand duplicated his 1999–2000 points-per-game total of 20.1 and, showing equal consistency, improved his rebounds per game from 10.0 to 10.1; his 3.9 offensive rebounds per game were the second best in the NBA. The Bulls' fortunes did not improve, however, and in August of 2001 Brand was traded to the Los Angeles Clippers; the Bulls received two players in exchange. Regardless of where he played, it seemed likely that he would continue to offer fans some basketball heroics and to support his teammates with that rare quality called leadership.

Sources

Periodicals

Basketball Digest, Summer 2000, p. 50.

Chicago Sun-Times, March 29, 2000, p. 125.
Jet, May 29, 2000, p. 47; August 6, 2001, p. 55.
New York Times, February 25, 1996, p. Westchester-1;
    January 10, 1997, p. B12; March 23, 2000, p. D1.
Sport, January 1999, p. 84.
The Sporting News, November 20, 2000, p. 46.
Sports Illustrated, November 1, 1999, p. 180.

Online

http://www.nba.com.
http://www.usatoday.com/sports/basketba/99draf/
    brand.htm.

—James M. Manheim

Jesse Leroy Brown

1926-1950

Naval aviator

Jesse Leroy Brown was the first African American to complete Navy pilot training and become a Naval aviator. Doing so was one of his greatest challenges—fighting his way to such an illustrious place in the armed services at a time when the military was still segregated and most traditionalists felt that there was no place of honor in the Navy for anyone who was not a white male. Born on October 13, 1926 in Hattiesburg, Mississippi, Brown grew up poor, the son of a sharecropper. He graduated second in his class from Eureka High School in 1944 where he excelled as both an athlete and a scholar.

Despite suggestions that he attend a traditionally "black" university, Brown applied for and attended Ohio State University, studying engineering from 1944 to 1947. On July 8, 1946 he enlisted in the U. S. Navy Reserves, and in 1947 he joined the Navy proper as an aviation cadet. He attended pre-flight school in Ottumwa, Iowa, and after that moved to Pensacola and Jacksonville, Florida to attend flight school. In 1948 Brown became the first African American to earn his Navy wings despite what the *Acepilots* web site called "racist resistance to an African-American studying aeronautics and aviation." Out of 100 candidates to enter the aviation program at Pensacola, Brown was one of only six men who completed it.

On April 15, 1949 Brown was commissioned an ensign in the United States Navy, and in October of 1950, he embarked on the *USS Leyte* (CV-32) to join the United Nations Force in Korea. While there, Brown was a pilot with the 32nd Fighter Squadron flying F4U-4 Corsair

fighters. He rose quickly to the position of section leader. He was of great help in the Korean conflict, winning an Air Medal and a Korean Service Medal for his 20 daring air combat missions over such places as Wonsan, Songjin, Sinanju, and Chongjin where he attacked military installations and transportation routes. According to the *Crosswinds* web site, "Leading his section in the face of hostile anti-aircraft fire, he courageously pressed home attacks that inflicted heavy losses on the enemy and provided effective support for friendly ground troops."

On December 4, 1950, while Brown was again attacking enemies in defense of the United States Marines near the Chosin Reservoir, his plane was hit by enemy fire and Brown was forced to land his plane in "a wheels-up landing in the best place he could find—a clearing that looked reasonably flat. . . . when it slammed into the ground, it bent 30 degrees at the cockpit," according to *Air & Space* magazine. The Chosin Reservoir was notorious for being overrun with Chinese Communists, and all the men flying with Brown that day knew that meant he could be found by the enemy at any time. While one of the men flew to a higher altitude to radio to the ship to send a medical emergency helicopter, the other men circled around the crash site to see if there was any sign that Ensign Brown was still alive.

Captain (then Lieutenant, Junior Grade) Thomas J. Hudner who was flying alongside Brown at the time as his wingman, saw Brown waving from his cockpit. Because he was not extricating himself from the crash, which had begun to smoke and seemed to be in danger of going up

At a Glance . . .

Born on October 13, 1926 in Hattiesburg, Mississippi; died at war in Korea on December 4, 1950; married Daisy Pearl; daughter: Pamela. *Education*: Attended Ohio State University, 1944–47.

Career: U.S. Navy Reserves, 1946–47; Aviator, U.S. Navy, 1947–49; Ensign and Aviator, U.S. Navy, 1949–50.

Awards: Air Medal; Korean Service Medal; Purple Heart; Distinguished Flying Cross; *USS Jesse L. Brown*, named for Brown, 1972; Ensign Jesse L. Brown Memorial Combined Bachelor Quarters, named for Brown, 1997; County Tax Services Building, Hattiesburg, Mississippi, named for Brown, 2000.

in flames at any minute, Hudner figured either Brown was so hurt he couldn't move, or that he was stuck. Before he even received approval from his flight leader, Hudner crashed his plane alongside Brown's in order to save him. He figured that the helicopter could come and pick them both up. The Navy Public Affairs Library records Hudner as having said in an interview with *Jax Air News*, the newspaper at the Naval Air Station at Jacksonville, Florida, "I knew what I had to do. I was not going to leave him down there for the Chinese. Besides, it was 30 degrees below zero on that slope, and he was a fellow aviator. My association with the Marines had rubbed off on me. They don't leave wounded Marines behind."

Hudner crashed a bit more violently than he had meant to but was still able to get out of his plane and run over to Brown's plane to see what had happened. Brown was indeed stuck in the plane; the cockpit had buckled in quite a lot upon impact, and his leg was crushed and jammed between equipment and the metal hull. Hudner tried to keep Brown warm, but even by the time he reached him 30 minutes after his crash, Brown's hands were completely frozen. Not knowing what else to do, Hudner radioed to the helicopter pilot to bring an ax to try to free Brown from the wreckage. When the helicopter pilot came, the two men tried vainly to free him, but were unable to break the metal surrounding Brown's leg. Despite these heroic efforts to save him, Jesse Leroy Brown died that day, perishing in the wreckage of his plane. According to *Discovering Multicultural America*, "Brown was the first African-American naval officer to lose his life in combat." He was posthumously awarded the Purple Heart and the Distinguished Flying Cross for his exceptional courage, airmanship, and devotion to duty.

In March 18, 1972 Brown was honored with a ship named after him, the *USS Jesse L. Brown*, a Knox class

destroyer escort. It was the first ship named after an African American. It was built at the Avondale Shipyards in Westwego, Louisiana and was commissioned in February 1973—both Daisy Brown, Brown's widow, and Thomas Hudner went to the commissioning ceremony. The ship was decommissioned in 1998 at the Pensacola Naval Air Station and given to the Egyptian Navy. According to the *Acepilots* web site, "retired Captain Thomas Hudner decried the sale and the neglect of Brown's ship, saying, 'We need everything we can in race relations.'" This might not be the end of Brown's name on a ship; however, for according to *Jet*, "The ship's former spokesman, Lt. J.G. John Rec, said the Navy is considering naming another ship for Brown."

In 1997 another honor was bestowed upon the ensign from Mississippi. The Naval Air Station Meridian in Mississippi dedicated the Ensign Jesse L. Brown Memorial Combined Bachelor Quarters to his memory. And according to *Jet*, in November of 2000 "a $2.6 million county tax services building was dedicated in his memory in Hattiesburg, [Mississippi]." A biography was written about him in 1998 called *The Flight of Jesse Leroy Brown*, written by Theodore Taylor with full cooperation from Daisy Pearl Brown Thorne. It is hoped that Brown's story will remain one of inspiration and honor for years to come.

Sources

CD-ROM

DISCovering Multicultural America, Gale Research, 1996.

Periodicals

Air & Space, June/July, 2000.
Jet, August 22, 1994, p. 38; November 10, 1997, p. 17; March 19, 2001.

Online

http://www.plateau.net/usndd/ff1089.
http://www.crosswinds.net/~jessebrown/jlb.html.
www.history.navy.mil/photos/pers-us/uspers-b/j-brown.htm.
http://www.acepilots.com/korea_hudner.html.
http://www.chinfo.navy.mil/navpalib/news/navywire/nwsb97/nwsb0203.txt.
http://216.85.248.206/brotherhood/hudner.html.
http://www.drum.ncat.edu/~carter/jessel.html.

—Catherine Donaldson

Kobe Bryant

1978-

Professional basketball player

At the age of 18 years 2 months and 11 days, Kobe Bryant became the youngest man ever to play in the National Basketball Association (NBA). Bryant bypassed college and moved straight from high school to the NBA, a feat accomplished by only 27 other players in the long history of the league. Drafted by the Charlotte Hornets on July 11, 1996, Bryant soon found himself traded to the Los Angeles Lakers, where he became the youngest player ever to make that West Coast team. He has been a Laker ever since, joining stars such as Shaquille O'Neal and Nick Van Exel in the team lineup.

Basketball players who have had some college experience often find the move to the NBA a tough adjustment. How much harder it must be, then, to arrive in the league as an 18-year-old high school graduate. Bryant's transition was hardly a smooth one, but he handled the media attention, the new expectations, the travel, and all the challenges with a dignity and determination far beyond his years. Asked about his sudden stardom in the *Los Angeles Times*, Bryant responded: "It's crazy. If you sit back and start thinking about it, maybe you could be overwhelmed by the situation. You've just got to keep going slowly and keep working hard on your basketball skills. Then, I don't think your head can swell because

you won't have time to think about it."

At six-feet seven-inches tall and 210 pounds, Bryant was hardly too small or frail to compete in the NBA. Observers cited his size, agility, and shot-making ability when predicting his future contributions to pro basketball. Another asset was his awareness of both the perks and the pitfalls of life as an NBA star—an awareness fostered by watching his own father play professional ball. "Basketball is kind of like life," Bryant explained in the *Philadelphia Inquirer*. "It can get rough at times. You can get knocked on your butt a couple of times. But what you have to do is get up and hold your head high and try again."

The youngest of three children born to Joe and Pam Bryant, Kobe Bryant was born in Philadelphia in 1978—the year before Magic Johnson joined the Lakers. The Lakers press guide stated his parents named him after a type of steak they saw on a restaurant menu shortly before he was born. Bryant's father was in the midst of a 16-year pro basketball career that first took the family through Philadelphia, San Diego, and Houston, and then took them overseas to an Italian league. When not

At a Glance . . .

Born on August 23, 1978, in Philadelphia, PA; son of Joe (a professional basketball player and coach) and Pam Bryant; married Vanessa Laine, 2001. *Education:* Graduate of Lower Merion High School, Ardmore, PA.

Career: Professional basketball player, 1996-. Drafted 13th pick in the first round of the 1996 National Basketball Association (NBA) draft by Charlotte Hornets; traded to Los Angeles Lakers, July 1996; signed with Lakers, July 24, 1996.

Selected awards Named National High School Player of the Year by *USA Today,* 1996; named Naismith Player of the Year, 1996; named Gatorade Circle of Champions High School Player of the Year, 1996; named to McDonald's All-American team, 1996; played in NBA Rookie All-Star Game, 1997; won Slam Dunk competition during 1997 NBA All-Star Weekend.

Addresses: *Home*–Pacific Palisades, CA. *Office*–Los Angeles Lakers, P.O. Box 10, Inglewood, CA 90306–0010.

traveling with his team, Joe "Jellybean" Bryant played sports with his children, teaching them his moves. Kobe proved to be a particularly apt student, and he adored his father. Said Bryant in the *New York Times*: "Other kids don't have a father. I don't have anything in common with them. My father's my best friend. Those kids say I lead a Beaver Cleaver life. I don't care."

Kobe was five years old when his father left the NBA and moved the family to Pistoia, Italy. There the elder Bryant competed eight more years in the Italian Professional Basketball League. Since no one in the Bryant family could speak Italian at first, the bonds between members grew even closer as they struggled with learning another language. "We didn't have anybody to depend on but our family. We had to stick together," Bryant remembered in the Riverside, California, *Press-Enterprise*. Kobe got along well with his sisters Sharia and Shaya, and—when time allowed—he played hoops with his dad. He also played soccer, a favorite sport in Italy.

High School Standout

When Joe Bryant's pro career ended in 1991, the family returned to the United States and settled in a comfortable home on the Main Line—the most prestigious of Philadelphia's suburban areas. Thirteen-year-old Kobe surprised his fellow students at Lower Merion High School

in Ardmore: they marveled at the young black man who could speak Italian fluently but who was relatively unaware of the hip urban attitudes popular among teens. In a *Los Angeles Times* profile Bryant recalled that time: "It was kind of strange because, being away, I didn't know a lot of the slang that kids used. Kids would come up to me and say whatever, and I'd just nod."

Basketball helped bridge the gap between Bryant and his classmates at Lower Merion High. Tall and skilled, Bryant quickly became a starter for the varsity team and just as quickly began to make a name for himself in the greater-Philadelphia region. While Bryant became a national star in the late 1990s, he was a local celebrity for years—and that level of attention helped to prepare him for the heightened attention he received in the NBA. He refused to make his ambitions to play in the NBA secret even though many people advised him to pursue safer goals. His parents, however, supported his dreams, and his high school coach, Gregg Downer, offered encouragement. "When I first met [Kobe], at age 13, and I saw him play, after five minutes I said, 'This kid is going to be a pro,'" Downer told the *Los Angeles Times*. "Never was there one moment I doubted that. That it would happen so quickly, I may have doubted that. But I knew if he progressed so quickly and continued to make good decisions, he would someday get there."

Bryant concluded his high school career as the all-time leading scorer in the history of Southeastern Pennsylvania basketball. His 2,883 points far surpassed the 2,359 points of Hall-of-Famer Wilt Chamberlain. As a junior, he was named Pennsylvania's high school player of the year. In Bryant's senior year he led the Lower Merion Aces to a season record of 31–3 and the Class-AAAA state championship. He averaged 30.8 points, 12 rebounds, 6.5 assists, 4 steals, and 3.8 blocked shots per game. Accolades poured in from both local and national sources. *USA Today* named him National High School Player of the Year, and he also won the Naismith Player of the Year citation. Downer told the *Los Angeles Times*, "I know the high school market very well and I've watched it for close to 20 years, and to think there could be another player come into my hands and be this good, that's an abstract concept. [Kobe's] blessed with a lot of natural ability and great genes, but the work ethic is his and it's very strong. Kobe has the skills and the maturity and everything you could want."

Bypassed College for the Pros

Not surprisingly, Bryant was offered scholarships to almost every major college and university in the country. Not only was he a brilliant basketball player, he was also a good student, scoring an above-average 1100 on his Scholastic Aptitude Test (SAT). Bryant and his parents remained coy about his future, however. They realized that they faced a momentous decision: whether to bypass college completely and go straight into the NBA draft. In the meantime, Bryant leaped into national prominence when the media learned that he would be escorting pop star Brandy to his high school prom in downtown Philadelphia.

Just before prom time, Bryant called a news conference to declare his decision to make himself available for the 1996 NBA draft in June. Philadelphia sports fans who had expected Bryant to enroll at one of the local colleges greeted the announcement with jeers. The criticism escalated when Joe Bryant quit his job as an assistant coach at La Salle University in order to manage his son's career. Answering all his detractors in the *New York Times*, Joe Bryant stated, "Would Kobe be more accepted going to the NBA if he'd been a dummy? Do you have to be poor, with five kids, living on welfare?" He concluded, "Kobe should have had the key to the city. Instead they tried to crucify him. No one saw how special he is."

No one, that is, except the Charlotte Hornets, who chose Bryant as the thirteenth pick in the first round of the 1996 NBA draft. No one but Adidas, who swooped in to sign the young star to a product endorsement contract. No one but Brandy, who praised her prom date as a terrific guy and invited him to guest-star on her television show, *Moesha*. And no one but the Los Angeles Lakers, who traded veteran center Vlade Divac to obtain the untested rookie. A month shy of his eighteenth birthday, Kobe Bryant signed a three-year, $3.5 million contract with the Los Angeles Lakers and moved into a mansion in Pacific Palisades, California. If anyone could be said to be "on top of the world," it was Bryant.

Faced Reality Check

Poised for greatness, Bryant took the Southern California Summer Pro League by storm. He appeared in four games—drawing huge overflow crowds— and netted 27 points in one game and 36 in another. Then, just before training camp was due to start in September, he broke his wrist playing pickup ball and could not practice for five weeks. This setback effectively undercut his first chance to learn the NBA style of play. To make matters worse, he took a body shot from an opponent in Philadelphia during an exhibition game in October of 1996 and missed not only the rest of the preseason but also the season opener in November.

The injuries gave Bryant a huge disadvantage during the Lakers' regular season. Lakers coach Del Harris explained in the Riverside, California, *Press-Enterprise* that "You've got to figure that not only did [Kobe] skip college, he also skipped training camp. Given that, the fact that he was able to compete at this level by January [1997] is incredible—especially with a team that's been in first or second place all year, rather than a team that might say, 'Well, we're not going anywhere anyway, so let's play the young guys.'"

Harris saw Bryant as a journeyman who needed more training in the pro game and restricted his playing time accordingly. Bryant warmed the bench, averaging 15.5 minutes, 7.6 points, 1.3 assists, and 1.9 rebounds in 71 regular season appearances. Naturally the former high school star who had pretty much carried his previous team on his back felt frustrated by the limited play. "One of the hardest things this year was not knowing whether you're going to play or how many minutes you're going to play," Bryant acknowledged in an Associated Press report. "But at the same time that kind of helps you, because you just have to be ready every night."

Bryant's chance to shine as a rookie came during the All-Star break, when he scored 31 points in the Rookie All-Star Game and aced the slam-dunk title with a dramatic shot that began between his legs. That moment of fame was some compensation for his slow start as a professional, and it served to reinforce his coaches' conviction that he would make an impact within a year or two.

In the meantime, the debate still raged over whether Bryant took a wrong turn when he decided to skip college. As Theresa Smith observed in the *Orange County Register*, "It's still too early. . . . If he hadn't turned pro, he'd be learning strategy and refining skills in frequent practice sessions, and starring for a Top 25 team two days a week. Instead, his practice time is limited by a rigorous game and travel schedule and his game time is limited by Harris, who has the incongruous task of developing young talent and winning at the same time." *The New York Times* quoted Harris as expressing similar frustrations: "I don't want to be remembered .. .. [as] the guy who wouldn't let Kobe Bryant play." He also observed, "I have to do it. I can't give him special treatment just because he's 18. He elected to come into a man's world and he'll have to play by a man's rules."

That "man's world" presents many challenges for a person of Bryant's age. Not yet old enough to order an alcoholic beverage legally and enormously wary of the multitude of other temptations beckoning NBA players, he generally kept to himself both at home and on the road. His parents often traveled with him, and they lived in his Pacific Palisades home. Bryant had no regrets about his busy schedule or his level of responsibility, however. "It's fun," he enthused in an Associated Press report. "I'm in the NBA. No way I'm bored. In four years, then I'll probably be like, 'Oh, God. We've got another road trip.' Right now, it's great."

Bryant's regrets did not extend to missing college, either. In fact, he said he planned to get a degree some day, either in basketball's off season or after he retires. "I know I would have liked college, but if I was there, I'd be thinking, 'Man, I should be in the NBA,'" he told the *New York Times*. "NBA life is fun."

It was also lucrative. In addition to his multi-million dollar contract, Bryant also had endorsement deals from Adidas and other companies who liked his clean-living persona and his appeal, especially among young people. He has a Screen Actors Guild card and is in demand for guest spots on television shows. Bryant welcomed these opportunities to add to his wealth and fame. "I like getting out there for promotional appearances and having a good time and meeting people," he said in the *Los Angeles Times*. "I like to see the end product, and I take pride in it. I want my product to be one of the best things out there. And I love going in front of the cameras and learning something new." At the same time, he added, "I understand basketball is what got me here and on top of that, I love to do it so much that it will always be my focal point."

His family loved him, the Lakers loved him, and his fans loved him. He attained celebrity status at lightning speed, "Most players have shoe deals and one or two others, but the opportunities Kobe has had are far greater than any other team athlete, aside from Jordan and Kobe's, have come quicker,"explained Kobe's agent, Arn Tellem. By the age of twenty, Bryant lived the American dream: money, good basketball moves, good looks, and a big smile. But, as could be expected, Bryant had some difficulties adjusting to the demands.

Off season, he had a rigorous schedule traveling and promoting consumer goods for several large corporations including Sprite, Spalding, and Adidas. In addition, Kobe had his own Nintendo game! When he was not traveling, he spent his time with his family. According to *Newsweek*, "Bryant says he doesn't have a single close friend on the team or in the city." Bryant was described as a loner.

By age twenty-one, Bryant landed millions of dollars in endorsement deals and had an All Star NBA status. Rather than squander his money on the high life, Bryant became co-owner of an Italian basketball league, Olimpia

Milano. He also released a hip-hop album, K.O.B.E. Inevitably, kids grow up. 76ers coach, Larry Brown, told *Sports Illustrated*, "Kobe's a model of what a young player should aspire to be. Year by year he has learned and made his game more solid, and now he's not just a highlight-film guy but an accomplished NBA player." But Bryant was not perfect. During a Spring of 2000 game with the New York Knicks, Bryant entered into a half-time scuffle with the Knicks guard, Chris Childs. Both players were ejected from the game, fined, and suspended. Bryant kept his focus throughout the rest of the season, however, and along with the NBA's Most Valuable Player, Shaquille O'Neal, Bryant helped the Lakers win their first championship in 12 years. The media paid a lot of attention to both Shaq and Kobe and tended to exaggerate any hint of tension between the two hoop stars. The fact is, Shaq and Kobe are two very different people. According to *Los Angeles Magazine*, "Shaq had never become an adult, while Kobe had never been a child."

Sources

Associated Press, November 10, 1996; April 29, 1997.
Jet, April 24, 2000; July 10, 2000.
Los Angeles Times, October 15, 1996, p. C1.
Los Angeles Magazine, June 2001, p. 58.
New York Times Magazine, January 19, 1997, p. 23; January 1999, p. 66.
Orange County Register, January 5, 1997, p. C10.
Philadelphia Inquirer, November 3, 1996, p. C1, C6.
Press-Enterprise (Riverside, CA), October 29, 1996, p. C1; February 8, 1997, p. C1.
San Diego Union Tribune, October 22, 1996, p. D2.
Sports Illustrated, April 24, 2000 p. 38.June 25, 2001, p. 42.

—Mark Kram and Christine Miner Minderovic

Solomon Burke

1936-

Soul vocalist and songwriter

Not the best known star in the firmament of 1960s soul music but perhaps the one with the most intensely emotional vocal style, Solomon Burke transplanted elements of black church services into secular music more effectively than any other artist except for perhaps Aretha Franklin. Burke enjoyed his greatest renown as part of the stable of soul vocalists under contract with the Atlantic record label in the mid-1960s. He remained a consistent crowd-pleaser into the twenty-first century thanks in part to his luxurious self-presentation on stage; dubbed the "King of Rock and Soul," he once had an exact replica of the British crown jewels made for his onstage "coronations."

Solomon Burke was born in Philadelphia, Pennsylvania, in 1936. His family was religious: he attended church services at the House of God for All People and sang gospel music all through his childhood. His musical solo debut came with the church's choir when he was nine, but it was preaching, not singing, that first marked him as something special. Soon he was giving sermons and becoming known as the Wonder Boy Preacher. He began hosting a gospel program on Philadelphia radio by age 12 or 13, broadcasting from a church of his own that he called Solomon's Temple.

Recorded Song Written for Grandmother

Burke's radio program mixed preaching and gospel singing, and in his late teens the power of his voice caught the attention of the wife of a Philadelphia disc jockey who in turn pitched Burke to record label executives of his acquaintance. Burke's recording debut came in 1955 with a song he had written for his grandmother entitled "Christmas Presents from Heaven." Recording for the New York-based Apollo label he soon began to make forays into the secular field; whether the rock-and-roll-oriented "Be Bop Grandma" of 1959 referred to the same grandmother is not known.

Reaping few financial rewards from his early recordings, Burke made a living by learning the mortuary trade. He remained involved in the funeral business after becoming a star, investing some of his earnings in a chain of funeral homes on the West Coast. "Solomon Burke knock you dead from the bandstand," fellow soul vocalist Joe Tex observed to writer Gerri Hirshey who authored *No Where to Run.* "Then he gift-wrap you for the trip home."

At a Glance . . .

Born 1936 in Philadelphia, Pennsylvania. *Religion:* Attended Church of God for All People before founding own church, Solomon's Temple, at age 12.

Career: Soul vocalist and songwriter. Gave sermons and sang gospel music broadcast on Philadelphia radio through his teen years; signed to Apollo label, ca. 1955; worked as mortician, late 1950s; signed to Atlantic label, 1960; recorded first major hit, "Just Out of Reach," 1961; reached R&B Top Five with "Cry to Me" (1962) and "If You Need Me" (1963); topped R&B charts with "Got to Get You Off of My Mind," 1965; moved to Bell label, 1969; recorded for Dunhill, MGM, and Chess labels, 1970s; continued to tour with 21-piece band through 1990s.

Awards: Inducted into Rock and Roll Hall of Fame, 2001.

Addresses: *Agent*–Thomas Cassidy, Inc., 11761 E. Speedway Blvd., Tucson, AZ 85748.

Burke's fiery yet controlled vocal style caught the attention of Atlantic Records, the leading rhythm-and-blues label of the day. Atlantic sensed that Burke had the potential to connect with diverse audiences. "He had a kind of gospel feeling to his singing, and he was also a little bit country," Atlantic executive Ahmet Ertegun told author Gerri Hirshey. Signed to Atlantic in 1960, Burke was brought under the influence of Atlantic producer Jerry Wexler's instinct for unexpected style mixtures. Burke's first major hit came in 1961 with a country song, "Just Out of Reach." Although vocalist Ray Charles is usually credited with developing successful country-soul fusions in the 1960s, Burke's effort preceded Charles's major country-style hits and may have helped to inspire them.

Southern Performances of Country Material

The country side of his work set Burke apart from other singers. "That got me a lot of bookings in the Deep South, in some places no other black artists could get into," Burke told Hirshey. "That kind of country soul bridged a lot of waters. Of course, once or twice it darn near killed me." The singer was referring to a bizarre incident in which he and his band were booked to provide entertainment for a Ku Klux Klan rally—from which the group nevertheless emerged unscathed as hooded Klansmen repeatedly requested Burke's hits.

In 1962 and 1963 Burke cracked the Top Five of *Billboard* magazine's rhythm-and-blues chart with "Cry to Me" and "If You Need Me," two recordings that fit the mold of what would soon be called soul music—songs in established rhythm-and-blues forms augmented by vocal devices and a fervent emotional tone borrowed from the world of gospel. In one section of "Cry to Me," Burke broke into an ecstatic high stutter that helped pave the way for some of the other acrobatic vocal devices of soul. Always appreciated by his fellow musicians, Burke numbered among his musical descendants the British rock band the Rolling Stones, which recorded covers of "Cry to Me" and several other Burke songs. Burke finally topped rhythm-and-blues charts in 1965 with "Got to Get You Off My Mind."

Fathered 21 Children

Record sales, however, were always less important to Burke than his flamboyant live appearances. Described by Gerri Hirshey as "a great, undulating vision of sea-green satin and rhinestones" and often appearing on stage in an ermine-trimmed cape or a gold lamé jacket, Burke played on the tension between his gospel roots and his sensual appeal. "It would be a sin to pass up the pleasures the Lord made just for us," Hirshey quoted him as saying, and indeed Burke has fathered 21 children, large groups of whom he has sometimes dressed identically. Long after his era of hitmaking had ended, Burke continued to tour with a 21-piece band and to command strong attraction from female fans.

By the late 1960s the focus of soul music had shifted south, to the Stax label in Memphis and Fame Records in Muscle Shoals, Alabama, and Burke fell out of the limelight. In part Burke blamed Wexler. "My relationship with Jerry Wexler is like a two-way street," Burke told *Billboard* in 1997. "There's one side where I'm angry for a lot for things that didn't go down and one side where I'm very grateful that he was there, because he did develop Solomon Burke to a certain point and then he stopped." Nevertheless, Burke included a Wexler-produced track on his 1997 album, *Definition of Soul.*

Leaving Atlantic in 1969, Burke recorded for the Bell label (for which he cut several fine tracks in Muscle Shoals) and for the Dunhill, MGM, and Chess labels through the 1970s; he has continued to record intermittently. The 1981 album, *Take Me, Shake Me,* recorded for the Savoy label, showcased his gospel skills. In 1987 he appeared in the film, *The Big Easy.* Burke's stage show survived little altered through the 1990s, and various collections of his recordings that appeared became, in the words of allmusic.com's Richie Unterberger, favorites of those "who want to experience a soul legend with talent and stylistic purity relatively intact." Solomon Burke was inducted into the Rock and Roll Hall of Fame in April of 2001.

Selected discography

Solomon Burke, Apollo, 1962.
Solomon Burke's Greatest Hits, Atlantic, 1962.
If You Need Me, Atlantic, 1963.
Rock 'n' Soul, Atlantic, 1964.
The Best of Solomon Burke, Atlantic, 1965.
King Solomon, Atlantic, 1967.
I Wish I Knew, Atlantic, 1968.
Proud Mary, Bell, 1969.
Electronic Magnetism, MGM, 1972.
We're Almost Home, MGM, 1973.
I Have a Dream, Dunhill. 1974.
Music to Make Love By, Chess, 1975.
Back to My Roots, Atlantic, 1977.
Take Me, Shake Me, Savoy, 1981.
Soul Alive!, Rounder, 1984.
The Best of Solomon Burke, Atlantic, 1989.
Home in Your Heart: The Best of Solomon Burke, Rhino, 1992.
Soul of the Blues, Black Top, 1993.
Solomon Burke Live at the House of Blues, Black Top, 1994.
Definition of Soul, EMI, 1997.

Sources

Books

Hirshey, Gerri, *Nowhere to Run,* Times Books, 1994.
Larkin, Colin, ed., *The Encyclopedia of Popular Music,* Muze UK, 1998.
Romanowski, Patricia, with Holly George-Warren, *The New Rolling Stone Encyclopedia of Rock and Roll,* Fireside, 1995.
Shaw Arnold, *The World of Soul,* Cowles Book Co., 1971.
Stambler, Irwin, *Encyclopedia of Pop, Rock & Soul,* St. Martin's, 1989.

Periodicals

Billboard, January 25, 1997, p. 13.
Jet, April 9, 2001, p. 34.

Online

http://allmusic.com.

—James M. Manheim

Stephen Burrows

1943—

Fashion designer

Stephen Burrows, called "one of the most audacious and auspicious talents in contemporary fashion" by *Contemporary Fashion,* was one of the first African Americans to become famous as a fashion designer, after Ann Lowe. He spent the 1970s, clothing a great portion of New York City and beyond. He made clothes that made a woman feel beautiful and considered his work "art."

Burrows was born September 15, 1943 in Newark, New Jersey. He came to the field of fashion design honestly, starting to make clothes with his grandmother when he was very young. He enjoyed helping his grandmother sew so much, that when the time came for him to choose a profession it seemed natural to follow his textile creativity into design. In order to do that, he attended first the Philadelphia Museum College of Art and later went to New York City to study at the Fashion Institute of Technology.

In 1968 after graduating from the Fashion Institute of Technology, Burrows opened a boutique in New York City with a partner. Around the same time, in 1969, he obtained employment with the prestigious Henri Bendel clothing store on Fifth Avenue whose upper floors are home to the work of the fashion world's top designers.

The NY.com web site said that Henri Bendel is a place only for those women with "a strong heart and a robust bank account." There he designed clothing that made him "the quintessential fashion expression of the 1970s in a disestablishment sensibility, young nonchalance, and unfailing insistence on looking beautiful," said *Contemporary Fashion.* In 1974 he stopped work at Bendel to try his hand with a more mainstream clothing firm, but in 1977 he returned to Henri Bendel, preferring to work in an environment where he could be creative without barriers.

The mainstream company had been afraid of risks and would only purchase cheap, artificial materials. This situation frustrated Burrows because he did not want to make safe and boring clothing with imitative and mundane materials. To him clothing is an art, and the best designs, while borrowing ideas from existing compositions, are still daring and make a statement. They are also patterned out of the most comfortable and luxurious materials available, making women feel slinky and feminine while at the same time evoking a mood of playfulness. "I make colorful adult toys because I think fashion should have a sense of humor, and I want people to be happy in my clothes," Burrows told *Contemporary Fashion.* Bur-

At a Glance . . .

Born September 15, 1942 in Newark, NJ. *Education:* Attended Philadelphia Museum College of Art, 1961–62; attended fashion design, Fashion Institute of Technology, New York City, 1964–66.

Career: Fashion designer, Weber Originals, New York, 1966–67; designer, Allen & Cole, c. 1967–68; co-founder, proprietor, "O" boutique, 1968; in-house designer, Henri Bendel store, New York City, 1969–73; founder-director, Burrows, Inc., New York City, 1973–82; designer, Henri Bendel, 1977–82, 1993–; designer, ready-to-wear design, 1989; designer, custom design, 1990; designer, Tony Lambert Co., 1991. Exhibition: Versailles Palace, 1973.

Awards: Coty American Fashion Critics, "Winnie" Award, 1973, 1977, and Special Award, 1974; Council of American Fashion Critics Award, 1975; Knitted Textile Association Crystal Ball Award, 1975.

Addresses: *Office*—550 Seventh Avenue, New York, NY 10013.

rows was obviously not meant to be a mass market designer. His pieces were originals, one-of-a-kind items. In fact, later in his career he began insisting on making only one-of-a-kind dresses. His reasons? "Why not?" he told the *New York Times,* "I have plenty of ideas-I don't have to repeat myself."

By the mid-1970s, Burrows was a Coty-Award winning designer who was also chosen, in 1973, as one of only 5 designers to represent American fashion at the world famous fashion show at Versailles. His clothing, well accepted at the show, proved to have a sexy, playful, and daring feel. He became famous for dresses that were made from clingy materials such as velour or jersey made into asymmetrical designs, using the bias cut, zigzag seams, and shirring to create startling and fun effects. He liked clothing that made a woman stand out in a crowd, and he received inspiration from just about everything found in American culture, but especially the American craze for sports and athletic events. This influence can be seen most evidently in some of his separates—skirts made out of comfortable, soft fabrics with elastic waistlines, and tops to match with large buttons and a relaxed feel that could be worn buttoned all the way up or left partly open for a flirtatious effect. He was also influenced by modern art. When he designed a dress made out of jersey with a large circular hole at the midriff, some people saw graphic modernism in his creation. "'Designers were inspired by two-dimensional art-like Stephen

Burrows and Pop Art,' Mr. Martin, exhibit curator, said to the *New York Times,* 'I am not saying that he was doing Jasper Johns's targets, but that there was something about a big circle that was in the air.'"

In the 1980s Burrows stepped back a bit from the fashion spotlight. Writers, in fact, penned articles in which they praised Burrows's individuality while also mourning his recent absence from the world of fashion design. The *New York Times* stated, "[f]inancial success [is not] the only measure of fashion greatness. Can anyone really say that Ralph Lauren is a better designer than Stephen Burrows?" And also, it asked, "But where is Stephen Burrows?" His might not be a household name, but among the knowledgeable, Stephen Burrows will always be highly praised and appreciated for his artistic creations.

In the 1990s Burrows returned wholeheartedly into the public fashion design scene, this time with a line of dresses that were both comfortable and sensual. "The dresses are sexy," he told the *New York Times,* "Women should have an escort when they wear them." In 1993 Burrows returned to Henri Bendel to design eveningwear. In 1999, *Ebony* gave proof to the fact that Stephen Burrows was back, and was the same designer whom people loved and missed. "Stephen Burrows designs kneelength, chiffon cocktail dress with haltered asymmetrical neckline and circular ruffle." Back are the sexy dresses done in soft fabrics and the asymmetrical designs. A man with a gift for designing clothes that make women feel beautiful, sexy, and noticeable, may he not disappear again. The world of fashion design needs innovative and creative thinkers like Stephen Burrows to challenge the norms, and it certainly needs his beautifying influence.

Sources

Books

Contemporary Fashion, St. James Press, 1995, 1997.

CD-ROM

DISCoveringMulticulturalAmerica, GaleResearch, 1996.

Periodicals

Ebony, May, 1999; February, 2000.
Jet, May 17, 1999, p. 33.
New York Times, May 1, 1990; October 7, 1997; November 4, 1997; February 15, 1998; April 3, 1998; August 29, 2000.

Online

http://www.ny.com/shopping/department/bendel.html.
http://wwwhenribendel.com/about/ben.asp.

—Catherine Donaldson

Juanita Bynum

1959-

Author

In a time when sexuality permeates the culture, there is a woman who encourages women to find closure for previous relationships, live chaste, and be the kind of people they hope to attract. Using her own mistakes as a basis for her sermons, prophetess Juanita Bynum has dedicated herself to reaching others with a message from God, a message that offers healing and encouragement through suggesting celibacy for singles. Treading on territory where few women have ventured, Bynum has allowed herself to be God's vessel, telling her colorful story to the masses, in hopes of saving souls from following the same dark paths she once walked.

As a child in Chicago with her parents, Katherine and Thomas, and siblings Janice, Kathy, Regina, and Thomas, Bynum embraced the church as a distinct part of her life. The family were members of St. Luke Church of God in Christ, where the father was an elder. According to *Ministries Today,* Bynum was an outgoing child. Her charisma became apparent to those outside her immediate realm, when she landed a starring role in her middle school's production of *My Fair Lady.* Her performance grabbed the attention of television show agents who wanted to cast her in programs similar to *Julia,* starring Diahann Carroll. Bynum's mother, however, declined the offers. "I used to make her stop playing outside and come in the house and just sit still," she told *Ministries Today.* "I wanted my daughter to listen to the voice of God," she added.

Though she later admitted in *Ministries Today,* "Every time I got on my knees I kept hearing [God] say, 'Before I knew you, I formed you in your mother's womb to be a prophet to the nations,'" she struggled in her youth to obey instructions from God. Still, Bynum had hopes of being a servant. She attended Saints Academy of the Church of God in Christ (COGIC) high school in Lexington, Mississippi and graduated second in her class. Soon after her graduation, Bynum, still a teenager, began preaching at churches and revivals. Eventually, she traveled to Port Huron, Michigan, to minister for pastor William T. Nichols and his wife, and ended up on an unanticipated journey that changed the course of her life.

Choices Led to Hardship

At the age of 21 Bynum married, despite the warnings of her loved ones. "Everybody told me he wasn't right, but I was screamin', I'm in love. I can change him," she told *Essence.* As Bynum later found out, she could not change her husband, and she had married him for all the wrong reasons.

A virgin until her marriage, Bynum admitted in *Essence,* "I married for sex—and what the man looked like." Her husband left her in 1983 and divorced her in 1985. The pain of the failed relationship landed her in an institution, battling anorexia nervosa, and questioning her life's turn of events. She lost sight of God's path, and eventually sought refuge and healing in empty sexual affairs. In addition to her emotional state, her financial state crumbled. She was forced to go on welfare to survive.

At a Glance . . .

Born Juanita Bynum on January 16, 1959; divorced, 1985. *Education*: Saints Academy of the Church of God in Christ (COGIC) high school in Lexington, Mississippi. *Religion*: raised COGIC.

Career: Author. Recorded videos include: *No More Sheets; Are You Planted for the Kingdom* (also available on CD); *I'm Too Fat For the Yoke* (also available on CD); *Limp of the Lord; Now That's Dominion; The Refiner's Fire; My Delivery; The Spirit of Isaac; The Umpire of my Soul; Tied to the Altar*. Wrote: *No More Sheets; Don't Get off the Train*. Speaker. Engagements include T.D. Jakes' Singles Conference ("No More Sheets" message),1997; T.D. Jakes' "Woman, Thou Art Loused!" conference, 1998; Women's Weapons of Power Conference, 2001.

Address: c/o Juanita Bynum Ministries, 415 North Crawford St., Waycross, GA, 31510.

Struggled to Rebuild Her Life

In 1990 Bynum returned to Chicago, became a hairdresser, and managed to leave government aid behind. Her next steps led her to New York as a flight attendant for Pan American Airways, a job she held until the company went out of business in 1991. Bynum told *Essence* that friends believed the fate of Pan Am was God's way of telling her that she was supposed to be a preacher. "I knew God was saying that this was my destiny, but I didn't want to hear it."

In New York, Bynum joined a new church and began ministering again. In 1996 she met a man who would prove to be a key figure in her transformation into a renowned prophetess. Though he knew nothing of her story, Pentecostal evangelist Bishop T.D. Jakes invited her to the singles' conference in Dallas—a step that, according to *Essence,* was the result of his obedience to God's instruction.

Life Story Became Testimony to Singles

Jakes' obedience turned out to be the stepping stone for Bynum's explosive break into national popularity, when two years after attending the singles' conference, Bynum's role changed from attendee to keynote speaker. In 1998 she delivered a message titled "No More Sheets" to 17,000 people, the majority women, and brought the crowd to their feet with praise and deliverance.

"No More Sheets" proved to be a testimony of Bynum's sexual deviation and her process of purification. She reached out to the crowd with brutal honesty, honing in on the concept that "single" is not synonymous with unmarried; instead "single" refers to those who are free from the remnants of past relationships. "In order for God to bring somebody else in your life, there's got to be room for that person in your life. You're not single yet," she told the crowd. "You're still attached."

Wrapped in sheets, Bynum explained that each sheet represented a past relationship and only God could peel those layers away in order to make people truly single—ready to receive their ordained mates. She shared a story of poverty that placed her in roach-infested projects, using McDonald's napkins as toilet paper. Bynum told the crowd that by allowing her to struggle, God was reconditioning her to release her dependence on men and embrace her dependence on Him. It was a sacrifice that she made in order to be blessed.

Bynum told *Essence* that when she was on stage, her message had a life of its own. "It wasn't me—it was God." By the end of the video, the camera captured thousands in a moment of spiritual awakening, chanting, "No More Sheets! No More Sheets!"

Bynum's endeavors have taken her across the country to deliver her untraditional message to the masses at numerous venues including Jakes' 1998 "Woman, Thou Art Loused!" conference. With her popularity came the conception of Morning Glory Ministries, a venue that allows people to find out exactly where Bynum will be delivering messages and to obtain information about the prophetess. Videotapes like the now famous, "No More Sheets," and other tapings like "I'm Too Fat for the Yoke" and "The Limp of the Lord," as well as books including *Don't Get Off The Train*, which was written about her experiences in Port Huron, are available for purchase through the ministry. Her lessons are also available through her ministry's television program, *Morning Glory,* which according to *Ministries Today,* was airing on 15 television stations throughout the country in 1999.

Despite the great success Bynum has found in ministry, her fulfillment comes from one-on-one contact with people. "I really love people," she was quoted as saying in *Ministries Today.* "My biggest joy is the individual contact I have with them." In fact, when she isn't traveling, she runs a bible institution training ministry at her church, New Greater Bethel Ministries in Hempstead, New York.

Bynum is constantly reminded of the rough days from which strength arose, and told *Essence* that the memories are still a great part of her existence. "If I close my eyes right now, I can see myself in the snow, wearing a black $2 coat and tennis shoes with no socks, waiting to get my $76 in food stamps. I can see myself in the hospital after my nervous breakdown, crying and throwing myself against the walls of the padded cell they put me in. When I remember the process it took to get myself from there to where I am today—and then I see a sister with no hope—I'm driven to get to that sister. I believe that the pain in each of our pasts gives us an opportunity to help others. If I honestly tell somebody what has happened to me, then maybe that person will be transformed."

From the pages of her electronic guestbook on www.nosheets.com, it appears that her mission to help others make a transformation is working. One message was just one of many that speaks to miraculous change. It read, "Sister Bynum, I want to thank God for you. I just read *No More Sheets* and I can't begin to tell you it has changed my life. I thought I knew, but am now aware that I knew nothing. Everything is so clear to me now. I can't explain how your book has changed me. . . . If it weren't for you and your message, I would still be lost. . . . I can proudly say no more sheets for me and I love you so much for what you have given me."

While Bynum has touched the hearts and souls of many, she is still cognizant of life's little lessons. In fact she found one in her dog, Corky. According to her website, www.nosheets.com, Bynum purchased the red-pepper poodle at a time when her heart was heavy. "The Lord explained to me that the dog was feeling what I was feeling, which was rejection. He said the poodle is thinking: What's the use in going to the window and barking?

She's not going to choose me anyway," she was quoted as saying.

Bynum did choose Corky. Something as small as reaching out to this dog quite possibly brought healing to both Bynum and Corky. Those who truly believe in God's wonders have testified that He works in mysterious ways. An example of his mystery, Bynum is on fire for the Lord, and she intends to do His work until the flame is extinguished.

Sources

Periodicals

Ministries Today, July/August 1999.
Essence, May 2001, p. 185.

Online

http://www.nosheets.com.

Other

Additional information was obtained from the video *No More Sheets,* T.D. Jakes Ministries, 1997.

—Shellie M. Saunders

Naomi Campbell

1970–

Model, actress

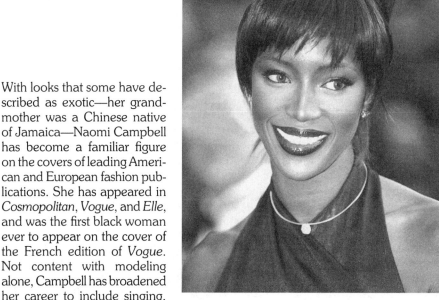

With looks that some have described as exotic—her grandmother was a Chinese native of Jamaica—Naomi Campbell has become a familiar figure on the covers of leading American and European fashion publications. She has appeared in *Cosmopolitan*, *Vogue*, and *Elle*, and was the first black woman ever to appear on the cover of the French edition of *Vogue*. Not content with modeling alone, Campbell has broadened her career to include singing, acting, and a variety of business ventures.

Campbell was born on May 20, 1970, in Streatham, London, England. Her father, a Jamaican immigrant who was part Chinese, left the family before she was born. Her mother, Valerie Campbell, was born in Jamaica but grew up in London. A modern ballet dancer, Valerie spent much time traveling throughout Europe with her dance troupe, so a nanny was hired to help raise Naomi and her brother. Like her mother, Campbell was also interested in ballet. At age ten, Campbell was accepted to London's prestigious Italia Conti Stage School to study ballet. She also attended the London Academy of Performing Arts. During this time, Campbell landed bit parts in two films: *Quest for Fire* (1981) and Pink Floyd's *The Wall* (1982).

Discovered in Shopping Arcade

When she was 15, an agent discovered Campbell in a shopping arcade at Covent Gardens, which Campbell frequented after school. Campbell described the encounter to George Wayne in *Interview*: "I was just hanging out, and this woman comes up to me and says, 'I'm a modeling agent.' I didn't believe her, but I took her card home and gave it to my mother. And then I saw an interview of her in *Tatler*, so I knew she was legitimate. After that I started pleading with my mother to let me go see her. At the end of the school year, I did. She took a picture of me in my school uniform . . . . then she sent me to a photographer who was working on an assignment for British *Elle* in New Orleans, and he booked me."

Signed to the Elite Modeling Agency, Campbell was soon working with some of the biggest names in the fashion industry, including Isaac Mizrahi, Calvin Klein, and Azzedine Alaia. She described in *Interview* some of her favorite fashion photographers: "I like working with Herb Ritts, and I do very much like working with [Francesco] Scavullo. He makes me feel like a woman. Herb makes you feel very innocent. Steven [Meisel] makes you feel like a character. When you work with him he'll give you

At a Glance . . .

Born on May 22, 1970, in London, England; daughter of Valerie Campbell (a ballet dancer). *Education*: Attended London Academy of Performing Arts, c. 1985.

Career: Model, 1986-; appeared on London stage in *The King and I*; film appearances: *Quest for Fire*, 1982; *The Wall*, 1982; *Cool as Ice*, 1991; *The Night We Never Met*, 1993; *Miami Rhapsody*, 1995; *Girl 6*, 1996; *Invasion of Privacy*, 1996; *Trippin'*, 1999; *Prisoner of Love*, 1999; *Destinazione Verna*, 2000; television guest appearances: *The Cosby Show*, 1988; The Fresh Prince of Bel-Air, 1990; albums: *Love and Tears*, 1994; *Babywoman*, 1995; author (with ghostwriter), *Swan*, 1994; co-owner, The Fashion Café, beginning 1995.

Addresses: *Agent*–International Creative Management, 8942 Wilshire Blvd., Beverly Hills, CA 90211.

postcards and books to look at and study. He makes me look different in every picture."

Earning more than $1 million a year, Campbell's assignments have taken her to many locations around the world. For one of her most exciting—and harrowing—photo shoots, she found herself, standing atop a volcano in Lanzarote, Spain—in heels. Her face was emblazoned on the French, Italian, American, and British editions of *Vogue* in the late 1980s. In 1988, she made a guest appearance on *The Cosby Show*.

One reason Campbell was so highly sought after is what many in the fashion industry have praised as her natural modeling ability. "She's one of the most delightful girls I've ever worked with, one of my favorite models," exalted fashion photographer Francesco Scavullo said in *Harper's Bazaar*. "No one else has such an amazing body. She makes clothes come alive." Fashion coordinator Audrey Smaltz also commented in *Harper's Bazaar* on Campbell's magnetism on style show runways: "She doesn't realize how wonderful she is . . . . She has terrific body language—most models don't—and can translate this into whatever she's wearing."

Expanded Career With Music and Acting

In the early 1990s, Campbell began to focus more on her other interests. In addition to appearing in Vanilla Ice's film *Cool as Ice* (1991), she also contributed vocals to a track on the soundtrack. She then recorded two albums of her own: 1994's *Love and Tears* and *Babywoman*

(1995). Campbell also recorded "La, La, La Love Song" with Japanese singer Toshi, and the song reached number one in Japan. In addition, she appeared in several music videos, including Michael Jackson's "In the Closet" video and George Michael's "Freedom."

In 1994 Campbell published a novel. The ghost-written *Swan* presents the story of a successful supermodel who has decided to quit modeling. The novel was a critical disappointment. Jonathan Van Meter of *Vogue* called the book "a laughingstock."

She commented about her hopes to expand her acting career in *Interview*: "You can't learn it all. As they tell you, acting is reacting. So it's all about going through life, having experiences." She won a small role in *The Night We Never Met* (1993), and in 1994 played a model in Robert Altman's *Pret-a-Porter (Ready to Wear)*. The following year, she had parts in *To Wong Foo, Thanks for Everything, Julie Newmar* and *Miami Rhapsody*, which starred Sarah Jessica Parker and Mia Farrow. She also showed talent in a cameo in Spike Lee's *Girl 6* (1996). Campbell continued to make guest appearances on such television shows as *The Fresh Prince of Bel-Air* and *New York Undercover*, in addition to a cameo appearance on the British comedy series *Absolutely Fabulous*.

Campbell continued to model, earning fees of $10,000 a day. She was reportedly paid a six-figure sum to appear in Madonna's book *Sex*, which featured erotic photographs, and she selected all of the pictures for another photo book called simply *Naomi*, which consisted of favorite shots of herself taken by top photographers. *Naomi*'s proceeds were donated to the Red Cross, for use in Somalia relief efforts.

A bonafide supermodel with several films behind her, Campbell had risen to megastardom. Tabloids and gossip columns could not print enough about her personal life. She has been linked to Mike Tyson, Robert DeNiro, who Campbell initially denied dating but later revealed that they had a four-year relationship, and flamenco dancer Joaquin Cortes. Campbell was also briefly engaged to Adam Clayton, a member of the band U2. The rumor mill has also suggested romantic connections with Sylvester Stallone, Sean "P. Diddy" Combs, and Gabriel Byrne.

Opened Fashion Café

Campbell's next venture was the restaurant business. In 1995 she, along with fellow models Elle MacPherson, Claudia Schiffer, and Christy Turlington, and Italian restaurateur Tommaso Buti, launched the Fashion Café. The restaurant and coffee house first opened in New York City, and was situated in Rockefeller Center. Patrons entered the restaurant through a door shaped like a giant camera lens and serving staff carried cuisine down a catwalk. The decor included a collection of fashion memorabilia, from Madonna's famous Jean-Paul Gaultier bustier to one of Elizabeth Taylor's wedding gowns. Branches in London, Jakarta, Barcelona, Mexico City, New Orleans, and Manila soon followed.

By 1997, however, Turlington had pulled out of the company, and the next year, investors accused the Fashion Café of mismanagement. The New Orleans and Barcelona franchises were shut down, and Buti resigned after selling his stake in the firm. New management was called in to restore order, however, and the business continued at other locations. The New York branch, however, was later closed and the London restaurant was placed in receivership in 1998. Buti, accused of defrauding investors, was arrested in 2000 and charged with wire fraud, conspiracy, money laundering, and transportation of stolen property.

Developed Reputation for Being Difficult

Throughout her career, Campbell has developed a reputation for being notoriously difficult to work with. Her temper reportedly possessed a short and fiery fuse. She has also been known to be perpetually late to assignments or appointments. In addition, she has earned a reputation for making selfish demands, such as insisting on being the first and last to appear on the runway at fashion shows. It was this difficulty which supposedly led to her temporary dismissal from Elite. Other reports, however, indicated that she resigned and was later hired back.

During a film shoot in September of 1998 for *Prisoner of Love*, according to Joe Warmington in the *Toronto Sun*, several crew members called Campbell "a 'nightmare' to work with," and one anonymous crewman called her "a spoiled child." In addition Georgiana Galanis, a Canadian assistant who had worked for Campbell for only nine days, claimed the model grabbed her by the throat, assaulted her with a telephone, and punched her in the shoulder twice. Campbell was arrested and charged with assault causing bodily harm.

Campbell did not attend the February of 2000 court hearing, but pleaded guilty in absentia to the lesser charge of assault. The court gave her an absolute discharge, which meant that she did not have to serve jail time and that she would not have criminal record in Canada. Galanis filed a civil suit, and an undisclosed settlement was reached out of court.

Aware of the problems caused by her incendiary temper, Campbell took steps to learn how to control her anger. In 1999 she spent four weeks at the Cottonwood Center in Tuscon, Arizona. While at the clinic, Campbell shared a room with three other patients, and learned several anger management techniques. Part of what drove her to seek help was Campbell's fear that her anger was having

a damaging effect on her relationship with Flavio Briatore, a businessman from Italy who Campbell began dating in 1999.

Campbell has given much of her time to charitable works. She has worked with the Dalai Lama rasing money to build kindergartens for poor communities. In February of 1998, she was involved with a fund raising event in Johannesburg, South Africa, for the Nelson Mandela Children's Fund. Campbell continued to work with the Children's Fund, developing a close friendship with Mandela.

Launched Signature Fragrance

The next step in Campbell's ever-diversifying career was the development of her own line of fragrances. Produced by Cosmopolitan Cosmetics, her first perfume, Naomi Campbell, hit stores in Japan, Germany, the United Arab Emirates, and Australia in the fall of 1999. U.S. stores welcomed the fragrance to their shelves in June of 2000.

Campbell was involved in every aspect of the production process. "I didn't want to just put my name on something, like I did with the Fashion Café," she told *WWD*. "I wanted to be involved with my fragrance every step of the way, and that meant committing myself in every way—to the promotion, to the formulation of the scent, to everything." Not only did Campbell work with Givaudan Roure to create the perfume, but she also worked with Thierry de Baschmakoff to design the bottle and outer packaging.

Naomi Campbell was only the first in a whole line of fragrances. Campbell's second fragrance, Naomagic, was released in the fall of 2000. According to *European Cosmetic Markets*, this follow-up was "said to free the magical attraction of a woman." Campbell turned to her favorite flower, the lily of the valley, for inspiration in creating this scent. The design for the flacon containing the perfume was also inspired by two stones that she has always carried in her handbag: a rock crystal for energy and a stone talisman for good luck.

With the success of these fragrances, Campbell planned to expand her line to include cosmetics, candles, and perhaps even skin care products. "I'm not doing this because I'm forced to financially," she told *WWD*. "Instead, I'm doing it because it touches me. It makes a statement about my sense of smell to the world."

In February of 2000 Campbell was still in demand as a model. However, she decided to reduce the number of runway shows she appeared in. "I find it really stressful," she told the *South China Morning Post*. Besides, there was only so much time in a day for the model/actress/entrepreneur, and she had several goals yet to accomplish. "Oh God, there's a lot more," Campbell said in her book *Naomi*, as quoted in the *African News Service*.

"I've got motherhood to achieve, marriage and family life. That for me would be a lot more than I've achieved in my career. That's something I would really love to do in my life."

Sources

Books

Contemporary Theatre, Film and Television, Vol. 31, Gale 2000.
Newsmakers, Gale, 2000.

Periodicals

Africa News Service, March 11, 2001.
Cosmetics International, October 10, 2000, p. 11.
Entertainment Weekly, April 4, 1995, p. 6.
European Cosmetic Markets, October 2000, p. 420.
Harper's Bazaar, March 1990; June 1992, p. 90.
Independent, October 21, 1998, p. 7.
Interview, May 1990; February 1998, p. 56.
Jet, May 31, 1993, p. 5; November 16, 1998, p. 63; February 21, 2000, p. 53; March 6, 2000, p. 37.
Maclean's, March 24, 1997, p. 12; February 14, 2000, p. 9.
Mademoiselle, February 1989, p. 122.
Nation's Restaurant News, December 18, 2000, p. 4.
Newsweek, June 18, 2001, p. 62.
New York Times Magazine, November 24, 1996, p. 60.
People, June 11, 1990, p. 44; December 30, 1991, p. 82; November 23, 1998, p. 132.
People Weekly, January 20, 1997, p. 37; September 8, 1997, p. 45.
Restaurants & Institutions, February 1, 2001, p. 21.
South China Morning Post, December 13, 1999; February 3, 2000.
Toronto Sun, December 13, 1998, p. 4.
Vanity Fair, December 1990, p. 194.
Vogue, March 1999, p. 438.
WWD, June 16, 2000, p. 6.

Online

Amazon.com. http://www.amazon.com (July 16, 2001).
Fashion Café, http://www.fashion-cafe.com (January 5, 2000).
Internet Movie Database, http://us.imdb.com.
http://mrshowbiz.go.com (February 8, 2000).

—Michael E. Mueller and Jennifer M. York

Morris Chestnut

1969-

Actor

Morris Chestnut's career trajectory has paralleled the film industry's belated realization that audiences enjoy films that present a more balanced view of contemporary African-American life: he made his debut in the early 1990s in the seminal urban culture film, *Boyz N the Hood*, but later found success as a handsome lead in several romantic comedies. Chestnut has often been described as one of Hollywood's new breed of black heartthrobs, with his "cool liquid eyes, a killer smile, and a fleet, almost musical way with dialogue," noted *Entertainment Weekly* reviewer Owen Gleiberman, each of which "hints at something held back, a hidden force behind his lightness. That force is what makes him a potentially major actor."

Chestnut was born in Cerritos, California on January 1, 1969. He took acting courses in college along with his business studies at California State University's Northridge campus. He claimed to have never planned on making a career of acting, and described himself to *Ebony* as "really the shy type."

His career path was affirmed when he made his feature film debut in 1991 with *Boyz N the Hood*, the first effort from a young writer-director named John Singleton.

Chestnut was cast alongside Ice Cube and Cuba Gooding, Jr. as one of two brothers in a coming-of-age tale set in violence-torn South-Central Los Angeles. Gooding's character lives with his former military man father, but Chestnut's Ricky and his brother are raised by their single mother, and know no real strong male presence in their lives. Ricky marries young, excels in athletics, and aims for a college scholarship, but meets with a tragic, avoidable demise. *National Review* film critic John Simon faulted some of the performances, except Chestnut's, and asserted that the actor "makes Ricky's almost too-good-to-be-true goodness sweetly believable," Simon gave *Boyz N the Hood* high marks: "It accomplishes most of its bitter aims with unsensationalistic honesty."

Chestnut was next cast in a 1992 made-for-television movie, *Street War*, part of NBC's "In the Line of Duty" series about actual crime-file cases. The film starred Mario Van Peebles as a housing project police officer in Brooklyn, while Chestnut and Courtney B. Vance played the possible suspects in a slaying. Chestnut also won a plum role for the fall season in 1992 on *Out All Night*. a new sitcom that featured Patti LaBelle as a night-club owner.

At a Glance . . .

Born on January 1, 1969, in Cerritos, California; married Pam. *Education:* Studied finance and acting at California State University-Northridge.

Career: Actor. Made feature film debut in *Boyz N The Hood,* 1991; television series: *Out All Night,* 1992; *C-16,* 1997; tv movies: *The Ernest Green Story,* 1993; *The Killing Yard,* 2001; film roles: *Under Siege 2,* 1995; *G.I. Jane,* 1997; *The Best Man,* 1999; *The Brothers,* 2001; *Two Can Play That Game,* 2001; *Scenes of the Crime,* 2001.

Addresses: *Office—*c/o The Agency, 10351 Santa Monica Blvd., Suite 211, Los Angeles, CA 90025.

Later that year he appeared in a movie made for the Disney Cable channel, *The Ernest Green Show.* in the title role. The work was a dramatization of the events resulting from the landmark 1954 U.S. Supreme Court order that declared all-black public schools unconstitutional. The real Ernest Green was one of nine students transferred, in 1957, to all-white Central High School in Little Rock, Arkansas. The transferred students were met with jeering crowds who attempted to bar them from entry. Even the Arkansas governor opposed their transfer, and sent National Guard troops to keep them out; President Dwight D. Eisenhower countered with federal troops. "Chestnut turns in a sturdy performance as the tenacious Green, who as the senior took on a leadership role, encouraging persistence and the 'creative nonviolence' advocated by Martin Luther King Jr.," remarked *Multichannel News* writer Rod Granger.

In the mid-1990s Chestnut appeared in the feature films *Under Siege 2* and *G.I. Jane,* but returned to the small screen after an offer from ABC to star in a new hour-long drama, *C-16* that debuted in the fall of 1997. The title referred to a special Federal Bureau of Investigation unit that deals with kidnaping cases, hostage crises, and other such matters. Chestnut was cast as an earnest young rookie, Mal Robinson, whose off-duty life is troubled by his drug-addict brother.

Chestnut's breakthrough role came in a 1999 romantic comedy, *The Best Man,* which starred Taye Diggs in the title role. Chestnut played the groom, a man who might soon discover that his best man once slept with his bride-to-be. The film was directed by Malcolm D. Lee, cousin of Spike, and earned rave reviews for its ensemble cast that included Nia Long and Sanaa Lathan. The wedding serves as an impromptu reunion for the group of college friends: Diggs plays a first-time novelist whose book and its scarcely concealed revelations threaten to undermine

several friendships. Chestnut, wrote *Newsweek* critic David Ansen, plays "a pro running back as devoutly Christian as he is piggishly male chauvinist," and *Variety* reviewer Emanuel Levy stated that the actor delivers "a strong and touching rendition of a jealously aggressive yet Bible-reading guy coerced to examine his double-standard ethics." Levy called the film "well-mounted and engaging" and "an honorable addition to the reunion genre."

Chestnut was next cast in another ensemble film, *The Brothers* (2001). Starring alongside Shemar Moore, D.L. Hughley, and Bill Bellamy, Chestnut plays a philandering physician. "Chestnut's character is desperate for intimacy but deathly afraid of commitment, while Moore's character is a reformed bachelor who's about to tie the knot," wrote *Ebony's* Aldore Collier about the plot. Chestnut, a married man, admitted that he drew upon his own personal experience for the role. "There was one time in my life when I was commitment phobic, and I had to go back to that time and imagine what it was like," he told the *Atlanta Journal-Constitution.* In his review of the film, *Entertainment Weekly's* Gleiberman proclaimed himself "struck, much as I was when I saw the exuberant matrimonial comedy *The Best Man,* by the way that the heroes voice their amorous doubts and drives with a bemused, honestly libidinous, nonexploitative joy and self-perception, something that happens all too rarely in movies these days."

Chestnut was next slated to appear in a film about the infamous early 1970s Attica prison uprising in New York, *The Killing Yard,* as well as a feature-film thriller alongside Jeff Bridges and Noah Wylie titled *Scene of the Crime.* He talked about the positive changes in Hollywood that have taken place just during the decade of his career alone in the *Atlanta Journal-Constitution,* agreeing that the film industry now offered black actors a far wider range of roles. From playing the good guy in a gangster film to one of the more unsympathetic characters in a film about four African-American professionals, Chestnut said he himself has evolved as an actor as well. "When I did 'Boyz,' I didn't really know the whole dynamic of this industry and what it was about, and the little intricate things that the public doesn't know goes on in this industry," he told the *Atlanta Journal-Constitution,* and described himself as a more self-assured player. "I know the industry, and I know how it works. I'm a veteran now, and I'm treated as such."

Selected filmography

Boyz N The Hood, 1991.
Under Siege 2, 1995.
G.I. Jane, 1997.
The Best Man, 1999.
The Brothers, 2001.
Two Can Play That Game, 2001.
Scenes of the Crime, 2001.

Sources

Periodicals

Atlanta Journal-Constitution, March 30, 2001 p. P15.

Ebony, April 2001, p. 148.

Entertainment Weekly, August 13, 1993, p. 82; October 3, 1997, p. 66; August 20, 1999, p. 38; October 29, 1999, p. 84: March 30, 2001, p. 44.

Essence, October 1999, p. 70.

Jet. November 22. 1999, p. 44; March 19, 2001, p. 18.

Multichannel News, December 21, 1992, p. 9.

National Review, September 23, 1991, p. 54

Newsweek, October 25, 1999, p. 80;

People, May 11, 1992, p. 15; September 28, 1992 p. 13; November 1, 1999, p.41.

Time, July 22, 1991, p. 65.

Variety. September 29, 1997, p. 39; September 20, 1999, p. 83; March 19, 2001, p. 30.

Online

Internet Movie Database, http://www.imdb.com.

—Carol Brennan

William "Bootsy" Collins

1951–

Funk vocalist, bassist, songwriter

When the history of modern African-American popular music is written, Bootsy Collins will be remembered as an influential figure, as one of the architects of the funk style. As a member of James Brown's band in the late 1960s, as a collaborator in the explosion of creativity that resulted in the bands Funkadelic and Parliament in the early 1970s, and as an immensely successful solo artist, Bootsy (as he was known) opened new creative frontiers with his bass playing, his songwriting, his vocals, and his stage performances. Yet a focus on Bootsy's influence and historical importance should not be allowed to obscure the sheer sense of fun that has infused much of his music.

Bootsy was born William Boyd Collins in Cincinnati, Ohio on October 26, 1951; he was introduced to music by his older brother, Phelps "Catfish" Collins, who played the guitar. Both brothers gravitated toward the studios of King Records, the legendary Cincinnati independent label whose rhythm-and-blues roots stretched back to the 1940s and which had given birth to the career of the inexhaustibly explosive soul-music original, James Brown, in the mid-1950s. By 1968, Bootsy had formed a group of his own, the Pacesetters.

The following year, Bootsy met Brown himself as Brown was walking from his car to the entrance of the King studios. Brown at the time was in the process of assembling a band to replace his decade-old backing group, the Famous Flames; in the sound of the ambitious teenage bassist he recognized a player who could help him take his music in a revolutionary new direction. Bootsy joined the JBs, as Brown's new band was called, just as the term "funk" was coming into general use. His bass playing is heard on such major Brown hits of the 1969–71 period as "Sex Machine" and "Super Bad," compositions whose heavy, rhythmically sharp bass lines would influence the basic sound of black music for decades to come.

Joined with George Clinton

In 1971, Bootsy found that the experience he had gained working with Brown opened up various new career possibilities. He was offered a slot with the hugely successful mainstream R&B group, the Spinners, but instead threw in his lot with a group of other Brown alumni who had begun to work with the wildly creative Detroit-based funk musician, George Clinton. Clinton's interrelated bands, Parliament and Funkadelic, seemed to offer to Bootsy a chance to develop his own artistic personality, but he likewise brought out new facets of Clinton's musical thinking.

Before he emerged as a solo act, Bootsy was also partially responsible for the adventurous music and stage shows of Clinton's "P-Funk" bands—involving a science-fiction "mothership"; innovative musical electronics; a big, spacy funk beat; and experimental word play that had deep African-American roots. He co-wrote most of the songs on the definitive Parliament album *Mothership Connection* and developed his own stage persona, "Bootzilla," for Funkadelic's live appearances. By the time Clinton moved from Detroit's Westbound Records to the major Warner Brothers label in the mid-1970s, he believed his protégé was ready for prime time.

"Bootsy and his group came in and that was a whole different concept within itself," Clinton was quoted as saying in the *Encyclopedia of Pop, Rock & Soul.* "So what I did was record Bootsy by himself with another group, recorded Parliament . . . which sounded like that but was a little more grown up. Bootsy was aimed more at kids—we called it silly serious—Parliament was a little older and Funkadelic was for a little older than that." Backed by his so-called Rubber Band, which also included JBs saxophonist Maceo Parker, Bootsy released

his first album, *Stretchin' Out with Bootsy's Rubber Band*, in 1976.

Topped the Charts

The title track of that album, "Stretchin' Out," broke into the R&B top 20, and Bootsy's band, with its strong appeal to young listeners, grew into a bigger commercial success than either of the other Clinton projects. Bootsy's second and third solo LP releases, *Ahh . . . The Name Is Bootsy, Baby!* (1977) and *Bootsy? Player of the Year* (1978), each were certified gold for sales of 500,000 copies; the latter album topped R&B album charts. Altogether Bootsy placed ten singles in the R&B top 30 over a five-year period. Such hits as "The Pinocchio Theory" ("If you fake the funk, your nose will grow") and "Bootzilla" became major dance-club hits that expanded Bootsy's popularity beyond a base of R&B and funk enthusiasts.

Part of the reason for Bootsy's success lay in his irrepressible stage presentations. Drawing on the Bootzilla image he had created as part of Clinton's band, Bootsy developed a full-fledged stage character with giant sunglasses studded with rhinestones in star shapes. "It's not just about doing records," Bootsy explained in a *Vogue* interview quoted in *Contemporary Musicians.* "It's got to be a circus, with a three-headed man and everything." He also adopted other stage personalities aimed at younger listeners, including one drawn on the television cartoon character, Casper the Friendly Ghost. In contrast to the often drug-inspired messages of Funkadelic, Bootsy exhorted young audiences to avoid drugs and alcohol.

Bootsy released six albums on the Warner Brothers label between 1976 and 1982, but in the early 1980s, burned out by a decade of role playing and on his own after the Parliament-Funkadelic organization fragmented, he temporarily called it quits as a solo performer. Moving to an estate where he lived with his mother and a group of hunting dogs, he kept a hand in music by performing, writing, and doing production work for a variety of innovative acts that included Johnnie Taylor, Bill Laswell, Malcolm McLaren, and Zapp. He emerged from semi-retirement with the 1988 album *What's Bootsy Doin'?*

In the 1990s Bootsy continued to find himself in demand, working with the groups Deee-Lite and Simply Red, among others. The year 1994 saw the release of a successful greatest-hits compilation and two more experimental Bootsy outings, but he seemed reluctant to return to the stage. "I'd become a so-called star, and I just didn't know how to handle it," he was quoted as saying in the *Rolling Stone Encyclopedia of Rock & Roll.* Another new album, *Fresh Outta "P" University*, was initially released in Europe and Japan in 1997.

Bootsy had always enjoyed considerable international popularity, and the album did well in several countries. It was released in the U.S. on the Private I label. Much of his older music was reissued as a general interest in the influence of funk on the following generation stimulated listeners to explore the work of all the artists in Clinton's stable. Of Bootsy specifically, *Entertainment Weekly*'s Josef Woodard noted that "[h]is loose-limbed soul sounds even better these days, an escapist's treat that paved the way for hip-hop." The year 2001 brought a new Bootsy compilation, *Glory B da' Funk's On Me!*

Selected discography

Stretchin' Out, Warner Bros., 1976.
Ahh . . . The Name is Bootsy, Baby!, Warner Bros., 1977.
Bootsy? Player of the Year, Warner Bros., 1978.
Ultra Wave, Warner Bros., 1980.
The One Giveth and the Count Taketh Away, Warner Bros., 1982.
What's Bootsy Doin'?, Columbia, 1988. *Jungle Bass,* 4th and Broadway, 1990.
Back in the Day: The Best of Bootsy, Warner Bros., 1994.
Fresh Outta "P" University, Warner Bros., 1997.
Glory B da' Funk's on Me!, Rhino, 2001.

Sources

Books

Contemporary Musicians, volume 8, Gale, 1992.
Larkin, Colin, ed., *The Encyclopedia of Popular Music,* Muze UK, 1998.
Romanowski, Patricia, and Holly George-Warren, *The New Rolling Stone Encyclopedia of Rock & Roll,* Fireside, 1995.
Stambler, Irwin, *Encyclopedia of Pop, Rock & Soul,* St. Martin's, 1989.

Periodicals

Billboard, December 6, 1997, p. 23.
Entertainment Weekly, June 28, 1996, p. 107.

Online

http://allmusic.com
http://www.bootsycollins.com

—James M. Manheim

Common

1972-

Rapper

In a time when most of rap and hip-hop's lyrics are centered on attaining wealth and fame, rapper Common stands out as one of the few who are trying to raise the consciousness of the youth. He joins a long list of rappers who feel a responsibility to the community at large. With keen and thought-provoking poetics, Common is giving music listeners a choice.

Born in Chicago in 1972, Common was named Lonnie Rashid Lynn after his father, Lonnie Lynn. He grew up on the south side of Chicago in an economically diverse Black neighborhood called Avalon Park with his mother, Mahalia Ann Hines, a teacher for the Chicago Public Schools; his stepfather, Ralph Hines; and his grandmother.

Two major passions of his early years were basketball and rap. As a young teen, he worked one season as a ball boy for the Chicago Bulls. His love of hip-hop began in the early eighties with a trip to visit his cousin in Cincinnati. When he returned to Chicago, he began, breakdancing, emceeing, and writing rap songs. In 1986, while attending Luther South High School, a Catholic school on Chicago's South Side, he formed his first rap group, called CDR for group members Corey, Dion, and Rashid. Dion, a friend of Common's from the fourth grade at

Faulkner Elementary School, later became rapper and producer NO I.D., and continued to work with Common on stage and in the studio after both had started to perform independently.

While Common continued to perform through high school and after, he also continued his education. After high school, he studied at Florida A & M in the College of Business for two years. But then in 1991, Relativity Records, which had begun to move into hip-hop from a straight rock line-up, offered him a contract, and Common decided to stop attending college to become a full-time performer.

Kept It Real

Lonnie Rashid Lynn began recording under the name Common Sense. The title of his first album, *Can I Borrow A Dollar?*, produced on Relativity's label in 1992, was an allusion of his place as a Chicago rapper on the hip-hop scene. The title seemed to ask if there was room in hip-hop for rappers who were not from the east or west coast. Common has always had a strong sense of place, and he gives much credit to his early experiences in Chicago as having been an important influence on his musical style.

At a Glance . . .

Born Lonnie Rashid Lynn in Chicago. IL on March 13, 1972; parents Mahalia Ann Hines and Lonnie Lynn; child: Omoye Assata Lynn. *Education*: Attended Luther South High School and Florida A & M University.

Career: Rap artist. Formed his first rap group in high school. Signed a contract with Relativity records in 1991; produced his first album *Can I Borrow A Dollar?*, 1992; *Resurrection*, 1994; *One Day It'll All Make Sense*, 1997; *Like Water for Chocolate,* 2000.

Awards: His fourth album, *Like Water for Chocolate,* went gold; Grammy Awards, nominated for best rap solo performance, "The Light," 2001.

Addresses: MCA Records, 2220 Colorado Ave, Santa Monica, CA, 90404. *Website*—mcahiphop.com

In the area around 87th Street and Stony Island, the neighborhood in which he grew up, Blacks with middle class aspirations, working-class Blacks, and young gang members lived side by side In a fall 2000 letter to the *Chicago Sun-Times*, he said, "That area kind of shaped me. It taught me . . . to be real with myself and to be real with people. It taught me to speak the truth."

Common moved to Brooklyn early in his career to have greater access to the music industry, but he retained his Chicago-based version of reality. Music reviewers and fans generally find Common's raps more wide-ranging and thoughtful than most other rap artists. In an article in the *Minneapolis Star-Tribune*, Britt Robson said, "Common's most noteworthy contribution to hip-hop has been his definition of 'keeping it real.' The phrase, often used by gangsta rappers to justify their grisly themes, has devolved into a lazy cliché . . . Common's reality is braver, broader, and more down to earth."

One way that Common has "kept it real" is by rapping about some uncommon themes. His 1997 album, *One Day It'll All Make Sense*, included the song "Retrospect for Life," about parenthood and abortion. It also featured rapper Lauryn Hill, and was recorded when both Hill and Common were expecting the birth of their first children. In fact, they shared the same due date for their children, August of 1997. The song's last line comments on the emotional price tag of abortion: "315 dollars ain't worth your soul." On the same album, in the song "G.O.D." which also featured artists Cee-Loo of the Goodie Mob, Common comments on world religions, rapping about the Koran and the Bible and concluding, "Who am I or they to say to who you pray ain't right?" Other albums include raps about how it feels to come home and find

your place has been robbed, and a series of raps by his father, Lonnie Lynn, called "Pop's Raps."

Common has a solid reputation among fans of hip-hop for his thoughtful lyrics and creative rhymes. *The Source*, a hip-hop magazine, has described him as "Chicago's lyrical warrior." While his songs offer biting and clever commentaries on contemporary topics, they are definitely not sermons. He told Soren Baker, a *Los Angeles Times* writer, that rap, while it needs to be socially conscious, needs to stay true to its tradition of word play and creativity. "I believe in balance." he said. "If you're going to educate people, then you've got to entertain them too."

A conflict came up in 1994 concerning his name. Though Common's lyrics represent his own version of common sense, another group—a California-based reggae group going by the same name—challenged his right to call himself "Common Sense." Faced with a lawsuit, Common shortened his performance name to Common.

Albums Reflect Common's Evolution

Common's own education, both formal and informal, is a consistent influence on his music. As his social consciousness expanded, his ideas are reflected in his songs' themes and lyrics. And as his knowledge of music expands, his records show the influence of a wider bandwidth of musical styles. His album, *Like Water for Chocolate* (the title of which is taken from a highly acclaimed novel by Laura Esquivel), released in March of 2000, is a good example of this interplay. One track on the album is a result of an educational journey that Common took. In 1997, he read a biography of Assata Shakur, a former Black Panther accused and convicted of being involved in the killing of a New Jersey policeman, an event that happened the year before Common was born. Shakur escaped from prison and fled to Cuba in 1979, where she has lived ever since. Common penned a rap to her, "A Song For Assata," and went to visit her in Cuba to add her voice to the song.

The album also reflected Common's musical growth. After the release of *Resurrection*, his 1994 album, Common decided to study more music theory. At the same time, he continued his informal musical education, listening to a wide range of artists including John Coltrane, Curtis Mayfield, Herbie Hancock, and Miles Davis. Many tracks on *Like Water for Chocolate* pay homage to the rich tapestry of African-American musical tradition. The first track, "Time Travelling," is a tribute to the legendary Nigerian musician Fela Kuti. It features his son, drummer Femi Kuti, and contemporary jazz trumpeter, Ray Hargrove. Other tracks reflect strong influences of R&B, of jazz, and of James Brown's driving guitar work. While the album is solidly in the genre of rap, it includes a wider range of music than mainstream hip-hop albums typically neglect. The album's cover also makes a statement: it's a black and white photo, taken by photographer Gordon Parks, of a well-dressed African-American woman in the 1950s drinking from a water fountain marked "Colored Only."

Each of Common's albums has done well. His third album, *One Day It'll All Make Sense*, sold a respectable 435,000 units. However, in 1998, MCA heard a rumor that Common was not happy with Relativity Records. MCA had already signed artists with a similar vision and style, Mos Def and Roots. MCA executives began talking to Common, and MCA bought out his contract that December. Common was given free artistic license on the album, The resulting album, released under Common's imprint, Madame Zenobia, was well-received, selling enough units to go gold. The *Village Voice's* reviewer described it as "an honorable and beautiful continuation of Common's longtime project of bridging the life of the street and the life of the mind."

A Common single, "The Light," had gotten him a Grammy nomination for best rap solo performance. He had also performed at Havana's fifth annual Hip-Hop Conference. Common often performs at concerts, on videos and on albums with other well-known artists, including Erykah Badu, De La Soul, and members of Roots.

He is most famous in the hip-hop community for the allegorical song from *Resurrection*, "I Used to Love H.E.R." The song describes his relationship with a girl that he met when he was 10, a funny, fresh, creative girl. She moved to L.A. after a few years and got involved with a negative scene, including some folks who, as the song says, "told her if she got an image and a gimmick that she could make money, and she did it like a dummy." Common says that even though he sees her being dragged through the sewer, he hasn't given up on her. He's going to try to help her turn herself around because, as the song's last line reveals, " . . . who I'm talkin' 'bout y'all is hip-hop."

West Coast rapper Ice Cube took Common's attack on West Coast rap as a personal affront and came back with a cut on his album with Mac10, *West Side Slaughterhouse*. Common responded with another rap single. Apparently fearful of a rap war of words that might lead to physical violence, Louis Farrakhan of the Nation of Islam called the two together at a conference in 1997, and the two rappers declared a truce.

However, the target of Common's criticism wasn't Ice Cube or any one rapper, but his view of the dangerous state of hip-hop because of the tendency for rappers to bend to the will of commercialism and produce tracks that will sell, without regard for the ideas that they put forth. In a Thanksgiving message published in the *Chicago Sun-Times* in 2000, Common commented on the positive turn he saw hip-hop taking, stating, "I'm definitely grateful that I'm seeing a lot of hip-hop artists out there doing stuff for the community. I'm grateful that I see artists taking a stand in their music. They're saying important things that can affect some lives." As his words indicate, Common sees contemporary hip-hop as a vehicle for conveying messages of importance at the same time that it is generating good music and entertaining its audience. It is his vision that makes him stand out from other rappers. At the same time, his musicality, his blending of multiple musical traditions, and his creative poeticism make his fans want to hear what he has to say.

Selected discography

Can I Borrow A Dollar?, 1992.
Resurrection, (songs include "I Used to Love H.E.R.") 1994.
One Day It'll All Make Sense, 1997.
Like Water for Chocolate, (songs include "The Light" and "A Song for Assata") 2000.

Sources

Periodicals

Billboard, Feb 19, 2000, p. 25.
Chicago Reader, Oct 10, 1997.
Chicago Sun-Times, November 23, 2000, page 9.
Los Angeles Times, March 19, 2000, Calendar page 5.
The Source, March, 2000.
Star Tribune (Minneapolis, MN), November 10, 2000, Freetime section, p. 3.
Village Voice, April 12–18, 2000.

Online

Biography Resource Center, Gale, http://www.galenet.com/servlet/BioRC.
Pop Matters Columns, http://www.popmatters.com.
Pound Magazine, http://www.pound.com.
Westword, http://westword.com.

Other

Additional material for this profile was obtained from an interview with *Contemporary Black Biography*, July 31, 2001.

—Rory Donnelly

Marvel Cooke

c. 1901-2000

Journalist and activist

Marvel Cooke's life story is an exceptional one, from her upper-class upbringing in a politically progressive Minnesota family to her adult life as a journalist, trade unionist, and political activist. Cooke came to New York City during the Harlem Renaissance and befriended some of history's leading artists and intellectuals, including W.E.B. Du Bois and Richard Wright. As a journalist, her landmark series, "The Bronx Slave Market," exposed the exploitation of black women by wealthy white women in New York. She fought for workers' rights as a member of the Newspaper Guild, and was called to testify before Senator Joseph McCarthy about her membership in the Communist Party. In the seventies, she worked on behalf of the defense of radical icon Angela Davis. Friend Lloyd Brown called Cooke "one of those unsung heroines of our people," according to Philly.com.

Cooke was born Marvel Jackson c. 1901, in Mankato, Minnesota, and was raised in an upper-class, white neighborhood in Minneapolis. Her father, Madison Jackson, was an Ohio State University law school graduate who, unable to find a law firm that would hire a black lawyer, was forced to work as a Pullman sleeping-car operator; her mother, Amy Wood Jackson, was a former teacher who once lived on an Indian reservation. Her parents were "Eugene V. Debs socialists," Cooke later claimed, her father being more politically active than her mother, who was kept busy with the children. Though her father died in 1927, Cooke's mother was politically supportive of her later in life. Cooke graduated from the University of Minnesota with a degree in English in 1925. She planned to take a teaching job in the South, but was offered a job at the NAACP's monthly publication, the *Crisis,* as an editorial assistant to W.E.B. Du Bois, and headed off to New York City.

Immersed in the Harlem Renaissance

Cooke arrived in Harlem at the tail end of the Harlem Renaissance. Du Bois, who had once dated Cooke's mother, recognized Cooke's talent for writing, and put her in charge of a column. Her column consisted of a summary of items of interest to African Americans that Cooke culled from a variety of publications. Du Bois, who is credited by many as the intellectual force behind the civil rights movement was "a very warm human being; despite what other people thought about him," according to an interview found online at Philly.com. Du

At a Glance . . .

Born Marvel Jackson c. 1901, in Mankato, Minnesota; died on November 29, 2000; daughter of Madison Jackson and Amy Wood Jackson; married c. 1929. *Education:* Graduated University of Minnesota, 1925.

Career: Moved to New York City; worked as an editorial assistant to W.E.B. DuBois at NAACP's *Crisis* magazine, 1927; helped form the Newspaper Guild's first unit in New York City; became a member of the Communist Party in the 1930s; wrote features for the *Amsterdam News*, 1928–37; was assistant managing editor of *People's Voice*, 1940–47; campaigned for Progressive Party presidential candidate Henry Wallace, 1948; joined the staff of the white-owned *New York Daily Compass*, 1950–52; was New York director of the Council of Arts, Sciences, and Professions, 1950s; took the Fifth Amendment when called to testify before Sen. Joseph McCarthy about her activities in the Communist Party, 1953; was legal defense secretary of the Angela Davis Defense Fund, 1970s; served as national vice chairman in the National Council on American-Soviet Friendship; wrote for the *New World Review* until the magazine's demise in the eighties; appeared in the documentary *W.E.B. DuBois—A Biography in Four Voices*, 1995.

Bois called Cooke "daughter" and often accompanied her to social events.

Harlem was thriving when Cooke moved to New York, and she moved in elite artistic and intellectual circles. She became friends with some of the leading figures of the era, including singer-actor/activist Paul Robeson and artist Elizabeth Catlett. She was engaged for a time to Roger Wilkins, a future leader of the NAACP. Cooke's sister married Wilkins's younger brother, Earl Wilkins. Cooke and her writing group, which included novelist Richard Wright and Langston Hughes, read the first chapter of Wright's landmark book, *Native Son,* "a million times" while the author reworked it, she recalled in the Philly.com interview. During the next two decades, Cooke's own writings delved into such issues as segregation in New York. She lived in an apartment at 409 Edgecombe Ave., a legendary Harlem address which has been home to Du Bois, Wilkins, and Supreme Court Justice Thurgood Marshall, among others. She remained at the same address for 70 years.

Cooke left the *Crisis* in 1928 to take a job at the *Amsterdam News.* Her editors there sent her to report crime stories, which she disliked. "Working at the *Crisis* was an editorial experience, and working at the *Amsterdam*

News was a street experience," she told Philly.com. Newly married to Cecil Cooke in 1929, Cooke took a break from the *News* to teach with him at North Carolina A&T in Greensboro, North Carolina. She returned to the *Amsterdam News* in 1931. Cooke helped form the Newspaper Guild's first chapter in New York City with several co-workers, and held union meetings in her home. The editorial workers' union was locked out of the *Amsterdam News* and picketed for "eleven long, cold weeks," Cooke told Philly.com. "It was the worst experience of my life." In a series of interviews Cooke later did with the Washington Press Club Foundation, she recalled being asked, "What's a nice girl like you doing on a picket line?" and replying, "The bosses are not necessarily in your corner, even if they are your own color." She was jailed twice during the strike, which finally ended Christmas Eve 1934. In 1937, Cooke quit the *Amsterdam News* in protest over a sensational headline that read: "Killed Sweetheart, Slept With Body."

Refused to Testify During Communist "Witch Hunt"

It was during the *Amsterdam News* strike that Cooke joined the Communist Party. She was recruited on the picket line by Benjamin Davis, a future New York councilman. Cooke told an interviewer in 1989 that the professed goals of American Communists were her goals, including racial equality and expanded welfare programs, according to the *Washington Post*. She felt, after her politically progressive upbringing, it was a natural step for her. Many American Communists left the Party in the thirties, forties, and fifties. As she told a *Washington Post* reporter in 1993, Cooke never held party office, but remained a member. In 1953, Cooke was called twice to testify before Sen. Joseph McCarthy on Capitol Hill about her involvement with the Communist Party. She was asked to provide information about a clerk at the *People's Voice*, but she refused to cooperate and took the Fifth Amendment. She referred to McCarthy as "a peanut," according to Philly.com, and laughingly recalled the clerk in question as a strident anti-Communist.

Cooke regularly walked picket lines during the twenties and thirties, not only for the Newspaper Guild, but also for civil rights demonstrations, many of which were led by Adam Clayton Powell, a Harlem pastor who became a Democratic congressman. She campaigned for Progressive Party presidential candidate Henry Wallace in 1948. When Paul Robeson was barred for his political activism from traveling outside the United States in the fifties, he called on Cooke for help. She attended an international peace conference in East Germany in Robeson's place, and later called the trip the "greatest experience of my political life," according to Philly.com. When she returned to the States, Cooke's passport was confiscated by federal agents, but activist attorney William Kunstler later worked to get it back.

In 1940, Cooke took a job as assistant managing editor of a new publication founded by Adam Clayton Powell, called the *People's Voice.* The publication was "just the kind of paper that we envisioned coming out of Harlem," she told *Philly.com.* "It was a people's paper dedicated to making things better in this community." She remained with the paper until it closed in 1947.

Exposed "The Bronx Slave Market"

Cooke took a job at the white-owned *Daily Compass* in 1950. Not only was she the only African American on the staff, she also was the only female. She later told *Philly.com* that she was not treated differently from anyone else on the staff, and "It never occurred to me that it was strange. . . . In retrospect, I do think it was a very progressive move." She laughingly recalled one editor who was unduly tough on her, but when confronted by co-workers, confessed he was uncomfortable because he felt he could not swear in front of her. She told him that, although she did not swear, she had heard the language all her life and it did not bother her. She wrote about the arts and life in New York's black neighborhoods for the *Compass,* and went undercover for a landmark series called "The Bronx Slave Market." She stood on a Bronx street corner with other black women, as they did every morning, and waited to be chosen by white housewives for housework. Cooke recounted in her story that the strongest-looking "slaves" were hired first, and that she had to argue to get 80 cents an hour to wash floors. The series sold a lot of papers, and Cooke remained with the paper until it closed in 1952. Paula Parker, a journalist and cousin of Cooke's, told *Philly.com,* "She cut a path that was just so wide and so clear that you can't help but be inspired by her and her work."

After the demise of the *Compass,* Cooke focused more on activism. She became New York director of the Council of Arts, Sciences, and Professions, and was national vice chairman of the National Council for Soviet-American Friendship. She volunteered as legal defense secretary of the Angela Davis Defense Fund in 1971. Davis, the sixties radical activist/professor charged with murder and kidnapping, was once on the FBI's "Ten Most Wanted" list, but was eventually acquitted. Cooke wrote for the *New World Review* until its demise in the eighties. She died of leukemia at a New York Hospital at age 99. "I didn't realize," she told *Philly.com,* "until much later looking back on my life, that I was having such a great experience."

Sources

Periodicals

Washington Post, December 2, 2000, p. B7.

Online

Southcoast Today (Massachusetts), http://www.s-t.com/daily/12–00/12–05-00/a11wn064.htm (August 3, 2001).
Philadelphia Inquirer Online, http://www.philly.com/packages/history/people/cbmoore/MARV22.asp (July 12, 2001).
Women in Journalism homepage, http://npc.press.org/wpforal/ohhome.htm#topWPCF Oral History Project (August 3, 2001).

—Brenna Sanchez

Michael Cooper

1956-

Basketball player and coach

"I love the sounds of basketball," Michael Cooper told a *Los Angeles Times* reporter as he sat out a game in a locker room after a technical-foul ejection, confident that his superbly trained Los Angeles Sparks team could function without him. "I even love being off the court, in a locker room, when a game is underway and hearing the crowd react—I can almost see what's happening." The love of basketball shown in that statement manifested itself in Cooper's lifelong dedication to the game—as a key player on the legendary Los Angeles Lakers squad of the 1980s; as a scout, as an assistant coach; and then as head coach of the Los Angeles Sparks of the Women's National Basketball Association (WNBA).

Michael Jerome Cooper was born on April 15, 1956, and grew up in Pasadena, California, outside Los Angeles. His parents divorced when he was a child; as his mother Jean struggled to survive working double shifts as a nurse, Cooper was left in the hands of his grandmother, Ardessie Butler. "Everybody gave me something different," Cooper told *Sports Illustrated*. "My mother and grandmother gave me love. Then they gave me to my uncles."

It was Cooper's uncles who spotted and encouraged his athletic talent. Small in comparison with most basketball players, Cooper tried other sports first as a student at Pasadena High School. His uncles pushed him toward baseball, but, as he explained to *Sports Illustrated*, "I didn't like hitting, standing there and letting somebody throw a rock at my head." He moved on to the position of wide receiver in football, but his uncles disparaged that idea, arguing that Cooper's slender six-foot-six-inch frame would not long withstand football's constant physical abuse.

Cooper did excel at track and field at Pasadena High; he was especially adept as a high-jumper, and even during his years in pro basketball a Los Angeles track coach tried to tempt him back to the high jump, arguing that he might have Olympic-level abilities. Finally Cooper settled on basketball. He was, then, not a basketball prodigy but an athlete of tremendous all-around ability who took up basketball as a career. His college career began not in a high-flying Division I basketball program, but at Pasadena City College. Later he transferred to the University of New Mexico, from which he graduated in 1978. There he met his wife Wanda; the couple has three children.

At a Glance . . .

Born April 15, 1956, in Pasadena, CA; parents: Marshall and Jean; partly raised by grandmother: Ardessie Butler; married: Wanda; three children: Michael Jr., Simone, Miles. *Education:* Attended Pasadena City College; University of New Mexico, B.A., 1978.

Career: Professional basketball player and coach. Played for Los Angeles Lakers, NBA, 1979–90; played on five championship teams; played professional basketball in Italy, 1990–91; special assistant to the general manager, Los Angeles Lakers, 1991–94; assistant coach, Los Angeles Lakers, 1994–97; assistant coach, Los Angeles Sparks, WNBA, 1998–99; head coach, Los Angeles Sparks, 1999–.

Awards: Selected nine times to All-Defensive First Team in NBA; NBA Defensive Player of the Year, 1987.

Address: *Office*—Head Coach, Los Angeles Sparks, 3900 W. Manchester Blvd., The Forum, Inglewood, CA 90301.

Signed to the Los Angeles Lakers in 1979, Cooper soon displayed his all-around abilities. "In an era of specialization, Mike does many things," legendary Lakers center Kareem Abdul-Jabbar told *Sports Illustrated.* "He's a true swing man, a backup point guard, a three-point shooter. And yes, a true stopper. He challenges everybody." Cooper was indeed known for his stubborn defensive skills. In 1987 he won the NBA's Defensive Player of the Year award, and he was selected for the league's All-Defensive first or second teams for eight seasons in a row—an especially noteworthy accomplishment in view of the fact that Cooper was often not part of the Lakers' set of five players who started the game. NBA offensive great Larry Bird once called Cooper the best defensive player he had ever faced.

Shots Inspired Nicknames

In fact, Cooper was once named by *Sporting News* to a list of basketball's all-time greatest reserve players or "sixth men." "He could do everything well," the magazine noted, and it was that versatility that made him so important to the Lakers as they notched five NBA championships (out of eight appearances in the finals) during his playing career. No slouch on offense, he inspired a set of nicknames for his various distinctive shotmaking capabilities: the "Coop-a-Loop," "Cooper Hoop," and "Cooper Scoop." Cooper led the Lakers in three-point shots five times, and once scored six three-pointers in a championship game—a feat matched by only two other NBA players.

After wrapping up his NBA career in 1990, Cooper played briefly in an Italian pro basketball league. In 1991 he returned to the Lakers as a special assistant to the team's general manager, Jerry West. He served in that front-office post for three years. In March of 1994 Cooper was named assistant coach for the Lakers, working for a short time under his old teammate Earvin "Magic" Johnson and then under Del Harris. Cooper first worked as a head coach during one 1994 game when a prior engagement called Johnson away, and he also got a taste of women's basketball when he coached a team that participated in the annual "Say No" women's tournament.

Cooper's defensive skills showed through in the Lakers' performance in the mid-1990s, as the team placed near the top of the league in steals and blocked shots and in the 1995–1996 season limited its opponents to a franchise record low of 98.5 points per game. With accomplishments like these under his belt, Cooper began to hunger for a chance to show what he could do at a team's helm. The formation of the new WNBA at the end of the 1990s gave him his chance.

Became Sparks Head Coach

Serving briefly as an assistant coach, Cooper was named head coach of the Los Angeles Sparks WNBA franchise on October 14, 1999. His penchant for hard work began to show immediate results with the Sparks, as the team consistently outlasted its opponents in tough contests. "We are the best conditioned team in the league, we've shown that," Cooper boasted to the *Los Angeles Times,* and his contention was backed by the Sparks' eight wins out of nine games decided by six or fewer points in the 2000 season. The Sparks narrowly missed winning the WNBA 2000 league championship, losing to the Houston Comets in the championship finals.

Cooper's success with the Sparks was recognized when he was named the WNBA's Coach of the Year in 2000. Redoubling his efforts for the 2001 season, Cooper scored the success that had eluded him the previous year; the Sparks won the WNBA championship over the Charlotte Sting. Over Cooper's two seasons at the helm, the Sparks' record was an impressive 56 wins and eight losses. A well-rounded figure who devotes time to several charitable causes, Cooper was often mentioned as a possible addition to the NBA's slender roster of African-American head coaches. In the summer of 2001, however, he indicated a desire to remain with the Sparks and was in the process of negotiating a new contract with the team.

Sources

Jet, September 11, 2000, p. 48.
Los Angeles Times, August 2, 2000, p. D8; August 8, 2000, p. D3; August 23, 2000, p. D3; September 6, 2001, p. D1.

The Sporting News, April 10, 1995, p. 20.
Sports Illustrated, May 11, 1987, p. 50.

Online

Los Angeles Sparks, http://www.wnba.com/sparks.

—James M. Manheim

Carl Craig

1969-

Electronic festival founder, musician

More than a million people flooded downtown Detroit over Memorial Day weekend in 2000. They were music lovers who had come to hear their favorite artists play the first annual Detroit Electronic Music Festival, which set the record as the largest electronic music event in history. If over a million fans came to listen to the sounds of artists like DJ Spooky, Mos Def, and the Roots, among many others, the artists themselves were there because of their allegiance to the festival's creative director, celebrated techno artist, DJ, and producer, Carl Craig.

Though acknowledged internationally as one of the genre's most influential and visionary artists, Craig's music has gone relatively unheard of in his hometown. However, he has gained recognition for breaking new ground in techno by incorporating jazz, soul, hip-hop, and avant-garde music influences. Throughout his career, Craig has used an alias for each of his musical moods. He has recorded futuristic house beats under the moniker Paperclip People, Psyche has been reserved for his more ambient sounds, 69's ("six-nine") recordings have a harder techno edge, and he has explored his experimental jazz tendencies with Innerzone Orchestra. According to the *Washington Post*, "Craig's musical expression has always gone beyond the artistic purity associated with techno." Craig admitted in *Billboard*, "I've always had a concept of dodging boundaries."

Experimented with Electronica

Born in 1969, Craig listened to a variety of music that included Prince, the German avant-garde duo Kraftwerk, Parliament, Led Zeppelin, and the Smiths as a teen while attending Detroit's Cooley High. He found great inspiration in the music of Motown legend Stevie Wonder. "Stevie just did it," Craig said in an interview with *MUSE* online. "He was bad; he was doing techno before it was techno. . . . Stevie just had it." As a teen Craig fiddled around making music on his guitar, and was exposed to the dance-music scene by a cousin who was doing lighting for parties around Detroit. He first became interested in electronic music while listening to Detroit techno pioneer Derrick May's radio show on WJLB. Craig experimented with recording on dual-deck cassette players until he convinced his parents to spring for a synthesizer and sequencer. He studied electronic music, including artists such as Morton Subotnick, Wendy Carlos, and Pauline Oliveros.

In an electronics course, Craig passed along a tape of his homemade productions to a friend of May's. May was taken with Craig's work and invited him to re-record one track, "Neurotic Behavior." Craig did not own a drum machine, so the track's original mix was completely beatless, but inspired nonetheless. As the British became solidly fascinated with Detroit techno music, May invited Craig to join his Rhythim Is Rhythim DJ group on its 1989 European tour. Craig subsequently lent his hand to May's classic "Strings of Life" and the Rhythim Is Rhythim single, "The Beginning." While on the tour, he also recorded several of his own tracks at Belgium's R&S Studios, some of which were released on the *Crackdown*

At a Glance . . .

Born on May 22, 1969, in Detroit, MI; married Hannah Sawtell; children: one.

Career: Joined Derrick May's Rhythim Is Rhythim DJ group, 1989; co-founded RetroActive label, 1990 (label dissolved); founded Planet E Communications record label, 1991; signed with Blanco Y Negro; released *Landcruising*, 1995; released *More Songs about Food and Revolutionary Art* on Planet E, 1996; organized and served as creative director of Detroit Electronic Music Festival and Ford Focus/Detroit Electronic Music Festival, 2000–01; released *Designer Music: The Remixes (Volume One)*, 2000.

Awards: Best Label Award for Planet E and Best Remix Award for "The Climax (Basic Channel Remake)," Musik Und Maschine Awards, 2001; honored by Detroit's mayor for contributions to music and the Detroit community, 2001.

Addresses: *Record Company*—Planet E Communications, P.O. Box 27218, Detroit MI 48207. *Website*—http://www.planet-e.net.

EP that Craig recorded as Psyche on May's Transmat record label.

Craig and partner Damon Booker founded RetroActive Records in 1990. Between shifts at a copy shop, Craig recorded tracks in his parents' basement, and from 1990 to 1991 he released six slick singles on RetroActive under his own name and the monikers BFC and Paperclip People. A falling out with Booker led to RetroActive's demise, but Craig wasted no time and founded his own Planet E Communications to record a deliberately lo-fi and funky EP called *4 Jazz Funk Classics*, which he released under the name 69. Craig's work during the rest of 1991 bounced from hip-hop to techno. His 1992 single, "Bug in the Bassbin," which he recorded as Innerzone Orchestra, was considered an early influence on the British drum 'n' bass and jungle genres—DJs and producers played the 33-rpm single at 45-rpms to create a ready-made, high-speed beat. His Paperclip People release "Throw" showcased Craig's disco and funk influences.

Remixing As Modern-Day Songwriting

"In the past, remixing was simply layering some percussion over a track and maybe adding a few samples," Craig said in an interview with *Billboard*. "Now, it seems as though the art of remixing has morphed into an almost completely new method of songwriting." Though he turns down more remix opportunities than he's offered, he made his mark in 1994 on the music of Tori Amos in a ten-minute rendition of her song "God," and on songs by Maurizio, La Funk Mob, and others. The Amos remix led to Craig's first deal with a major label and he signed with the Blanco y Negro European imprint of Warner Bros. Records. *Landcruising*, Craig's subsequent first full-length release, exposed his broad range and vision to a market far wider than he'd known before. The swell of popularity led to R&S Records re-releasing 69's *The Sound of Music*, a compilation of two previously released EPs.

Craig's 1996 single with Paperclip People, "The Floor," released on Britain's Ministry of Sound label, was so complemented by a grooving bassline and disco sample that it found favor in many house-music clubs. Craig began to be recognized more for his broad vision and drifted from his Detroit-techno contemporaries. He became increasingly uncomfortable putting the Detroit-techno label on his music, and opted to call it "urban" or "soul" if it need be labeled at all, he told the *Washington Post*. Craig released arguably his most important full-length collection, *More Songs About Food and Revolutionary Art*, on Planet E in 1997.

In 1999 Craig released Innerzone Orchestra's *Programmed*, and played a number of very well-received dates with what *Billboard* called the "free jazz meets techno" group. Craig remixed live instrumentation by former Sun Ra drummer Francisco Mora, jazz keyboardist Craig Taborn, and bassist Paul Randolph, and added vocals and digital enhancement. The result, according to *Billboard* critic Amanda Nowinski, was "21st-Century jazz whose roots are grounded in the past but technologically enhanced." The release, she continued, "signifies the aesthetic maturity of an artist whose training began in the early days of techno." Citing what experimental artists like Sun Ra, Miles Davis, and John Coltrane did with jazz, Craig told *Billboard*, "You need to know the history in order to learn and develop the future."

Craig showcased an extensive collection of his remixes from the previous eight years in 2000's *Designer Music: The Remixes (Volume One)*. *Rolling Stone* music critic Pat Blashill wrote that Craig reworked the music of such artists as R&B's Incognito, Belgian Euro-disco act Telex, Ron Trent, and Italian synth-pop/disco artist Alexander Robotnik "with the discipline of a gene splicer." The release's standout piece was Craig's rewiring of Detroit techno pioneer Kevin Saunderson's 1988 anthem, "Good Life," renamed "Buenda Vida" on *Designer Music*.

Festival Brought Fans to Detroit

In 2000 Craig served as creative director for his brain child, the first Detroit Electronic Music Festival. He used his influence in the music industry to get big names to perform, and expected a turnout of maybe 200,000 to 300,000 over the course of three days. His estimate was wrong—over a million dance-music fans flocked to downtown Detroit to listen to acts on four stages. Though national and international acts performed, Craig's emphasis was on Detroit talent. The festival "instantly catapulted Motown's techno artists from almost total anonymity in their own hometown to front-page news in the local papers," according to writer Mike Rubin in *Rolling Stone.* "It was definitely a feeling of vindication for all the Detroit-based artists that have been in the business for the past ten or 15 years," Craig told *Billboard.*

The second annual festival in 2001 was even bigger than the first. The world-class artist roster, which included Kid Koala, Mix Master Mike, and De La Soul, still emphasized Detroit talent, with performances by Stacey Pullen, Kenny Larkin, Juan Atkins, and Kevin Saunderson, among many others. Eighty artists played on four stages. The crowd grew and downtown hotels were packed full of foreign tourists. Ford Motor Company and Miller Genuine Draft beer, honing in on the festival's prime promotional value, sponsored the event and it was renamed the Ford Focus/Detroit Electronic Music Festival, much to the chagrin of fans, who lamented the festival's commercialization.

In an abrupt turn, festival organizer Carol Marvin fired Craig days before the festival for "very murky reasons," according to Rubin in *Rolling Stone.* A subsequent outcry and e-mail campaign flooded Marvin's inbox and those of higher-ups at Ford and J. Walter Thompson, Ford's advertising company. Ford responded by claiming it was not "the corporate monster you worry about," according to the *Wall Street Journal.* Craig struck back by suing Marvin for breach of contract.

Honored by Detroit

Despite the controversy, Craig was validated when, on the final day of the festival, he was honored by Detroit's Mayor Dennis W. Archer. Just as the second DEMF was coming to a close, Craig accepted a special commendation from the mayor that recognized his founding role in the festival and Detroit music. "Craig has endeared himself to an international audience of electronic music lovers with his artistic vision, intellectual curiosity, and his willingness to identify with and promote the work of other artists," the mayor's proclamation read. "He has . . . . enhanced the image of the city of Detroit"

Craig's vision extended far into the future. He told *Code* magazine, "It's about making your mark and leaving something behind for the generations to come, so they can expand on the concepts and ideas and take them to the next level." He believed, as he told *Code*, that contemporary music, "especially black music, is just so stagnant. It's so focused on materialism . . . Chasing money, being greedy . . . there's just no future in it." But,

he continued, he understood his calling: "To get people to understand what it means to go beyond the norm and push the boundaries. . . . Someone has to stick his neck out and take that chance. The way I see it, if that person isn't me, then who's it gonna be?" In 2001, Planet E celebrated its ten-year anniversary. Craig and wife and business partner Hannah Sawtell were expecting their first child.

Selected discography

Landcruising, Blanco Y Negro, 1995.
Stevie Knows, Planet E, 1995.
More Songs About Food and Revolutionary Art, SSR, 1996.
Intergalactic Beats, Planet E, 1992.
DJ Kicks, !K7, 1996.
Acid Tunes, Nova Tekk, 1997.
House Party 013: A Planet E Mix, Next Era, 1999.
Designer Music: The Remixes, Vol. 1, Planet E, 2000.
Onsumothasheeat, Shadow, 2001.
Problemz/The Truth (vinyl 12"), Planet E.
The Climax (original mix and "Basic Channel Reshape" mix) (vinyl 12"), Planet E.

As 69

4 Jazz Funk Classics (vinyl EP), Planet E, 1991.
Sound on Sound (CD), released with R&S Records.

As Paperclip People

Remake (vinyl 12"), Planet E.
Throw/Remake (remix) (vinyl 12"), Planet E.
The Floor (vinyl EP), Planet E, 1996.
Secret Tapes of Dr. Eich (CD), Planet E.
Steam (vinyl 12"), Planet E.
For My Peepz (EP), Planet E.

As Innerzone Orchestra

Bug in the Bass Bin (vinyl EP), Planet E, 1992.
Programmed (LP/CD), Planet E, 1999.
People Make the World Go Round (Carl Craig and Kenny Dixon Jr. remixes) (vinyl 12"), Planet E.
People Make the World Go Round (Jaydee and Lacksidaisycal remixes) (vinyl 12"), Planet E.

Sources

Books

Larkin, Colin, editor, *Encyclopedia of Popular Music,* Muze UK Ltd., 1998.

Periodicals

Billboard, July 17, 1999, p. 29; August 5, 2000, p. 34.

Code, October 2000, p. 28.
Rolling Stone, September 28, 2000, p. 60; July 5, 2001, p. 40.
Wall Street Journal, May 25, 2001, p. B2.
Washington Post, August, 30, 2000, p. C5.

Online

All Music Guide, http://www.allmusic.com (July 10, 2001).
MUSE Online, http://www.muse.ie/archive/icon/carl_craig.html (September 6, 2001).
Planet E Communications, http://www.planet-e.net (August 22, 2001).

—Brenna Sanchez

Damon Dash

19(?)(?)–

Record producer, executive

When rap surpassed country to become the third-best-selling music genre after R&B and rock in 1998, a spotlight was cast on rap-industry executives. "It's become part of the hip-hop culture now to become a business mogul," L. Londell McMillan, an entertainment attorney, told *Black Enterprise*. Unlike other music genre executives, those in the business of rap and hip-hop were quick to sell not just records, but to market a culture. With a diverse spread of film interests, a successful clothing line, and other marketing tie-ins, in addition to backing multi-platinum records, Damon Dash has become one of music's most prominent moguls. As CEO of Roc-A-Fella Records, the Roc-A-Fella film division, and the Roc-A-Wear clothing line, "I'm a millionaire after taxes," Dash said in an interview with *Black Enterprise*.

Street Kid Went to Boarding School

Though he was raised in Harlem, Dash was a scholarship student for a time at the South Kent School in Connecticut. He got his start in the entertainment business at age 19, when he and his cousin, Darian Dash, started Dash Entertainment, an artist-management company. After finding record company executives uninterested in their artists or ideas, the pair, frustrated, quit the business.

Roc-A-Fella's most prominent artist has emerged in Brooklyn-raised rapper Jay-Z. Dash met struggling rapper Jay-Z after the dissolution of Dash Entertainment, and the two became fast friends. Dash became the rapper's manager, but couldn't get him signed to a record deal. Finally, they decided they had "better insight" into how to market urban music and style, according to writer Charles Whitaker in *Ebony*. "We knew that people liked our music and were imitating our style, the way we dressed," Dash told *Ebony*. "So from the start we said we wanted a company that would promote that urban culture to a mass audience." They wanted to do it all—music, clothes, film—and believed they could do it better than a lot of the competition.

So Dash, Jay-Z, and third partner Kareem "Biggs" Burke put their money together, pressed some records on their own, and secured a distribution deal, launching Roc-A-Fella Records in 1995. After the independent album went gold, selling 500,000 copies, the same record companies that had turned down Dash and Jay-Z were eager to do business with them. "When record companies were first courting us, they came to me with the nigga

At a Glance . . .

Born and raised in Harlem, NY.

Career: Founded Dash Entertainment with cousin Darien Dash at age 19; founded Roc-A-Fella record label partnership with Kareem "Biggs" Burke, Jay-Z, and Def Jam Records, 1995; started Roc-A-Wear clothing line and Roc-A-Fella Films, 1998; produced Jay-Z's *Hard Knock Life...Volume 2,* 1999; produced *Streets Is Watching* film and *Backstage* documentary; organized *Hard Knock Life* tour with Jay-Z, Redman, DMX, and Method Man, 1999.

Addresses: *Office*–Roc-A-Fella Records, 825 8th Ave., New York, NY 10019. *Website*–http://www.rocafella.com.

predominantly denim, with a selection of T-shirts, sweatshirts, sweaters, jackets, leather, and accessories. After launching in 1999, Roc-A-Wear reportedly did $100 million in sales in 2000, putting it in competition with Def Jam-founder and rival Russell Simmons's Phat Farm line, as well as more high-profile lines by such designers as Calvin Klein and Tommy Hilfiger. Dash also planned a women's Roc-A-Wear line.

Dash road-tested the Roc-A-Fella brand name in 1999, with the "Hard Knock Life" tour, a 50-city, large arena tour headlined by Jay-Z, and featuring Redman, DMX, and Method Man. Though he encountered resistance because of the perceived threat of violence at the events, Dash researched every detail and the tour was notable for its lack of incidents among fans and performers. The artists played to mostly sold-out crowds, and the tour broke rap-genre records for ticket sales. The tour reportedly grossed over $13.7 million, ranking it at Number Ten in sales for the first half of 1999.

Harlem in Hollywood

Despite having to fight for attention as an unknown film producer in the Hollywood establishment, Dash launched Roc-A-Fella Films in 1998. Dash's goal with the production company was to create urban films that did not glorify sex and violence, but illustrated the consequences of his character's actions. Dash turned out two reasonably successful straight-to-video films—*Streets Is Watching,* the semi-autobiographical movie based on Jay-Z's songs, and the concert documentary *Backstage,* which went behind the scenes of the "Hard Knock Life" tour.

Boston Globe critic Loren King called *Backstage* a "gritty and freewheeling documentary." The film follows the artists of the "Hard Knock Life" tour with a "raw, behind-the-scenes peek that strips away preconceptions (often stereotypical and judgmental) about the rappers," King wrote, "revealing the drive, brains, anger, pain, and humanity of the urban hip-hop scene." *New York Times* critic Elvis Mitchell wrote that the film captures the "standard life of revelry and exhaustion" that is typical of concert music, as well as "the performers' awareness of the way rappers are perceived." Mitchell summed up: "*Backstage* isn't as good as the rap documentaries *Rhyme and Reason* and *The Show,* but it still casts a keen, observant eye (even though video fatigue sets in) on this world."

Dash's ambition and business acumen has helped him succeed in a variety of endeavors. As a producer and founder of his own record label, Dash has earned the title of music mogul, and, with his forays into fashion and film, he has brought hip-hop culture to a wider audience. But perhaps his greatest achievement still lies ahead.

deal where they make you think you own a label and you really don't," Dash told *Black Enterprise.* "I wanted a joint venture because I knew I was going to be successful and the equity would be worth something down the line." In most joint-venture arrangements, major labels retain more power, but Dash finally struck a joint-venture deal with Def Jam Records in which Roc-A-Fella owns one-half the master tapes of all recordings. Since its start, Roc-A-Fella Records has produced eight albums that have earned either gold or multi-platinum status.

Sewed Up Success With Clothing Line

Dash also was not going to give away the upper hand in setting up his and Jay-Z's clothing line, Roc-A-Wear. Rather than license the name to a manufacturer, he found a New York manufacturer who would go into business 50–50 with him. "I may not know how to manufacture and design clothing but I have a brand that I can bring to it," Dash told *Black Enterprise.* Though many Jay-Z fans could be seen sporting Roc-A-Wear gear, "It's been more about the clothes and the quality than the artist," Dash said in an interview with *USA Today.* "People look at the clothes as being good clothes, as opposed to being Jay-Z's line. That might have gotten their curiosity going, but it's not that easy. You have to make quality clothes to stay in the business." That said, Dash admitted that a lower-level artist than Jay-Z might not have been able to launch a successful clothing line. He told *USA Today* that only a few artists "are influential enough and business savvy enough to make it lucrative for them."

The line was targeted at males between 14 and 30 years old, and included men's clothes in the $23 to $600 price range; kids clothes ran from $15 to $60. The clothes were

Sources

Periodicals

Black Enterprise, December 1999, p. 78.
Boston Globe, September 6, 2000, p. D6.
Ebony, January 2001, p. 32.
New York Times, September 6, 2000, p. E5.

USA Today, August 29, 2001, p. D10.

Online

All Music Guide, http://www.allmusic.com (August 3, 2001).

—Brenna Sanchez

Craig David

1981-

Singer

In the summer of 2000, Craig David's debut recording, *Born to Do It*, made him an instant celebrity at 19 in his native Britain. The assemblage of dance-oriented R&B songs earned accolades from critics and achieved platinum several times over. The recording's first single, "Fill Me In," made David the youngest British male singer to have a No. 1 hit in his country. Journalists called him a talent to watch, praising David's impressive tenor as well as his song-writing abilities. "David has a genuinely remarkable vocal style, displaying a luxurious tone and athletic flexibility of a kind rarely heard in British pop," declared music critic Neil McCormick of London's *Telegraph* newspaper. Not long after *Born to Do It* was released in the United States, the record made it into the Top 20 on the charts.

Observer journalist Akin Ojumu described David as "that rarest of things: a homegrown soul star." The young singer is a product of Britain's multicultural society, born to a white Jewish mother and a Grenadian carpenter in 1981. But the Davids separated not long after their son's birth, and David was raised by his mother, a sales clerk. They lived in a relatively impoverished area of Southampton, a port city on the English Channel, where David grew up listening to the records of American stars like Stevie Wonder and Michael Jackson. He had little knowledge of his father's previous career as a reggae musician with a group called the Ebony Rockers, but when he himself showed an interest in making music, his father attempted to steer him toward classical guitar. "I loved the guitar, but I wasn't really feeling these classical songs," David told *Entertainment Weekly* writer Rob Brunner. "I wanted to sing."

Teen DJ Sensation

His chance came one night when he was just 14, at the West Indian social club to which his father belonged, when the DJ handed him the microphone. "I was just kind of harmonizing, singing, ad-libbing," David recalled in the interview with Brunner. He began MC-ing, or rapping over the songs of others, with the DJ and others, and soon gained a measure of local celebrity. The extra-curricular activities often kept him out quite late, but David recalled that his parents were supportive. "I chose my friends carefully, and they knew I had my head on my shoulders," he said in the *Entertainment Weekly* interview. "I wasn't gallivanting around being an idiot." At home, his bedroom contained an array of instruments

At a Glance . . .

Born Craig Ashley David on May 5, 1981, in Southampton, England; son of George (a carpenter) and Tina (a sales clerk) David. *Education:* Attended Southampton City College.

Career: Worked as a disc jockey in Southampton, England, and host of pirate radio show, mid-1990s; signed to Wildstar Records, c. 1999; debut LP, *Born to Do It,* released in the United Kingdom, 2000, released in the United States, 2001.

Addresses: *Record company*—Atlantic Records, 9229 Sunset Blvd., 9th Floor, Los Angeles, CA 90069-2474.

and turntables, and he began writing songs on his own. Entering a contest at the age of 15, he won first prize with "I'm Ready," a song recorded by a successful group in the United Kingdom called Damage. He also hosted his own show on a pirate, or unlicenced, radio station.

Though David worked toward an engineering degree at Southampton City College, his career plans took a new turn in 1997 when he struck up a friendship with an older musician, Mark Hill, of Artful Dodger. The band was a well-known "garage" outfit, the term used to denote a style of drum-and-bass, house-music, and R&B elements in the U.K. music scene also called two-step. David worked with Hill in the studio and appeared as a guest vocalist on an Artful Dodger track, "Re-Rewind," in late 1999. David and Hill also had a minor hit with "What Ya Gonna Do?," which "caused a storm on the underground scene," David recalled in the article by Brunner. "Bristol, London, Manchester . . . we were just amazed. We were these guys from Southampton, and we'd made a record that was getting five-star reviews. It was crazy." The success led David to a contract with Wildstar Records to record his own songs.

Vaulted to Top of Charts

Produced by his friend Hill, David's *Born to Do It* appeared in British record stores in early 2000. Its soulful R&B songs, like "Last Night" and "Follow Me," appealed to fans, and the first single, "Fill Me In," about a girl whose budding romance is repeatedly thwarted by her parents, reached No. 1 in April. David was amazed at its success, for he could easily recall the day when he had written it in his bedroom. "Like, in a small confined space writing a song to then be embraced by thousands of people, millions of people, it's like I can't believe it," he enthused in an interview with Carol McDaid of the *Observer.*

The work won positive accolades from the music press. Ojumu called it "an inoffensive, sunny confection, sprinkled with Spanish guitar touches and accessible lyrics" in the *Observer* article, while the *Telegraph*'s McCormick commended its "superbly crafted songs" that proved David's talent as "a clever lyricist with a knack for concise story-telling and an unerringly melodic sensibility." McDaid, writing for the *Observer*, praised the work as possessing "something for everyone: Spanish guitar, tasteful strings, great melodies, storyboard lyrics, two-step basslines and that gorgeous, athletic voice." David noted that his experiences as a DJ were crucial to his success as a songwriter. "It gave me a really good idea of what works and what doesn't in terms of structure," David told another *Telegraph* writer, Ben Thompson. "Even in the course of a three-and-a-half minute tune, the crowd gets tired, and you have to know how to get them going: do they want to hear the bridge again?"

Achieved International Success

Soon David was a bona-fide celebrity in the United Kingdom, selling out concert arenas and his every move chronicled in the press. In late 2000, the *Observer*'s Ojumu reviewed a performance in David's hometown of Southampton, where his popularity had reached massive proportions. During the show, David sang much of *Born to Do It*, but also performed songs from Usher ("Nice and Slow") R. Kelly ("Did You Ever Think")-a choice of covers, Ojumu noted, that "hints at something more interesting in his future. The former is a showy ballad that lets his heartfelt voice soar and the latter gives the audience a rare chance to jump up and down as David raps and stomps across the stage."

David and his debut LP earned nominations for six "Brit" awards, the United Kingdom's equivalent to the Grammy but lost in all categories. Still, the record had attracted some notable fans, including Sir Elton John, Macy Gray, Sean "P-Diddy" Combs, and Sisqo, and went on to sell 5 million copies around the world. It was released in the United States on the Atlantic label in the summer of 2001, but David was cognizant of the fact that few male British pop acts had achieved lasting stardom in the North American market. "There are so many great artists here in the U.S.," David told *Los Angeles Times* writer Steve Hochman. "It's a different culture. I feel I have a different approach, being a DJ and rapping in my songs as well as singing." Again, the record garnered positive critical accolades. David's voice, noted *Entertainment Weekly* critic Will Hermes, "slides and skips over sparkling arrangements. Melodies get sketched out by acoustic guitar, harp, or harpsichord; bells and wind chimes up the tinkle factor. And the rhythms bump along, busy but refined, nodding to American R&B scientist Timbaland just as he nods (admittedly or not) to British DJ music."

"David seems devoid of the egotism that so often accompanies youthful success," observed McCormick in the

Telegraph. Though his daily life and possible romantic links were avidly chronicled in the British press, he rarely gave the tabloids any salacious headlines for bad behavior. "I don't feel like I've achieved anything yet," he told McCormick. "I've got such a long way to go, I don't want to get caught up in any of the rock and roll kind of lifestyle because these early stages of my career are the most important and to throw it all away by making stupid mistakes is something I'd regret for the rest of my life."

Selected discography

Born to Do It, Wildstar, 2000, Atlantic, 2001.

Sources

Entertainment Weekly, May 11, 2001, p. 80; July 20, 2001, p. 64; August 3, 2001, p. 30.
Essence, June 2001, p. 64.
Los Angeles Times, February 4, 2001, p. 66.
Observer (U.K.), July 16, 2000 p. 6; November 26, 2000, p. 14.
Telegraph (U.K.), August 24, 2000; October 14, 2000; March 2,

—Carol Brennan

Kenneth "Babyface" Edmonds

1959-

Producer, singer, and songwriter

Kenneth "Babyface" Edmonds has emerged as one of the most prolific producers, songwriters, and performers in popular music. Much of the artist's success has been achieved in tandem with Antonio "L.A." Reid, with whom he founded the LaFace record label in 1989; at one point, the duo was responsible for six singles appearing simultaneously in the R&B Top Ten. Described by Gordon Chambers of *Vibe* as "clearly an architect of today's black pop scene," Edmonds has written songs for such pop luminaries as Michael Jackson, Whitney Houston, Boyz II Men, Mariah Carey, Toni Braxton, Aretha Franklin, Vanessa Williams, TLC, and Madonna. A *Keyboard* magazine writer deemed him "that rarest of creatures, a producer with a Midas touch." Not content to remain behind the recording console, however, Edmonds, who reluctantly adopted the nickname Babyface, given to him by guitarist Bootsy Collins, has also pursued a successful career as a solo recording artist.

Love and music have always been inextricably combined for Edmonds. He grew up in the Midwest, the second youngest of six boys, and—as he told David Ritz in *Essence*—"I fell in love almost every day. I fell in love at the drop of a hat. I can remember falling in love as far back as kindergarten." These episodes of infatuation always had a soundtrack. "When I was falling in love with love, I was also falling in love with melody. [Soul superstar] Stevie Wonder's melodies, [British pop icons] the Beatles' melodies—any pretty melody might move me. Melodies spoke to me about the state of my own heart."

At a young age he learned guitar. When he was in eighth grade, Edmonds's father died of lung cancer, leaving his mother to raise her sons alone. At this stage, Edmonds became determined to have a career in music.

While in the ninth grade, Edmonds used this determination to devise a way to meet some of his musical idols. He confided to Jack Baird of *Musician* that he would phone concert promoters pretending to be his teacher, asking if the musicians would grant his gifted young charge— namely himself—an interview. Civic-minded chart-toppers like the Jackson 5, Stevie Wonder, and funk hitmakers Earth, Wind and Fire agreed, and Edmonds was able to chat with them. Baird theorized that young Babyface made very good mental notes of whatever they divulged and stored them away for later use.

At a Glance . . .

Born Kenneth Edmonds on April 10, 1959, in Indian-apolis, IN; son of Marvin and Barbara (a pharma-ceutical plant manager) Edmonds; married Denise (di-vorced, c. 1980s); married Tracey, 1992; children: Brandon, Dylan.

Career: Producer, songwriter, arranger, keyboardist, gui-tarist, and solo performing and recording artist, late 1970s-; member of groups ManChild, mid-1970s, and the Deele, mid-1980s; with L.A. Reid, writer and pro-ducer of recordings by the Deele, Shalamar, the Whis-pers, After 7, Karyn White, Bobby Brown, Johnny Gill, Whitney Houston, Paula Abdul, TLC, Boyz II Men, Toni Braxton, and others, 1987-; released debut solo album, *Lovers*, 1989; *Tender Lover*, 1989; *For the Cool in You*, 1993; *The Day*, 1996; *Christmas with Babyface*, 1998; *Face 2 Face*, 2001; co-founded LaFace Records, 1989; co-founded Edmonds Entertainment, 1997.

Awards: (With L.A. Reid) songwriter of the year, Broad-cast Music Inc. (BMI), 1989, 1990, 1991, 1995; double platinum awards, 1990, for *Tender Lover*, and 1994, for *For the Cool in You*; Lifetime Achievement Award, NAACP, 1992; ten Grammy awards; American Music Award for favorite male R&B artist, 1995; Trumpet Award, Turner Broadcasting Systems, 1998; Image Award, NAACP, 1998; had a federal highway named in his honor.

Addresses: *Home*—Beverly Hills, CA. *Record company*—Arista Records, 6 West 57th St., New York, NY 10019. *Fan club*—Babyface, 14755 Ventura Blvd., 1–710, Sher-man Oaks, CA 91403.

Met L.A. Reid

In Indianapolis, Edmonds played in Top 40 bands and then in a funk group called ManChild and another called the Crowd Pleasers. While with ManChild he realized that, as he explained in a *Keyboard* interview, "the only way I'd really be able to grow in terms of my writing was to pick up keyboards." In 1981 Edmonds first hooked up with Antonio "L.A." Reid, who was performing with a group called the Deele. Edmonds later joined the band, and he and Reid soon began to attract attention. After Dick Griffey, the head of Solar Records, noticed the duo's producing skills on their own work, the two were enlisted to write and produce for the Whispers and Shalamar. Soon after, they were producing big-name acts like the Jacksons and newcomers like Karyn White, After 7 (featuring two of Edmonds's brothers and one of his cousins), and Pebbles (who married Reid). The pair's

work with up-and-coming soul crooner Bobby Brown—particularly his hits "Don't Be Cruel" and "Every Little Step," both of which were written by Edmonds—helped Edmonds and Reid break through to the next level.

In 1987 Edmonds and Reid went out on their own and began writing and producing independently of Solar Records. Soon they were working with some of the biggest stars in pop, notably Paula Abdul, Whitney Hous-ton, and Sheena Easton. With the exception of R&B stalwarts Jimmy Jam and Terry Lewis, they had little competition among production duos.

Two years later, in 1989, Edmonds and Reid, with the financial backing of Arista Records, formed the LaFace label to develop and produce talent and make records that Arista would distribute. "With the importance that black music plays in the overall scheme of music," Reid said in a *Grammy* interview, "to not have more success-ful black owned and operated record companies is really sad. We obviously have the talent and capable execu-tives who help run so many other labels." The company, based in Atlanta, Georgia, soon attracted an impressive array of talent.

Edmonds and Reid were honored by Broadcast Music Inc. (BMI) as songwriters of the year in 1990. They had emerged as two of the biggest players on the music scene, but this didn't shield them from criticism. In a more delicate assessment, Robert L. Oderschuk of *Keyboard* called them "craftsmen" rather than "innovators," citing their commercial savvy at the expense of risk-taking. *Musician*, noting some more harsh criticism, pointed out that "critic Nelson George castigated the Reid/Edmonds sound as the epitome of homogenized L.A. pop." Edmonds and Reid fended off claims that such "homog-enization" represented an attempt to soften the distinc-tively African-American traits of the R&B form. "We're Black artists creating out of a Black bag [of styles and influences]," Edmonds insisted in *Essence*.

As the decade progressed, the duo launched a number of successful new acts, most notably Johnny Gill, TLC, and Toni Braxton. "With TLC, it was their personalities," Edmonds told Franklin in *Interview*. "They gave off the vibe that made you feel, O.K., these kids are stars, and you just needed to put the right music with them and let them go. Toni Braxton auditioned with her sisters, and she just shined. And I thought, 'I can write for her.' She can deliver something emotional and get it across. That's really what I look for—someone who can pull off that emotion." In *Dollars & Sense*, Perkins wrote about Edmonds's nurturing of Braxton's meteoric rise in pop and R&B: "He signed Braxton to his LaFace label in 1991 and brought her along slowly, giving her a duet ('Give Us Heart') before settling in for a debut album. And for that effort, he wrote 'Breathe Again,' 'Seven Whole Days,' 'Another Sad Love Song,' 'Love Shoulda Brought You Home,' and 'You Mean the World to Me,' all hits that have established Braxton as the industry's most promising star."

Second Solo Album A Success

While writing and producing for other acts as a part of LaFace, Edmonds was also working on his solo career. In 1989 he released his second solo album, *Tender Lover*, which went double platinum, thanks in large part to singles like the smash hit "Whip Appeal." The recording's success, he told *Billboard*, "was so gradual, and so quiet, that I didn't realize how well it was doing." He was equally surprised, he said, by the response of concert audiences when he went on tour with Pebbles before recording the album. "I was blown away by the audience's reaction," he said.

The fame that has come with Edmonds's success has at times been disconcerting. He told Ritz of *Essence*, "I wish being a public person came easier to me, but I can't change my character. I can't betray my privacy." Edmonds's self-effacement in interviews has been almost proportional to his huge success. "I don't call myself a keyboard player," he claimed in his *Keyboard* interview. "I'm a writer who uses keyboards to get the songs done. I'm not even close to being a keyboard player." He evinced similar modesty in *Musician*: "I don't claim to be a great vocalist, but I know how to work my voice with its limitations. My talent is I know how to work what I have. It might not always be a picture-perfect performance, but what we look for is the emotion. Sometimes the emotion comes from it being just a pinch sharp or flat."

Looking back on his quick rise in a business in which many artists struggle for years, Edmonds was philosophical. "I kind of just stumbled into producing," he told Franklin in *Interview*. "It was more that I was a writer, and the only way you were going to get your songs done was to do them yourself." Yet he and Reid synched more than sounds in the studio: "Our musical souls blended," he told Ritz of *Essence*. "We shared a similar drive for success." With Reid programming the drums, Edmonds playing keyboards and guitar and handling most of the backup vocals, their friend Kayo laying down the basslines, and Darryl Simmons providing production assistance, the team developed a distinctive and very influential style. *Musician*'s Baird wrote, "The core L.A. & Babyface sound has always included spunky electronic textures, explosive percussion and complex, rubbery bass lines, even as it's changed to stay ahead of an army of imitators." Oderschuk of *Keyboard* described the duo's trademark sound as "built on crystalline [electric piano] Rhodes-like timbres, light but stinging backbeats flicking through layers of gauzy echo, radical scratch-like gating on the snare in upbeat tunes, sparse synthetic strings, lush backup harmonies, an overall delicacy even on dance tracks."

In 1992 Edmonds, who had been married for three and a half years during his twenties, wed again, this time to Tracey, a model whom he first met at an audition for a part in the "Whip Appeal" video. Edmonds recalled in *People*, "She didn't get it because she caught chicken pox." They later ran into each other and, Edmonds explained in *Jet*, "It was like a 'meant to be' kind of thing." He and Tracey, who managed Yab Yum Entertainment—a record label and publishing company financed by Sony—lived in Beverly Hills in a French Regency-style mansion. Married life, Edmonds told *People*'s Preston, had a positive effect on him: "I'm more stable, more confident, and more satisfied. It's a cool thing to know you have somebody who's there for you and you're there for them."

Boomerang Soundtrack a Hit

The 1993 soundtrack to the Eddie Murphy film *Boomerang* featured a song Edmonds wrote for Boyz II Men called "End of the Road," which became one of the best-selling singles of all time, eventually breaking Elvis Presley's record for number of weeks at Number One on the *Billboard* singles chart, which he had held for decades with "Heartbreak Hotel." Edmonds told Ken Parish Perkins of *Dollars & Sense* that "End of the Road" was "a great song. I felt something when I wrote it. But I knew someone out there would be better [as a singer], and that was Boyz II Men. And I was right. They did a terrific job with the song." In 1995 another Edmonds-produced Boyz II Men hit, "I'll Make Love to You," broke the record for number of weeks in the top spot of the charts, this time surpassing Whitney Houston's "I Will Always Love You," which had beaten "End of the Road."

In 1993, after winning a Grammy Award for producer of the year for the Boomerang soundtrack, Edmonds and Reid dramatically altered the nature of their relationship and the structure of LaFace records. It was widely reported in the press as a split, but Edmonds described their partnership in 1995 to Preston, saying, "We have defined our relationship. He's an executive, so he deals with the ins and outs of the company. I deal with the creative." Edmonds was frequently asked about the timbre of his relationship with Reid, after Edmonds essentially took control of the creative end; he responded to Preston, "It was a natural evolution that things would change. At the end of the day, [Reid is] probably one of the most important songwriters of all time."

Perhaps the most significant reason behind the restructuring of LaFace and the assumption of creative control was Edmonds's desire to put more effort into his solo career. He predicted in *Entertainment Weekly* that his solo output would now take up more of his time: "It's satisfying to see Boyz II Men or Whitney [Houston] singing one of my songs. But I've never given my own career as an artist 100 percent. I do wonder if I can turn it into something bigger."

Edmonds answered that with the release of his third album, *For the Cool in You*, which was co-produced by Reid. The record went platinum in early 1994. "Babyface continues the nearly forgotten tradition of solo black R&B lover men," wrote *Rolling Stone's* Touré, who generally praised the album despite taking issue with its stylistic conservatism. Chambers noted in *Vibe*, "The subtle soul man uses his seductive falsetto, passion-over-precision phrasing, and well-timed growls to woo his listeners," and found the album "a perfect vehicle for his vocal melisma." And Danyel Smith commented in the *New York Times*, "[*For the Cool in You's*] themes—love and relationships—are commonplace, but the album is not. It is deceptively low-key, a quiet little opus etched from the duo's [Edmonds and Reid's] romantic sensibilities."

The hit single from *For the Cool in You* was an acoustic guitar-based love song called "When Can I See You," which the *New York Times* called "the best cut on the album. . . . With its acoustic flavor, it sounds like a cross between [folk musician] Tracy Chapman and the British soul singer Tasmin Archer." Summing up the Edmonds and Reid sound, the *Times* observed, "Yes, Babyface and L.A. Reid produce mushy souls. No, it isn't Motown; it's contemporary rhythm and blues. Rather than actual innocence, there is hope for it. Rather than bouncy tambourines and chirpy background vocal, there are soaring keyboards and profound bass lines."

Late in 1994 and into 1995, Babyface went on a 27-city sold-out U.S. tour, opening for Boyz II Men, whose popularity, it could be argued, was won in large part by Edmonds's songwriting. One striking feature of Edmonds's show was when he brought a woman from the audience onto stage with him and hands her five 100 dollar bills as he sang "As Soon As I Get Home." Reviewing the San Diego show for the *Christian Science Monitor*, Yoshi Kato noted: "He sang about treating women right and, after an exchange with a woman from the audience, elicited a roar of approval from the audience. 'I feel that women demand respect. Rather, I feel that women deserve respect,' he announced, before inviting the woman to join him on stage. Once in the spotlight and seated atop a stool, she was serenaded and then given $500 dollars to pay her rent." *People* asked an Edmonds assistant about this unique promotional tool and was told that it was slated to be done at every one of the 27 shows planned for the tour.

Edmonds's tour ended in mid-February of 1995, giving him the time to do what he really enjoys: shopping, skiing, and songwriting. Reflecting on his tour, he declared in *People*, "I'm not like the regular artist who needs that attention, getting on-stage. They need to feel people. That's not important to me. I feel the people when they buy the records."

Recognized Again at Grammys

In 1995 Edmonds was recognized for his solo work when he was nominated for five Grammy Awards, including one for best male R&B vocal performance for his 1994 hit "When Can I See You." At the ceremony held in Los Angeles on March 1st, he was awarded two statues—one for "When Can I See You" and the other for his songwriting efforts on Boyz II Men's "I'll Make Love to You."

Edmonds next wrote and produced the soundtrack for the 1995 film *Waiting to Exhale*. Featuring numerous female artists, the album produced several hits—most notably "Exhale (Shoop Shoop)" performed by Whitney Houston and Brandy's "Sittin' up in My Room." Yet, despite great commercial success, Jeremy Helligar of *People Weekly* commented that with this project Edmonds "seems to be overextending himself, trying too hard to give these 15 sister acts something to say."

The Day, Edmonds's fourth solo album, was released in 1996. Several artists contributed to the album, including Stevie Wonder, Kenny G, and Eric Clapton. Edmonds's duet with Wonder, "How Come, How Long," lamented domestic abuse. "The Day (That You Gave Me a Son)" chronicled his feelings about the day his son, Brandon, was born. David Browne of *Entertainment Weekly* called the album Edmonds's "most cohesive and confident work. . . . a sumptuous blend of elegance and sensuality."

Formed Film Production Company

In 1997 Edmonds and his wife decided to extend their partnership into the professional realm. The couple formed Edmonds Entertainment, a film production company. *Soul Food*, executive produced by Edmonds and co-produced by Tracey, was the company's first film. The film was a hit and the soundtrack went double platinum.

Edmonds Entertainment's next project, *Hav Plenty*, was released in 1998, but could not duplicate the success of *Soul Food*. In 2000, however, with *Soul Food* the television series airing on Showtime, Edmonds Entertainment had produced another hit. *Variety* writer Laura Fries called the series "a welcome addition to the ethnically-challenged TV landscape" and praised producers Edmonds and his wife for keeping "the integrity of the story well intact, focusing on the volatile personalities and unique family dynamics."

Along with fellow Grammy-winning songwriters Carole Bayer Sager and David Foster, Edmonds launched Tonos.com in 1999. Described by *PR Newswire* as "the ultimate digital 'insider' music network," Tonos.com offered music enthusiasts and aspiring musicians an inside look at every aspect of the record business. The site also offered contests for undiscovered talent. First

Prize winners in the Composer Lyricist and the Vocalist contests would be flown to Los Angeles where Edmonds and Foster would record and produce a demo for them.

Edmonds then branched out into professional sports in 2000, forming, along with attorney Ken Harris, Edmonds Sports Group. The company would provide agent representation for players from all sports, though it initially focused on signing NFL players. Also in 2000, Edmonds signed a multi-year and multi-record contract with Arista Records.

In 2001 Edmonds released *Face 2 Face*. This album was an attempt at reinvention. When the first single, "There She Goes," was released, Arista executive Lionel Ridenour told *Entertainment Weekly*, "We're [thinking] nobody is going to believe this is Babyface." Critics did not respond as positively as Ridenour had hoped. In *Entertainment Weekly* Craig Seymour called the album "a poorly executed composite intended to appeal to a younger fan base" and "a monstrous waste of talent and time."

Many have hailed Edmonds the next Quincy Jones. And no wonder. With so many multi-media irons in the fire, from his work as a recording and film executive to his artistry as a singer and songwriter, Edmonds has, according to *Variety*, "parlayed his success into a diversified entertainment conglomerate." Edmonds has accomplished all this by following a simple philosophy: "The whole idea," he told *Variety*, "is whatever you do, have fun with it, try to make sure that it's quality, and something you don't mind putting your name on."

Selected discography

With the Deele

Street Beat, Solar/Epic, 1984.
Material Thangz, Solar/Epic, 1985.
Eyes of a Stranger, Solar/Epic, 1987.

Solo releases

Lovers, Solar/Epic, 1989.
Tender Lover, Solar/Epic, 1989.
For the Cool in You, Epic, 1993.
The Day, Epic/Legacy, 1996.
Christmas with Babyface, Epic, 1998.
Babyface: A Collection of His Greatest Hits, Epic, 2000.

Face 2 Face, Arista, 2001.

Sources

Books

Who's Who Among African Americans, 13th ed., Gale, 2000.

Periodicals

Billboard, December 1, 1990; June 15, 1991; August 28, 1993; March 26, 1994; May 27, 1995.
The Business Journal Serving Charlotte and the Metropolitan Area, October 6, 2000.
Christian Science Monitor, January 17, 1995.
Dollars & Sense, September/October 1994.Ebony, May 1995.
Entertainment Weekly, September 10, 1993; November 1, 1996; April 13, 2001; September 14, 2001.
Essence, September 1990.
Grammy, December 1992.
Interview, March 1994.Jet, July 16, 1990; March 14, 1994; May 8, 1995.
Jet, October 13, 1997; April 16, 2001.
Keyboard, November 1990.
Los Angeles Times, July 25, 1993.
Musician, October 1990; March 1994.
Newsweek, January 16, 1995.
New York Times, August 5, 1993.
People, January 23, 1995; February 27, 1995; May 8, 1995.
People Weekly, December 11, 1995.
PR Newswire, November 3, 1999; October 19, 2001.
Rolling Stone, October 28, 1993; December 1, 1994.
Upscale, June 1994.
Variety, June 26, 2000; November 13, 2000.
Vibe, September 1993; December 1993; September 1995.

Online

All Music Guide, http://allmusicguide.com.

Other

Additional information for this profile was obtained from Epic Records publicity materials, 1993.

—Simon Glickman, Jim Henry, and Jennifer M. York

Missy "Misdemeanor" Elliott

1971–

Singer, composer, producer

As a singer/rapper, songwriter, arranger, and producer with three successful albums under her belt, Missy "Misdemeanor" Elliott has taken the recording industry by storm. The head of her own record label, Elliott has become known for her versatility and originality. "Missy is one of those talented artists who always finds a way to reinvent herself," Sean R. Taylor, music director for WQHT in New York, told *Billboard*. "Her music is always pounding, moving, vibrant."

dom. "I remember in school writing Janet Jackson and Michael Jackson and asking them to come get me out of class," she told *Interview*. "I would imagine them running down the hall and asking my teacher, 'Ms. Daniels, can we get Missy out of class? We're here to see Missy.' My imagination was always wild like that. So when I got a call from Janet, just to hear her say she loved my music, it was like a blessing. It was a dream come true to get a call from Mariah [Carey] . . . and now I'm just waiting for Michael Jackson to call."

Melissa Elliott was born in Portsmouth, Virginia. Her earliest musical experiences were with a church choir. Elliott knew at an early age that she was going to be a star, and she told her mother so repeatedly. She began playing the part of the star singer early, too. Elliott would sing in her room with a broomstick microphone to an audience of her dolls. "In my mind I pictured them screaming for me. I would go into a whole other zone," she told of *Essence*. Elliott wrote her own songs about butterflies, birds, whatever happened to be around. She sang them to passing cars from overturned trash cans, or to her family from atop picnic tables in the park.

Elliott not only vividly imagined herself on stage, she could see her heroes coming to take her to music star-

Despite the fact that many of her dreams came true and the impressive power she accumulated in the recording industry, Elliott remained a little star-struck by the artists who used to be just voices on records. Whitney Houston once called her, and, she told *Interview*, "when I got off the phone I screamed so loud." Elliott's feet remained firmly planted on the ground, however, and often signed autographs patiently for the fans who recognize her on the streets of Manhattan. More significantly, Elliott has courageously made public her father's physical abuse of her mother and her own sexual abuse at the hands of a cousin. For her, speaking out publicly was a way of taking control of a past that had previously controlled her, as

At a Glance . . .

Born Melissa Elliott in 1971, in Portsmouth, VA.

Career: Auditioned with group Sista for Devante Swing of Jodeci, 1991; with partner Timbaland, began writing and producing 1992; Sista cut first and only album, *Brand New*, 1995; wrote seven tracks for Aaliyah's *One In A Million*, 1996; received major songwriting, recording and production deal, including a label of her own from Elektra Entertainment, 1996; worked with Jodeci, Raven-Symone, 702, Whitney Houston, Janet Jackson, Mariah Carey, Paula Cole, Scary Spice, and Nicole; released debut solo album, *Supa Dupa Fly*, 1997; *Da Real Life*, 1999; *Missy E . . . . So Addictive*, 2001.

Addresses: *Record company*—East-West Records, Elektra Entertainment Group, 75 Rockefeller Plaza, New York City, NY 10019. *Fan club*—Missy Elliott Fan Club, c/o Gejel Enterprise, P.O. Box 923, Temple Hills, MD 20757.

well as drawing attention to a serious social problem that frequently gets swept under the rug.

Elliott got her first musical break in 1991 when the group Jodeci, came to Portsmouth. She took her group, Sista, made up of some of her friends from junior high, to the hotel where Devante Swing, one of the members of Jodeci was staying. He was so impressed by their performance—a set of original tunes written by Elliott—that he signed them to his production company. "We thought we were too hot," Elliott told Imusic.com. "We tried to look just like Jodeci during that audition. We had our pants tucked in our boots. We had begged our mothers to get us these outfits. We even had our canes. We thought we were four hot Devantes."

Teamed up With Timbaland

Sista cut their first album in 1995, and broke up when it became clear that Elektra Records could not afford to release it. Elliott then formed a production team at the company with Timbaland, a childhood friend, and began writing songs for artists such as Jodeci, Raven-Symone, and 702. Timbaland produced the records. It was a combination that worked. "When we come together, we are able to be a lot more creative because there are no bars," Elliott told the *New York Times Upfront*. "We're just, 'Let's do it,' instead of worrying about what people might say."

Despite Sista's apparent failure, Elliott had gotten noticed. "People started to call for songs, or ask me to rap or something," she told Imusic.com. One call came from the

late singer Aaliyah, who was looking for a new producer. Elliott and Timbaland entered the picture and the result was four big singles from Aaliyah's CD *One In A Million*: "4 Page Letter," "Hot Like Fire," "If Your Girl Only Knew" and the title track. Sylvia Rhone, the chairman and CEO of the Elektra Entertainment Group, took notice. She offered Elliott, then a mere 22-year-old, a deal that included writing and producing opportunities, her own recording label (The Gold Mind, Inc.), and eventually a contract as an artist. "You could recognize instantly that Missy possessed star potential," Rhone told *Essence*.

Elliott has since worked with a number of other superstar singers, including Whitney Houston, Janet Jackson, Mariah Carey, Paula Cole, and Scary Spice. In addition to writing, arranging and producing, Elliott began making guest appearances, notably on Gina Thompson's "The Things You Do," in which she displayed her infectious laughter and did a one-of-a-kind slide. "That one caused people to start coming up to me on the street and say 'Ain't you the 'Hee Ha' girl?,'" she told Imusic.com. "They don't even know my name and they'll say, 'Hee Ha girl, do that slide across the floor.'"

Michael Musto asked Elliott in *Interview* if she ever worried that her work as a label executive, songwriter, and producer would distract her from making her own music. "No," she replied, "because I really enjoy writing and producing for other artists. Some people save their best songs for their own albums. I'd rather give another artist one of my songs. At the end of the day, it still represents me."

Released "Supa" Debut Album

Despite the fact that the world seemed to be waiting with baited breath, it took Elliott some time before she finally released the first CD of her own. "I was not going to make a record just to make one, if you know what I mean," she told Imusic.com. "I wasn't going to do a record if I couldn't mix it up." The result was 1997's *Supa Dupa Fly*, a record critically praised as forging an innovative new direction for hip-hop. John Bartleson wrote that "open-minded hip-hop heads may find Elliott's intelligent yet indulgent, anesthetized electro-funk flow a persuasive argument for the unification of rap and R&B." In "The Rain (Supa Dupa Fly)," for example, she deliberately distanced herself from the violent themes that run through so much other hip-hop. "I don't knock nobody's hustle," she told Imusic.com, "but everybody don't want to hear that. You get that on the news and it depresses you enough." *Supa Dupa Fly* ended up going platinum and receiving a Grammy nomination.

Her second album, *Da Real World*, had more of a street feel. It produced a controversial single, "She's a B****," a song which addressed her power—and attitude—as a woman. "Music is a male-dominated field," Elliott explained to *Interview*. "Women are not always taken as seriously as we should be, so sometimes we have to put our foot down. To other people, that may come across as being a b****, but it's just knowing what we want and being confident." *Da Real World* also went platinum, and garnered both a Grammy nomination and three MTV Video Music awards.

Elliott stepped back out of the spotlight in 2000, concentrating on her record label. With releases from Gold Mind artists T.C., Mocha, and Nicole slated for release that year, Elliott found herself busy overseeing these new projects. "These are my babies," Elliott said in *Billboard*. "I'm very proud of the work they're doing; they're kicking it hard."

For the 2001 film *Moulin Rouge*, Elliott produced and was briefly featured in a cover of Patti LaBelle's "Lady Marmalade." Performed by Christina Aguilera, Lil' Kim, Mya, and Pink, the song was an instant hit. The video for the song went into heavy rotation, and won both the Best Video from a Film and Video of the Year awards at the MTV Video Music Awards.

Stars Collaborated on Third Album

Also in 2001, Elliott released her third album, *Missy E . . . . So Addictive*. Dimitri Ehrlich, *Interview*'s Music Editor at Large, said that the album served "up frenetic, freaky soundscapes that seem to have no precedent anywhere." The album's first single, "Get Ur Freak On," featured, according to Gareth Thomas of *Music & Media*, "a hypnotic, looped riff that sticks in your head." Pop singer Nelly Fertado appeared on the remixed version, much to Elliott's delight. "People are going to bug out when they hear it," Elliott enthused in *Billboard*.

Produced by Timbaland, the album also included several collaborations. "One Minute Man," the album's second single featured Jay-Z and Ludacris on two separate versions. On "This Is for My People," rising rap star Eve added, according to *Billboard*'s Marci Kenon, "an out of character flow on the hot techno number." R&B singer Ginuwine appeared on "Take Away" and gospel singers Kim Burrell, Yolanda Adams, and Mary Mary joined Elliott on the inspirational "I'm Moving On." Elliott was accompanied by Redman and Method Man on "Dog in Heat." "They can always add party to a track," Elliott told *Billboard*. "There's something about both their voices that gives energy to a track."

Elliott's artistic success was reflected in the prices she has been able to command for her services. Earning six-figure checks for single tracks, Elliott has used her wealth to buy three Mercedes Benzes, a Cadillac SUV, a Lexus, and a Jaguar XK8. She has also lavished gifts, including flowers, minks, and cash, on her mother with whom she remained very close. She was even building a small mansion in Portsmouth for the two of them. She has

invested part of her fortune in her own lipstick brand, Misdemeanor Lipstick, produced by a cosmetic company headed by former super-model Iman. Part of the profits from the product go to Break the Cycle, a group that helps victims of domestic violence.

While already spending mornings in meetings at her label and afternoons and evenings in the studio, Elliott intended to continue expanding her activities. She has done ads for Gap and Sprite, made television appearances, and hoped to break into movies. "It ain't easy but I've got goals in life. And I'm going to step forth and do all of them," she told *Essence*. But with her music, Elliott remained committed to creating something fresh and new. "Once you make an impact on the world you kinda gotta come back and make sure your new music don't really sound like the last time," Elliott told *Interview*. "I'm never scared to try whatever," she later added, "and I feel that's what people like me for, for doing something different."

Selected discography

With Sista

Brand New, Elektra, 1995.

Solo

Supa Dupa Fly, East-West, 1997.
Da Real World, East-West, 1999.
Miss E . . . So Addictive, 2001.

Sources

Books

Contemporary Musicians, Volume 30. Gale Group, 2001.

Periodicals

Billboard, March 11, 2000; April 14, 2001.
Dallas Morning News, September 7, 2001.
Essence, March, 2000.
Interview, June, 1999; May 2001.
Music & Media, April 28, 2001.
New York Times Upfront, May 14, 2001.

Online

All Music Guide, http://allmusicguide.com (September 21, 2001).
Biography Resource Center, Gale, 2001, http://www.galenet.com/servlet/BioRC.
Elektra Records, http://missy-elliott.com (September 18, 2000).
Imusic, http://imusic.com/showcase/urban/missy.html (September 18, 2000).

MTV Online, http://www.mtv.com/sendme.tin?page=/ news/gallery/m/missyfeature99.html (September 18, 2000).

—Evelyn Hauser and Jennifer M. York

Dale Emeagwali

1954—

Microbiologist, cancer researcher

Renowned microbiologist Dr. Dale Emeagwali excels in the fields of microbiology, molecular biology, fermentation, enzymology, virology, cell biology, and biochemistry. She earned a Scientist of the Year award for her cancer-research work. Emeagwali has been commended for her contributions to and accomplishments in medical science and, as a minority in an overwhelmingly white field, she works to expose minority youth to the sciences, which she feels they are discouraged from pursuing.

Emeagwali was born Dale Brown on December 24, 1954, in Baltimore, Maryland, to Johnnie Doris Brown, a public school teacher, and Leon Robert Brown, who worked as a superintendent of the production department of *Afro-American* magazine for 42 years. The youngest of three children, Emeagwali grew up in the Poplar Grove-Lafayette Avenue area of Baltimore and went to Alexander Hamilton Elementary School #145 and Northwestern High School, graduating in 1972.

As a girl, Emeagwali enjoyed science and excelled in math at school. "Black people are told, 'You can't do math,'" she said in an interview with the Morgan State University *Spokesman*. "We were taught inadvertently,

and sometimes directly, that we couldn't do that." Fortunately, though neither of her parents was involved in academia or science, Emeagwali received the support she needed from her parents to become one of relatively few blacks in science. According to the *Afro-American,* she credits her parents for her success as a scientist. She remembers her parents mentioning entertaining science facts and doing simple experiments with her and her two brothers. Her father was interested in mathematics, had a small collection of books on the subject, and would show the kids tricks using numbers. "Parents must always stress the importance of education and achievement to their children," she told the *Afro-American,* "When kids know there are low expectations, they won't rise."

Emeagwali earned her bachelor's degree from Coppin State College in Baltimore in 1976, with a biology major and chemistry minor. She then left Baltimore to attend Georgetown University Medical School in Washington, D.C. Leaving her family behind for Georgetown was a "cultural shock," she told the *Afro-American.* But she coped with the move by striving to achieve. "I was always ahead in my class and I held on to that ambition," she

At a Glance . . .

Born Dale Brown, December 24, 1954, in Baltimore, MD; daughter of Johnnie Doris (a school teacher) and Leon Robert Brown (magazine production department superintendent); married Philip Emeagwali, August 15, 1981; son: Ijeoma. *Education:* Coppin State College, B.A., biology, 1976; Georgetown University, Ph.D., microbiology, 1981.

Career: Microbiologist and cancer researcher; co-author, "Evidence of a Constitutive and Inducible Form of Kynurenine Formamidase," *Archives of Biochemistry and Biophysics,* 1980; postdoctoral fellow, National Institutes of Health, 1981–84; co-author, "Sequence Homology Between the Structural Proteins of Kilham Rat Virus," *Journal of Virology,* 1984; co-author, "Purification and Characterization of Kynurenine Formamidase Activity from S Paravulus," *Canadian Journal of Microbiology,* 1986; postdoctoral fellow, Uniformed Services University of Health Sciences, 1985–86; research associate, University of Wyoming, 1986–87; senior research fellow, University of Michigan, 1987–88, assistant research associate, 1988–91; co-author, "Modulation of Ras Expression by Antisense Non-ionic Deoxyoligonucleotide Analogues," *Journal of Gene Research,* 1989; co-author, "Amplified Expression of Three Jun Family Members Inhibits Erytholeukemia Differentiation Blood," 1990; research associate, University of Minnesota, 1992–95; Morgan State University, 1996-.

Member: Sigma Xi, 1983-; American Association for the Advancement of Science, 1985-.

Awards: Biomedical Fellowship Award, Meharry Medical College, 1974; Third Place Award, Best Presentation, Beta Kappa Chi and the National Institute of Science, 1976; Biomedical Research Award, Coppin State College, 1976; Postdoctoral Fellowship Award, National Science Foundation, 1981; Postdoctoral Fellowship Award, American Cancer Society, 1981; Scientist of the Year, National Technical Society, 1996.

Address: *Office*—3713 Sylvan Dr., Baltimore, MD 21207–6364.

Not long after, the two were wed. Though they both are scientists, they practice in different disciplines: she is a medical scientist; he is a leading research scientist involved with supercomputers and the Internet. Together, they make an effort to motivate minority students to pursue careers in science. While living in Minnesota—he was working as a research fellow, she as a research associate at University of Minnesota—they began working with the Science Museum of Minnesota on the annual African-American Science Day there. The science-fair-type event, which also includes other professional scientists, is designed to give fourth- through twelfth-graders from inner-city neighborhoods an idea of what scientists do. "We make it seem like an everyday thing so it isn't a shock that we do science," Dale Emeagwali told the *Star Tribune.* "The purpose of science is to do something useful," she told the *Bog Hopper,* "Plants and trees, soap bubbles and toys—simple, everyday things—are science. What I do in the lab, a lot of it is 'cooking' and 'cleaning.'" She believes that this is most beneficial to minority kids, who are often discouraged from pursuing an interest in science. "When a black child said he wanted to be a doctor," she told the *Afro-American,* "he was slapped upside the head and told to stop being simple." Dale Emeagwali also teaches undergraduate-level college science courses. The Emeagwalis have a son, Ijeoma.

After she earned her Ph.D. in microbiology from Georgetown, Emeagwali earned postdoctoral fellowships at the National Institutes of Health and the Uniformed Services University of Health Sciences. In 1987, she and her husband moved to Ann Arbor, Michigan, where she worked as a senior research fellow, then as an assistant research associate, while he worked as a researcher. They both then worked for the University of Minnesota.

Emeagwali's scientific accomplishments so far include the discovery of isoenzymes of kynurenine formamidase in the bacteria Streptomyces paravulus. Prior to her discovery, the isoenzymes were thought to exist only in higher organisms. Her finding is important because a better knowledge of this enzyme in particular could lead to further understanding of what causes cancers of the blood, like leukemia. She was among the first to prove that the cancer gene, or oncogene ras, could be inhibited by a technique known as antisense methodology. This discovery has therapeutic potential because oncogene ras is overexpressed in most cancers.

Her findings in the field of biochemistry have pointed out shortcomings of current research and data interpretation involving proteins. She developed a system for the analysis of a significant cellular protein. The results will affect the current understanding of how some proteins work. In the field of virology, Emeagwali worked with a DNA virus and found the existence of overlapping genes. This discovery sheds light into how organisms may be able to more efficiently use limited genetic material.

continued in the *Afro-American.* "I felt I had the ability to easily assimilate, regardless of race or class."

While on a bus trip back to Georgetown after a school break, Emeagwali met Philip Emeagwali, a Nigerian doctorate student in civil engineering at Georgetown.

In 1996, Emeagwali was named Scientist of the Year by the National Technical Society. The honor is given each year to a scientist who is regarded as a role model and inspiration to other scientists and whose work has somehow benefitted mankind. Emeagwali earned it for her contributions to the fields of microbiology, molecular biology, and biochemistry.

After years of pursuing science and academics all over the United States, Emeagwali moved back to the Baltimore area with her husband in 1996. She took an associate professor position at Morgan State University there, while Philip Emeagwali works as an independent consultant. She enjoys exercise, reading, painting, and has a yellow belt in karate. One of her poems has been published in the *Atlantic Monthly.*

Sources

Books

Black Scientists and Inventors Year 2000 Calendar, BIS Publications, 1999.

Henderson, Ashyia, ed., *Who's Who Among African Americans,* The Gale Group, 2000.

Periodicals

Bog Hopper (a science publication for secondary teachers), January-March 1995.
Insight, January 24, 1995, p. 1A.
Journal of the NTA (National Technical Association), Fall 1998, p. 15.
Spokesman (Morgan State University), November 19, 1996, p. 1.
Star Tribune (Minnesota), January 28, 1995, p. 1B.

Online

Dale Emeagwali Homepage, http://www.emeagwali.com/dale (July 20, 2001).

Other

Additional material was provided by Dale Emeagwali, 2001.

—Brenna Sanchez

Jacqui Frazier-Lyde

1961–

Professional boxer

Jacqui Frazier-Lyde is a lawyer with a successful practice and a devoted mother of three children. She speaks Spanish and French and has an understanding of Arabic. She's a shrewd businesswoman and an upstanding citizen of her native Philadelphia. She also knows how to duck and jab and throw a right hook that would knock the wind out of most women half her age. As a professional boxer, she has scored a series of knockouts and helped put women's boxing on the road to respectability. There is one word to explain the contradictions she embodies: Frazier. Jacqui Frazier-Lyde is the daughter of boxing great Smokin' Joe Frazier. At the unlikely age of 38 Frazier the younger decided to follow in her father's footsteps and become a professional boxer.

Born Jacquelyn Frazier on December 2, 1961, Frazier-Lyde moved from Beaufort, South Carolina, with her family to Philadelphia when she was just four. With her mother Florence, father Joe, brother Marvis and sister Natasha, she grew up in Philadelphia but continued to visit Beaufort during summers. There she enjoyed working with her hands and knew how to change oil and repair brakes by the time she was 13. "I wanted to be a mechanic," she told *Philadelphia People.* In high school she directed her energies into sports instead of shop and

excelled in basketball, hockey, lacrosse and softball. Not content to just score on the field, Frazier-Lyde also snagged the role of class president and was voted Best Personality and Most Likely to Succeed.

Frazier-Lyde's prowess as an athlete scored her a scholarship to American University in Washington D. C. where she majored in Justice and learned Spanish and French. She continued her higher education by earning a juris doctorate in 1998 from Villanova University in Pennsylvania. In the years following graduation she practiced law and soon founded her own law firm, Frazier-Lyde and Associates, LLC, with offices above her father's gym in Philadelphia. She also married Peter Lyde and gave birth to three children, Peter Jr., Sable, and John-Joseph. For many women, this would have been enough—successful career, healthy family, devoted husband—but not many women carry the name Frazier.

Her Mouth Made Her Do It

In October of 1999 Laila Ali, daughter of boxing legend and Frazier's main opponent Muhammad Ali, made her professional boxing debut. Women's boxing was just beginning to garner public interest and with a name like Ali, Laila was bound to draw the spotlight. Following Ali's boxing debut, the media frenzy ensued. Every angle of women's boxing was pursued. Experts debated the value and sportsmanship of the event. A once dismissed sport was finally in the national spotlight. One foresighted reporter, boxing expert Bernard Hernandez, decided to play up the "daughters of boxing greats" angle and called up Frazier-Lyde at her law firm in Philadelphia. "[He] asked me how I thought I would measure up to Laila," she told CBS News, "I just said—it just came out—'Oh I could whip her butt'." With those few words, a mother and lawyer turned herself into a boxer and a fighter. "Since that day I've been training two hours a day, every day, at my dad's gym."

With characteristic ferocity, Frazier-Lyde quickly made her decision to become a professional boxer a reality. She got herself a team of trainers, including brother Marcus and many Philadelphia-based professional boxers. Just three months after that fateful phone call, she applied for her professional boxing license, and in four months she was stepping into the ring as a professional boxer. Frazier-Lyde enjoyed the support of her family, with her husband stepping in as promoter and her brother as trainer; however, father Joe, was a bit more hesitant. *Jet* printed Frazier's comment on Frazier-Lyde's decision to become a boxer, "You get your head shook, your money took, and your name in the undertaker's book." However, it wouldn't be long before her father threw his support and respect behind her and even joined her training team.

Motives Questioned by Boxing Experts

With the ring name of Sister Smoke, ironically given to her years earlier by Muhammad Ali, Frazier-Lyde made

her boxing debut in February of 2000. Not only did she knock out her opponent in one round, she also scored the largest purse ever for a professional woman boxer's debut—a whopping $25,000. This figure immediately started the critics speculating that Frazier-Lyde was in boxing only for the publicity and attendant dollar signs. They accused her of using her father's legacy for marketing and hype. The fact that the company promoting the fights, SoReal Communications, was owned by Frazier-Lyde and her husband only added fuel to the controversy. Frazier-Lyde responded by telling *Philadelphia People*, "I'm not in this for the fame or the money. I'm in it for the history and the competition of the game."

Still, boxing experts loudly questioned her motives as illustrated by *Sports Illustrated's* Rick Reidel who wrote, "[Frazier-Lyde didn't start boxing until last year, after she saw Ali doing it and a great big dollar sign flashed before her eyes." Her arrogant attitude also discredited her in the critic's eyes. She told *Jet* just a month before her pro debut, "I fight in court every day with people who are not the nicest . . . Boxing? That is easy compared to who I really have to fight." Frazier-Lyde mostly dismisses this criticism as recorded by www.blackvoices.com, "A lot of people in the boxing business are not all that happy with women boxers. Too bad. They weren't too happy about the WBA (Women's Basketball Association) or the women's soccer team. They were trailblazers. I am a trailblazer." Though critics still question her motives and credibility, no one can question the dedication she has shown in training and in the ring.

Fought for Frazier Family Name

Between February of 2000 and March of 2001, Frazier-Lyde fought and won seven fights. Though critics derided Frazier-Lyde's opponents as unskilled hacks, her trajectory along the boxing path often seemed nothing more than a way to get to Laila Ali. From the onset of her boxing career, Frazier-Lyde called for a fight with Ali. She claimed to want to have the fifteenth round of the "Thrilla in Manila," the famed 1975 fight between Joe Frazier and Muhammad Ali that ended in the fourteenth round with a loss for Frazier. *Jet* quoted Frazier-Lyde discussing a bout with Ali, "It's about history, competition, family and legacy." Still the businesswoman, she didn't ignore the financial windfall such a fight could create, both for her and Ali. In an oft-quoted remark Frazier-Lyde said, "[The fight] would establish Laila financially, then I would establish her horizontally." Through it all, Laila, unlike her verbose father, kept quiet on the matter.

Amid fanfare and media spotlights the Frazier-Ali rematch was scheduled for June 9, 2001 at Turning Stone Casino in Verona, NY. As the hype built up, so did the criticism. Of the fight, Jay Larkin, senior VP of event programming at Showtime told New York's *Daily News*, "It has nothing to do with sports. It's a spectacle that has appealed to the paparazzi mentality." He continued, criticizing Frazier-

Lyde: "Jacqui Frazier has zero ability. Women's boxing has a hard enough time gaining credibility. This isn't going to help." Still others criticized the profit motive behind the bout. However, Ali and Frazier-Lyde's respective husbands didn't see a problem, as they co-promoted the event.

Frazier and Ali in the Ring Again

Both women entered the fight with perfect records behind them, Ali with eight wins, zero losses; Frazier-Lyde with seven wins, zero losses. However, there the similarities ended. Frazier-Lyde was nearly fifteen years older than Ali and had been fighting for far less time than Ali. The public perception of the two women also greatly varied. Ali was viewed as a seasoned professional, while Frazier-Lyde was decried as a publicity hound who had only stepped up to the ring to make money by exploiting her last name. Critics pointed to Frazier-Lyde's short career and the cavalier attitude that propelled her into boxing. Aficionados of women boxing were angered that Frazier-Lyde seemed to be making a spectacle of a sport they revered, while critics of women's boxing used the fight as an example for what is wrong with the sport. As the fight ensued, many of those critics changed their minds.

With a crowd of over 7,000 people in attendance and tens of thousands more watching on pay-per-view, Ali and Frazier-Lyde entered the ring. They went after each other with the ferocity all the hype had promised. The true rivalry between the Ali's and Frazier's played out on the mat. They met each other blow for blow. Frazier-Lyde proved to be a wild card. Mid-fight, just as it looked as if Ali had beaten Frazier-Lyde down, Sister Smoke came barreling back, drawing on a wellspring of energy many compared to her father's. After eight grueling rounds, Ali bleeding from the nose, Frazier-Lyde with a swollen eye, the final bell rang, and the judges ruled Ali the winner by a close margin.

Fighting for Herself and Women's Boxing

Though Frazier-Lyde had lost her bout with Ali, she had gained a lot. Critics began to change their minds about her. "That a 39-year-old woman could come back the way Jacqui did is really something," Al Bernstein, longtime ESPN boxing commentator told *The Philadelphia*

Inquirer. "Laila is more skilled but she nailed Jacqui with punches and Jacqui kept coming." Boxing Hall-of-Fame inductee Emanuel Steward told www.jacquifrazier.com, "If Jacqui was slightly more fine tuned, she'd have won the fight but even now she's won my respect by fighting so hard."

The bout also brought new respect to the sport of women's boxing. Bernstein told *The Philadelphia Inquirer,* "Both women showed grit and determination. They are in the embryonic stages of their boxing careers, sure, but they gave it everything they had and you can't ask for much more than that." Fightnews.com called the fight, "so wild and thrilling that even the staunchest opponent of women's boxing couldn't possibly deny the excitement." Though many critics, including other professional women boxers still dismiss the fight as a media farce, no one can deny that the brawl between the Frazier-Ali brought unprecedented attention to the oft-misunderstood sport. It put women's boxing on the front page of newspapers around the world and padded the pockets of both Ali and Frazier nicely. Early in her short career Frazier-Lyde told *The Detroit News,* "I want to be a positive influence on this sport." With the publicity she brings to the sport she is sure to draw more young women into it, helping women's boxing to gain acceptance from sports critics and fans alike.

Sources

Periodicals

The Hartford Courant, June 6, 2001.
Jet, January 10, 2000, pg 52.
The Philadelphia Inquirer, June 7, 2001; June 9, 2001.
Philadelphia People, June 9, 2001.
USAToday, June 6, 2001.

Online

www.blackvoices.com/sports/ali-frazier/highlights/html.
www.cbsnews.com/earlyshow/entertainment/sports.
www.detnews.com.
www.fightnews.com.
www.jacquifrazier.com.
www.phillynews.com (June 7, 2001; June 9, 2001).
www.usatoday.com, (June 6, 2001).
www.temple.edu/philapeople.

—Candace LaBalle

Joe Gilliam, Jr.

1950-2000

Former professional footbal player

Joe Gilliam, Jr. was the first African-American quarterback to start a regular-season National Football League (NFL) game. Although he was a highly talented player, his career was cut short when he became involved in drugs. But Gilliam persevered and got his life back in order before his untimely demise.

Gilliam's father, Joe Gilliam Sr., coached football for more than forty years, most of them at Tennessee State University. He passed on his talent and love for the game to Gilliam, who grew up on the campus, helping his father. When Gilliam was eight years old, he began going into the opposing teams' locker rooms at halftime, posing as a team helper. He cleaned the other team's shoes, listened to the enemy coach's halftime talk, and then went back to tell his father and the other coaches what he had learned. He continued this until he was in eleventh grade, when a player recognized him and ended his spying career.

Two years later, he was the star quarterback at Tennessee State University. Between 1969 and 1972, he led the team to a 39–3 record as well as two Division II national championships. In 1971 and 1972, he was an AP All-American and was the National Black College Player of the Year.

In 1972 Gilliam was picked in the 11th round of the draft by the Pittsburgh Steelers. In 1974 he led the Steelers to a 30–0 win over Baltimore in the season opener, and became the first African-American quarterback to start a regular-season NFL game. He got his chance because other players, including quarterback Terry Bradshaw, were on strike, and coach Chuck Noll said Gilliam could start if he crossed the picket line.

However, even though he had a 4–1-1 start that year and a three-game winning streak, coach Chuck Noll took his spot as starter away, saying the team needed a change. According to a Nando.net reporter, Gilliam said he thought the reason was "race, hate mail, and rumors of threats to Three Rivers Stadium." For the rest of the 1974 season, Gilliam played backup, but was closely involved in the team, helping with play selection when the Steelers won the Super Bowl against Minnesota.

Began Taking Drugs

Gilliam remained a backup in 1975, and his involvement lessened. He threw only 48 passes for the entire season. Late that year, he was injured and began using drugs.

At a Glance . . .

Born on December 29, 1950 in Nashville, Tennessee; died on December 25, 2000 in Nashville, Tennessee; *Education:* Tennessee State University.

Career: Pittsburgh Steelers, quarterback, 1972–75; became first African-American quarterback to start a regular season game, 1974; New Orleans Saints, 1976; U.S. Football League; wrote autobiography, *In Spite of Myself;* ran football camp at Tennessee State; rehabilitation counselor.

Awards: AP All-American, 1971, 1972; National Black College Player of the Year, 1971, 1972.

According to John Pruett of the *Huntsville Times,* Gilliam said, "A guy came by and said, 'Take these and you won't feel the pain.' He was right, I took 'em and I didn't feel the pain. That's how I got involved with drugs. But he didn't hold a gun to my head and say, 'Take this dope.'" Gilliam acknowledged to Pruett that he knew using drugs was wrong.

"A person can be raised in a good home and still make the wrong life decisions," he said many years later, according to the *Detroit News.* He also said, according to Pruett, "A person is responsible for his own actions. I wasn't abused. I didn't go to school hungry. I was loved. My people were educated. I still made a poor life decision." Gilliam's decision to use drugs led to a downward spiral of addiction, homelessness, and crime.

In 1976 he was picked up by the New Orleans Saints, but didn't last long on that team; he was fired for breaking team rules. Gilliam turned to playing semipro football, and played with the U.S. Football League, but by then, drugs had taken hold in his life. Stories of his football career were interspersed with tales of arrests, stays in drug rehabilitation centers, and his work as a rehabilitation counselor.

Pawned Super Bowl Rings for Drugs

In the late 1970s he pawned his Super Bowl rings to get money to buy drugs. Pruett noted in the *Huntsville Times* that the worst aspect of Gilliam's life as an addict was the fact that sometimes people would recognize him and mock his failure. Pruett wrote, "In his shame and despair, he climbed the Shelby Street bridge in east Nashville, intending to jump off." He slipped and almost fell, and in that split second, he realized that he really didn't want to die.

At other times, Gilliam was shot at and held up. In one case, two other people were wounded, but Gilliam was unhurt, and in two other incidents, the attacker's gun misfired. "In spite of myself," Gilliam said, according to Pruett. "I was always lucky in a lot of ways." In 1988 a television report on Gilliam's life led a group of fans to buy back one of his Super Bowl rings, and eventually the other was also returned. His father kept them in a safe place.

In 1996 a Nando.net reporter found Gilliam on the streets of Nashville, and asked him if he would be watching the Steelers play in that year's Super Bowl. Gilliam said he would, but he had no idea where he would do so—or where he would sleep that night. "I take one day at a time, you know. A couple of days, that's too far down the line at this point," Gilliam told the reporter. He also said that, although he had quit using heroin in 1991, he was still addicted to crack. "I stopped doing the things that I was supposed to be doing, the things that helped me with my sobriety," he said.

Turned His Life Around

In the last few years of his life, Gilliam managed to reclaim his life. According to Pruett, he said, "It took me hundreds and thousands of dollars, lots of pain, jail, a lot of heartache and a lot of misery to come to the conclusion that the things my parents kept telling me were true." He was sober for three years, and during that time he ran a football camp for teens at Tennessee State and counseled drug addicts. He also wrote an autobiography, *In Spite of Myself,* describing his experiences. A CNNSI.com reporter quoted James Hefner, president of Tennessee State, who said, "He reestablished himself as a role model and an inspiration not only to athletes and young people, but to us all."

Gilliam died on Christmas Day, 2000, while watching football. According to CNNSI.com, his father said, "There was an exciting play, and someone said, 'Joey, did you see that?' They shook him and he didn't respond. Joey passed away in his sleep, sitting there on the couch." According to the coroner's report, he died of a cocaine overdose. Gilliam's funeral was at Tennessee State, and he was buried in Nashville. In *Nashville Sports Weekly,* Gilliam summed up his personality and life: "I'm a positive person. I love God. I love myself. And I try to respect all human beings. And be respectful to them. Even though one might not respect me, I give them respect, too."

Sources

Periodicals

Detroit Free Press, January 13, 2001, p. 3C.
Detroit News, December 30, 2000.
Huntsville Times, April 26, 2000.

Nashville Sports Weekly, May 16, 2000.

Online

http://sportsillustrated.cnn.com/football/nfl/news/
  2000/12/26/Gilliam_dead_ap/ (March 7, 2001).
http://detnews.com/2000/lions/0012/30/sports-
  169344.htm (March 7, 2001).

http://www.al.com/columnists/Huntsville/jpruett/
  04262000-e27348.html (March 7, 2001).
http://www.nando.net/newsroom/ap/fbo/1996/nfl/nfl/
  feat/archive/012196/nfl13510.ht ml (March 7, 2001).
http://www.nashvillesportsweekly.rivals.com/?sid=
  632&p=2&stid=207850 (March 7, 2001).

—Kelly Winters and Ashyia N. Henderson

Pam Grier

1949-

Actress

Film critic Roger Ebert, in his *Movie Home Companion*, referred to Pam Grier as "one of the most intriguing action stars of the 1970s." Though she continued to work in the ensuing decades, Grier established herself as a box-office draw in the "blaxploitation" genre, generally playing tough, sexy crimefighters. *Vibe*'s Darius James—an expert on the genre—rhapsodized, "Grier reigned over the altars of adolescent onanism in a dangerous double-D cup like a black-skinned [Hindu religion deity of destruction] goddess Kali."

Some twenty years earlier, *Ms.* contributor Jamaica Kincaid dismissed the films themselves as "mostly simplistic, sensational, violent, and technically faulty" but celebrated their presentation of "a woman who is independent, resourceful, self-confident, strong, and courageous. Above all, they are the only films to show us a woman who triumphs!" Yet rather than be hemmed in by such roles, Grier took a break from her film career that began to look like retirement until she returned in a challenging, unglamorous role in 1981's *Fort Apache: The Bronx*. Since then she has pursued a variety of film and television work, though 1970s nostalgia has only made her blaxploitation heroines—Friday Foster, Coffy, Foxy Brown, and others—loom ever larger.

"When I was a young girl, I never thought of acting," Grier claimed in an *Ebony* profile. "I never thought of television, of fans, movie stars, signing autographs. It never crossed my mind." She was born in Winston-Salem, South Carolina; her father's military job kept the family traveling, and she grew up in Europe, returning to the United States when she was 14.

Military jargon prevailed even at home: "It was a [totally] different mentality, a way of life," she told *Los Angeles Times* writer Bob Ellison. "Like, 'Daddy, can I go to the movies?' 'Negative!' 'Why can't you say 'No,' like anybody else's father?' He'd say 'Negative!' or 'Affirmative.'" They settled in Denver, Colorado, which she described to Kincaid as "rough." With her slight English accent, fastidious manners, hand-me-down clothes, and fondness for afternoon tea, she scarcely fit in with her peers. "I wasn't popular with boys, and I almost didn't have a date for the senior prom," she recalled. "I felt strange, and I just couldn't find a balance."

Spotted by Agent in Pageant

Having enrolled at Denver's Metropolitan State College, Grier envisioned a career in medicine. It was the death of her boyfriend in the Vietnam war that made her consider acting, for the catharsis it allowed. High tuition costs, meanwhile, drove her to enter the Miss Colorado Universe contest in hopes of winning prize money. As the only black contestant in the 1967 pageant, she knew she faced an uphill battle; though she did not win, she placed second and attracted the attention of agent David Baumgarten, who handled comedians Rowan & Martin, among others. Baumgarten invited her to Hollywood, having immediately recognized her star quality. In a reversal of the traditional story, Grier was disinclined to

At a Glance . . .

Born Pamala Suzette Grier on May 26, 1949, in Winston-Salem, NC; daughter of a U.S. Air Force maintenance mechanic. *Education*: Attended Metropolitan State College, Denver, CO.

Career: Worked as switchboard operator at talent agency and American International Pictures, c. 1969. Film appearances include: *The Big Bird Cage*, 1969; *Beyond the Valley of the Dolls*, 1969; *Black Mama, White Mama*, 1972; *Scream, Blacula, Scream*, 1973; *Coffy*, 1973; *Foxy Brown*, 1974; *Friday Foster*, 1975; *Sheba, Baby*, 1975; *Drum*, 1976; *Greased Lightning*, 1977; *Fort Apache: The Bronx*, 1981; *Something Wicked This Way Comes*, 1983; *Stand Alone*, 1985; *On the Edge*, 1986; *Tough Enough*, 1987; *Above the Law*, 1988; *Class of 1999*, 1989; *Bill and Ted's Bogus Journey*, 1991; *Posse*, 1994; *Original Gangstas*, 1996; *Escape from L.A.*, 1996; *Mars Attacks!*, 1996; *Jackie Brown*, 1997; *Jawbreaker*, 1999; *In Too Deep*, 1999; *Holy Smoke*, 1999; *Fortress 2*, 1999; *Snow Day*, 2000; *3 A.M.*, 2000; *Ghosts of Mars*, 2001; *Bones*, 2001; *Love the Hard Way*, 2001; *Pluto Nash*, 2002. Television appearances: *Badge of the Assassin*, *The Elizabeth Morgan Story*, *Miami Vice*, *Knots Landing*, *Frank's Place*, *The Cosby Show*, and *Monsters*. Stage appearances: *Fool for Love*, *Frankie and Johnny at the Clair de Lune*, and *The Piano Lesson*.

Awards: NAACP Image Award for best actress, for *Fool for Love*, 1986; National Black Theatre Festival Achievement Award and African American Film Society Achievement Award, both 1993; Career Achievement Award, Chicago International Film Festival, 1998; Golden Globe nomination for *Jackie Brown*, 1998.

Addresses: *Agent*—Gold/Marshak/Liedtke Talent and Literary Agency, 3500 West Olive Ave., Suite 1400, Burbank, CA 91505.

go, but she was encouraged by her mother to take the agent up on his offer.

Signed to his Agency of the Performing Arts, Grier attended acting classes and worked the office switchboard. But the film roles didn't come; eventually she took a switchboard operator job at the famed low-budget studio American International Pictures (AIP), earning a higher salary. She claimed to be well versed in AIP's more complicated system, then came in early to work every day until she learned it. She also uncovered a great deal about the film business by listening in on the calls she routed.

Eventually she visited producer Roger Corman—arguably the era's king of bare-bones moviemaking—and asked for a part in his film *The Big Bird Cage*. She landed a small role. "I thought she had everything we were looking for in an actress to play in our action-adventure films," Corman recalled to *Moviegoer* years later. "She was a big, good-looking girl with a lot of energy, and I knew those qualities would come through on the screen. She was an untrained actress, but she always had a natural ability. And as she learned she became very skilled."

Even so, the education came at a price—minor parts in "B" pictures like *Twilight People* and *Beyond the Valley of the Dolls*—before Grier secured a lead in Black Mama, White Mama, a prison escape melodrama loosely modeled on the Tony Curtis-Sidney Poitier vehicle *The Defiant Ones*. This Corman outing got Grier noticed, and she went on to stardom in the burgeoning black exploitation, or "blaxploitation," field.

Established Reputation in Blaxploitation

After hits like *Shaft* and *Superfly* demonstrated the box-office potential of black-themed action pictures, the market was more or less flooded with attempts to cash in. Aside from the profitable *Cleopatra Jones*, starring Tamara Dobson—with whom Grier has often been confused—nearly all the blaxploitation features with a female lead starred Grier. In *Coffy*, she portrays a nurse who takes revenge on the drug dealers who destroy her sister; the film is often remembered for the title character's emasculation of her adversaries with a shotgun. As *Foxy Brown* she arranges the castration of a nemesis and sends the severed member to his girlfriend, while *Sheba, Baby* concludes with Grier's character dispatching the primary evildoer with a speargun.

Alongside her starring roles in action vehicles were appearances in such fare as the black horror sequel *Scream, Blacula, Scream* and the plantation melodrama sequel *Drum*, which *VideoHound's Golden Movie Retriever* described as "bad taste at its best." Yet Grier had become that rarity—a bankable female star. Only Barbara Streisand and Liza Minelli shared that distinction during the 1970s. Ebert, quoted in *Moviegoer*, compared Grier to venerable action hero and dramatic star "Sean Connery, in that she knows how to keep her action in character, make it believable. She remained likable in those roles while doing some truly horrible things to her enemies. She should have done them to her directors."

It was a formative period for modern feminism, but Grier's tough-sexy image was sufficiently malleable to accommodate both a cover story in feminist journal *Ms.* and a pictorial in *Playboy*. Her self-sufficient heroines managed to commit their mayhem in skimpy outfits and usually enjoyed a tender tryst with a sensitive man, thus staying within the realm of acceptability for the largely male audience her films attracted.

Grier herself expressed dissatisfaction with AIP's editing of her films, complaining to *Ms.* that the company took *Coffy* and "cut it up—taking out the most important parts, like tender scenes between me and my sister. So all you see is *bang, bang, bang*, shoot 'em up tits and ass, *bang, bang, bang*, shoot 'em up tits and ass. But they kept saying, people will love it now. It's entertainment." She added, "AIP policy is to give the niggers shit." Even so, she insisted to Stephen Farber of Moviegoer years later, "I learned a lot about the business from making those movies."

She moved in a more conventionally dramatic direction for 1977's *Greased Lightning*, portraying the wife of a race-car driver played by Richard Pryor. It was a small role in a critically praised though relatively minor film, but it initiated a romantic relationship between Grier and Pryor; the actor-comedian encouraged her to expand her repertoire. Despite admonitions that she was endangering her career, she began turning down work. "I said, 'I think I'll sit back and see who I am, see if I want to remain in the business—and on whose terms,'" she told Farber. "Everyone warned me that it's usually hard to make a comeback when you drop out. I said, 'Well, if I want it that badly, I'll just have to work real hard, won't I?'"

"I played those [*Coffy*-type] parts because they had women in positions of power," Grier told *Los Angeles Times* contributor Dennis Hunt. "It was a good positive image for black women. But the films became redundant and I don't like being redundant." As it turned out, Grier jumped off the blaxploitation ship just before it began to sink; by the late 1970s, box-office returns for "ghetto" action films were virtually nonexistent. Unfortunately, so were roles for the performers who had helped create the genre. Rather than lobby for acting work, however, Grier pursued other interests, among them intensive dance training, singing, and piano; aside from appearances on television's Love Boat and the *Roots II* miniseries, little was heard from her during this period.

Death of Friend Marked Return to Acting

It was the loss of a friend, singer Minnie Riperton, that drove her back to film work. "I watched Minnie struggle with cancer for a year and a half," Grier recounted to Farber. "I saw her trying to make her last album in extreme pain, raising her family at the same time, loving and giving and sharing without one complaint. She said to me, 'We live such a very short time. You have a lot to give, and you should be giving.' So just from watching her try to live and live fully, I started to realize a lot about myself. After she died, I withdrew for several months. But when I came out of it, I decided to go back to work."

This time, however, Grier asked her agent to seek more demanding roles; soon she was offered the part of a murderous, drug-addicted prostitute in the drama *Fort Apache: The Bronx*. "If people thought of me as glamorous before," she told Hunt, "they will change their minds after seeing this film." She called the part "the hardest role I've ever played and I couldn't have played it as effectively without getting really into the character. I've never gotten that deeply [into] a character before." Her preparation, by her own reckoning, required radical self-neglect. "I stopped shaving. I let the hair grow under my arms and on my legs. I painted my nails and let it chip away. During the three months of shooting I wasn't getting much sleep. I was losing weight. I was eating a pizza a day to keep weight on, but it wasn't working. I was so skinny in the film you can almost see my jawbones sometimes. People thought makeup made me look that way but it wasn't makeup. Those dark circles were real. My friends thought I was sick. They said I looked like death."

Grier also researched her character by hanging out on the street, lingering long enough to blend in and acquire "her [character's] moves, her attitude and everything else about her." Farber quoted venerable *New Yorker* film critic Pauline Kael's remark that "each time Pam Grier's angel-dusted hooker appears, making snaky movements with her tongue, she gives us a feeling of obscene terror." For his part, Hunt called the actress's performance "stunning."

The success of this performance led to appearances in *Tough Enough* and the Disney screen adaptation of Ray Bradbury's fantasy-horror novel *Something Wicked This Way Comes*. The latter allowed her to play the Dust Witch, a belly dancer. She told *Moviegoer*'s Farber that Bradbury was one of her favorite science fiction authors and that she enjoyed working with both Disney and the splendor of her character. "What a great fantasy, to play someone described as the most beautiful woman in the world!" Director Jack Clayton explained, "Pam was the most exotic person I could find. So we changed the character to a black lady. I chose her because she was beautiful and strange and exotic. She has remarkable presence, but she doesn't have to depend on that. She is also a very good actress."

Grier worked sporadically during the rest of the 1980s, appearing as Steven Seagal's partner in *Above the Law*, as Bruce Dern's lover in *On the Edge*, and on television's *Miami Vice*. She also appeared on stage in Los Angeles in the acclaimed Sam Shepard play *Fool for Love*, for which she was honored with an NAACP Image Award for best actress. By the 1990s, Grier's cult status—thanks to the roles she'd spent two decades trying to transcend—was assured. Despite this cult status, however, Grier was only offered small roles in such films as *Bill and Ted's Bogus Journey* (1991), the all-black western *Posse* (1993), and *Mars Attacks!* (1996). She told Farber that the lack of leading roles "doesn't disturb me. I feel that even in a small part, people will see my work. The performance isn't judged by the size of the role."

Grier found great happiness in her personal life after she met former RCA Records executive Kevin Evans. Though Evans was 13 years younger than Grier, the couple fell deeply in love and became engaged. "Age is irrelevant!" Grier told *Jet*. Evans agreed, telling *Jet*, "It was always about the personality, about the inside qualities Pam possesses."

Landmark Performance in Jackie Brown

Noted filmmaker Quentin Tarantino, whose work owes a substantial debt to 1970s exploitation films, was among Grier's many admirers. Grier had auditioned for a role in Tarantino's career-making 1994 film *Pulp Fiction*, but lost the role to Rosanna Arquette. However, a year later, Grier ran into Tarantino and he told her that he had a part for her. Tarantino had been working on the script for *Jackie Brown*, and Grier possessed, according to Rebecca Ascher-Walsh in *Entertainment Weekly*, "the exact beauty-cum-wisdom quality he was looking for." Tarantino explained to *Entertainment Weekly*, "One thing you get with someone like Pam is they've been up and down and sideways and out. And it's all there, in their body and their face, ready to be drawn upon."

Although *Jackie Brown* was Grier's 50th film, it was her first starring role in over twenty years. In this adaptation of Elmore Leonard's 1992 novel, *Rum Punch*, Grier took on the title role of a flight attendant smuggling money and drugs for Odell, an arms dealer played by Samuel L. Jackson. The film also featured Michael Keaton, Bridget Fonda, and Robert DeNiro.

Reviews for the film were mainly positive, and of those reviewers who found the film disappointing most praised Grier's performance. Owen Gleiberman of *Entertainment Weekly* noted that Grier "is, as always, a commanding actress; she blends street smarts and melancholy the way she used to blend street smarts and Amazonian hauteur." The *New Republic*'s Stanley Kauffmann commented, "Tarantino's best achievement in this film is his casting and use of her." For her work in the film, Grier received a Golden Globe nomination.

While promoting the film, Grier revealed to the press that she had been diagnosed with cancer in 1988. "My doctor gave me 18 months to live," Grier told *Entertainment Weekly*'s Rebecca Ascher-Walsh. "My whole life changed. I became a different person at that point." She underwent treatment for two years, and there were times when she considered ending the pain. "Dr. Kevorkian wasn't around back then," she told Ascher-Walsh. "There would be days where I thought, Take bottles of pills. I would look at the ceiling, saying 'Should I live? Should I die?'" Grier took those two years one step at a time, and in the

end, Grier had survived not only the deadly disease, but its difficult treatment.

Following *Jackie Brown*, Grier appeared in several 1999 films, including *Jawbreaker*, *In Too Deep*, *Holy Smoke*, and *Fortress 2*. For *In Too Deep*, Grier shared the screen with a veritable cornucopia of stars, not the least of whom were LL Cool J, Omar Epps, Stanley Tucci, Veronica Webb, and Nia Long. *Holy Smoke* placed Grier alongside Harvey Keitel and Kate Winslet.

Career Booming in the Millennium

After a small role in 2000's *Snow Day*, Grier won a starring role in the Showtime film *3 A.M.* (2001). Here Danny Glover plays a New York cab driver who works the late shift and is dating Grier's character, a waitress named Georgia. Reviews for the film were not glowing, but Kirk Honeycutt of the *Hollywood Reporter* noted that Grier and Glover, "anchor the wispy film."

Also in 2001, Grier appeared alongside Ice Cube in John Carpenter's *Ghost of Mars*, as well as in *Bones* with Snoop Doggy Dogg. In the latter, Dogg plays a ghost who, twenty years after his death, awakens, seeking out revenge on those who killed him. Grier plays his clairvoyant girlfriend. Grier was also seen that year in the role of a New York City police detective in the independent *Love the Hard Way*. In addition, she began working with Eddie Murphy on *Pluto Nash*, a futuristic film set for release in 2002.

Throughout her career, Pam Grier has known many ups and downs. Recognizing the fickle nature of show business, she has never allowed herself to get caught up in the Hollywood hype. She told *Interview*, "I always thought that not living here in Hollywood was a way of showing that I'm not afraid of losing my career; I'm afraid of losing me."

Selected filmography

Beyond the Valley of the Dolls, 1969.
Black Mama, White Mama, 1972.
Scream, Blacula, Scream, 1973.
Coffy, 1973.
Foxy Brown, 1974.
Friday Foster, 1975.
Sheba, Baby, 1975.
Drum, 1976.
Greased Lightning, 1977.
Fort Apache: The Bronx, 1981.
Something Wicked This Way Comes, 1983.
Stand Alone, 1985.
On the Edge, 1986.
Tough Enough, 1987.
Above the Law, 1988.
Class of 1999, 1989.
Bill and Ted's Bogus Journey, 1991.

Posse, 1994.
Original Gangstas, 1996.
Escape from L.A., 1996.
Mars Attacks!, 1996.
Jackie Brown, 1997.
Jawbreaker, 1999.
In Too Deep, 1999.
Holy Smoke, 1999.
Fortress 2, 1999.
Snow Day, 2000.
3 A.M., 2000.
Ghosts of Mars, 2001.
Bones, 2001.
Love the Hard Way, 2001.

Sources

Books

Contemporary Theatre, Film, and Television, Volume 20, Gale, 1998.
Ebert, Roger, *Roger Ebert's Movie Home Companion*, Andrews & McMeel, 1993, p. 2.
VideoHound's Golden Movie Retriever, Visible Ink Press, 1993, p. 199.

Periodicals

Ebony, June 1976, pp. 33–40.
Entertainment Weekly, December 19, 1997; January, 9, 1998; August 7, 1998.
Hollywood Reporter, October 1, 1998; November 20, 1998; February 7, 2000; November 13, 2000; February 1, 2001.
Interview, January 1998.
Jet, March 2, 1998; April 13, 1998.
Los Angeles Times, August 19, 1979, calendar section, p. 34; March 12, 1981, section 5, pp. 1, 7.
Moviegoer, May 1983.
Ms., August 1975, pp. 49–53.
Multichannel News, June 18, 2001.
New Republic, January 26, 1998.
New York, May 19, 1975, pp. 43–6.
Vibe, September 1994.

Online

Internet Movie Database, http://us.imdb.com.

Other

Additional information for this profile was provided by the Irv Schecter Company, 1994.

—Simon Glickman and Jennifer M. York

Buddy Guy

1936-

Guitarist

George "Buddy" Guy, hailed by Eric Clapton in *Musician* magazine as "the greatest guitar player alive," Guy remains as one of the last links to a blues tradition that began before Robert Johnson and continued most notably through Muddy Waters and other Chicago blues players. Though the legendary bluesman is internationally famous today, he began his life as a sharecropper's son. Today Guy owns a mansion outside of Chicago where he presides over his own blues club in his adopted home town, but the middle child of the five children of Sam and Isabell Guy began his life picking cotton.

Guy was born in Lettsworth, Louisiana on July 30, 1936. Life was difficult in rural Louisiana especially when the weather did not cooperate and the cotton harvest was poor. To help feed his family Guy fished and hunted raccoon, muskrat, and possum. His mother had a vegetable garden and grew food for the family in the summer and made it last all the way through the winter. Guy worked on his family's farm, but on Saturdays he would pick cotton for a half day to earn money for himself.

From the beginning Guy spent his hard-earned money on the blues by sending away for old 78s of Howlin'

Wolf, Muddy Waters, and John Lee Hooker. Guy made his first guitar out of old paint cans and wire from the front screen door. When his father got tired of all the mosquitoes that came into the house, he bought his son an old acoustic guitar with only two strings on it. Soon Guy was able to pick out a passable version of Hooker's "Boogie Chillen." The first time he heard an electric guitar occurred when a man who was passing through town playing for change plugged in his amp in front of a local store. Guy threw the man his 35 cents allowance and the rest was history.

As many kids his age were forced to do in his circumstances, Guy quit high school to work—pumping gas and washing cars in Baton Rouge. It was at the gas station that Guy got his introduction to show business. A local bandleader, John "Big Poppa" Tilley, heard of a young man who was changing tires at the local service station who could play guitar. The 300-pound Tilley brought his guitar and amp to the pumps, and Guy got an audition right there. Guy roared through a rendition of Eddie "Guitar Slim" Jones's version of "Things I Used To Do." Not only did the playing attract a crowd of people who wanted to buy gas, but Tilley hired Guy on the spot.

At a Glance . . .

Born George Guy on July 30, 1936 in Lettsworth, LA; parents: Sam (a sharecropper) and Isabell Guy.

Career: Blues guitarist. Went to Chicago, 1957; signed with Cobra Records and cut two singles, 1958; signed with Chess Records where he recorded numerous singles, including "Stone Crazy" which became a number 12 R&B record; became a valued session musician for Chess artists such as Muddy Waters, Sonny Boy Williamson, Little Walter, and Howlin' Wolf among others, 1960–67; released one album, *A Man and His Blues*, 1968; began a long association with harmonica player Junior Wells, 1970s; owner of a blues club, the Checkerboard Lounge, 1972–83; released breakthrough album, *Damn Right I've Got The Blues*, 1990; owner of another blues club, Legends, 1989-.

Awards: Grammy Award for Best Blues Album of the Year for "Damn Right I've Got The Blues," 1990, and for "Feels Like Rain," 1992; Billboard's Century Award for lifetime achievement, 1993.

Addresses: *Home*—Chicago, IL. *Office*—Legends, 754 South Wabash, Chicago, IL 60605.

After a dubious beginning in which Tilley fired the shy, nervous young player because he would not face the crowd, Guy became a regular with the band. By this time he had secured a job as a custodian at Louisiana State University. He had all but given up on the idea of being a professional musician. His mother, however, disagreed with her son's assessment of his abilities. Isabell, who was recovering from a stroke, regained her ability to speak and told him that he was good enough to be a professional but that Baton Rouge was not the place where he could follow his dream. With the help of a local disc jockey, Guy made two demos—"The Way You've Been Treating Me" and "Baby, Don't You Wanna Come Home." Guy sent them to the preeminent blues label of the day, Chess Records in Chicago, sure that he would be a star.

On to Chicago

On September 27, 1957 with his two recordings in hand, his Gibson Les Paul guitar, and $500, Guy bought a one-way train ticket to Chicago to find Leonard Chess, owner of Chess Records. He knew a friend of his sisters in Chicago but spent most of his time wandering the streets day and night, trying to work up the courage to make an appearance at Chess Records. When he finally did show up, he found that no one had listened to the demos he had sent and that an unknown guitarist could not just walk in off the street for a meeting with Leonard or his brother Phil Chess.

After spending another few months in Chicago unsuccessfully looking for work or an opportunity to play, Guy was down to his last dime ready to call home for train fare back to Louisiana. He met a man purely by chance who guided him to the 708 Club, a local blues hot spot. When the young man with the guitar walked in, he found none other than Chicago blues legend Otis Rush presiding over a jam session. Rush brought him up on the stage and Guy, near swooning from hunger, plugged in his guitar and released all of his frustration and loneliness. After a short but spectacular set, which included "Things I Used To Do" and "Further On Up The Road," Guy walked off the stage and out of the bar certain that he had performed his swan song in Chicago.

But word of his performance had spread. Several days later a man approached him on the street and introduced himself as "Mud." Guy was dumbfounded, because the man turned out to be blues icon Muddy Waters. Waters had heard about the young guitarist's epic impromptu performance; besides feeding the starving young man, Waters introduced him to some of the most important people on the Chicago blues scene.

Guy was suddenly appearing in top flight blues guitar competitions with other young guitarists such as Earl Hooker, Magic Sam, and even B. B. King in which first prize was a bottle of whiskey. With such talent, Guy knew he had to find a way to distinguish himself. He found his trademark one night at the Blue Flame club while Otis Rush and Magic Sam were on stage. Guy told Timothy White of *Billboard* what happened: "I got a new extra-long cord, and I told this fella who was with me to take the wire, unroll it, and bring his end all the way to the stage where Magic and Otis were. I would hide in the bathroom, and when they call my name, he'd jump up and plug me in!"

Guy was introduced, but instead of appearing on stage he came out of the back of the club ripping through his solo at maximum volume. He walked through the stunned crowd, out the front door of the Blue Flame, and then back up to the stage to join the other musicians. The stunt worked so well that Guy made his stroll through the crowd a mainstay of his show for the next forty years.

Signed with Chess

In 1958 Guy signed with Cobra Record and cut two singles. The next year Cobra went under, and this time it was Chess Records that came looking for him. He signed with Leonard Chess in 1960 and became a noted session musician while recording his own singles. Besides such singles as "Stone Crazy" which became a number 12

Billboard R&B record, Guy played with Sonny Boy Williamson, Little Walter, Howlin' Wolf, Koko Taylor and others.

In an interview conducted with John Lee Hooker with Jas Obrecht of *Guitar Player*, Guy talked about his attitude when playing as a session musician with some of the masters: "When I got to Chicago, there were so many great guitarists around that I went to work a regular job. When I saw these people play, I just knew that there was no way I had a chance. I just wanted to meet these great musicians, and I woke up and they was askin' me to play with them. One thing helped me a lot was I was a good listener, and if they would ask me to play with them, I didn't go tell John Lee or Muddy Waters or the Howlin' Wolf or Walter what to play . . . When I went into the studio with them, I got in the corner and said, 'I'm at school now. It's time for me to learn my lesson, not teach.'"

Guy even appeared on an acoustic record of Muddy Waters, *Folk Singer*. When Leonard Chess objected to the electric guitarist being included on an acoustic album, Waters told the record label owner to "shut up and sit down." Guy stayed with Chess until 1967, but the company released only one album, *A Man & His Blues*, in 1968.

Though Guy received a measure of success and notoriety in Chicago, few outside the blues capital of the world knew about him. But those that did know his style were devoted and influential. Jimi Hendrix used to tape Guy's concerts, and in trips to England he first met Clapton and Jeff Beck in the sixties. Clapton co-produced Guy's collaboration with harmonica legend Junior Wells in 1972, *Buddy Guy and Junior Wells Play the Blues*, and the artist was instrumental in Guy's later ascent to stardom. Guy continued to tour, most of the time without a recording contract, though he did release a live album, *Stone Crazy,* of a performance in France in 1978. In 1972 he opened a blues club in Chicago, the Checkerboard Lounge, which he ran until 1983. His days as a club owner resumed when he opened another Chicago blues club, Legends, in 1989.

A Breakthrough Year

In 1990 Guy was invited by Clapton to be part of his historic string of London's Royal Albert Hall concerts. The concerts were recorded on Clapton's *24 Nights* album, and suddenly everyone wanted to know who Buddy Guy was. After the appearance in England, Guy returned there in 1990 with a new recording contract with Silvertone to record "Damn Right, I've Got The Blues."

After all those years of playing in anonymity Guy wanted this album to be just right. He was resolved to capture the Buddy Guy live sound that he was never able to or allowed to capture before. He told Ed Enright of *Downbeat* about the negotiations leading up to the groundbreaking recording: "They told me, 'We'd like to sign you, and we would want to support you.' And I said, 'Well, I really want to play Buddy Guy, because I never had the chance to play Buddy Guy before. I want you to hear that, because I'm a Johnny Come Later now; everybody else says these are Buddy Guy licks, and Buddy Guy has never played them himself.' They said, 'We're not going to tell you what to play, just give you a good supporting band. Won't you come to London and make this session?' And I said, 'Thank you, I'll sign.'"

Damn Right I've Got The Blues included guest appearances from Clapton, Beck, and Mark Knopfler and went on to receive a Grammy. The album reached gold record status in Canada, New Zealand, and in England, and made Guy a star on the international blues scene. A book with the same title quickly followed which featured interviews with Wells, Clapton, Beck, Willy Dixon, Robert Cray, and Stevie Ray Vaughn.

Guy followed up his hit record with *Feels Like Rain* in 1992. For his new album Guy wanted to make more of an ambitious statement. He told Jim Washburn of *The Los Angeles Times* that he wanted a wider audience: "We got down in the alley on it, but also we were trying to get some of the bigger radio stations that do not play Muddy Waters or Howlin' Wolf to hopefully feel that maybe some of it would fit on their station. . . . I told myself if I get slick enough, they might play it on this big rock station. Then, if a kid buys the album, he'll find (Waters') "Nineteen Years Old" right next to that song."

Guy repeated the success of his previous album including the Grammy Award for Best Blues Album of the Year. The following year *Billboard* presented Guy with its highest honor, the Century Award for lifetime achievement. The man who went almost thirteen years without a recording contract was now recording soundtracks and going on tour with the Saturday Night Live Band. His club, Legends, which he had struggled at times to keep open as so many other blues clubs closed, was finally secured as a place where new blues talent could develop just as the master did. Though he recorded another successful album, *Slippin In*, and continues to tour around the world, Guy never strays far from his Chicago home and Legends, often popping in to the bar to mingle with the crowd and see the local talent. Guy told Enright of *Downbeat* that he will always remember where he came from: "Sometimes entertainers get so big, they have to isolate themselves. Please believe me, I don't ever want to get like that. I think that's the time I would start thinkin' maybe I should quit playin'. Because I would miss people."

Sources

Books

Contemporary Musicians, Volume 4. Gale Research, 1990.

Periodicals

Billboard, December 4, 1993.

Downbeat, February 1995.
Guitar Player, June 1996.
The Los Angeles Times, April 22, 1993.

Online

Biography Resource Center, Gale, 2001, http://www.galenet.com/servlet/BioRC.

—Michael J. Watkins

Mary Styles Harris

1949—

Geneticist

The daughter of a doctor, Mary Styles Harris developed an interest in science at an early age. By the time she was in high school, she was entering local science fairs and volunteering in a medical laboratory. Harris pursued graduate studies in molecular genetics and was later in charge of the Sickle Cell Foundation of Georgia. After several years of teaching and consulting, Harris became the head of BioTechnical Communications, which produces health care communication, product, and research materials for radio, television, and the Internet.

Mary Styles Harris grew up in a scientific environment. She was born in Nashville, Tennessee, on June 26, 1949. Her father, George Styles, was finishing his studies at Meharry Medical College, and her mother, Margaret, had completed her degree in business administration at Tennessee State University. Soon after her father's graduation, the family moved to Miami, Florida, where her father opened a medical practice near the city center.

In 1963 Harris was one of the first African Americans to enter Miami Jackson High School. At that time, schools in the city were just beginning to desegregate. Four years later, she graduated 12th out a class of 350.

Harris's pursuit of science increased during her high school years by her after school work. Harris entered the local science fair each year. She also volunteered evenings and weekends at the first black-owned medical lab in Miami. While there, lab technicians showed her the use of various laboratory equipment and items. By the time she was ready to graduate from high school, she could perform simple routine biological tests, such as counting red cells in blood samples.

After high school, Harris enrolled in Lincoln University, located in Lincoln, Pennsylvania. She was one of the first women to be accepted there, so her classmates were almost entirely male. Although she basically followed a pre-med program in college, Harris also took advanced algebra and chemistry courses. It was generally assumed, certainly by her classmates, that she would enter medical school. In fact, her father's colleagues in Miami had been able to assure a place for Harris, through a minority program, at the University of Miami Medical School.

What young pre-med student would turn down an assured place in medical school? Harris did, much to the surprise of her classmates. But by now she had decided that her true passion was not in treating patients, but research. Upon graduation in 1971 with a B.A. in biology, her overall academic performance earned her a Ford Foundation Doctoral Fellowship to study molecular genetics.

Soon after graduation, Mary Styles married Sidney Harris, who had just graduated from Morehouse College in Atlanta, Georgia. The young couple decided to pursue their careers at Cornell University in Ithaca, New York. Her husband had been accepted in the graduate engineering program, and Harris entered the well-regarded molecular genetics research center at the university.

At a Glance . . .

B orn Mary Styles on June 26, 1949, in Nashville, TN; daughter of Dr. George and Margaret Styles; married Sidney E. Harris; children: one daughter. *Education*: Lincoln University, BA, Biology, 1971; Cornell University, PhD, Genetics, 1975; Rutgers Medical School, Postdoctoral study, 1977.

Career: Sickle Cell Foundation of Georgia, executive director, 1977–79; Morehouse College, assistant professor, 1978; Atlanta University, assistant professor, 1980–81; Georgia Department of Human Resources, director of genetic services; Harris and Associates, founder, president, until 1987; BioTechnical Communications, president.

Memberships: Public Health Association, 1977-; American Society of Human Genetics, 1977-; Congressional Black Caucus Health Brain Trust; Georgia Board of Regents, University of Georgia, 1979–80; Women's Forum of Georgia; Governor's Advisory Council on Alcohol and Drug Abuse; Georgia Human Genetics Task Force; CDC Foundation, board member.

Awards: Outstanding Working Woman, *Glamour* magazine, 1980.

Addresses: *Office*—BioTechnical Communications, 5920 Roswell Rd., Bldg. B107, PMB 190, Atlanta, GA 30328.

Barbara McClintock, a Nobel Prize-winning geneticist, had conducted her experiments at the Cornell labs and returned there frequently while Harris was a student. Harris also benefitted from the fact that her own faculty advisor, Dr. Gerry Fink, had been a close colleague of McClintock's over the years.

This was a rewarding time for those in the study of genetic research. Harris graduated from Cornell with a Ph.D. in genetics in 1975. Her dissertation was entitled "An Investigation of Several Aspects of the Killer Character in Saccharomyces Cerevisiae," dealing with yeasts. Following that, she received a National Cancer Research postdoctoral fellowship to study the structure of viruses. For this work, Harris spent the next two years at the New Jersey University of Medicine and Dentistry. Although she found the work rewarding, after completion of a project involving the chemical structure of viruses and molecules, Harris decided that she needed a career change.

Harris became the executive director of the Sickle Cell Foundation of Georgia in 1977. This was an administra-

tive, rather than a research-based, position. Besides raising money to fight sickle-cell anemia, a disease that afflicts mainly African Americans, she was in a position to inform the public about this very serious condition.

This administrative position was new to Harris in many respects. She had to learn how to direct an organization whose basic aim is public service. She also had to mix advances in science with meeting the practical health problems of the public she served. But Harris did her job well, and she was awarded a Science Residency Award by the National Science Foundation.

With this aid and recognition, Harris was able to publicize other diseases in addition to sickle-cell anemia. Her face became familiar to television viewers when she hosted a series of documentaries, which she wrote and produced, explaining health and science issues to the general public. Largely because of these, she won *Glamour* magazine's Outstanding Working Woman of 1980 award. The award ceremony took place at the White House with then-President Jimmy Carter presiding.

After a period spent in Washington, D.C. completing her Science Residency, Harris became the State Director of Genetic Services for the Georgia Department of Human Resources. From this position, she could also influence health policies nationwide, and her advice was sought by health officials in other states. In addition to work in Genetic Services, Harris was a part-time assistant professor at Morehouse College in Atlanta and at Atlanta University. To make life even busier, the couple's daughter was born during this period.

After three years at Georgia's Department of Human Resources, Harris took charge of a program encompassing seven states for the genetic screening of newborns. Next, she founded Harris and Associates, a consulting firm she ran until 1987 for companies with products that are based on genetic research.

Harris moved to California when her husband was offered a teaching position at Claremont College. But they later returned to Atlanta, where he became head of the Georgia State University College of Business. Harris headed up BioTechnical Communications, which actively focuses on health issues by producing audiovisual materials on such health topics as breast cancer, an issue of major concern among minority women. She produced a 40-minute television special called "To My Sisters . . . A Gift for Life" and hosted by Debbie Allen that examined breast cancer among black women. Harris remained a firm backer of public health education, focusing on the need for cooperation between government officials and scientists so that vital health information is made available and understandable to the people who can most benefit from it.

Sources

Books

Kessler, James H., et al. *Distinguished African American Scientists of the 20th* Century, Oryx, 1996.
Notable Black American Scientists, Gale, 1998.

Who's Who Among African Americans, 14th edition, Gale, 2001.

Online

http://www.princeton.edu/˜mcbrown/display/mary_harris.htm (July 13, 2001).

—Corinne J. Naden and Jennifer M. York

Charlayne Hunter-Gault

1942–

Journalist

Charlayne Hunter-Gault has staked her claim as one of the leading journalists in the United States, having won many of the top honors in her field for excellence in investigative reporting. One of the springboards into her career came when she herself was the subject of journalistic investigation at the height of the civil rights era: In 1961, Hunter-Gault was one of two black students who first broke the color barrier in higher education in Georgia. While braving the protests of white students during that tumultuous time in American history, she also underwent an important learning experience by observing the styles and techniques of reporters who chronicled the event.

Hunter-Gault has built a reputation as a keen investigator of social injustice, especially among African Americans. She became known to millions of television viewers as the national correspondent on PBS-TV's *MacNeil/Lehrer NewsHour* and has also written landmark articles on subjects ranging from the ravages of heroin addiction to the evils of apartheid in South Africa.

Born in 1942 in the small town of Due West, South Carolina, Hunter-Gault was one of three children of Charles and Althea Hunter. Her father was a Methodist Army chaplain who often served long tours of duty away from home, leaving the care of the children to Charlayne's mother and grandmother.

The resilience and pride that have served Hunter-Gault well in her career owe a lot to the strong values passed on to her during her formative years. She has often cited her grandmother as a key role model. Though not educated beyond the third grade, her grandmother read three newspapers a day and helped spark a healthy curiosity about the world in the future award-winning reporter. Hunter-Gault's father was also a critical influence, despite his frequent absences. "He was an important part of my life and development because he set standards for me that were very high," Hunter-Gault told *Southern Living.*

Hunter-Gault's first encounter with prejudice over race occurred when she was a child: she was mocked by other black children for having a light complexion. Her early childhood years were spent in Covington, South Carolina. But in 1951 the family moved to Atlanta, and by age 12 Charlayne had decided to pursue a career in journalism. "With a passion bordering on obsession," she revealed in her autobiography *In My Place,* "I wanted to be a journalist." Her hero at the time was Brenda Starr, the comic-strip reporter.

Hunter-Gault excelled at Turner High School in Atlanta, the top black school in a city where black and white students were still educated under separate roofs. She edited the school newspaper and wrote for a community weekly during her high school years. Much to her disappointment, though, the family went to Alaska in the mid-1950s to live where her father was stationed at the time. Hunter-Gault attended a school there that had no other students of color, and she had to enter a lower grade because her school in the South lagged academically behind white schools. The entire family returned to Georgia after a year, and Hunter-Gault went back to

At a Glance . . .

Born Charlayne Hunter on February 27, 1942, in Due West, SC; daughter of Charles S. H., Jr. (a Methodist Army Chaplain) and Althea Hunter; married Walter Stovall (a journalist and writer), 1963 (divorced); married Ronald Gault (an investment banker), 1971; children: Susan, (with Stovall); Chuma (with Gault). *Education*: Attended Wayne State University, 1959–61; University of Georgia, Athens, B.A., 1963; Russell Sage Fellow at Washington University, St. Louis, c. 1967–68.

Career: Wrote for the *New Yorker*, 1964–67; *New York Times*, 1968–77, became Harlem bureau chief; *MacNeil/Lehrer NewsHour*, New York City, general correspondent, 1978–83, national correspondent and substitute anchor, 1983–97; National Public Radio, chief correspondent for Africa, 1997–99; CNN, Johannesburg Bureau Chief, 1999-.

Awards: *New York Times* Publisher Awards, 1970 (with Joseph Lelyveld), 1974, and 1976; George Foster Peabody Broadcasting Award, 1986; named Journalist of the Year by the National Association of Black Journalists, 1986; *Good Housekeeping* Broadcast Personality of the Year Award; American Women in Radio and Television Award for excellence in journalism; Woman of Achievement Award from the New York Chapter of the American Society of University Women; Newswomen's Club of New York Front Page Award; two National News and Documentary Emmy Awards; National Urban Coalition Award for distinguished urban reporting; Lincoln University Unity Award; Peabody Award, 1999; Lifetime Achievement Award, Annenberg School of Communication, University of Southern California, 2000.

Addresses: *Office*—CNN, One CNN Center, P.O. Box 195366, Atlanta, GA 30348–5366.

Turner High School. She became the school's homecoming queen and graduated number three in her class in 1959.

Future Reporter Became Important Newsmaker

The University of Georgia's practice of barring black students made it impossible for Hunter-Gault to attend the only college in her state that had a journalism school. Her opportunity to overcome that restriction came when she, along with fellow Turner High student Hamilton Holmes, was recruited by civil rights leaders who wanted to break the color line in Georgia education. Georgia State University was originally selected as the school to be integrated. However, Holmes suggested that they go to the University of Georgia because it offered a better quality education, and Hunter-Gault agreed. Despite the historic significance of entering a previously whites-only college, Hunter-Gault said that she was not motivated to be such a symbol. Quoted in *Essence* magazine, she said, "To become a historic symbol was not the point of what I did. The point of what I did was to have access to the best education I could in the state to become a journalist."

Hunter-Gault attended Wayne State University in Detroit for a year and a half before the courts opened the door to her entry into the University of Georgia. When she and her mother finally arrived on the Georgia campus in 1961, white students converged on their car and started rocking it until they were chased away by a dean. Two nights later, a crowd 1,000-strong gathered outside her dormitory, one of them heaving a brick through a window. According to an article in *Essence*, during these riots a white woman went up to Hunter-Gault and tossed a quarter at her feet, saying, "Here, nigger, do my sheets." Hunter-Gault and Holmes were suspended for their own safety, then ordered by a federal court to return the next day.

Although Hunter-Gault was occasionally threatened during her stay at the university—and faculty members often stood guard outside her classes to make sure she was not abused—she never considered leaving. She stated in *Southern Living*: "I think it was the result of having a goal and having support for that and being supported by a lot of really good people who made sacrifices for us." Shortly before earning her journalism degree in 1963, Hunter-Gault secretly married fellow journalism student Walter Stovall, who was white. Although they were divorced several years later due to diverging career paths, they have remained close friends. (Hunter became Hunter-Gault in 1971 when she married Ronald Gault, an investment banker.)

Part of Hunter-Gault's training for her career turned out to be her exposure to the throng of journalists who followed the story of her enrollment at the University of Georgia. Her observations of reporters in action served as an apprenticeship in the art of interviewing. During the summers of her college years, Hunter-Gault further honed her reporting skills by working for the *Inquirer*, a black Atlanta newspaper.

After graduating in 1963, Hunter and her husband moved to New York City and had a daughter. Her first job was as a secretary at the *New Yorker*, a position she accepted on the condition that she be considered for future writing assignments. From 1964 to 1967 she contributed pieces to the "Talk of the Town" feature section of the magazine, and she also wrote short stories. Then she received a Russell Sage Fellowship to study social science at

Washington University in St. Louis. During that study period she also edited articles for *Trans-Action* magazine.

Attacked Prejudiced Editorial Policy

While covering a story in Washington, D.C., Hunter-Gault was hired by WRC-TV, an NBC affiliate, as an investigative reporter and anchor of the local evening news program. In 1968 she accepted a position with the metropolitan staff of the *New York Times* and later created the post of Harlem bureau chief. During this tenure she wrote a scathing memo to top editors objecting to their practice of changing the term "black" to "Negro" in her pieces; she went on to attack the presumptions her white bosses seemed to be making about people of color. Her points were taken to heart, and the Times adopted the word "black" as standard usage. "Nowadays it seems almost silly," she was quoted as saying in *People* magazine. "But it was one of those defining moments in the history of black journalism in major white institutions."

Her next stop on the journalism career track came in 1978 when she became a correspondent for the *MacNeil/Lehrer Report*, later renamed the *MacNeil/Lehrer NewsHour*. Five years later, she was promoted to national correspondent and fill-in anchor. Her skills as an interviewer resulted in her meeting with some of the most famous people in the world, including British prime minister Margaret Thatcher, archbishop of Capetown Desmond Tutu, U.S. president George Bush, U.S. Army general Norman Schwarzkopf, German statesman and chancellor Helmut Schmidt, and comedian and business mogul Bill Cosby. Hunter-Gault was one of the first correspondents allowed into the West Indian nation of Grenada after the American-led invasion in 1983, and also reported on location during the Gulf War. She won an Emmy Award for her Grenada coverage, as well as one for her report on Admiral Zumwalt, who authorized the spraying of Agent Orange in Vietnam and unwittingly poisoned his own son. In 1986 Hunter-Gault was named Journalist of the Year by the National Association of Black Journalists. Most cherished among her honors, though, is the George Foster Peabody Broadcasting Award presented to her in 1986 by the H. W. Grady School of Journalism at the University of Georgia for her documentary *Apartheid's People*.

Hunter-Gault has striven to find the essence of her investigative subjects and remain objective in her reporting. Both as a television journalist and a writer, she has produced riveting stories about racial prejudice, the underclass in the United States, and a host of other pressing social concerns. Throughout her successful career, she has never lost sight of herself as a black journalist, and in a piece for *Fortune*, she emphasized the need for the media to present African Americans "as whole people." In his 1989 book *I Dream a World: Portraits of Black Women Who Changed the World*, Brian Lanker

quoted her as saying: "You have to assess every situation that you're in and have to decide, is this happening because I'm black? Is this happening because I'm a woman? Or is this happening because this is how it happens?"

Acclaimed Memoir Put Life in Perspective

In 1992 Charlayne Hunter-Gault produced a much-praised account of her life entitled *In My Place*. In it she recalls her early years growing up black and female in the Deep South, as well as the turmoil of entering the University of Georgia. Her book downplays her own courage in living through the adversity of her college years, giving credit instead to the black community and her family for supporting her and paving the way for her giant step forward.

In My Place is a stirring story of Hunter-Gault's journey from a world of segregation—attending schools in the South where children often had no textbooks—to a world of international exposure—covering events of worldwide impact for a major news show. Most vivid of all is her recounting of the injustice and horror of her first days at the University of Georgia, when riots ignited around her. As she noted in the book's prologue: "We would be greeted by mobs of white students who, within forty-eight hours would hurl epithets, burn crosses and black effigies, and finally stage a riot outside my dormitory while nearby state patrolmen ignored the call from university officials to come and intervene." The impact of *In My Place* was not lost on the critics, either. *The New Yorker* concluded: "This book is a vivid retelling of history, and should take its place as one of the informal literary classics of the civil rights movement."

In fitting recognition of her personal success—and the social, economic, and political advancements people of color have been making in the United States over the past few decades—Charlayne Hunter-Gault was asked to deliver the commencement address at the University of Georgia in 1988. She was the first African American to do so in the school's history. In an interview with *Southern Living*, Hunter-Gault said, "I knew that we had really reached a significant milestone in the reconciliation between the Georgia we entered and the Georgia that I wanted it to be." As recounted in the *Atlantic*, Hunter-Gault's address to the university stressed the need for "acknowledging the guiding principles of fundamental human decency and then living by them" in "a waiting and needful world."

After nearly twenty years at PBS, Hunter-Gault left *The MacNeil/Leher NewsHour* in 1997 for a position with National Public Radio (NPR). She moved to Johannesburg, South Africa, joining her husband, who had moved there the year before for a position with J.P. Morgan. In Johannesburg, Hunter-Gault acted as NPR's chief correspondent for Africa. "Africa conceivably could be one of the most exciting places in the world this coming decade," she told *Jet*.

Two years later, Hunter-Gault left NPR and returned to television. She accepted an offer from CNN to become the network's Johannesburg Bureau Chief. "In Africa, every restaurant you walk into has CNN on the television," Hunter-Gault told *Electronic Media*. "That kind of power is something you don't treat lightly."

Hunter-Gault has held her ground against racism to become a voice of consciousness in the field of American broadcast journalism. During her years with *MacNeil/Leher*, her face became a well-known symbol for accuracy and integrity. After moving on to NPR and then CNN, Hunter-Gault remained dedicated to her journalistic ideals.

Selected writings

In My Place, Farrar, Straus & Giroux, 1992.

Sources

Books

Contemporary Heros and Heroines, Book IV, Gale, 2000.

Hunter-Gault, Charlayne, *In My Place*, Farrar, Straus & Giroux, 1992.
Lanker, Brian, *I Dream a World: Portraits of Black Women Who Changed the World*, Stewart, Tabori & Chang, 1989, p. 62.

Periodicals

Atlanta Journal and Constitution, October 25, 1992, p. N-1; January 12, 1993, p. D-1.
Atlantic, December 1992, p. 151.
Boston Globe, January 31, 1993, sec. BGM, p. 9.Essence, March 1987, pp. 41–42, 110.
Editor & Publisher, January 31, 2000.
Electronic Media, March 15, 1999.
Fortune, November 2, 1992, p. 118–19.
Jet, March 1, 1993, p. 30; May 26, 1997; June 7, 1999.
Los Angeles Times, December 17, 1987, sec. VI, p. 1; June 12, 1988, p. I-4; November 30, 1992, p. E-1.
New Yorker, December 21, 1992, p. 135.
New York Times Magazine, January 25, 1970, pp. 24–25, 50.
People, December 7, 1992, pp. 73–76.
Southern Living, June 1990, pp. 78–83.
USA Today, July 16, 1993, p. A-13.

—Ed Decker and Jennifer M. York

Ice-T (Tracy Marrow)

1958–

Rapper, actor, social commentator

Ice-T appeared on the music scene in 1987 with a new style, gangster rap, which offers rhymes about crime—and street life in general—in unflinching detail. His tough, ground-breaking records paved the way for the wave of younger gangster-rappers that included Ice Cube and N.W.A. Before Ice-T's arrival on the scene, rappers devoted most of their lyrics to partying. But Ice-T, an ex-criminal from South Central Los Angeles trying to go straight by way of his music, sang about what he knew: robbery, murder, pimps, hustlers, gangs, and prison. In his own words: "I try to write about fun/ And the good times/But the pen yanks away and explodes/And destroys the rhyme."

By the early 1990s, however, Ice-T had reached such a level of success as a recording artist and film star that his gangster image began to give way to that of a teacher. *Newsweek* referred to him as "a foulmouthed moralist." *Entertainment Weekly*'s James Bernard declared that "Ice-T has something to teach anyone concerned about the rotting core of America's cities." As his success broadened, Ice-T continued to sing about the street—but with a determination to help black kids escape the ghetto and make white kids understand it. He also considered his financial future a matter of strategy: "The name of the game is capitalism," reads a typical Ice-T quote from his publicity packet, "and I aim to win that game, too."

Ironically, when Ice ventured into rock 'n' roll—generally a less controversial music form than rap—he touched off his greatest controversy: a furor arose over his incendiary 1992 song, "Cop Killer," recorded with his hardcore rock band Body Count. After breaking ties with his record company, he signed with the independent rap label, Priority, and continued his assault on racism and mainstream sensibilities.

From Crime to Rhyme

Ice-T was born Tracey Marrow on February 16, 1958 in Newark, New Jersey. By the time he was in the seventh grade, both his parents had died, and he went to live with an aunt in Los Angeles. While at Crenshaw High School, he wrote rhymes for local gangs and was soon drawn by his friends into petty crime. At age 17, he left his aunt's home and, in his words, "started hanging out in the 'hood with my friends." By the early 1980s, Ice was also drawn to rap music, thanks to the success of artists like

At a Glance . . .

Born Tracey Marrow (some sources say Morrow) on February 16, 1958 in Newark, NJ; raised by an aunt in Los Angeles, CA, after the death of his parents; married Darlene; one child.

Career: Recording artist and film actor. Wrote rhymes for Los Angeles gangs in 1970s; recorded "The Coldest Rap" in 1982 for independent label; released first album, 1987; released first album with band Body Count, 1992; signed with Priority records, 1993, and released *Home Invasion*. Joined Lollapalooza concert tour, 1991. Appeared in films *Breakin'*, 1984; *Breakin' 2: Electric Boogaloo*, 1984; *Rappin'*, 1985; *New Jack City*, 1991; *Ricochet*, 1992; *CB4*, *Trespass*, and *Who's the Man*, all 1993; and *Surviving the Game*, 1994; *Tank Girl*, 1995; *Johnny Mnemonic*, 1995; *Players*, 1997; *Judgment Day*, 1999; *The Heist*, 1999; *Leprechaun in the Hood*, 2000; *3000 Miles to Graceland*, 2001; Appeared in television series *New York Undercover*, 1994–98; *Players*, 1997–98; *Law and Order: Special Victims Unit*, 2000– ; Made for TV movie, *Exiled: A Law & Order Movie*, 1998; Author, with Heidi Siegmund, of *The Ice Opinion*, 1994.

Addresses: *Record company*—Priority Records, 6430 West Sunset Blvd., Hollywood, CA 90028. *Publicist*—Susan Blond, Inc. 250 West 57th St., Suite 622, New York, NY 10107.

Kurtis Blow. In 1982 he recorded "The Coldest Rap" for an independent label and was paid twenty dollars for it.

Naturally, this kind of money was nothing compared to what he and his friends could make illegally. Although he claimed to have never been a "gangbanger" himself, he was close enough to see that world as a dead end. Eventually his friends starting being sent to prison. "Then one of my buddies got life," he told *Musician*. "And they were all calling me from jail, saying, . . . Stay with that rap. Stay down." He stayed with it, honing his style and landing a part as a rapper in the 1984 movie *Breakin'*.

In addition to the advice and admiration of his friends, Ice relied on his girlfriend, Darlene, who stayed with him through the lean years and finally shared his success with him. "Even though we were broke," Ice told Scott Cohen in *Details*, "she knew that I could take five minutes out and go scam $20,000. I needed a girl who was ready to say, 'Don't do it, Ice. It's O.K.'" Darlene added that for a long time they were too broke to go to the movies: "We just lived in one little room and paid rent. We didn't have a car for two years."

By the mid-1980s rap had grown from an urban phenomenon to a national one, but New York City's rappers had a monopoly on street credentials. California, which had produced the good-natured surf pop of the Beach Boys and psychedelic rock bands like the Grateful Dead, hardly seemed a source of rhymes about urban strife. But Ice-T's 1987 debut, *Rhyme Pays*, put South Central Los Angeles on the nation's cultural map with its disturbing stories of inner-city warfare.

This new approach took the music community by storm; it also provoked charges from watchdog organizations like the Parents' Music Resource Center and from critics on the political left and right who felt that Ice glorified violence, theft, and sexism. Subject matter aside, he drew fire—and the first warning sticker placed on a rap record, by his reckoning—for using "profanity." "No one has yet been able to explain to me the definition of profanity anyhow. . . . I can think of ways to say stuff—saying things using legitimate words but in a context—that makes a more profane comment than any bullshit swear words." The album's rap, "6 in the Morning," telling the story of a handful of gang members escaping the police became particularly well-known.

Ice returned in 1988 with *Power*. The cover of the album featured a bikini-clad Darlene pointing a gun at the camera; Ice hadn't softened his approach. The album yielded two hits, "High Rollers" and "I'm Your Pusher." Ice's face began to appear more regularly on MTV, and he contributed the title song to the soundtrack of the 1988 film, *Colors*. His high-profile gangsterism provoked more attacks from various authorities, particularly when he began speaking to students in schools. In a discussion with Arion Berger in *Creem*, Ice presented his imitation of an FBI agent opposed to his school tours: "'He has a record here called, um, "I'm Your Pusher." 'Well, have you played it?' 'Oh, we don't have a phonograph here at the Bureau.'"

Ice's frustration at attempts to suppress his music motivated a change of direction on his next LP, *The Iceberg/ Freedom of Speech . . . Just Watch What You Say*, released in 1989. A drawing of his face appeared on the cover with a gun to either side of his head and the barrel of another in his mouth. He enlisted punk politician and former Dead Kennedys lead singer Jello Biafra to deliver an announcement of right-wing martial law over a sampled piece of deathmetal guitar, setting the tone for a relentless counterattack on conservative thinking. The record also featured, "Peel Their Caps Back," which Berger called Ice-T's "most vicious criminal record so far."

Ice later reflected that the Iceberg album was too preoccupied with censorship and free expression. "Sales were good on that album," he told Dennis Hunt of the *Los Angeles Times*, "but [I can see where] some of the raps made some people think I was going soft. I just got caught up in messages—about freedom of speech. People at the record company wanted me to do that and I'm sorry that

I listened to them." In the meantime, he added, the rising stars of gangster rap had upped the ante of street-tough rhyming. In 1991, though, he would come roaring to the forefront of the scene once

Original Gangster—and Actor

Ice-T landed the role of an undercover cop in the smash 1991 film *New Jack City* and his song, "New Jack Hustler," appeared on the film's soundtrack and was later nominated for a Grammy Award. He received excellent reviews for his acting in the film; Alan Light of *Rolling Stone* called his performance "riveting." "It was scary," Ice told Dave DiMartino of *Entertainment Weekly*. "I didn't know how the actors were gonna react, and in music I'm in my own domain. But when I got there, the first thing I found out was that they were, like, in awe of me—they wanted, like, autographs and stuff." Soon he had signed on to play a drug dealer in another film, *Ricochet*.

Ice's 1991 album, *O.G.—Original Gangster*, contained twenty-four tracks of uncompromising and often violent raps. Rather than pursue the anti-censorship course of the *Iceberg* album, *O.G.* returned to Ice-T's earlier turf with a vengeance. The album's themes are summed up by titles like "Straight Up Nigga," "Prepared to Die," and "Home of the Bodybag." Ice's raps, though laced with the "profanity" of earlier records, had become tougher and leaner; "Mic Contract" likened rap competition to gang warfare and suggested that Ice-T was ready to face off with young gangster-rappers. The album also included a rock and roll song, "Body Count," named for the hardcore band he had assembled. Ice enlisted four different producers to work on the album, and DJ Evil E. provided the eclectic mix of beats and samples.

Reviews of *O.G.* were mostly very positive. Even as Jon Pareles of the *New York Times* acknowledged contradictions between Ice's "trigger-happy machismo and his increasing maturity." He remarked that "[*O.G.*] works to balance the thrills of action and the demands of conscience." A notice in *Musician* commented, "It's his candor that really draws blood," while *Stereo Review* insisted that Ice-T's rhymes "cut to the bone with lack of pretense or apology." And in his *Rolling Stone* review, Mark Coleman noted that "*O.G.* can be heard as a careening, open-ended discussion. Of course Ice does tend to follow his sharpest points with defiant kiss-offs. . . . But get past his bluster and this guy is full of forthright, inspiring perceptions."

Warnings and Promises

For its unsparing language and content, *O.G.* received a parental warning sticker; Coleman claimed that such warnings were "like sticking a Band-Aid on a gunshot wound." Ice-T's response to the sticker, in a quote which

appeared in his publicity materials as well as ads for the album, was as follows: "I have a sticker on my record that says 'Parental Guidance is Suggested.' In my book, parental guidance is always suggested. If you need a sticker to tell you that you need to guide your child, you're a dumb f—kin' parent anyhow."

Also in 1991, Ice-T joined the ambitious traveling rock festival known as Lollapalooza. Organized by Perry Farrell—whose band, Jane's Addiction, was the headlining attraction—the tour included such divergent acts as Black Rock Coalition founders Living Colour, the industrial dance outfit Nine Inch Nails, and British postpunk veterans Siouxie and the Banshees. As the only rapper on the tour, Ice-T faced Lollapalooza's predominantly white audiences with a positive attitude: "All I want them to do is come out and say 'I like him.' Not get the message, not understand a word I'm saying. Just think, 'Those black guys on the stage I used to be scared of, I like 'em.' I want to come out and say, 'Peace.' If I can do that, that's cool." His participation in Lollapalooza attested to his belief that rap had the same rebellious and unifying quality that rock and roll had when it first appeared: "White kids will continue to get hipper to black culture. With R&B, the kids didn't want to meet us, but this is rock & roll all over again—everybody chillin' together."

Ice-T began as a controversial rapper in the late 1980s, throwing around gangster slang and strong language and provoking anxiety in many listeners. By the early 1990s, however, he had matured into a thoughtful, charismatic performer with strong careers in at least two media. Despite his newfound success, though, Ice insisted that he still made a lot of people nervous: "Parents are scared because my record is Number One on the campus charts of Harvard for three months," reads a quote in his publicity packet. "These kids are being trained to grow up and become Supreme Court justices and politicians."

"Cop-Killer" Debate

Little did the rapper realize how politically important he would become. Soon after the long-promised Body Count record hit the stores, a firestorm surrounded the song, "Cop Killer." Though Ice explained the track away as the fantasy of a downtrodden but sick man driven over the edge by police brutality, police groups and conservative politicians condemned it for advocating the killing of police officers. Even then-President George Bush and Vice President Dan Quayle—admittedly not figures Ice ever cared to please—took the opportunity to lambast the record publicly. *Time* quoted Doug Elder, head of a Houston police organization, as saying, "You mix this with the summer, the violence and a little drugs, and they are going to unleash a reign of terror on communities all across this country." Though the quote provided no clarification of who "they" were, Elder clearly appealed to fears aroused by the upheaval in Los Angeles and other cities after the 1992 acquittal of four white police officers in the beating of black motorist Rodney King.

Ice expressed no surprise about the riots—he called them a "revolution" in a *Rolling Stone* interview—as he'd been predicting such a turn of events for years. He was adamant in his public statements about a point few authorities cared to acknowledge: that rap, Ice's included, had opened the ears of a lot of white kids. "For the first time there was something like a riot and the white parents weren't able to say 'Look how terrible they [people of color] are,' because the white kids said, 'We know why they did it,'" he insisted to *Spin*. "Why? Because there's been a dialogue through rap music to let them know we're really ready." Ultimately, however, he elected to have "Cop Killer" removed from the album and later gave *Musician* magazine seven reasons why. Among them was his claim that "it was a good way to let people know what censorship is like." In addition, giving the single away at concerts neutralized the charge that he was motivated by greed. Finally—and perhaps most importantly—removing it helped to restore the focus on police brutality.

Surprisingly, the result of the controversy left no obvious rancor between Ice and Warner Bros./Sire. Apparently, the company never demanded that Ice-T pull the record; "So I have a lot of loyalty to them," he remarked. Even so, star and label elected to part company. Ice, after reviewing his options, signed with Priority, a Los Angeles-based label best known for releasing records by Ice Cube and N.W.A. In 1993 he came roaring back into the public eye with the album, *Home Invasion*, in which he continued to mine the theme of rap's infiltration of young white minds. *Time* called the record "for the most part, balanced and coherent," adding, "With his gangsta posturing, Ice-T is far from a role model for urban youth, but his real goal is to expose suburbia to inner-city anger."

Ice continued appearing in films—he co-starred with Ice Cube in the thriller, *Trespass,* and in late 1993 was at work on Ernest Dickerson's *Surviving the Game,* in which he plays a homeless man hunted for sport. In addition, Ice collaborated with speedmetal rockers Slayer on a song for the *Judgment Night* soundtrack. He also announced plans for a new Body Count album. "We wanted a group that has the attack of Slayer, the impending doom of [British metal pioneers Black] Sabbath, the drive of [U.K. punk-metal trio] Motorhead and [is] groove-oriented," he explained to *Musician*, "to come up with what I call consumable hardcore music—a record that once you hear it you can sing it." Despite his declared revolutionary principles, his lyrics for Body Count were lambasted by critics for their perceived misogyny.

Clearly, Ice-T came through the onslaught of negative publicity he received for "Cop Killer" with a redoubled sense of purpose and a diversified career portfolio. In addition to his film and recording work, he announced his intention to publish a book, *The Ice Opinion,* through

St. Martin's Press. Whether he would set off a new controversy with his future work remained to be determined, but he demonstrated that he was less interested in shock than in dialogue. "I write to create some brain-cell activity," he insisted in *Time*. "I want people to think about life on the street, but I don't want to bore them. I want them to ask themselves, 'Does it matter to me?'"

Apparently, what Ice thought mattered to many. Ice continued to represent the voice of street after the 1994 release of *The Ice Opinion* even though as an entertainer, he was several thousand dollars and many years from the streets. The book touched on Ice's views of sex, religion, education, and drugs. And in a review of *The Ice Opinion*, *Artforum International Magazine* noted Ice's own contradictions. They describe the book as, "On the one hand a profound critic of crime and the injustice of the prison system, coupled with an urgent call for access to education; on the other, a seriously seductive glamorization of the criminal life as the ultimate independent free space."

Ice-T took that contradictory stance to the networks and producer Dick Wolf in 1997 when he proposed his crime fighting drama, *Players*. The show followed a group of ex-convicts who were working with the Feds to fight crime with crime. Ice was accustomed to television roles and Dick Wolf's style after guest appearances on Wolf's Fox Network show *New York Undercover*. The foray from "Cop Killer" to the "right" side of the law didn't concern Ice either. "I'm not going to do anything that isn't me," he explained to *People Weekly*. "I still gotta go back to my neighborhood." Each of the roles allowed Ice to stand behind his view on law enforcement. "I believe in doing the right thing," He told *Entertainment Weekly*. "But I don't believe that just because you put on a uniform that makes you right." Ice must have enjoyed working with Wolf, he signed on to play Detective Odafin (Fin) Tutuola on *Law & Order: Special Victims Unit* in 2000.

Ice-T's next album release was *7th Deadly Sin*, with Body Count. To promote the release, he entered into a groundbreaking partnership with Atomic Pop, a full-service, internet music company. Atomic Pop provided an aggressive online marketing program for the release but ultimately lacked the marketing force outside the Net that was necessary to push the album. In an interview with *Hollywood Reporter* Ice T explained, "Atomic Pop did an excellent job in setting up a website, but honestly, they lacked in the offline promotion department." He added, "I am trying to work with labels over the Net, but at the moment, I really only use the Net as a promotion device."

The importance of cyberspace not being lost on Ice-T, he took a less than popular stance in the discussions surrounding Napster, a website that provided easy access to MP3 sharing software. Although he understood musicians' views against Napster, he labeled record executives that conspired to shut the website down "gangstas."

Ice also said that he understood how fans could feel vindicated in ripping off the labels by sharing music because labels had historically abused artists.

Ice-T's willingness to seek out the Net as a viable outlet for music led to an appointment to the advisory board of Solutions Media Inc. (SMI) in 2000. After hosting the unveiling of SMI's Internet music division, SomeMusic.com, SMI president and CEO Wayne Irving II welcomed Ice-T's business sense and input as a songwriter, actor, author and musician. "Knowing that he participates or speaks at just about every music conference in the world and promotes exactly what we are providing," explained Irving, "I knew he would be a great addition to our team." As a member of the SMI board, Ice contributed to the development of viable electronic applications for the consumer market. "For example, I don't have time to burn up MP3s and deal with the technology," he told the *Hollywood Reporter*. "I love (MP3) . . . but I don't think they have gotten user-friendly enough to where I would listen to an MP3 over a CD."

Ice T also ventured into the fun part of the computer world as the voice of Agent Nathaniel Cain in Fox Interactive's *Sanity, Aiken's Artifact,* a science-fiction fantasy adventure game. Ironically, his participation in bringing the Net and computer futures to the forefront is as important as his past foray's to bring street life into the spotlight. "Ultimately, there has to be a paradigm shift, and I think it will be here soon." he told the *Hollywood Reporter*. "Once you get into the Internet, you tend to think that everyone knows what you know. But you really are still a minority. People are just now getting cell phones, and people are also just now getting into computers." Staying on top of music innovations, Ice still gets people to think about life. His presence on the net has merely added the streets to the net and forces them to question; "Does it matter to me?"

Selected works

(films)

Breakin,' 1984.
New Jack City, 1991.
Trespass, 1993.
Surviving the Game, 1994.

(television)

New York Undercover.
Players, 1997.
Law & Order: Special Victims Unit, 2000.

albums

Rhyme Pays (includes "6 in the Morning"), Sire, 1987.

Power (includes "High Rollers" and "I'm Your Pusher"), Sire, 1988.
The Iceberg/Freedom of Speech . . . Just Watch What You Say (includes "Peel
O.G.—Original Gangster (includes "New Jack Hustler," "Straight Up"
Body Count (includes "Cop Killer"; song deleted from second version),
Home Invasion, Priority, 1993.
Return of the Real, Priority, 1996.
7th Deadly Sin, Priority, 1999.

With other artists

Colors (motion picture soundtrack; appears on title song), Sire, 1988.
New Jack City (motion picture soundtrack; appears on "New Jack Hustler").
(With Ice Cube) *Trespass* (motion picture soundtrack; appears on title song).
(With Slayer) *Judgment Night* (motion picture soundtrack.

Sources

Artform, Summer 1994.
Billboard, June 8, 1991.
Broadcasting & Cable, August 7, 2000.
Business Wire, March 23, 2000, pp. 350; May 11, 2000, pp. 77.
Creem, April/May 1991; June 1993, pp. 58–67.
Details, July 1991.
Emerge, September 1992, p. 30.
Entertainment Weekly, May 24, 1991; May 31, 1991; February 12, 1993, pp.
Hollywood Reporter, July 14, 1999, pp. 18; August 2,2000,pp. 5; August 7, 2000, pp. 4; February 14, 2001, pp. 7.
Jet, August 17, 1992, pp. 35.
Los Angeles Times, April 21, 1991.
Musician, June 1991; August 1991; January 1993.
Newsweek, July 1, 1991.
New York Times, May 19, 1991.
Option, March 1992, pp. 75–79.
Parade (Detroit), June 6, 1993, p. 2.
People Weekly, June 30, 1997, pp. 16
Publishers Weekly, June 28, 1993, p. 17; January 24, 1994, pp. 45.
Rolling Stone, May 16, 1991; June 13, 1991; September 19, 1991; June 25,
The Source, May 1991.
Spin, May 1991; July 1993, pp. 71–75, 92–93.
Stereo Review, August 1991.
Time, June 22, 1992, pp. 66–68; May 3, 1992, p. 81.

Online

Internet Movie Database, http://www.imdb.com

Other

Ice-T press release, Warner Bros./Sire 1991.

—Simon Glickman and Leslie Rochelle

Monte Irvin

1919—

Baseball player

Monte Merrill Irvin was considered by the owners of the old Negro Leagues to be the ideal candidate to integrate Major League Baseball. As early as 1942 his name was being mentioned as the player to break the color barrier in the big leagues. He could hit for power and average, was fast with an excellent glove, and perhaps more importantly, was level-headed and mature. But instead of taking the field in Brooklyn instead of Jackie Robinson, Irvin was shipped overseas to serve in the Army during World War II. Though Irvin eventually made it to the major leagues and performed well, he was 30 years old when he signed with the New York Giants, and he was not the player he had been before serving in the military.

Born Hubert Merrill on February 25, 1919 in Haleburg, AL, Irvin was the eighth child of Cupid Alexander and Mary Eliza Henderson Irvin. His father was a sharecropper, and his family picked cotton and lived on a farm that kept hogs and cows. When food ran low his father would hunt for wild game. Monte Irvin's given name was Hubert, but everyone called him Pete except for his sister Eulalia, who died of a burst appendix at 17. She called him Monford. When he was eight years old, he officially changed his name to Monford Merrill Irvin. Irvin adjusted his name again when he was a professional baseball player, changing Monty to Monte because it was easier to sign.

Irwin's first exposure to the game of baseball came on Saturday afternoons when men came from neighboring towns to play with homemade bats and balls and then picnic after the game. In the spring of 1927 his father felt the overseer of the land he worked was cheating him. Since Cupid Irvin had no legal recourse, he was forced to take the injustice or leave. Irvin's father decided to leave his family behind, move north, and look for work there. Soon his family joined him because men working for the landowner tried to intimidate Irvin's mother into telling them where her husband was. The family eventually migrated to Bloomfield, NJ when Irvin was eight.

Living in the North

Irvin's father soon found work at a dairy in Orange, New Jersey, so the family moved there. Irvin's life revolved around family, the church, and sports—especially baseball. He made the local team, the Orange Triangles, at the age of 13 in 1932. When it came time to go to high school, Irvin competed in football, basketball, baseball, and track earning 10 varsity letters. Irvin set a state record throwing the javelin. His track coach even asked him to think about trying to qualify for the Olympics. Irvin played baseball in the spring and continued throughout the summer with the Triangles and another team in nearby Paterson, New Jersey, the Paterson Smart Set.

Irvin contracted hemolytic streptococcus during basketball season. Since medications to combat the infection had not been invented, he was forced to undergo an operation. Doctors cut a hole in his chest and one under his arm to let the infection drain. At one point doctors asked his mother if they could amputate his left arm, but his mother would not allow it. Irvin stayed in the hospital for six weeks, at times, near death. He was hospitalized from the beginning of February to the middle of March and lost 30 pounds.

When he got out, however, he was able to graduate with his class in 1938. He joined the local Negro league team, called the Newark Eagles. Since Irvin wanted to attend college and play sports, he needed to protect his amateur status. He played only in Newark away games and took the field as "Jimmy Nelson." For college, Irvin wanted to attend the University of Michigan, but he attended Lincoln University in Oxford, Pennsylvania, on a scholarship. But Irvin stayed in college only for a year and a half. During his spring break of his sophomore year, Irvin left school and signed with the Newark Eagles. He traveled with the Eagles to spring training and never made it back to school. He played regularly during his rookie year but broke out his second year after changing his batting stance to emulate Joe DiMaggio's. Irvin estimated that he hit around .400 and hit 40 home runs. He was selected to the East-West All-Star game in Chicago, which in the mid-thirties was one of the social and sporting highlights for African Americans all over the country.

Irvin's life revolved around baseball. He played winter ball in Puerto Rico among the greats of black baseball such as Satchel Paige, Roy Campanella, and Josh Gibson. In 1942, Irvin began the year with Newark, but when

he was offered too little money he looked to Vera Cruz of the Mexican League. Irvin was making $150 a month and was offered $500 a month to play in Mexico. Since he was getting married and needed the extra money, Irvin and his new wife, Dee, headed to Mexico City. Irvin played with fellow Eagle Roy Dandridge and had an excellent year, leading the Mexican league in batting average (.398) and home runs. Irvin wanted to return to Mexico for the 1943 season, but his life was about to take a dramatic turn.

A Career Interrupted

Irvin remembered standing on second base in Puerto Rico when it was announced that the Japanese had bombed Pearl Harbor. After returning from Mexico, Irvin was drafted and served in an all-black engineering unit. Irvin spent 19 days crossing the Atlantic bound for England on a ship so packed with soldiers that they had to sleep in shifts. Irvin made it to France after D-Day and was stationed in Paris during the Battle of the Bulge. He never saw combat and was discharged after contracting an inner ear imbalance. In September of 1945 he returned home and reported to the Newark Eagles right away. He found out that after three years of no baseball, he was not the same player he had been before he left. Not only was he still sick and worn out, but also he was out of practice. The Brooklyn Dodgers approached him about signing with them, but he told them he was not ready yet. During the winter of 1945, he played in San Juan, Puerto Rico, and then rejoined Newark for the 1946 season.

In 1946 Newark was loaded with talent, including Larry Doby, the first African American to play in the American League. Leon Day pitched a no-hitter on the first day of the season, and the Eagles won their league. Irvin batted .394 to lead the league in hitting. The Eagles played the Kansas City Monarchs in the 1946 Negro League World Series. The Eagles stretched the series to seven games and won when the Monarchs' Paige did not show up to pitch the deciding game seven. Newark won and Irvin was the key factor in the Eagles' championship batting .462 during the series. Irvin played two more years in the Negro Leagues until the league folded after the 1948 season. By that time, Irvin's former teammate was playing for the Cleveland Indians in the American League, and many wondered why Irvin was not playing Major League Baseball. Branch Rickey, owner of the Brooklyn Dodgers who had signed Jackie Robinson, also signed Irvin, but there was a dispute over money with the Eagles' owner. Rickey would not pay compensation, so Irvin's rights went to the New York Giants for $5,000.

Major League Talent

Irvin started the 1949 season with Jersey City, the Giants Triple A affiliate, living in his own house with his wife and daughters. Irvin was hitting .373 and tearing up the minor leagues. He was called up to the Giants on July 15, with Cuban League teammate Hank Thompson. Neither man got much of a chance to play that first season, but the climate in the clubhouse between the black and white players was much more easygoing than in Brooklyn where Jackie Robinson was playing for the Dodgers.

In 1950, Irvin reported to his first Major League spring training. He was sent down to the minors but quickly made it up to the Giants on the strength of a .510 batting average with 10 home runs after only 18 games. In 1951 he established himself as one of the most complete players in the game. He led the National League with 121 runs batted in (RBI) to become the first former Negro League player to lead the league in RBI. Besides the impressive RBI total, Irvin finished that season with 24 home runs and a .312 average to place third in the National League MVP voting. As a team the Giants won 16 games in a row and 39 out of 47 to catch the Dodgers. The team came from 13 and a half games out of first place in mid August to tie first-place Brooklyn on the last day of the season. The Giants beat the Dodgers in a three-game series on Bobby Thomson's famous "shot-heard-round-the-world" home run. Irvin had been up before Thomson in the ninth inning with two men on base, but he fouled out. Irvin told John Shivers of the *Shepherd Express Metro* that he was the happiest man in the world after Thomson's hit cleared the wall: "we won the game and were going to the World Series, but it almost meant that no one would remember that I popped out with runners on earlier in the inning. I could have easily been the goat of that series if it wasn't for Thomson." In the first inning of the first game of the World Series, Irvin stole home against the New York Yankees. Though Irvin knocked out 11 hits and compiled a .458 average in the series, the Giants lost to the Yankees. Irvin finished the season as the Giants MVP.

Before the 1952 season, Irvin signed for $25,000 to become the first player to sign with the team. In spring training Irvin seemed to pick up where he left off during the 1951 season, but he broke his ankle in a pre-season game in Denver. He missed most of the season but returned in August to hit .310. The following year, Irvin batted .329 with 97 RBI and 21 home runs. In 1954 the Giants won the World Series in four games over the Cleveland Indians, but Irvin was relegated to spot duty as a pinch hitter.

The following year was his final one with the Giants organization. Irvin stayed 45 days with the big team and then was sent down to Minneapolis, the Giants' Triple A affiliate. Irvin spent the rest of the season in the minor leagues. Irvin led the league in hitting and his team won the pennant, but the Giants were no longer interested. In 1956 Irvin played for the Chicago Cubs. Irvin had a productive season with the Cubs platooning in left field. He finished the year with a .271 batting average and 15 home runs. Despite his solid numbers he was 37 years

old, and after just one season with the Cubs, he was released after the 1956 campaign. The next year Irvin caught on with the Los Angeles Angels of the Pacific Coast League. He started off well and then his back started to bother him. After one month of problems, Irvin consulted a doctor who told him that at 37, it was time to give up baseball. Irvin agreed and in May of 1957, after 20 years of professional baseball, called it quits.

Life After Baseball

Irvin worked for Rheinagold Brewery for ten years after leaving baseball. In 1968, Irvin came back to baseball to work in the commissioner's office. Irvin was with the office as a special assistant to the commissioner through some of the most important events in the history of the game. He was there when Curt Flood filed suit against Major League Baseball to challenge the owners' prohibition of free agency. He weathered two labor stoppages, owner Charles Finley of the Oakland As, and the introduction of the designated hitter in the American League.

One of Irwin's most important responsibilities was the formation of the commissioner's Negro Leagues' committee to pick out candidates for inclusion in baseball's Hall of Fame. Irvin acted as chairman of the committee and was instrumental in selecting nine former Negro League players for the Hall of Fame including Satchel Paige, Josh Gibson, and Buck Leonard. Though Irvin accomplished much in his efforts to recognize great black ballplayers who were being forgotten, he still had some regret over the matter, which he expressed to *The Los Angeles Times'* Larry McShane: "If they had let our guys play in the major leagues ten years sooner, they would have seen some great stars. There's still a lot that deserve the Hall of Fame."

Irvin himself was selected to enter the Hall in 1973. After selecting nine players to enter the Hall of Fame, the committee disbanded leaving the matter of the Negro League players to the regular Veterans Committee of the Hall. After his stint as a baseball executive Irvin retired with his wife Dee to Florida.

Sources

Books

Irving, Monte and James A Riley. *Nice Guys Finish First*, Carroll & Graf Publishers, Inc, 1996.
Who's Who Among African Americans, 13th ed. Gale Group, 2000.

Periodicals

The Los Angeles Times, June 14, 1998.

Online

Biography Resource Center, Gale, 2001, http://www.galenet.com/servlet/BioRC.

Shepherd Express Metro, http://www.shepherd-express.com/shepherd/21/7/this_and_that/talking _sports.html.

http://www.sportsline.com/u/baseball/bol/ballplayers/I/Irvin_Monte.html.

—Michael J. Watkins

Earl Jackson

1948–

Artist

An artist of originality and vision and an astute businessman as well, Earl Jackson has done much to define a contemporary visual style for African-American life. By the late 1990s, prints of his graceful, elegant artworks were widely and consistently sold in art stores and bookstores. A measure of their appeal to a wide cross section of Americans was that they appeared several times in hit films and television programs. "African Americans . . . . are hungry for images on their walls—positive images of African Americans," Jackson was quoted as saying in the *International Review of African American Art*. By responding to that hunger, Jackson became one of the few American artists unconnected with an educational institution to make a living from art full time.

Earl Jackson was born in 1948 in Ann Arbor, Michigan, and raised in nearby Willow Run, an unincorporated area west of Detroit that was largely dominated by auto manufacturing. He attended Willow Run High School (also the alma mater of the R&B vocalist and songwriter Nickolas Ashford, of the duo Ashford and Simpson), and graduated in 1966. Taking art courses at Washtenaw Community College and at Eastern Michigan University (both located in Ypsilanti near his Willow Run hometown),

Jackson worked for some years toward an art degree. He never finished that degree, but along the way he obtained an education of a different kind.

Worked as Picture Framer

Working for fifteen years as a picture framer at the Borders Book Shop in Ann Arbor (the original store in what became a nationwide chain), Jackson spent his evenings creating artworks—predominantly oil paintings—of his own. In 1970, he exhibited his works for the first time at the Ann Arbor Art Fairs, a huge outdoor event that draws hundreds of thousands of art enthusiasts. He continued to show and sell his works at similar events through much of the 1970s, but gradually he came to feel that the art fair scene was a poor fit with his own creative process. Producing large batches of original works in the weeks leading up to the fair season, Jackson would find himself completely burned out creatively for some time afterward.

Many working artists depend on art fairs for income, but Jackson chose a different approach. Instead of putting himself under the pressure of having to create large numbers of originals, he decided to channel his energies into more distinctive works that he would reproduce as

At a Glance . . .

Born 1948 in Ann Arbor, MI; raised in Willow Run, MI, near Detroit. *Education:* Willow Run High School, 1966; attended Washtenaw Community College and Eastern Michigan University, Ypsilianti, MI.

Career: Visual artist. Exhibited work publicly for the first time at Ann Arbor Art Fairs, 1970; continued to exhibit and sell work at art fairs, 1970–78; worked as picture framer, Borders Book Shop, Ann Arbor, ca. 1974–1989; solo exhibition, *Blues, Sippie Wallace and Eureal Montgomery,* University of Michigan, Ann Arbor, 1983; traveled to Africa, 1985 and 1988; completed painting "Following the Path," 1988; strong sales of painting in print form; solo exhibition *Journey with the Blues Gods,* St. Louis, MO, 1992; moved to Atlanta, GA, area, late 1990s.

Awards: Best Miniature Paintings, African World Festival, Detroit, MI, 1983.

Addresses: *Home*—1063 Seven Springs Circle, Marietta, GA 30068.

prints and distribute as widely as possible. Between about 1980 and 1985, Jackson created several black-and-white works that he made into prints and built a network of distribution contacts. The new depth in his paintings was recognized when they were included in group exhibitions at galleries, corporate offices, and educational institutions around Detroit and beyond. Several solo exhibitions of Jackson's work were also organized in the early 1980s.

Paintings Depicted Musicians

One of those exhibitions, *Blues, Sippie Wallace and Eureal Montgomery,* held in 1983 at the Eva Jessye Afro-American Music Collection at the University of Michigan in Ann Arbor, demonstrated one of the emerging themes of Jackson's art: the role of music in African-American life in general and the lives of African-American musicians specifically. Jackson went on to create a number of paintings on musical subjects. A series of "Jazz Greats" depicted such figures as Louis Armstrong, John Coltrane, and Dizzy Gillespie, while such works as "Crooners" and "Left Hand Like Thunder, Right Hand Like Lightnin'" evoked not specific musicians but more general types.

A crucial experience in the formation of Jackson's mature artistic personality was two trips he made to Africa in

1985 and 1988, first to Senegal and then to Kenya. After these voyages, Jackson's art was deepened by a layer of awareness of the way that many aspects of African-American life had their roots in African backgrounds. The culmination of this new awareness was "Following the Path," a painting that took Jackson a year and a half to complete. The painting depicts a group of women and girls, several holding parasols, walking along a stone wall. Influenced by music, they seem to be reenacting some ancient practice or ritual. Rendered in pastels and composed of an unusual collection of geometric shapes (the curves of the women's dresses, the circles of the parasol tops, the long rectangles of the wall), "Following the Path" suggests both lightness and strength.

Print Run Sold Out

Just as he made this creative breakthrough, Jackson also was on the point of perfecting his new business model. Ready to receive the 1,000 prints of "Following the Path" that Jackson had made was a nationwide network of galleries, distributors, and wholesalers, including 20 shops specializing in African-American art to which Jackson shipped prints directly. The results were startling. Jackson's initial run of 1,000 copies sold out, as did a second run of 600 more. Fourteen months after the work's release in December of 1988, 2,300 copies were in print and Jackson was a full-time artist—a picture framer no longer.

Jackson's art practice combines his creative concerns, retains elements that characterize his work at one stage of his career and incorporates them into new contexts at another stage. For example, Jackson continued to paint works based on musical subjects, but the paintings also showed the impact of the new spiritual ideas that were finding their way into his art. Jackson's solo exhibition, *Journeys with the Blues Gods,* shown at the Lithos Gallery in St. Louis in 1992, depicted blues singers, but represented them to some extent as religious icons; in one painting, several musicians' heads grew from a single body, and the paintings also included dowels or staffs, made of handmade paper, that suggested the heavy walking sticks used in a religious procession.

Through much of the 1990s, Jackson's art gained showings around and beyond Michigan; in addition to exhibitions at the University of Michigan Museum of Art in Ann Arbor and the Creative Arts Center in Pontiac, Michigan, Jackson's works have been displayed at Museum of Science and Industry in Chicago and in the National Gallery of Art in Dakar, Senegal. He has painted several murals in southeastern Michigan (including one at Detroit's impressive Museum of African-American History), and has taught art and mentored young artists in local schools. In the late 1990s, attracted by the vibrant African-American culture of the city of Atlanta, Georgia, Jackson moved to the Atlanta suburb of Marietta.

Sources

Periodicals

Ann Arbor News, February 21, 1988; February 17, 1990, p. B1; November 3, 1991, p. F6; April 16, 1996, p. C4; July 14, 1997, p. C4.
International Review of African-American Art, volume 14, number 1.

St. Louis Post-Dispatch, May 19, 1992.

Other

Additional information for this profile was obtained from a biography provided by the artist.

—James M. Manheim

Rodney Jerkins

1978(?)–

Producer and songwriter

When young people achieve major success in popular music, it is usually as performers, as charismatic figures who win the hearts of their youthful contemporaries. Pop producers and songwriters, who in some sense are the music's real creators, tend to have spent at least a few years mastering the complex crafts of record-making and musical composition. One startling exception to this generalization, however, is Rodney Jerkins. Active as a songwriter since childhood and as a producer since his mid-teens, Jerkins emerged in 1997 with a Midas touch that put him in demand not only in the R&B and gospel styles with which he was most familiar, but also in pop, Latin, and even country music circles.

Jerkins was born in small-town Pleasantville, New Jersey, around 1978; he later opened the headquarters of his burgeoning Darkchild Entertainment company just a short distance from where he grew up—and from the Holiness church where his father is pastor. Jerkins's mother was the church's choir director, and his childhood musical experiences revolved around playing drums in the church and around lessons in classical piano. When Jerkins was 12, his father gave him as a present the basic tools of contemporary musical creation—a keyboard and a drum machine.

Father Had Divine Vision

By the time he was in junior high school, Jerkins had set his sights on becoming a record producer. The Rev. Fred Jerkins was initially dismayed about his son's secular ambitions but agreed to them after receiving a divine vision regarding the success of which Rodney was capable. Jerkins's father continues to serve as his son's manager. When he was 15 Jerkins made a gospel album of his own, and his gospel roots continue to show through in his songwriting and choice of material. Unlike a large majority of his peers in urban music, Jerkins avoids sex and violence in his music. "I kinda want to do things that my mother can hear," he told *Time*. "If my mother can listen to it, then I'll work on it."

Amassing a stock of demo recordings he had made for local rap acts, Jerkins sought an entry point into the big-time music industry. His breakthrough came in 1992, when he buttonholed and impressed producer Teddy Riley, the 'new jack swing' pathbreaker who infused tune-based R&B with some of the street intensity and rhythmic edginess of hip-hop. Jerkins made his way to Riley's Virginia studio, five and a half hours from home, and "just waited to see him," he told *Billboard*. "I owe him a lot of credit because he told a lot of people about me."

The following year Jerkins produced two songs for the female vocalist Casserine, part of the roster of the major Warner Brothers label, and then was signed to a production deal at rival label Mercury. At Mercury he worked on high-profile remixes, including one for former beauty queen Vanessa Williams's "The Way That You Love" single, and produced tracks for vocalist Gina Thompson. All of a sudden the producer prodigy found himself the target of a great deal of attention. Hip-hop mogul Sean "Puffy" Combs (later known as P.Diddy), renowned as a talent spotter in his own right, tried to sign Jerkins to a production deal.

Turned Combs Down

But Jerkins turned him down. "I wanted to prove that I could make it on my own," he told *Billboard.* And he went on to prove just that: in 1995 he wrote, arranged, and produced five tracks that appeared on Mary J. Blige's 1997 album, *Share My World.* Blige encountered Jerkins while working next door to a studio in which he was doing remix work on a single by the late singing star Aaliyah, entitled "Everything's Gonna Be Alright." Blige's album went on to sell over two million copies; the single "I Can Love You," written and produced by Jerkins, hit Number Two on *Billboard*'s R&B chart, and Jerkins

went from being a young phenomenon with potential to being a proven hitmaker. Numerous production jobs began to flow his way.

One production effort took Jerkins to a higher level still. In 1998 he served as lead producer on teen vocalist Brandy's second album release, *Never S-a-y Never,* contributing 11 tracks to the album as producer and co-writing "The Boy Is Mine." That song evolved into an entertaining mock-argument duet involving Brandy and fellow teen star Monica; it rose to Number One on *Billboard*'s pop chart, remained there for 13 weeks, and became the top single of 1999. Jerkins has also worked with a roster of stars that reads like a Who's Who of contemporary urban pop, including Whitney Houston ("It's Not Right But It's Okay"), Will Smith, Deborah Cox, and, keeping a hand in gospel music, Kirk Franklin.

Along the way it became clear that Jerkins was offering a sound distinct from that of other producers, one that relied less on digital devices and more on traditional musical instruments, sometimes played by Jerkins himself. "I definitely feel responsible for [the diminished use of] sampling," Jerkins told *Entertainment Weekly.* "From 1990 to 1997, all you heard was samples. Then I came with 'The Boy Is Mine' and we stayed No. 1 for 13 weeks . . . It made people switch their whole style up." "I want to be one of the ones that takes music back to where it was," he added in *Billboard.* Quincy Jones, Gamble & Huff, those guys made real music; they didn't focus on just drums and basslines. I want to make music that people can cry to and people can dance to." To *Time* he described his style as "an R.-and-B. pop classical sound."

After the success of the Brandy-and-Monica duet, Jerkins founded his own production studio, Darkchild Entertainment, and label, Darkchild Records. With the blessing of corporate parent Sony he began to branch out beyond urban contemporary music. He produced a remake of the Rolling Stones' "Satisfaction" for pop megastar Britney Spears, who forecast in conversation with *Entertainment Weekly* a still-greater future for her collaborator and near-contemporary: "He's so young he still hasn't gotten to show the world what he is capable of doing," Spears said. Jerkins also produced tracks for Latin star, Marc Anthony, and country diva, LeAnn Rimes.

By 2001 Jerkins had notched five Number One pop singles as producer, several of which he also wrote or co-wrote: in addition to "The Boy Is Mine," they were: "Say My Name" by the trio Destiny's Child; "If You Had My Love," by the Latina superstar Jennifer Lopez; Monica's "Angel of Mine"; and Toni Braxton's "He Wasn't Man Enough." "He's the bomb," Destiny's Child vocalist Kelly Rowland told *Time,* "and he drops nothing but hits." With a strong track record, a coterie of powerful admirers that included Sony CEO Thomas Mottola and veteran songwriter Carole Bayer Sager, and seemingly limitless inspiration, Jerkins seemed poised to dominate pop music in the new decade; he also hoped to break into films. In 2001 he undertook the delicate task of reviving the career of 1980s megastar Michael Jackson. A marker of his growing success was his purchase of a 12,000-square-foot home in an exclusive gated community in Florida.

Selected discography

As producer

"The Boy Is Mine," Brandy and Monica.
"Say My Name," Destiny's Child.
"Satisfaction," Britney Spears.
"If You Had My Love," Jennifer Lopez.
"Angel of Mine," Monica.
"He Wasn't Man Enough," Toni Braxton.

Sources

Periodicals

Billboard, April 29, 2000, p. 65; February 27, 1999, p. 12; May 15, 1999, p. 44.
Entertainment Weekly, June 2, 2000, p. 44.
Interview, March 2001, p. 90.
Time, May 22, 2000, p. 132.

Online

All Music Guide, http://allmusic.com.
Biography Resource Center Online, Gale Group, 2000.
http://rodneyjerkins.com.

—James M. Manheim

Mat Johnson

1971(?)—

Novelist

In 2000 Philadelphia native Mat Johnson published his first novel, *Drop*. Critics lauded Johnson's debut, often mentioning his name in the same breath as James Baldwin and Richard Wright. A former regular columnist for New York's *Time Out* magazine, the Harlem resident began work on his second novel shortly after *Drop*'s publication.

Johnson was born and raised in Philadelphia. While in his twenties, Johnson moved to London, where he remained for about three years. He spent some time at a university in Wales and also lived in Brixton, the south section of London below the Thames River that houses many black residents. Johnson found many similarities between Brixton and Harlem, the mainly black section of New York City. Like Harlem, Brixton is hip, set apart from the rest of the metropolis, and mainly populated by members of the working class.

When he ran out of money, Johnson returned to his hometown and worked for about a year as an electrician. He then moved to New York City, where he earned a master's degree at Columbia University. He also worked as a copywriter for MTV Networks during this time.

While at Columbia, Johnson began work on his first novel, and by graduation, he had completed a rough draft of *Drop*. The novel, however, was not Johnson's first attempt at fiction. "Before, I'd been trying to do Toni Morrison Knockoffs," Johnson told *Interview*. "That was my idea of what a writer should be." But with *Drop*, Johnson had found his own unique voice.

Drop was published in 2000, and Johnson's voice was praised by critics. "Johnson's talent is obvious from the get-go," *The Washington Post*'s Jabari Asim enthused. "I especially like the way he injects snappy jazz into his sentences, successfully deconstructing Big Ideas while resisting the urge to show just how smart he is."

As the story unfolds, several "Big Ideas" emerge. "Some people who first read the book said, 'It's about this guy who hates being black," Johnson told *Interview*. ". . . it's not that. He loves being black; he just doesn't like being poor." The protagonist, Chris Jones, is, like the author, a Philadelphia native. The novel introduces Jones as, according to *The Washington Post*, "poor and broke, alone, thirty-one-years-old and only just finishing as an undergrad at a third-rate Pennsylvania state college." With few prospects for a young black in the city, Jones accepts an offer to join another young black, David Crombie, in a start-up shop in London. "This is going to be massive," Crombie tells Jones, according to *The Washington Post*. "Two black boys, in pretty black Brixton town, in a very white and very old city that won't know what hit it." But Crombie is a drunk, and other complications eventually send Jones wearily back to West Philly, the city he despises. But with the help of his best friend, Jones reaches an understanding: "Funny how much nicer this town was when you couldn't feel it sitting on you," he concludes, according to *The Washington Post*.

Jones's journey reveals one of *Drop*'s "Big Ideas." A *Kirkus* review found at Amazon.com noted that one of the novel's themes was "the young American who travels

At a Glance . . .

Born Mat Johnson c. 1971; in Philadelphia, PA; married. *Education*: Columbia University, MFA.

Career: Author. MTV, copywriter; *Time Out* magazine, columnist, "Utter Matness," published novel *Drop*, 2000.

Awards: Thomas J. Watson Fellowship.

Addresses: c/o Bloomsbury Publishing, 175 Fifth Avenue, suite 300, New York, NY, 10010

abroad to forge a new identity but ends by discovering that he is far more American than he'd realized." Unhappy with his life in Philadelphia, Jones finds a sense of liberation in London. But "in scenes both corrosively funny and bittersweet," the *Kirkus* review stated, Jones "discovers that he has an innate American sensibility not so easily discarded."

In December of 2000 Johnson discussed *Drop* during an online chat found at About.com's New York: Harlem/Uptown site. In the book, Johnson portrays black Africans making fun of African Americans, and these scenes sparked several questions from readers. "I used to live with Nigerians, and it was a huge lesson, of class and of history," Johnson explained on About.com. Johnson's Nigerian co-habitants had launched cotton-picking jokes at him and acted more like well-to-do whites than the people he had grown up with. He explained on About.com, "I had never been around solidly upper-class black folks before who didn't care about slavery, had no concept of black as an identity." Johnson drew on these experiences in order to add another dimension to the novel. As he said on About.com, "*Drop* in many ways, not directly, is about looking at an international Black world, one you rarely see."

Johnson described his writing routine as sporadic. "I'm a streak writer," he said on About.com. Sometimes writing feverishly for a month or two, only to find himself out of creative fuel. "I can write 150 pages in a month then go dry for a year," Johnson said on About.com. Despite his speed, however, Johnson still labored over each word and line, carefully crafting his sentences like, as he said in the About.com online chat, "a castle of toothpicks."

Until 2000, Johnson was regular columnist for New York's *Time Out* magazine. His column, entitled "Utter Matness," dealt with a wide breadth of issues—some funny, some serious, but all thought-provoking.

Johnson began work on his second novel in 2000. The story, he decided, would center around a real estate agent who kills the poor in order to sell their apartments to rich buyers. Johnson planned to set the literary horror/suspense in Harlem's Mount Morris Park because, as he explained in the About.com online chat, "I love the creepiness of the brownstones." Although his second novel was set in Harlem, Johnson was sure that Philadelphia would be the subject future works. He said in the About.com online chat, "Philly is my home. [James] Joyce got Dublin, but Philly's mine."

Sources

Periodicals

Interview, September 2000.
Washington Post, October 17, 2000.

Online

http://www.amazon.com.
http://harlem.about.com/library/weekly/aa122100a.htm (July 14, 2001).

—Rose Blue and Jennifer M. York

Betty Lennox

1976–

Professional basketball player

In professional basketball it is often the imposing, aggressive, high-scoring centers and forwards who grab the limelight, but Minnesota Lynx guard Betty Lennox has been an exception to the rule. Standing five feet, eight inches tall, Lennox was named Rookie of the Year after the 2000 season of the Women's National Basketball Association (WNBA). Through an odyssey marked by sheer determination, Lennox had become one of women's pro basketball's brightest young stars.

Betty Bernice Lennox was born in small-town Hugo, Oklahoma, on December 4, 1976; her middle name Bernice was her mother's first name. The eighth of nine children, she had five older brothers who spent a good deal of time playing basketball. She loved the game from the start, once even dressing up as a basketball for Halloween. Her brothers let her join in their games, but never cut her any slack. "My brothers taught me: Don't be scared of anything," Lennox told the *Kansas City Star.* "I go into games and don't get intimidated by anyone. I'm not afraid of anything, except the Man upstairs."

Indeed, Lennox has been known to snare jump balls when facing off against the WNBA's seven foot players.

Lennox's positive attitude has helped her overcome a series of setbacks. The first came when the Lennox family moved to Independence, Missouri, outside Kansas City, when Lennox was in the ninth grade, and she tried out for the basketball team at Fort Osage High. In Oklahoma she had played under old-fashioned women's basketball rules that split teams into three offensive and three defensive players, with no crossing the center line allowed. Lennox, who was an offense player, remains most comfortable as a shooter.

"I didn't think I could cross," Lennox recalled to *Sports Illustrated.* "Everybody was laughing at me. I was like, Is there something on my pants?" Briefly cut from the varsity team, Lennox nevertheless bounced back to become a standout player at Fort Osage. Throughout her career she has had the support of Fort Osage coach Dale Williams, who jokingly calls her his "black daughter"; Lennox in turn calls Williams her "white father." Lennox seemed to be college scholarship material, but she lacked the grades to win admission to a major-college program. So in 1995 she enrolled at Butler County Community College across the river in Kansas.

That proved another temporary setback in her career, for the school's basketball program was weak indeed. "I knew it was all wrong when I saw our 300-pound, no-muscle post player," Lennox told *Sports Illustrated*. Transferring to Trinity Valley Community College in Athens, Texas, Lennox had better luck in her sophomore year. With a 26-point-per-game average, Lennox led the team to the national junior college women's championship and a record of 34–2.

Took Year Off for Academics

After amassing that impressive record, Lennox won a basketball scholarship to Louisiana Tech, a top Division I college program. But mindful of the problems that academics had caused her in the past, Lennox took a year off to devote herself exclusively to her studies. "It's more than just on the court for me," Lennox told the *Kansas City Star* after she graduated in 2000 with a psychology major. "I still consider myself an average student even though I put hours and hours of study in, worked so hard. But I tell kids, it all starts in class."

When Lennox returned to basketball she was once again discouraged to find herself on the bench instead of on Louisiana Tech's starting team. Her time at Louisiana Tech was stormy; at halftime of one game, angry with herself over her performance, she wrote "DON'T PUT ME BACK IN THE GAME!" on the locker room chalkboard and landed in hot water with the coaching staff. But her dedication impressed Louisiana Tech coach Leon Barmore. "Inside her gut, every day, she wanted to be good," Barmore told the Minneapolis *Star-Tribune*.

"When you run across someone like that, you treasure them."

Together with fellow guard Tamicha Jackson, Lennox came into her own during her senior year at Louisiana Tech. She still had a reputation for being mercurial—her teammates nicknamed her "Psycho"—but she began to reap the rewards of her work regimen, which included a weightlifting routine involving bench presses of up to 165 pounds. Lennox and fellow guard Tamicha Jackson became a much-feared duo, and Louisiana Tech was ranked No. 2 in the United States for much of the season before losing to Penn State in postseason tournament play. Lennox averaged 17.5 points per game and was named to the U.S.A. Basketball Writers Association All-America first team. Pro scouts came calling.

Joined Minnesota Lynx

In the 2000 WNBA draft Lennox was the sixth player picked; she was signed to the Minnesota Lynx. Once again the pattern of initial difficulties followed by hard work and standout play repeated itself. Struggling in preseason training, she clashed with Lynx coach Brian Agler and called Lousiana Tech coach Barmore for advice. "I said, 'Look. That guy can coach. Be patient. He has a game plan,'" Barmore told the Minneapolis *Star-Tribune*. Over her first four games with the Lynx, Lennox averaged only 8.2 points per game.

Then Lennox began to blaze across the court like the Tasmanian Devil cartoon character to which she sometimes likens herself (and which she had tattooed on her body twice). Scoring 24 points in a game against the WNBA's Orlando franchise, she never looked back. She ended up scoring 541 points for an average of 16.9 points per game. At the season's end she received 59 out of a possible 62 votes as the WNBA's Rookie of the Year. She was also selected as part of the WNBA All-Star Second Team.

A tireless worker who spends much of her spare time in her Minneapolis apartment watching herself on game films and trying to spot areas in need of improvement, Lennox spent the 2000–2001 off-season in Israel, playing on a pro team there in order to hone her competitive skills. In 2001 she was sidelined for 20 games by a strained left hip, managing to average 11 points per game in the 11 games she did play. Still, she returned to top form late in the Lynx season, and her goal of eventually winning the WNBA's Most Valuable Player award seemed well within reach.

Sources

Periodicals

Kansas City Star, August 2, 2000, p. D1; February 16, 2001, p. D1.

Minneapolis Star-Tribune, July 7, 2000, p. C1; August 11, 2000, p. C1; August 12, 2000, p. C4.
Sports Illustrated, February 7, 2000, p. 74.
USA Today, March 13, 2000, p. E22.

Online

Women's National Basketball Association, http://www.wnba.com.

—James M. Manheim

Lester Lawrence Lyles

1946–

U.S. Air Force General

In April of 2000 General Lester L. Lyles was named head of Air Force Materiel Command at Wright-Patterson Air Force Base in Ohio. As such, he was now in charge of keeping U.S. Air Force weapons systems ready for war. In addition, Lyles also supervised research, development, and test and evaluation programs at the base.

Lester Lyles was born in Washington, D.C., on April 20, 1946, the son of Ambrose and Gladys Hawthorne Lyles. In 1965 he married Mina McGraw, and the couple eventually had four children: Renee, Phillip, Leslie, and Lauren. Lyles was educated at Howard University, graduating in 1968 with a bachelor's degree in mechanical engineering. As a distinguished graduate of the ROTC program, he then entered the U.S. Air Force. From there he went to Las Cruces and the Air Force Institute of Technology Program at New Mexico State University, where he earned a master's degree in mechanical and nuclear engineering in 1969.

Lyles held various positions during his early years in the military. He was a propulsion and structures engineer for the Standard Space-Launch Vehicles Program Office in Los Angeles and was part of the Short-Range Attack Missile Program at the Headquarters of the U.S. Air

Force in Washington, D.C. From 1978 to 1980, he served as special assistant to the commander of the Air Force Systems Command at Andrews Air Force Base in Maryland. When he left that post for the Defense Systems Management College at Fort Belvoir, Virginia in 1980, he had achieved the rank of Major. The following year he graduated from the Armed Forces Staff College in Norfolk, Virginia.

By 1985, Lyles had completed the National War College in Washington and reached the rank of colonel at the end of that year. His was then assigned to Andrews Air Force Base as director of the tactical aircraft systems. In his next two positions, Lyles was stationed at the Headquarters of the Space Systems Division, located in Los Angeles. Here Lyles served as the director of the Medium-launch Vehicles Program, and then as assistant deputy commander for launch systems.

While Lyles was next serving as assistant deputy and then deputy chief of staff for requirements at Andrews Air Force Base from 1989 to 1992, he was promoted to the rank of Brigadier General. He then moved to Hill Air Force Base in Utah to become vice commander, and then commander, of the Ogden Air Logistics Center.

At a Glance...

Born Lester Lawrence Lyles on April 20, 1946, in Washington, D.C.; son of Ambrose and Gladys Hawthorne Lyles; married Mina McGraw, November 26, 1965; children: Renee, Phillip, Leslie, Lauren. *Education*: Howard University, BS, 1968; New Mexico State University, MS, 1969; Defense Systems Management College, 1980; Armed Forces Staff College, 1981; National War College, 1985.

Career: U.S. Air Force Officer. Promoted to 2nd Lt., 1968; lst Lt., 1969; Captain, 1971; Wright-Patterson Air Force Base, propulsion engineer, 1971–74; Headquarters Air Force Systems Command, assistant to the commander, 1978–80; promoted to Major, 1979; Lt. Col, 1982; Colonel, 1985; Headquarters AFSC, director, tactical aircraft systems, 1985–87; promoted to Brigadier General, 1991; Ogden Air Logistics Center, vice commander/commander, 1992–94; promoted to Major General, 1993; Lt. General, 1994; Ballistic Missile Defense Organization, director, 1996–99; promoted to General 1999; Headquarters, vice chief of staff, 1999–00; Air Force Materiel Command, Wright-Patterson, commander, 2000-.

Awards: Defense Distinguished Service Medal; Distinguished Service Medal; Defense Superior Service Medal; Legion of Merit with oak leaf cluster; Meritorious Service Medal with two oak leaf clusters; Air Force Commendation Medal; named Astronautic Engineer of the Year, National Space Club, 1990; Roy Wilkins Renown Service award, NAACP, 1994; Sociedad de Ingenieros Award, Hiram Hadley Founder's Award of Excellence, New Mexico State University, 1999; General Bernard A. Schriever Award, 2000.

Addresses: BMDO/Pentagon, U.S. Air Force, BMDO-7100 Defense Pentagon, Washington, D.C. 20301-7100 (703) 693-3025.

He was promoted to the rank of Major General in August of 1993.

Lyles then returned to Los Angeles in 1994, where he was named commander of the Space and Missile Systems Center. In November of 1994, he was promoted to Lieutenant General. Lyles left Los Angeles in 1996 to serve as the director of the Ballistic Missile Defense Organization (BMDO) for the Department of Defense, a position he held until 1999.

Lyles became a full General in July of 1999. He then served as the vice chief of staff at the U.S. Air Force Headquarters from May of 1999 until April of 2000, when he became head of Air Force Materiel Command at the Wright-Patterson Air Force Base.

From the beginning of his new command, Lyles made efficiency one of his top priorities. He believed that the key to a better military is better, more efficient military personnel. Lyles considered enlisting and retaining good people the number one problem for the Air Force. Toward that end, the Air Force has initiated television and other types of advertising to attract young Americans. "We need to make careers in the military . . . more attractive to people," Lyles was quoted as saying on the Tinker Air Force Base website. One way to do that was to offer better educational opportunities and financial bonuses.

For most of his military career, U.S. Air Force readiness has been of prime concern for Lyles. He considered Tinker Air Force Base in Oklahoma a possible model for the future. During a September of 2000 visit to Tinker Air Force Base, Lyles observed, as quoted on the Tinker Air Force Base website, that "Team Tinker" was "not just an Air Force team, it's not just a single multi-command team, it's a multi-service team." The base, Lyles added, was "probably a model for some of the things we'll see in the future." He cited the Air Force base as unique in that it also contained the U.S. Navy on base along with the 552nd Air Control Wing, an air logistics center, and other combat wings.

Lyles also believed that in the future the military should expand its partnerships with industry to outsource certain types of work. Tinker has teamed up with Lockheed Martin in the area of propulsion business. Such teamwork, Lyles believed, would allow advantageous use of facilities and personnel at the base. However, before dramatically increasing the amount of work contracted out to private businesses, Lyles warned that current and past outsourcing should be examined to determine, as he was quoted on the Tinker Air Force Base website, "Has it had any impact on mission and readiness and has it had any impact on work force, including their morale?"

Throughout his career, Lyles has received the following decorations: the Defense Distinguished Service Medal, the Distinguished Service Medal, the Defense Superior Service Medal, the Legion of Merit with oak leaf cluster, the Meritorious Service Medal with two oak leaf clusters, and the Air Force Commendation Medal. In addition, he was named Astronautic Engineer of the year by the National Space Club in 1990 and received the 1994 Roy Wilkins Renown Service award from the NAACP. In 1999 he received two awards from New Mexico State University: the Sociedad de Ingenieros Award and the Hiram Hadley Founder's Award of Excellence. Lyles was granted the General Bernard A. Schriever Award in 2000.

Sources

Books

The Complete Marquis Who's Who, 2001.
Who's Who Among African Americans, 14th ed, Gale, 2001.

Online

Lester Lyles United States Air Force Biography, 2000, http://www.af.mil/news/biographies/lyles_ll.htm (July 13, 2001).
http://www.stsc.hill.af.mil/Cross Talk, 2000 (July 13, 2001).
Tinker Air Force Base, http://www.tinker.af.mil/pa/Model/htm (July 13, 2001).

—Corinne J. Naden and Jennifer M. York

Helen Martin

1909-2000

Actress

Actress Helen Martin was a pioneer in theater. A founding member of the Harlem-based American Negro Theater, Martin was one of the first African-American actresses to appear on Broadway. In her prolific career she worked with such famed people as legendary director Orson Welles and screen giants Sidney Poiter, Warren Beatty, and Halle Berry. When she died on March 25, 2000 in Monterrey, California, Martin left behind an acting career that spanned sixty years.

Helen Dorothy Martin was born July 28, 1909 to William Martin, a minister, and Amanda Frankie (Fox) Martin. Though born in St. Louis, Missouri, Martin grew up in Nashville, Tennessee. She was drawn to performing at an early age and was active in local theater groups. Not limiting herself to acting, she also sang with her own band. However, her parents had other ideas for her future and insisted that she go to college. Wanting to please them, Martin dutifully went off to Fisk University in Tennessee where she studied for two years. She also did a stint at A&I State College, also in Tennessee, before finally breaking off on her own to pursue the acting career she longed for.

Martin moved to Chicago in the thirties and became active in theater under the Federal Theatre Project, which was part of the Works Progress Administration, WPA, established under President Franklin Roosevelt in 1935. By the end of the thirties Martin had made the leap to New York City's thriving theater scene. She made her stage debut there in 1939 with the Rose McClendon Players. McClendon was a driving force in the effort to

establish a black theater aesthetic, and Martin shared those aspirations. Along with black theater legends, Abram Hill and Frederick O'Neal, Martin became a founding member of the American Negro Theater. This groundbreaking company firmly established African-American theater and provided a training ground for African-American actors, actresses, and playwrights. In addition to Martin, the American Negro Theater launched the careers of Sidney Poitier, Harry Belafonte, Ruby Dee, and Ossie Davis—all legendary African-American performers.

In 1941 Martin made her Broadway debut as Vera Thomas, Bigger Thomas's sister in Orson Welles's production of *Native Son*. According to the *Los Angeles Times,* "Orson Welles personally cast her" in the role. Martin's performance in *Native Son* not only established her as a serious stage actress but as one of the first African-American actresses in a major role on Broadway. The performance also heralded the way in which legions of African-American actresses were to follow. Following its run on Broadway, *Native Son* toured the United States with Martin in her role.

Martin's talent took her from stage to screen and she made her film debut in the Allied Artist's production, *The Phoenix City Story* in 1955. Fifteen years would pass before she would appear on the big screen again and then only in minor parts. During this time her stage career flourished. Between her 1939 debut and her death in 2000, Martin performed in over 40 stage productions, including roles in such famed plays as *Cat on a Hot Tin*

At a Glance . . .

Born on July 28, 1909 in St. Louis, MO; died March 25, 2000; parents: William Martin, a minister, and Amanda Frankie (Fox) Martin; raised in Nashville, TN; *Education:* Attended Fisk University and A&I State College, both in TN.

Career: Stage and screen actress. Became one of the first serious African-American actresses to make a mark on Broadway; acted in Orson Welles's production of *Native Son,* 1941; appeared in over forty stage productions, over a dozen films, and countless television sitcoms, including *227; Baby, I'm Back.*

Memberships: Founding member of the American Negro Theater, Harlem, NY.

Roof, Raisin in the Sun, and *Purlie Victorious.* She also toured the United States in productions such as *You Can't Take it With You* and *Deep are the Roots,* the latter of which became a British Broadcasting Corporation, BBC, radio broadcast in 1947. She also performed onstage in London, England.

With the ascent of African-American themed sitcoms, Martin found a new career on the small screen. Throughout the sixties, seventies, and eighties she enjoyed continuing roles on hit shows such as *Sanford and Son, Good Times, Benson,* and *The Jeffersons* and landed her first featured role on a series in 1978 with the show *Baby, I'm Back.* However, it wasn't until 1985 when Martin was cast in the role of the grouchy neighbor Pearl Shay on the hit show *227,* that she gained national recognition. Her impeccable comic timing as an elderly busybody gained the attention of casting agents, and in her seventies veteran stage actress Martin found a new career as an acerbic grandmother character in a slew of contemporary movies, including 1987's *Hollywood Shuffle* by esteemed African-American director Robert Townsend—a role for which she received a nomination for an NAACP image award. She also appeared in 1991's *House Party 2,* 1996's *Don't Be a Menace to Society While Drinking Your Juice in the 'Hood,* a satire of Los Angeles ghetto-based movies, and 1998's *Bulworth* with Halle Berry and Warren Beatty.

In January of 1996, her public image firmly established as a sweet if mouthy grandmother, Martin appeared on the television show, *Late Night with Conan O'Brien,* ostensibly to promote *Don't Be a Menace.* Instead she shook up O'Brien and crew—not to mention her fans—with her raunchiness. According to transcripts of the show, O'Brien asked Martin what she would have done if she hadn't become an actress. After replying that she would have been a stripper, "she got up on the leg rest and then did a little dance while the band played a bump and grind," www.misfit.com/conan reported. A bit later in the show, referring to her pot-smoking grandmother character in the film, O'Brien asked her if that image bothered her. She responded by saying, "I love the reefer," and then asking O'Brien if he had any. Marijuana enthusiasts pounced on her pronouncement and quickly held her up as an example of the drug's presumed harmlessness. Whether O'Brien and Martin were playing a little gag on the audience or Martin was just letting loose is not known.

After nearly sixty years on stage and screen and a metamorphosis from color-barrier busting Broadway regular to quick-witted granny on the small screen, Martin filmed her last movie, *Something to Sing About.* On March 25, 2000, before the film debuted, Martin succumbed to a heart attack and died in her home in Monterrey, California. Her career, while not having the highest profile, was undoubtedly prolific. In her wake, thousands of African-American actresses and actors have walked across Broadway stages, their feet a bit surer because of the path she and her colleagues in the American Negro Theater trod. The little 'ole granny with a penchant for 'reefer' left a career legacy to be admired and emulated.

Sources

Periodicals

American Theatre, July 2000, p. 15.
Ebony, June 1998, p.36.
Jet, April 17, 2000, p.64.
Los Angeles Times, March 29, 2000.
Variety, April 10, 2000, p.75.

Online

www.misfitmedia.com/conan.

—Candace LaBalle

Jesse L. Martin

1969–

Actor

Jesse L. Martin's television roles have ranged from detectives to doctors, but the towering, well-built actor has been celebrated as the one of the medium's newest romantic leads. Martin began his career on Broadway, and has appeared on *Ally McBeal* and *Law & Order*. In 1999 he was named "Sexiest Newcomer" by *People* magazine in its annual "Sexiest Man Alive" issue. "Women do come up to me, and they tell me what they think!" Martin admitted to the magazine, "I've gotten great compliments on my eyes and my smile. But I don't see myself as sexy."

Martin was born on January 18, 1969, in Rocky Mount, Virginia, a small burg deep inside the Blue Ridge Mountains. His father was a truck driver, and his mother eventually became a career counselor at a local college, but the pair divorced when he was still young and Martin and his mother moved to Buffalo, New York. He was just nine at the time, and was teased at school because of his Southern accent. Being bused to an integrated school only added to his difficulties in adjusting to his new life. "It's always tough when you're a kid and you feel different from everybody else and you're picked on because of it," he told *In Style*. "But I got over it and learned to blend and I worked very hard to get rid of my accent."

The acting bug bit Martin when he was cast in his first play during his fourth-grade year. The production was *The Golden Goose*, and he was "the pastor, which I associated with a brimstone-and-fire, Southern Baptist sort of preacher, so that's the way I played it," he told *Entertainment Weekly*. "None of the white kids there had ever seen anything like that, and everyone was impressed, thought it was very funny. I got so much positive feedback, I knew I was on my way to being a performer."

Still, in his teens Martin was a self-professed nerd and shy despite his years in a performing-arts program for gifted students. At 16, he asked a girl on a date—for the first time—and planned to meet her at the movies to see *The Color Purple*, but she stood him up. After finishing high school, he attended New York University, where he majored in theater but did not graduate. "When I was accepted, my mother cried because she knew we couldn't afford it," he revealed to *Cosmopolitan*. "But I worked four or five jobs at a time to stay there. Then I had to leave because school was interfering with work—and I couldn't afford not to work." Martin revealed in the same interview that the most undignified job from these years he held was at a department store offering perfume spritzes to shoppers.

At a Glance . . .

Born on January 18, 1969, in Rocky Mount, VA; son of a truck driver and a college career counselor. *Education*: Studied theater at New York University.

Career: Actor. Began career off-Broadway; appeared in the original cast of *Rent,* 1996; television shows: *413 Hope St.,* 1997; *Ally McBeal,* 1998; *Law & Order* 1999-.

Addresses: *Home*—New York City. *Office*— c/o Law and Order Production Office, Pier 62, Hudson River at W. 23rd St., New York, NY 10011.

Martin's big break came, unbeknownst to him at the time, when he was cast in the original company of *Rent* in 1996. The play, a musical based on the 1896 Puccini opera *La Boheme*, opened to overwhelmingly positive reviews—a success made all the more poignant by the fact that its creator, Jonathan Larson, died suddenly just before opening night. *Rent* is set in modern-day New York City, in its own bohemian East Village quarter, and Martin was cast as Tom Collins, a character whose boyfriend is a transvestite. "Although characters appear and disappear, seemingly at will, memorable impressions are made by" Martin and several castmates, noted *Back Stage* critic David A. Rosenberg. Other characters include a woman dying of AIDS and those struggling with drug additions. Martin reprised his role on the London stage in 1998, which prompted *Variety* critic Matt Wolf to state that "Martin impresses with a sincerity that never once becomes stolid: His reprise of the wrenching 'I'll Cover You' emerges tearfully, from someplace within."

Though Martin would later segue successfully into television, he admitted to harboring a certain passion for the theater. "There's something exciting about being onstage, knowing anything could go wrong." he told *In Style*. In 1997 he was offered a lead role on a new hour-long drama series created and produced by Damon Wayans, *413 Hope St.* The show was set at a New York City teen crisis center, where Martin's character, Antonio, served as a staff psychologist. He also appeared in one episode of the *X-Files* as a Negro Baseball League star who was actually an alien. But Martin's more memorable television credit came when he was offered a recurring guest role on the hit Fox-TV show *Ally McBeal*. He played Dr. Greg Butters, a paramour of the star for a few episodes. Reportedly the actress Michelle Pfeiffer, wife of *Ally*

McBeal creative force David E. Kelley, had seen Martin in *Rent* and recommended him for a guest spot on the show. The interracial romance between the pair attracted some hate mail, but the issue was deliberately skirted in the scripts. "Calista [Flockhart as the show's star] and I loved that our characters never discussed race," he told *Cosmopolitan*.

In 1999 Martin replaced outgoing Benjamin Bratt on the hit television drama *Law & Order*. He was cast as Detective Ed Green, a new character. Martin's Green seems unflappable, but is in reality a brooder with a possible gambling problem. Martin had already auditioned for several other guest roles on critically acclaimed show, but was usually offered unsavory criminal parts that were not much of a challenge professionally. The new part gave Martin a chance to stretch his talents as a dramatic actor. "Green is not a predictable guy," he told *Entertainment Weekly*. "There's not a lot about him that I know," a secrecy that the show's producers fostered to maintain a sense of realism.

The longer contract with *Law & Order* meant that Martin had to move from Los Angeles to New York City, a change that pleased him immensely. He has maintained his six feet, two inch physique with a regiment of yoga and calisthenics. The actor has often been told that he resembles late soul singer Marvin Gaye, and has said that his dream project would be the starring role in a film biography about the troubled Motown star, slain by his own father in 1984. Meanwhile, he has claimed he is eager to rid himself of the "eligible bachelor" tag, as he told *In Style*. "Me, I don't want to be eligible," Martin declared in *In Style*. "I want to be one of those guys that's completely hooked up and can't be considered a bachelor."

Sources

Periodicals

Back Stage, May 10, 1996, p. 48.
Broadcasting & Cable, May 3, 1999, p. 60.
Cosmopolitan, May 2001, p. 232.
Entertainment Weekly, November 12, 1999, p. 33.
In Style, November 1, 2000, p. 207.
People, November 15, 1999, p. 102.
Variety, September 22, 1997, p. 88; May 18, 1998, p. 82.

Online

Internet Movie Database, http://www.imdb.com.

—Carol Brennan

Felicia Mason

1963(?)–

Writer, journalist

Called a "super storyteller" by *Publishers Weekly*, Felicia Mason did not choose to become a writer. She was interested in relaying the truth, through news, to the public, so her love for the writing of creative fiction came as a surprise. She soon discovered, however, that writing was very important to her. "I write because I have to," Mason told *The Virginian Pilot-Ledger Star*.

The daughter of a Baptist minister, Mason grew up in Pennsylvania. Her family moved to Virginia when she was young, and Mason has spent most of her life there. Graduating from Hampton University as a mass media arts major in 1984, she went on to become a staff developmental editor for the *Daily Press* in Newport News, recruiting and training for the newsroom.

It was her love of fiction and of writing that led to of her first novel, 1994's *For the Love of You*. With this book, Mason's writing career was off to a laudable start. The book received *Glamour* magazine's readers' all-time Favorite Love Stories award. Since that time she has won many other awards, including the Best Selling Multicultural Romance Award from Waldenbooks for both *Body and Soul* and *Seduction*. She was also a finalist for the 1999 *Romantic Times* Career Achievement Award.

Mason's next book, *Body and Soul* (1995) was called a "funny, warm, sensual novel," by Cheryl Ferguson of the *Romantic Times* website, "It's no wonder that in less than a year, Ms. Mason has gone from fledgling writer to award-winning author." The novel presents the story of a May-December romance between a successful business-

woman and a man 15 years her junior. Mason won an award for the Best Contemporary Ethnic Novel from Affaire de Coeur for *Body and Soul* as well as the Reviewer's Choice Award from *Romantic Times*. In addition, the book was also optioned by the African Heritage Network for a television movie.

1997's *Rhapsody*, according to Ferguson on the *Romantic Times* website, is "a compelling story of love, betrayal, and restoration that will make the reader sigh, cry, then shout for joy at the triumphant, healing power of true love." The story is about two college lovers who have been separated for years and brought back together with a friend's assistance. The friend has died and left a will giving the two a fortune if they'll live together for one week. Gwendolyn Osborne of the *Romance Reader* website said that Mason "injects humor, style, emotion, and even a few surprises" into the novel. "The dialogue is snappy and the pacing is rhythmic . . . [Mason] knows how to tell a great story and she has a healthy professional respect for the written word," Osborne concluded. *Publishers Weekly* said that in the novel Mason "creates magic."

In *Foolish Heart* (1998) Mason "reaches new levels of excellence," according to Ferguson on the *Romantic Times* website. The story starts with revenge, a woman revenging her family's humiliation on the man who's family caused the embarrassment, but in the tradition of all good romance novels, Mason manages to end the story with true love. Amazon.com called the book "a tale that deftly deals with the full range of human emotions,

At a Glance . . .

Born c. 1963, in Pennsylvania; daughter of a Baptist minister. *Education:* Hampton University, mass media arts, 1984.

Career: Writer, journalist. Author of: *For the Love of You,* 1994; *Body and Soul,,* 1998; "The Dreamers," published in *Man of the House,* 1999; "The First Noel," in *Something to Celebrate,* 1999; "In Love Again," in *Rosie's Curl and Weave,* 1999; *A Valentine Kiss; Island Magic,* 2000; *Forbidden Heart,* 2000; "Truly, Honesty," in *Della's House of Style,* 2000.

Awards: Favorite Love Stories award, for *For the Love of You, Glamour;* Best-selling Multicultural Romance, for *Body and Soul,* for *Seduction,* Waldenbooks; Best Contemporary Ethnic Novel, for *Body and Soul,* Affaire de Coeur; Reviewer's Choice award, for *Body and Soul, Romantic Times.*

Addresses: P.O. Box 1438, Yorktown, VA 23692.

from the dark instinct of revenge to the heady inspiration of love." *Publishers Weekly* said that "Readers will enjoy Mason's compelling characters and the ease of their dialogue."

Mason has also written a number of short stories that have been published in anthologies. "The First Noel" was published in 1999's *Something to Celebrate,* a collection of winter holiday romances. The story involves a woman raising her nephew and a woodworker. The two meet at a Christmas pageant rehearsal. *Library Journal* said of the book, "Although these enjoyable stories focus on the African American experience, they will bring holiday cheer to readers of all backgrounds and should not be considered a niche-market item." For a 1999 Father's Day anthology called *Man of the House,* contributed "Man of the House," a story about a father whose wife was killed by a drunk driver the day his daughter was born. He struggles alone to raise his daughter until he meets just the right woman to help him with his daughter and his own life.

Rosie's Curl and Weave (1999), with four stories centered on a hair salon, is another collection containing a Mason story. Mason's story, "In Love Again," shows the romance between Louis Sweet, the owner of the salon, and one of his customers. 2000's *Della's House of Style* is the sequel to *Rosie's Curl and Weave.* Mason's "Truly, Honestly" involves a successful and very conservative businesswoman who decides she's like to experience a little more in life.

About novels, Mason told *The Virginian Pilot-Ledger Star:* "The reason you pick up a novel is to go away for a while. Novels are places people go to experience something else. For two hours, you're Sam Spade." And many readers have certainly found themselves in another, pleasant world with Mason's books. There is no doubt that she will continue to help readers find another world to escape into for a long time to come.

Sources

Periodicals

Black Issues Book Review, September, 2000, p. 23.
Essence, August, 1999; September, 1999; January, 2000; October, 2000; November, 2000.
Library Journal, November 15, 1999, p. 56.
Publishers Weekly, May 5, 1997, p. 206; October 26, 1998, p. 63.
The Virginian Pilot-Ledger Star, June 22, 1997, p. 13.

Online

http://www.amazon.com.
http://www.geocities.com/SoHo/Lofts/2376/Mason.htm.
http://www.geocities.com/Paris/Gallery/9250.
http://theromancereader.com.
http://www.romantictimes.com.

—Catherine Victoria Donaldson

Mariétou (Bileoma) Mbaye

1948–

Writer

Senegalese author Mariétou Mbaye wrote of the particular challenges faced by women in her country. The legacy left by centuries of foreign rule, combined with a predominantly Muslim culture, made Senegal a place where women desiring independent lives faced unusually high barriers. Only one of Mbaye's books was translated into English: her 1991 memoir *The Abandoned Baobab: The Autobiography of a Senegalese Woman*. This and her subsequent novels sometimes appeared under the pen name, "Ken Bugul," a Wolof term that translates as "nobody wants this child."

Mbaye was born on November 28, 1948, in Louga, Senegal, when the country was still a part of French West Africa. Her father, Abdoulaye, was a marabout, or Muslim holy man, who was in his eighties at the time of her birth. She attended a school in her village as a youngster but was later sent to live with an aunt in a larger city so that she might attend its lycée, or French high school. For years, Mbaye battled anger and feelings of abandonment over her mother's decision to send her away. But the move was a positive one in many ways, for Mbaye went on to the University of Dakar, in Senegal's capital, and then won a government grant to study in Belgium. Her time in Europe, however, was anything but enriching: she was dismayed by the racism she experienced and felt bereft and cut off from her culture and homeland. She abandoned her studies and lived in a debauched state for some years, much of which she described in *The Abandoned Baobab*.

Mbaye returned to Senegal in 1980 and married an elderly marabout who died a short time later. She went to work for family-planning agencies and began writing in earnest. Her autobiography written in French, *Le Baobab Fou*, was published by Nouvelles Editions Africaines in 1984. Mbaye's Paris-based editors urged her to use the "Ken Bugul" pseudonym, a common one for women writers in West African literature. Mbaye pointed out, however, that the name is a blessing of sorts in Wolof culture, for it is sometimes bestowed on a child whose mother has suffered more than one stillborn birth-if "nobody wants" the infant, then neither will God, and so it might survive.

Le Baobab Fou's publication and shocking revelations of the author's life in Belgium caused a stir in Senegal, as its author told Bernard Magnier in an interview whose quotes were translated for a *Research in African Literatures* article. "[T]he fact that I had written this book," Mbaye recalled, "that I had dared to write it and publish it . . . they said it couldn't be true." The title of Mbaye's autobiography reflects her symbolic love for the large baobab tree that stood across from her family's home when she was a child. She wrote of the French presence in Senegal during her youth, her attempts to fit into a society where traditional African values and ways were disdained in favor of an idealized European image of the "native," and of a general sense that she did not belong, no matter where she went or how hard she tried.

Mbaye returned to her own village after a time at the lycée. Her colonial education set her apart, and as a teen

At a Glance . . .

Born on November 28, 1948, in Louga, Senegal, Africa; daughter of Abdoulaye and Aissatou (Diop) Mbaye; married Semiou Bileoma (a physician; deceased); children: Yasmina Ndella. *Education:* Attended University of Dakar; studied in Belgium. *Religion:* Muslim.

Career: ASBEF, Senegal, program coordinator, 1982–86; International Planned Parenthood Federation, Africa region, program officer in Togo, after 1986; Africans International, administrator; writer.

Addresses: *Home*—B.P. 1048, Porto Novo, Benin.

she turned away from her culture completely, speaking French, wearing dresses and high heels, and reading French fashion magazines. Her time in Belgium, recounted in what Publishers Weekly described as "a terrifying journey of self-discovery," involved drug abuse and prostitution; she also ended a pregnancy and had an affair with a woman-all of which are seriously proscribed in Senegalese society. "Europe is exposed as a hedonistic playground in which people communicate only through illusion," observed Research in African Literatures writer Nicki Hitchcott about Mbaye's memoir.

The Abandoned Baobab recounts Mbaye's return to Senegal and a reconciliation with her mother and her culture-though one that is forged on her own terms. "I couldn't be like those women who, every evening, would wait for their husbands whom they needed more than the air that they breathed," she wrote. "The women would burst out of themselves during the day and then, as soon as the men came home, everyone would withdraw." Published in the United States in 1991, *The Abandoned Baobab* was termed "a wise, lyrical account, superbly translated" by *Publishers Weekly*. Other critics considered it a benchmark work for West African women writers. "For the feminist reader, *Le baobab fou* is an important text because it recognizes feminism as a call for solidarity and not, as is traditionally maintained in Africa, for the promotion of the individual," declared Hitchcott in her *Research in African Literatures* critique.

Mbaye also wrote *Cendres et braises (Ashes and Embers)*, published in Paris in 1994. An autobiographical work as well, it begins with the female narrator recounting a story to a friend. She tells of her Paris lover, a married French man whom she calls "Y," who is physically abusive. Though she sometimes leaves him, the narrator feels compelled to return to what she terms la valse infernale, or infernal waltz. This dance conflicts with the rhythms of her native Senegal, where some of the action takes place. In the end, the listener is revealed as a marabout who guides the narrator back to her true Senegalese self-and in the final paragraph, the storyteller relates how her mother then sold her to the marabout. "While this story is very much a personal one, it provides a social commentary on woman's role, on differing perceptions of polygamy, on the importance of the mother-daughter bond, and on the postcolonial difficulties of finding one's identity," observed E. Nicole Meyer in a review for *World Literature Today*.

Though she held a job as an administrator for Africans International, a cultural organization that promotes African arts abroad, Mbaye continued to write. Her other works include *Riwan ou le chemin de sable (Riwan or the Sandy Track)* and *La Folie et la mort (Madness and Death)*. She lived in Porto Novo, Benin, and had one child.

Selected writings

Le Baobab Fou (The Mad Baobab Tree), Nouvelles Editions

Africaines, 1984; translation published as *The Abandoned Baobab: The Autobiography of a Senegalese Woman*, Lawrence Hill, 1991.

Cendres et braises (Ashes and Embers), L'Harmattan (Paris), 1994.

Riwan ou le chemin de sable (Riwan or the Sandy Track), Présence Africaine (Paris), 1999.

La Folie et la mort (Madness and Death), Présence Africaine, 2000.

Sources

Periodicals

Publishers Weekly, November 1, 1991, p. 75.
Research in African Literatures, summer 1997, p. 16.
World Literature Today, winter 1996, p. 226.

Online

Biography Resource Center, Gale, 2001.
Contemporary Authors Online, Gale, 2000.

—Carol Brennan

Michael Michele

1966—

Actress

Michael Michele is widely considered to be one of the most beautiful actresses working today. With exotic looks inherited from her interracial parents—flowing honey colored curls, hazel eyes, chiseled cheek bones—she could easily find fulltime work as a model. Instead, she proved herself as an actress on two of the most acclaimed dramas on television, *Homicide: Life on the Street* and *ER*. Michele is a major acting talent in the making and people are noticing.

Loved Basketball and Broadway

Michael Michele Williams was born on August 30, 1966 in Evansville, Indiana to Theresa and Jerry Williams. The masculine moniker was not a result of a subconscious wish for a boy on her parents' part. "I'm named after my mother's best friend, Michael Ann. In high school she agreed with my mother that whoever had a child first would name it after the other," she told *Maxim*. Theresa, a pharmaceutical company manager, is African American and Jerry, a shipping executive, is Caucasian. They also have a second child, Michele's younger sister Erica.

The Williams raised their family in Evansville and instilled in their daughters hearty Midwestern values—determination, hard work, and charity. At the age of 15, Michele began a lifelong commitment to disadvantaged youth by becoming a mentor. The Williams girls also enjoyed a healthy competitiveness and spent much of their energy on sports including volleyball and track. However, it was in basketball that Michele excelled.

Michele became a star player on her school team, Indiana's top-ranked Benjamin Bosse High School's women's basketball team. She could have probably pursued a college scholarship in the sport if it hadn't been for her other love—acting. As a child Michele was fascinated with Broadway and wanted a stage career. By high school she was already experiencing a bit of the limelight when she became a teen model for *Seventeen*. "My mother submitted my picture without my knowing," she insisted to *Maxim*, "I was a tomboy . . . totally embarrassed by the whole thing." Tomboy or not, she had stars in her eyes and would soon leave basketball to pursue her acting dreams.

Following her high school graduation in 1984, Michele left Indiana for the Big Apple and stardom. Instead she

At a Glance . . .

Born Michael Michele Williams on August 30, 1966 in Evansville, Indiana; parents are Theresa Williams, a corporate manager and Jerry Thomas, a shipping executive. *Education:* graduated from Benjamin Bosse High School in Indiana, 1984.

Career: Actress. Stage appearance: "Purlie Victorious;" "A Raisin in the Sun;" "The Owl and the Pussycat;" Television appearances include: *Homicide: The Movie,* 2000; *ER,* 1999-; *Creature,* 1998; *Homicide: Life on the Street,* 1998–1999; *Central Park West,* 1995; *New York Undercover,* 1994–95; *Trade Winds,* 1993; *Dangerous Curves,* 1992. Film work includes: *Def by Temptation,* 1990; *New Jack City,* 1991; *The Sixth Man,* 1997; *The Substitute 2: School's Out,* HBO Movie, 1998; *Ali,* 2001.

Awards: Nominated for an NAACP Image Award, "Outstanding Supporting Actress in a Drama Series" for *ER,* 2001; nominated for an NAACP Image Award, "Outstanding Actress in a Drama Series" for *Homicide: Life on the Street,* 2000.

Addresses: *Home*–New York, NY and Los Angeles, CA; *Studio*–Warner Brothers Studio, 300 Television Plaza, Burbank, CA 91505.

landed a job at the Gap. It paid the bills and gave her ample time to make the audition rounds. Like many beginning actresses, her first experience in front of the camera was in fast food commercials. "I'd walk in thinking, I'm a serious actress, then have to eat 20 burgers in half an hour," she told *Maxim.* Despite this diet, she managed to keep her figure and catch the eye of R&B artist Freddie Jackson who cast her in three of his music videos.

Michele also began her stage career, fulfilling a dream she had since childhood. She studied under acting coaches Wally and Joanna Strauss. She auditioned for many parts for the Negro Ensemble Company. She has appeared in "A Raisin in the Sun," "Purlie Victorious," and "The Owl and the Pussycat."

Michele's film career got off to a shaky start when rumors of problems with mega-star Eddie Murphy emerged in the late eighties. Considered for roles in the Murphy vehicles, *Coming to America* and *Harlem Nights,* Michele saw both of those parts dissolve, one under the veil of sexual harassment and the other for creative differences. Though rumors of a sexual harassment suit filed against Murphy by Michele and settled out of court have sur-

faced, Michele doesn't dwell on it, nor has it affected her steady rise to fame.

In 1990, six years after arriving in New York, Michele got a bit part in her first film, *Def by Temptation.* Barely a year later she appeared opposite Wesley Snipes in *New Jack City.* From there she moved to television and throughout the nineties Michele zigzagged across the channels with stops at nearly every major network. In 1992 she appeared in the CBS television series *Dangerous Curves* and a year later landed a leading role in the six-hour NBC miniseries, *Trade Winds.* From 1994 to 1995 Michele enjoyed a recurring role on the Fox drama *New York Undercover.* She finally landed her own series as a cast member of CBS's short-lived primetime soap opera *Central Park West.*

In 1997 Michele leaped from the small screen back onto the big screen with a starring role in *The Sixth Man.* She followed that with a role opposite Treat Williams in the 1998 HBO movie, *The Substitute 2: School's Out.* Despite these film roles, Michele was not yet a household name or face. That would begin to change with her role on the critically acclaimed, wildly popular NBC series *Homicide: Life on the Street.*

Found Her Star in Homicide

First airing in 1993, *Homicide,* quickly made a fan out of Michele. She told the *Detroit Free Press* that before landing the role, she felt as if *"Homicide* [was] my shining star. 'I gotta get on it,' I kept telling myself." In 1998 she got that chance when *Homicide* started looking for a new character. Of her first meeting with the producer of the show, she told the *Detroit Free Press,* "The first thing I said to him was, 'Look, I've waited six years to be on the show. I know this show. I know what I would have to deliver to be on this show.'" That season she joined the cast as Detective Rene Sheppard.

Though Michele was thrilled with her role, many seasoned fans of the show were not. Disparaging comments about her acting ability raged across the show's many fan site chat rooms. Many critics seemed only to be angry because Michele was 'too pretty' for the gritty police drama. Michele didn't take this criticism lightly and when a television interviewer brought it up, she exclaimed, "How dare you! Because YOU think I'm attractive, I can't do the job?" Still, she doesn't pretend that her looks don't affect the way she is perceived. "Does she look like a cop? That's what we thought viewers would wonder when Sheppard was introduced," Michele told the *Detroit Free Press.* "So we addressed that issue at the start of the season. We showed how the men in the squad room related to her, what they would say—'Ummmmm, baby!'—and how she would respond to that."

The show reflected Michele's own struggles to be taken seriously. She has lost auditions because she looked too much like a model. Still, she doesn't let this dampen her drive. "I hate, abhor, detest, when celebrities say that being attractive is a burden in show business. Get over it!" she told *Maxim*. And 'get over it,' she did. She didn't cave in to the easy life as a pretty face in a toothless Hollywood sitcom. She went after what she wanted despite the "handicap" of her natural beauty. "The worst thing in the world is to have to live by another person's idea of who you are," she told the *Detroit Free Press*.

With characteristic vigor, Michele dove into her role and proved that she wasn't at all "too pretty" for "Homicide." She particularly enjoyed getting to flex a little muscle on the show as she confronted murder suspects and drug dealers. She told *Maxim*, "I'm very physical, very hands-on. I love to wrestle. You can't be a wuss with me." Shot on location on the broken glass-littered streets of inner city Baltimore, *Homicide* also appealed to Michele's nature. "Baltimore itself was a very, very important character in *Homicide*. And it helped me to connect with Sheppard. I love working on the street. It offered a great deal of assistance to me as an actor," she told *The Bergen Record*. Sadly, against public protest, NBC cancelled the show at the end of the 1999 season.

Joined ER

The end of life on *Homicide* led to a beginning of life in the *ER*. Michele joined the cast of *ER* in 1999 as pediatric and emergency room doctor, Cleo Finch. Landing a role on such a highly acclaimed series is more proof of Michele's skill and willingness to challenge herself as an actress. "Playing these kind of characters raises the bar and makes you a better actor. Both *Homicide* and *ER* are fast-paced series with large ensemble casts and there's no time for even a hiccup. You have to be ready to walk on the set and do your job right away," she was quoted on www.tvschedules/about.com.

Having a role on such a popular show as *ER* has also raised Michele's public profile. She was named one of *People* Magazine's "50 Most Beautiful People in the World" in 1999 and has become a darling of the fashion press. Her presence on the red carpet is heralded with an explosion of flashbulbs as the paparazzi gather to see what she is wearing. Words like "elegant," "regal," and "sophisticated" are regularly used to describe her sophisticated, yet fashionable style.

In between filming in Los Angeles, and flights home to New York City, Michele continued to give back by working with underprivileged youth. She is a supporter and volunteer for New York-based Kids 'N Us, an organization that provides speakers to children in need of guidance and inspiration. She is a mentor to a number of children both in New York and in the Midwest. She also takes time to do one of her other first loves—basketball. You are more likely to catch Michele in a pair of gym shorts shooting hoops rather than attending trunk shows. "Being active is so deeply ingrained in me that it's become an integral part of who I am," she told www.efit.com. Between takes on the set of "ER" she is known not only for shooting baskets, but also for whipping anyone foolish enough to challenge her to a game. "I was an athlete first, and even though I'm not playing a team sport any longer, I still use that competitive drive," she explained to www.efit.com.

Michele may have to put away her gym clothes and slip into high fashion a bit more often in the coming years. With starring roles in two major motion pictures due to release in late 2001 and 2002—opposite Will Smith in *Ali* and Kurt Russell in *4–29-92* aka *The Plague Season*—Michele is poised to become major movie star. With the skills she has honed on two of the most popular dramas on television and her focused determination, Michele will no doubt have miles of red carpet to traverse.

Sources

Periodicals

The Bergen Record, (New Jersey), September 30, 1999.
Detroit Free Press, January 7, 1999.
Ebony, July 2000.
Maxim, June 1999.

Online

http://www.askmen.com/women/actress_60/65c_ michael_michele.html
www.efit.com
www.ertv.com
http://www.geocities.com/Linda_Whitlock_1999/
http://tvschedules.about.com/library/actors/ blmichaelmichelebio.htm

—Candace LaBalle

DeLisha Milton

1974—

Professional basketball player

From her upbringing in a small Georgia community, through the college ranks and ultimately to the pros, DeLisha Milton has created a marriage of sweetness, grit, and determination to become one of the country's dominant female basketball players. With extreme focus and dedication to the sport, Milton has proven success on every level of the game. Such a blend has put in her in the national spotlight in the Women's National Basketball Association and on the world's stage as a gold medal-winning U.S. Olympic athlete.

Born September 11, 1974 to Beverly Milton, DeLisha began developing her basketball skills in the southern rural region of Liberty County. Her court was a section of dirt and tree roots, the hoop, a bicycle rim nailed to a tree. There, Milton perfected her crossover dribbling, ball-handling skills, and leaping ability. She beat boys bigger than she and played well into darkness.

Tipped Off Early

According to an article appearing at www.afrocentricnews.com, Milton nearly drowned in a pool at age eleven. Author Dave Marks wrote that the incident served serious notice to Milton and those around her: "My philosophy on life is to live each day to the fullest because I feel that every breath that I take is a borrowed breath," Milton is quoted as saying. "At any moment it can be taken away." People in Milton's hometown thought she was rescued for a reason and destined for greatness. "I do have a true purpose here on Earth," Milton stated. "I don't know it's been shown to me yet. I may be living it right now. Who knows? But while I'm searching for that answer I'm definitely going to enjoy myself."

While a collegiate player at the University of Florida, Milton was a model of consistency on the court. Balancing her studies with athletics was no easy feat. However, she managed to succeed in both areas. While hitting the books and ultimately earning a degree in sports management with a minor in mass communications, Milton continued to excel on the court. According to statistical information found at www.usabasketball.com, Milton showed steady improvement during her college years.

In her first season at Florida, she averaged 11.7 points, 11.5 rebounds and 2 steals per game. Milton continually improved throughout her collegiate career. As a sopho-

At a Glance . . .

Born on September 11, 1974 in Riceboro, GA; mother: Beverly Milton; *Education*: University of Florida, 1997.

Career: Professional basketball player. Selected as second pick in first round of American Basketball League's 1997 draft by the Portland Power; ABL disbands in 1998; selected as the fourth pick by the Los Angeles Sparks in the first round of the Women's National Basketball Association's 1999 draft.

Memberships: U.S. Team, World Championships, 1997–1998; U.S. Team, Olympic Cup gold medal, 1999; participating U.S. National Team, Olympic Team, 2000.

Awards: Naismith High School Player of the Year, 1992, 1993; recipient, University of Florida President's Recognition Award, 1997; Wade Trophy recipient as top senior in the country, 1997 ; NCAA Mideast Regional Most Outstanding Player, 1997; All-America first team, 1997; Southeastern Conference Player of the Year, 1998 (All-SEC first team, 1996–97; All-SEC second team,1995 ; SEC All-freshman team, 1994; named to SEC All-Tournament team, 1994, 1997); named to WNBA All-Star team, 2000.

Addresses: c/o the Los Angeles Sparks, 555 N. Nash St., El Segundo, CA 90245

more, she improved her per-game average to 13 points and 6 rebounds. She averaged 15 points and nearly 9 rebounds per game as a junior before erupting her senior year. Milton capped her outstanding collegiate career with a whopping 19 points and 8 rebounds per game in 1997. For her work, Milton earned an avalanche of accolades. She paced her team to four consecutive NCAA Championship Tournament appearances, getting as far as the Final Eight her senior year. She won the Wade Trophy in 1997 as the top senior in the country. She received numerous All-America designations and Southeastern Conference honors, including: the 1997 SEC Player of the Year by both conference coaches and media, 1997 NCAA Mideast Regional Most Outstanding Player in 1998 and All-SEC first team in both 1996 and 1997.

Hard Work Led to the Pros

With such an impressive collegiate resume and her display of grit and tenacity on the court, Milton had no problem signing on with a professional team. In

1997, she was selected as the second pick of the first round by the Portland Power of the American Basketball League. Again, she wasted no time helping her team win. Despite folding as a league the following year, www.usabasketball.com reported that Milton "ranked among leaders twenty-first for scoring (11.9 ppg.), eighth for rebounding (6.9 ppg.), fifth (tie) for steals (2.4 spg.), ninth (tie) for blocked shots (9) and twelfth for field goal percentage (46.5 %)."

Just a year later, Milton was the fourth overall pick in the first round by the Los Angeles Sparks. She was now a member of the Women's National Basketball Association. In her professional debut for the Sparks, Milton was indeed the "spark" that lit a fire for the team. Milton helped power the squad to a 20–12 record and a second-place finish in the WNBA Western Conference. According to www.wnba.com, she averaged nearly 10 points per game in the regular season, third-best on the team, and maintained that average into the Western Conference finals. According to additional information found in the club's media guide, the 2000 season saw Milton "emerge in the spotlight this season, earning her first ever selection as a Western Conference All-Star." In that game, Milton had four points, four rebounds and three assists in 16 minutes.

Throughout the season, Milton started all 32 games, averaging 12 points and 6 rebounds per contest. According to the Sparks' media guide, 2000 was a breakout season for the 6-foot-1-inch forward. Milton "posted a career high 14 rebounds and six assists in the Sparks' 73–66 victory over Minnesota (7/31). Notched a double-double with 13 points and 11 boards in the victory over the Monarchs (7/23). Tied a career high 20 points, while grabbing seven boards in the Sparks' victory over Sacramento (7/5)."

Fulfilled Olympic-sized Dream

In 2000 Milton received one of the highest acknowledgments for nearly any athlete when she was selected to the U.S. National Team that would compete in the Olympic Games in Sydney, Australia. The opportunity gave her the chance to add to her gold medal resume, as found at www.usabasketball.com. It includes medals from playing on the 1999 U.S. Olympic Cup team, the 1998 World Championship team, the 1998 World University Games team and the 1994 U.S. Olympic Festival team. For Milton, the opportunity to play on the world's stage with the WNBA's finest was a crowning moment in her athletic career. In a live chat transcript from www.usabasketball.com, Milton summed up her feelings on the experience when the games first commenced. "I think it's an honor within itself being able to play with and against the best basketball players in the world," she said. "I'm pretty young in my basketball career and being able to be on the court with them and learn from them is really great. It's a confidence boost for me and it enables me to learn valuable lessons from great people and great players."

Team USA captured the gold medal of the 2000 Olympics, beating Australia 76–54. In eight games, Milton averaged 4.5 points and 2.6 rebounds, playing only 11 minutes per game. Milton took her role as a bench player seriously. The L.A. Sparks media guide cited her Olympic accomplishment. Milton, "scored eight points off the bench in the opener against South Korea. Tied for fourth on the team with seven offensive rebounds in the tournament." Prior to the Olympic games, Milton told the *Savannah Morning News*, in a September 18, 2000 article, that getting to the games had long been a dream of hers. "I always felt I was going to be in the Olympics one day," she said. "I would watch track and field on television, and I would be in awe of how smooth they made themselves look. They made it look so easy. I told myself I was going to do that. It didn't matter what sport it was."

By the 2001 season, Milton had earned the nickname "Sunshine," due to her ever-present smile. However, at the same time, head coach Michael Cooper had given Milton a different moniker. Thanks to her intense, scrappy play on the court, as well as her relentless, no-holds-barred dominance of the boards for rebounds, Milton has earned the name "D-Nasty." Milton's game is of merciless defense, yet incredibly smooth ballhandling.

Milton's prowess on the court, as well as her stunning physical stature and good looks, earned her commentary in *Esquire* magazine. In it's August 2000 issue, the publication profiled Milton under its section "Women We Love," along with the following assessment. "Her eighty-four-inch wingspan is longer than that of most heavyweights. It's no wonder, then, her childhood friends would stare at those long fingers and arms and call her E.T. Tree. Slim. Delicious. DeLisha Milton answered to all of 'em when she was practicing under the bicycle rim nailed to a tree in her grandmother's dirt backyard in Riceboro, Georgia. Her outta-this-world ballhandling was born in that soil. When you stand six feet one and can dribble around male opponents and between bony-fingered tree roots, you can go to the hoop anywhere, anytime."

In the *Savannah Morning News article*, writer Timothy Guidera cited the origins of Milton's alter ego. "She is one of the league's true intimidators, as much for her aggressive attitude as her ability to block shots. During a nationally televised game late in the season, Milton shoved Phoenix Monarchs' Michelle Griffith and then challenged her face-to-face before both players received technical fouls. It really wasn't anything uncharacteristic for a player who likes to let opponents know when she blocks one of their shots. 'That's D-Nasty,' Sparks coach Michael Cooper recently told the *Los Angeles Times*. 'She has the killer instinct.'"

Sources

Periodicals

Esquire, August, 2000, pp. 72–3.
Savannah Morning News, Sept, 18, 2000.

Online

www.usabasketball.com/usab/Women/
milton_transcript.html.
www.usabasketball.com/Women/milton_bio.html.
www.wnba.com/playerfile/career/delisha_milton/html].
www.afrocentricnews.com/html/
marks_milton_sparks.html.

Other

Additional information for this profile was obtained from the Los Angeles Sparks Media Guide, 2001.

—John Horn

Loften Mitchell

1919-2001

Playwright

As both a playwright and a theatre historian, Loften Mitchell has made an invaluable impact on American drama. His critical works, such as *Black Drama* and *Voices of the Black Theatre*, contain insights on the contributions of African Americans to the theatre. His plays address themes of unity, black pride, and perseverance.

Mitchell was born on April 15, 1919, in Columbus, North Carolina. Shortly after his birth, the family later moved to Harlem where, as a high school student, Mitchell wrote sketches for the Salem Church's Progressive Dramatizers Group. He then acted with the Rose McClendon Players. In Harlem, Mitchell was exposed to up-and-coming black theatrical performers, such as Ethel Waters and George Wiltshire. It was also in Harlem that Mitchell learned first-hand about the discrimination of blacks in America. When he was ten-years-old, Mitchell had a job selling newspapers on the streets of New York and once got into a fight with a white boy who informed him that the street belonged more to whites than to blacks. Mitchell also realized the theatre was not immune to racial discrimination. He saw the way African Americans were misrepresented in the theatre and decided to work toward shattering negative images of blacks. Mitchell dedicated himself to projecting blacks in a realistic way, and decided that the best vehicle to accomplish this was African-American history.

With limited opportunities for black actors in 1930s New York, Mitchell left the city to attend Talladega College in Alabama on scholarship. He recalled in a *Freedomways* interview, as quoted in *Negro Playwrights in the American Theatre, 1925–1959*, that, although many blacks during the Depression were either financially or academically ineligible, "Southern Negro colleges, offering athletic scholarships and grants-in-aid, rescued many from the despair into which they had been dumped." While at Talladega, Mitchell wrote the paper which later became the basis for his lauded collection, *Black Drama: The Story of the American Negro in the Theatre*.

During World War II, Mitchell spent two years in the U.S. Navy as a seaman second-class. He then enrolled in graduate school at Columbia University, where, from 1947 to1951, he studied playwriting. He accepted a job as a social investigator with the Department of Welfare in 1948, continuing his studies during the evening. During this period, Mitchell wrote one of his first successful plays, 1946's *Blood in the Night*. 1948's *The Bancroft Dynasty* and *The Cellar* (1952) followed. From 1950 to 1962, Mitchell wrote for and acted in *The Later Years*, a weekly program on New York's WNYC radio station. In addition to his work for WNYC, Mitchell wrote a daily show for WWRL called the *Friendly Advisor* in 1954.

For his 1957 play, *A Land Beyond the River*, Mitchell adapted the story of Joseph DeLaine, the South Carolina schoolteacher and pastor whose historic court case brought about the end of segregation in America's public schools. In Mitchell's dramatization a sickly but courageous black woman, Martha Layne, proposes the lawsuit, and her husband, Joseph, rallies the support of other black citizens and a sympathetic white physician. The couple struggles with intimidating threats, the burning of their home, and Martha's poor health. Their struggles convince most community members to accept a local court decision to provide a "separate, but equal" school for blacks. Joseph, however, argues that black children would not receive an equivalent education under such a system and convinces the community to appeal to a higher court. After a long run Off-Broadway, the play was published as a book. Mitchell won a Guggenheim award in 1958, allowing him to return to Columbia for one year and write.

With 1963's *Tell Pharaoh*, Mitchell surveyed African-American history. His characters reflect on their African heritage, their experiences as slaves, and the ongoing struggle for civil rights. The play recalls African-American martyrs and heros, celebrating their contributions to American life. Music sets the mood and underscores the play's sentiments.

A later work, *Miss Waters, To You* (1983), was based on the life of actress and singer Ethel Waters. Through a series of scenes and musical numbers, Mitchell depicts Waters's transition from a struggling 17-year-old divorcée to an accomplished performer. Other African-American figures that appear as characters in the play include Bessie Smith, Duke Ellington, Lena Horne, and Cab Calloway. These characters offer each other moral sup-

port and teach Waters how to endure racial prejudice in show business. However, some critics noted that such scenes weakened the play's credibility as a true portrait of Waters's life—her animosity toward black entertainers such as Horne was well known. The drama also glosses over Waters's less admirable traits.

Mitchell died on May 14, 2001, in Queens, New York. He was 82 years old.

Selected writings

Plays

Shattered Dreams, first produced in New York, 1938.
Blood in the Night, first produced in New York, 1946.
The Bancroft Dynasty, first produced in New York, 1948.
The Cellar, first produced in New York, 1952.
A Land Beyond the River, first produced in New York, 1957; published 1963.
The Phonograph first produced in New York, 1961.
Tell Pharaoh, televised 1963; first produced in New York, 1967; published 1970.
(with Irving Burgie) *Ballad for Bimshire*, first produced in New York, 1963; revised version produced Cleveland, 1964.
(with John Oliver Killens) *Ballad of the Winter Soldiers*, first produced in New York, 1964.
Star of the Morning: Scenes in the Life of Bert Williams, first produced in Cleveland, 1965; revised version produced New York, 1985; published 1971.
The Final Solution to the Black Problem in the United States; or, The of the American Empire, first produced in New York, 1970.
Sojourn to the South of the Wall, first produced 1973; revised version produced 1983.
The Walls Came Tumbling Down, music by Willard Roosevelt first produced in New York, 1976.
Bubbling Brown Sugar, concept by Rosetta LeNoire, music by Danny Holgate, Emme Kemp, and Lilian Lopez, first produced in New York, 1976; published, 1985.
Cartoons for a Lunch Hour, music by Rudy Stevenson, first produced in New York, 1978.
A Gypsy Girl, first produced in Pine Bluff, Arkansas, 1982.
Miss Waters, To You, concept by Rosetta LeNoire, first produced in New York, 1983.

Screenplays

Young Man of Williamsburg, 1954
Integration: Report One, 1960
I'm Sorry, 1965.

Novels

The Stubborn Old Lady Who Resisted Change, Emerson Hall, 1973.

Literary Criticism

Black Drama: The Story of the American Negro in the Theatre; Hawthorn, 1967.
Editor, *Voices of the Black Theatre*, James T. White,1975.

Sources

Books

Abramson, Doris E., *Negro Playwrights in the American Theatre 1925–1959*, Columbia University Press, 1969.
Afro-American Writers after 1955, Gale, 1985.
Contemporary Dramatists, 6th ed. St. James Press, 1999.
Notable Black American Men, Gale, 1998.

Periodicals

Choice, January, 1976.
Contemporary Literature, winter, 1968.
Crisis, February, 1965.
Nation, August 25, 1969.
Negro Digest, June, 1966.
New York Post, March 29, 1957.
New York Times, March 29, 1957; May 23, 2001, p. C19(L).

Online

Biography Resource Center, Gale, 2001, http://www.galenet.com/servlet/BioRC.
Contemporary Authors Online, Gale, 2001.

—Addell Austin Anderson and Jennifer M. York

Garrett Morris

1937–

Actor, comedian

He has been both reviled and revered by African-American audiences and artists alike. He both shined and shamed on the small and big screens. During the sixties he led a black consciousness raising theater group, and in the seventies as an original cast member of *Saturday Night Live,* he personified black stereotypes. In the eighties he almost lost himself to drugs, and in the nineties he almost lost his life to a bullet. Though his nearly half-centuy in the limelight has not always been bright, through it all—as an actor, comedian, and singer—Garrett Morris has survived.

Born in New Orleans, Louisiana on February 1, 1937 and raised by his grandfather, a Southern Baptist minister, Morris discovered a passion for music at an early age. Just five, Morris began singing with the church choir. "[My grandfather] heard me singing in the bathroom, and said 'Brothers, sisters, this boy can sing," he told *The Kansas City Star,* " . . . . and I haven't really stopped singing since."

As a young adult, Morris gained a degree from New Orleans's Dillard University and pursued formal musical training, including a stint at Julliard, New York City's famed performing arts school. In 1956 he received a scholarship to attend a music workshop at prestigious Tanglewood in Lenox, Massachusetts and received the Tanglewood Conductors Award. Then in 1958 on the way home from a National Association of Negro Musicians' music competition, Morris took a detour to New York City. There, Morris branched out into theater, joining the Harlem YMCA Drama Club, which counted among its members actress Cicely Tyson. Soon after arriving in New York, Morris received his first big career break when he auditioned for the Harry Belafonte Singers and was hired as a soloist. Though he spent the next ten years singing with Belafonte, Morris continued pursuing theater.

Actor, Activist, Struggling Artist

By the late sixties Morris was working as an actor, singer and playwright in New York. He appeared in such famed musicals as *Show Boat* and *Porgy and Bess* and dozens of smaller off-screen plays, many with black political themes. Proving his diversity, Morris also penned and produced his own plays. In 1970 he made the leap to screen actor with an appearance in Carl Reiner's *Where's Poppa?.* Other mostly forgettable parts followed, both in

At a Glance . . .

Born February 10, 1937 in New Orleans, LA; wife, Freda; *Education:* Dilliard University, BA; attended Julliard School and Manhattan School of Music; *Religion:* raised Southern Baptist.

Career: Actor, comedian, and singer. Soloist with Harry Belafonte Singers, 1958–68; cast member: *Saturday Night Live,* 1975–80; *Martin,* 1992–94; *The Jamie Foxx Show,* 1996; Films include: *Where's Poppa?,*1970; *Cooley High,* 1975; *Car Wash,*1976, *How to Beat the High Cost of Living,* 1980; *Children of the Night,* 1992; *Twin Falls Idaho,* 1999; *Little Richard,* 2000; and *Jackpot,* 2001. Stage credits include: *Porgy and Bess,* 1961, 1964; *Show-boat,* 1966. Worked steadily in film and on stage from the early sixties into 2001.

Awards: Tanglewood Conductors Award, 1956.

Addresses: *Home*—Los Angeles, CA; *Agent*—Stone Manners Agency, 8436 W. 3rd St., Los Angeles, CA, 90048, Phone (323) 655-1313.

film and television. The one exception was 1975's *Cooley High.* Cast as a high school principal, Morris and the film were well received by the critics.

As Morris added theater and singing credits to his professional resume, he added the role of activist to his personal accomplishments. With a group of like-minded performers, Morris formed a theater group designed to raise black consciousness and confront racial problems. Though the group endured political threats and police harassment, Morris, recalling the era, told *The Kansas City Star,* "I was in seventh heaven because this was my idea of what you should and could do with your talent. . . . There were problems out there in the country, and we had acting and writing talent to write plays that would demonstrate this." Sadly, his professional career would soon not only stifle his activist beliefs, but it would mock them.

By 1975, despite nearly twenty years of performing credits, Morris was still struggling. Like many working actors, he belonged to various professional associations. However, it was his membership in the Writer's Guild that propelled Morris from bit parts in films and off-Broadway plays to national celebrity and a permanent place in television culture. NBC was putting together the comedy show, *Saturday Night Live.* The show's producer, Lorne Michaels, had appealed to the Writer's Guild for apprentice writers that could be hired at a discounted rate. The Guild sent Morris. Though he had

proven skills as a playwright, his comedy writing ability did not impress Michaels. Rather than let Morris go, Michaels decided to make him a member of the cast largely based on Morris's *Cooley High* appearance. According to *Saturday Night: A Backstage History of Saturday Night Live,* it soon became apparent to the other actors and writers that Morris, despite his past acting history, did not have the skills for sketch comedy which requires an actor to quickly switch from one role to another. Still, had it not been for an unfortunate mix of factors, Morris may have overcome this.

Saturday Night Wasn't 'Berry Berry Good' to Morris

At 38 Morris was over a decade older than the most of the other "Not Ready For Prime Time Players" which included Chevy Chase, John Belushi, and Dan Aykroyd. Morris was also the only seasoned stage veteran. Finally, Morris was the only black actor on the show. As a result, Morris was often ignored by the other actors and writers. When they weren't ignoring him, they were often criticizing him. The authors wrote in *Saturday Night,* "Since Garrett was not a strong enough performer or writer to impose his own sensibilities on *Saturday Night, Saturday Night* imposed its sensibilities on him, and they were at best cruel, at worst racist."

With the exception of a few notable roles, especially that of ex-baseball player Chico Escuela, whose tag line "Bazboll's bin berry, berry good to me" became Morris's most famous line from the show, Morris had few roles in the sketches and many of those were as stereotypical black characters. By the third season, after an electrifying appearance as Tina Turner, Morris became the resident drag queen. In high heels and skirts, Morris finally got regular airtime on the show. However, some close to the show saw these roles as demeaning to Morris. "It was," said one observer, as if the show actually enjoyed making Garrett 'participate in his own degradation'," wrote the authors of *Saturday Night.* Never was this more obvious than in a show hosted by Cicely Tyson.

Morris, dressed as Tyson, had begun the opening monologue, when the real Tyson appeared on stage demanding to know what was happening. "I was hired by this show under terms of the Token Minority Window Dressing Act of 1968," Morris replied. Tyson went on to scold him, "Garrett, what is happening to you?" Referring to their work together in the sixties, she went on to say, "I expected something really big from you." She continued, "Where's your integrity?" Morris's response was a blithe, "Well, it doesn't look bad on my resume . . . and I get to keep the dresses." SNL writers had written the entire exchange, yet it illustrated what black audiences and performers had already been complaining about Morris.

Whether it was due to the isolation and racism that Morris suffered on the show, the criticism he received from black audiences and performers, or even the complications arising from national celebrity, by his third season with the show Morris had turned to cocaine. *Saturday Night* reported that his drug problem soon became a problem for the show: Morris began to miss rehearsals, spent hours locked in his dressing room, and avoided the rest of the crew. The book also detailed Morris's growing paranoia and his belief that a "hypnotist robot" was watching him. Of that time, Morris says little, though he did admit to *People Weekly*, "I was smoking a lot of cocaine." In 1980, after five seasons with the groundbreaking show, Morris left *Saturday Night Live*. Morris still doesn't discuss why he left. However, he did confess to *The Kansas City Star*, "By the time I left, I didn't have a lot of friends at NBC."

Built a Healthy Body, Mind, and Career

While his fellow SNL alums went on to major films, comedy tours, and fame, Morris received bit parts in short-lived television shows and regrettable films. He did, however, get his life in order. He quit drugs soon after leaving the show; "I ceased around 1981, 1982, just stopped," he told *People Weekly*. He also quit smoking and, in a move back to his activist nature, became a spokesperson for the American Cancer Society. Morris replaced his smoking habit with a jogging habit and in his fifties kept up a regimen of three mile runs every day. As his body and spirit improved, so did his career. He had memorable recurring roles on the popular television shows, *Hunter* and *Roc*, appeared in dozens of films, and wrote and produced another play. Finally, in 1992 he landed a part on the wildly popular *Martin*. Playing a womanizing radio manager given to polyester suits and hilarious antics, Morris was redeemed. *Martin*, aimed at black audiences, gave Morris a new chance with the black community, and they embraced him.

On February 24, 1994, Morris's renewed career—and his life—almost came to an end. Leaving a friend's shop in South Central Los Angeles, he was shot by two men in a botched robbery attempt. The bullet penetrated his arm, ripped through his abdomen, and lodged near his spine. He told *People Weekly*, "[I thought] 'I'm going to die.' I was only mad because someone else had chosen the time." Though the wound was serious and he would remain in the hospital for over a month, Morris amazed his doctors with an astounding recovery. He was moving about with a walker within a week of the shooting. He even filmed an episode of *Martin* from his hospital bed.

With the help of his wife, Freda, Morris undertook a rigorous exercise regimen to regain his strength, and with the help of comedy he has regained his early passion—using his art to help others. Barely four months after the shooting, he did a stand-up comedy routine for Los Angeles-based charity Kids Against Guns. "One thing the shooting has taught me is that humor is what it's really all about," Morris told *People Weekly*, "From the second night on, Freda and I were laughing about this thing. It's like something else inside me was causing me to see the bright side in everything." With a co-starring role in the 2001 film *Jackpot*, a new series in the works, and Freda by his side, the limelight is finally shining bright for Morris.

Sources

Book

Hill, Doug and Jeff Weingard, *Saturday Night: A Backstage History of Saturday Night Live,* Beech Tree Books, New York, 1986.

Periodicals

Entertainment Weekly, March 26, 1993.
The Kansas City Star, May 7, 1997.
People Weekly, July 11, 1994.
USA Today, November 16, 2000.

—Candace LaBalle

Ava Muhammad

1951–

Minister

"It is my fervent prayer that I succeed in my assignment in order to help the minister in his effort to destroy the myth that women are inferior beings who cannot preach the Word or shepherd the flock." These were the words of Minister Ava Muhammad on July 28, 1998, as she accepted her appointment as Southern Regional Minister with the Nation of Islam. The words held significance due to the unprecedented assignment she accepted from the Honorable Minister Louis Farrakhan. She stood that day before a capacity crowd in the Hillside Chapel Truth Center in Atlanta as the first woman in Islamic history to serve as a regional leader in the Nation and as minister of a mosque.

Muhammad, who was raised in a Methodist family, traveled a winding road into the Nation of Islam. She was grew up in a middle-class home in Columbus, Ohio, and to this day, still professes that she is a Christian. Both of Muhammad's parents were educators and some of her early influences included The Rev. Dr. Martin Luther King, Jr., Stokely Carmichael (Kwame Ture), and other civil rights activists that promoted equality and self-reliance. She earned a law degree graduating from Georgetown University Law Center in 1975. Muhammad was on a normal course in life for law students,

becoming a criminal defense attorney, and charting a successful career when she reached a turning point in her life in 1979, at the age of 28. She was diagnosed with cancer and began looking for spiritual support to deal with the fear of death that accompanied her cancer.

Muhammad first took refuge in the church of her youth, but it did not provide the comfort she was searching for and she found that she was still afraid of dying. Admiring the Nation of Islams focus on self-reliance for black people, she went to hear Louis Farrakhan speak in New York City and finally felt she was where she belonged. She had long been an advocate of the self-reliance message that she encountered in Farrakhans preaching, but in an interview with the *Atlanta Journal-Constitution,* she explained why this time it was a revelation. "When I heard him talk about Allah, it penetrated my very being," said Muhammad, "I knew that this was what I was born to do." She also avowed that her cancer disappeared after she heard Farrakhan's message.

Muhammad joined the Nation of Islam in 1981. As a member, she became a great help to Farrakhan, serving as his attorney in several significant court battles. President Reagan placed a ban on American travel to Libya in

At a Glance . . .

Born 1951, Columbus Ohio; married Darius Muhammad, 1988. *Education:* Graduate of Georgetown University Law Center, 1975.

Career: Appointed as first woman to head a Mosque, Muhammad Mosque No. 15, 1998; appointed Southern Region Representative of the Nation of Islam, 1998; author: *Real Love,* and *Queens of the Planet Earth: The Birth and Rise of the Original Woman.*

Memberships: Member of the New York Bar Association.

Addresses: Nation of Islam, 734 W. 79th St., Chicago, IL 60620.

1986. Muhammad was called to defend Farrakhan when an attempt was made to arrest him following a visit to that country. In an even higher profile case, she took on the *New York Post* in a defamation suit against Farrakhan. After several years in court, Muhammad convinced the courts that the *Post* deliberately and maliciously took Farrakhans words out of context to bolster a 1994 story that implicated him in the assassination of Malcolm X.

Muhammad gained prominence in the Nation throughout this time and was considered one of the future leaders of the Nation in spite of the past limitations the Nation had placed on women. During the later 1990s, part of the Nations goal was to not appear so extreme in their practice and Muhammad had evolved into a leader that could hopefully provide a link into the mainstream for the often-embattled religion. As one of the most visible women in the Nation, she was a key speaker at the 1997 Million Women March. She addressed the women at the march on the topic, "The Further Development of Black Women Who Are or Wish to Become Professionals, Entrepreneurs, and or Politicians." In the message she emphasized the importance of women to first establish a strong relationship with God when seeking to move forward in life.

As Southern regional minister, Muhammad still provided legal counsel to Farrakhan and even worked in the forefront to tear down obstacles that the Nation faced both nationally and internationally. She was one of the most outspoken and proactive members of the Nation to fight against the exclusion order placed on Farrakhan by the British government. The exclusion was issued in 1986 and presumed that Farrakhans presence in Britain would make a negative contribution to the public good. In 1999 She spoke at a rally by the London branch of the Nation of Islam to put fuel back into the fight against the ban. She was quoted in the *Final Call* as stating, "[f]or

you and I to be told that we lack the intelligence and the ability to discern his message is an insult to us as a people."

In spite of the historical value of being the first woman in Islams 1400-year history to be appointed to a leadership position of the cloth, Muhammad came across more ordinary than many imagined. She considered best selling author Iyanla Vanzant, and *Essence* Magazine Editor Susan Taylor among her closest friends. More importantly, in accordance with her down to earth qualities, she insisted that God welcomes people of all colors, religions and walks of life. "We are all one," she told the *Atlanta Journal-Constitution.*

Muhammad's 1998 appointments to Southern Regional Representative of the Nation and as minister of Muhammad Mosque No. 15 appeared to mark a departure from traditional Islamic faith for the Nation and Farrakhan. It differed in both its demonstration of acceptance of women as leaders in the nation, and in Muhammads message of inclusion, which was in opposition to Farrakhans past promotion of separation. But Muhammad insists that it actually marked a growth for the religious group. "We dont like being viewed as haters of people," she told the *Atlanta Journal-Constitution* interview. "It is the ego in us that assigns labels and names and creates division. We can never say that because youre Jewish, because youre Christian, because youre Muslim, youre not going to heaven and youre not right," she continued.

Muhammad felt that the Nations philosophy is not completely changing, but rather evolving. "This has been an evolution in the message," she told the *Atlanta Journal-Constitution.* "But it is not changing and going into a different direction. It is moving toward that which the Creator intended it to be." Muhammad also determined that part of her role as a leader in the Nation of Islam is to move toward being one who is within the will of God.

Selected writings

Real Love LoveKare Productions.
Queens of the Planet Earth: The Birth and Rise of the Original Woman.

Sources

Periodicals

The Atlanta Journal-Constitution, October 16, 1999
Essence, July 1997, pp. 65.
The Capital Times, November 18, 1999.

Online

Northern Star Online, www.star.niu.edu, April 6, 2001.
The Final Call, www.finalcall.com

Official   Minister   Ava   Muhammad   website,
   www.ministerava.com
Nation of Islam website, www.noi.org

—Leslie Rochelle

Khallid Abdul Muhammad

1948-2001

Activist, former Nation of Islam minister

Khallid Abdul Muhammad called himself a "truth terrorist" and a "knowledge gangsta," and he was clearly at war with the status quo. A spokesman allied with the Nation of Islam, Muhammad ignited a storm of controversy through his dynamic, emotional speechmaking. Having attacked Jews, homosexuals, the Pope, and white South Africans, Muhammad was labeled a dangerous racist and anti-Semite. To his followers, however, he was a force for positive change, empowerment, and cultural pride in the African-American community who simply told the truth as he saw it. According to Rogers Worthington in the *Chicago Tribune,* Muhammad "can be entertaining one moment, and chilling the next. He'll talk of the need for black self-love, self-help, discipline and independence in one breath, and in the next he'll launch into a fiery anti-white, anti Semitic diatribe assigning blame for all of black America's ills."

After 1992 Muhammad took his message all across the country, to colleges and lecture halls, attempting to reach troubled young African Americans. He has clashed—though not seriously—with Nation of Islam leader Louis Farrakhan, who noted in *Emerge:* "Brother Khallid is like a stallion, a beautiful black stallion. And it takes God to ride such a gifted horse. He will buck, that's his spirit, he's a warrior. His spirit is his love for his people."

One of Muhammad's favorite lecture topics was the "Black Holocaust," the sufferings of black people over the centuries as a result of slavery, colonial domination, and discrimination. Muhammad claimed that the black holocaust was "100 times" worse than the atrocities Jews suffered at the hands of the Nazis in World War II and that the problem was ongoing in America due to the racial climate. To make matters worse, he said, the black holocaust was ignored or glossed over by white historians, depriving blacks of a full recognition of the forces that have shaped them. "The worst crime that can be committed is to be robbed of self-knowledge," he asserted in the *Washington Post.*

While his theory was deplored by those who saw it as needlessly argumentative, Muhammad found a willing audience among the young, who sensed that they had been treated unfairly by the white majority. "Muhammad entered the public limelight at a time when there [was] a heightened sense of pessimism among blacks about their lot in America, and growing receptivity among young African-Americans for black nationalism," contended Worthington. "Media coverage and the storm of protest over his remarks seem[ed] only to [make] him more popular among young blacks, old-guard black nationalists, Afro-centrists and border-line middle-class blacks who ... turned out to hear him."

Devoted to Nation of Islam

Muhammad was born Harold Moore Vann in Houston, Texas, in 1948 and spent his childhood there with an aunt. He was an honor student and quarterback of the football team at the all-black Phyllis Wheatley High School in Houston. Muhammad wanted to go into the ministry and was nicknamed "the preacher" by his

At a Glance . . .

Born Harold Moore Vann in 1948, in Houston, TX; died February 19, 2001, in Atlanta, GA; divorced; children: Farrakhan. *Education:* attended Dillard University, 1966–70.

Career: Became member of Nation of Islam, 1967; became minister of Mosque 27, Los Angeles, c. 1974; minister at mosques in New York and Atlanta, c. 1977–87; named supreme captain of Fruits of Islam (security force for Nation of Islam), c. 1989; named top aide to minister Louis Farrakhan, c. 1990; demoted, 1994; left Nation of Islam; formed New Black Panther Party and New Black Muslims, c. 1995; organized Million Youth March, 1998, 1999.

classmates. So talented was he in his studies that he was placed in an accelerated learning program, one of only 27 students in the entire school to be given that opportunity.

After graduating from high school in 1966, Muhammad enrolled at Dillard University. Although some sources claim that he eventually earned a doctorate degree at that institution, the registrar's office told the *Chronicle of Higher Education* that he dropped out of Dillard in 1970 without having earned a diploma. Muhammad himself refused to discuss his formal education, deeming it worthless since it was achieved at institutions catering to a white majority, yet he was referred to as "Dr. Muhammad," and he claimed to have a Ph.D. in sociology.

Far more influential to Muhammad than his studies at Dillard was his introduction while on the campus to the Nation of Islam. A highly disciplined faith based on the teachings of Islam, the Nation of Islam was founded in 1930 by Elijah Muhammad. Members of Elijah Muhammad's sect were encouraged to abstain from alcohol, practice sexual monogamy, eat sparingly, and pray, meditate, and study. One of the secretive organization's basic tenets was the belief that blacks were chosen by God to form their own nation separate from whites. This radical notion gained ground among some blacks as the fight for integration in America became violent and frustrating. Speakers like Malcolm X and Louis Farrakhan—both members of the Nation of Islam—offered blacks another solution to their problems with racism, a homeland free of the white oppressor.

Farrakhan first met Muhammad at Dillard University in 1967. The young student came to hear Farrakhan speak and enthusiastically embraced the tenets of the Nation of Islam sect. Farrakhan recalled in *Emerge:* "In my effort to rebuild the work of the Honorable Elijah Muhammad, he

was one of the first to come by my side. And when I had no security, just standing up teaching, I would see Brother Khallid standing beside me with a Bible in his hands. And I wondered why he was standing with the Bible. And once he opened the Bible and he had cut the Bible out and in the Bible was a pistol that he had to defend his brother. I had to say, 'No, Brother Khallid, we don't need that." Having taken the name of Khallid Abdul Muhammad in repudiation of his "slave name," the young follower of Farrakhan and Elijah Muhammad began to study the tenets of his new faith and embrace its notions of black empowerment and black nationalism.

The Nation of Islam faltered after the death of Elijah Muhammad. In the early 1970s, Khallid Muhammad journeyed to the East African nation of Uganda to help dictator Idi Amin form a plan to overthrow the white government in South Africa. While there he heard that Farrakhan was trying to re-start the sect and return it to a more radical agenda. "I was in Kamapla, Uganda, ready to kill some white folks when I put the call through," Muhammad told an audience in Baltimore, as quoted in *Newsday.* "I thought the Nation of Islam was gone never to come back again. From that point on, I have been at the side of Minister Louis Farrakhan in the rebuilding of the Nation of Islam."

A "New Malcolm X"

Invited to be among the original group that reinstated the Nation of Islam, Muhammad rose quickly to prominence within the sect. In the late 1970s he was named minister of Mosque 27 in Los Angeles, and he set about doing what he could to end the gang warfare in the city. His chapter of the Fruit of Islam—a highly disciplined security force for the sect—won national honors at the organization's conventions and, with their crisp white shirts and imposing demeanor, provided an enticing model for black pride.

Muhammad was transferred to a mosque in New York City and later to one in Atlanta, where he ran into trouble with the law. In 1988 he was convicted in federal court of using a false Social Security number to obtain an home mortgage in Atlanta. Farrakhan wrote a letter to the judge asking for leniency, promising the Nation of Islam would descipline him. Instead, the judge sentenced Muhammad to three years in federal prison. The *Washington Post* quoted the judge in question as having told Muhammad: "Unlike some of your supporters, I feel that there is another side to you—a side maybe the devil got to." Muhammad served nine months in prison. When he was released, he returned to New York.

Soon thereafter, Muhammad was named "supreme captain" of the Fruits of Islam, in effect making him the leader of security for the Nation of Islam. In this role he traveled with Farrakhan when the minister had speaking engagements. He was responsible for the discipline and bearing of the other security officers. By 1991 he had been promoted again, to national assistant to Farrakhan. In this position he was for the first time given an opportunity to speak before national audiences. "Ironically, it was a position held by both Malcolm X and Louis Farrakhan under Elijah Muhammad," noted *Emerge* reporter Sylvester Monroe. "It also historically has been a post from which the holder has often gained a following and stature of his own, as both Malcolm X and Farrakhan did."

Indeed, by virtue of his fiery oratory and his uncompromising message, Muhammad did become known as the "new Malcolm X." He concentrated his message toward the young and found a ready audience among rap musicians and gang members in Los Angeles and elsewhere. Bits of Muhammad's speeches found their way onto the albums of Ice Cube, X-Clan, and Public Enemy. Professor Griff, a former member of Public Enemy, told *Newsday* that rappers responded to Muhammad because "the brother has a spirit....If you are about revolution and change you have to lend him your heart as well as your ear." Some Los Angeles gang members seemed to have been positively influenced by the dynamic minister as well. *Emerge* reported that several ex-gang members who played leading roles in the Los Angeles truce of 1992 joined the sect in response to Muhammad's calling.

Kean College Speech Caused Controversy

In November of 1993, Muhammad was invited by a student group to make an address at Kean College in Union, New Jersey. The quiet commuter campus with approximately 50 percent black enrollment hardly seemed a likely venue for a speech that would rock the nation. To quote Fred Bruning in *Maclean's* Muhammad unleashed a speech "as remarkable for its grandiloquent goofiness as its incendiary spirit....Muhammad's speech was a corker by any standard. Approximately 140 students and faculty heard Farrakhan's man launch attacks on a variety of targets—whites, Jews, homosexuals, the Pope—during a meandering three-hour presentation."

Among other assertions, Muhammad suggested murdering *every* white person remaining in South Africa and referred to the head of the Catholic Church as "the old no-good Pope," adding, "somebody need to raise that dress up and see what's really under there." The height of his vitriol was reserved for the Jews, however, whom he accused of participating in the slave trade and of hastening their own persecution by the Nazis. At one point he referred to Jews as "bloodsuckers of the black community." Muhammad also criticized a variety of black American leaders, characterizing them as "house niggers" who had sold out their people to a white power structure.

In the wake of the speech, the Anti-Defamation League of B'nai B'rith published a full-page advertisement in the *New York Times* with excerpts from the address under the headline: "Minister Louis Farrakhan and the Nation of Islam claim they are moving toward moderation … you decide." In fact, Farrakhan was trying to adopt a more moderate posture at the time, and he officially censured Muhammad and relieved him of his duties as top aide. At a press conference, Farrakhan declared: "During the speech, Brother Khallid made remarks that were not consistent with the proper representation of the Honorable Elijah Muhammad, his teachings and guidance, myself, and the Nation of Islam. Therefore, in that instance, he was not representing us; he was representing himself." Later, in a widely-quoted comment, Farrakhan admitted that he did not disagree with the "truths" in Muhammad's speech, but only in the manner with which they were

The break between Farrakhan and Muhammad was never serious or formalized. Each man continued to speak respectfully about the other, but Monroe contended in *Emerge* that Muhammad's continued diatribes were maybe "deliberately undermining the efforts of Minister Farrakhan to broaden his base" or may in fact have been "attempt[s] to 'sabotage' Farrakhan's apparent move toward moderation and his joining with mainstream Black civil rights leaders."

For his part, Muhammad remained adamantly unapologetic for his remarks or his views. *Newsday* quoted him in 1994 on the subject of Jews: "Never will I say I am not an anti-Semite," and on whites: "I don't have any love for the other side. It's not in me. I don't want no integration. I want independence for a nation of my own." On the other hand, Muhammad expressed nothing but respect and admiration for Farrakhan and would probably have been insulted by the notion that he was trying to undermine his mentor. "Minister Farrakhan is my spiritual father, leader, teacher and guide," Muhammad stated in *Emerge*. "And like any good son, I respect the discipline and judgment of my father, and I am not silly enough to run away from home....I am a soldier and I follow a divine chain of command, and I am going to complete my tour of duty."

Muhammad's "tour of duty" took him all across the country for speaking engagements that sometimes paid him as much as $10,000 per appearance. In May of 1994 he was shot in the foot by a former Nation of Islam minister but was not seriously injured. Muhammad was often accompanied to the podium by his son, Farrakhan, who occasionally introduced his father. Although not formally denounced by America's black leaders, Muhammed was quietly considered something of a pariah who was speaking his own mind and not necessarily representing the views of others.

Muhammad moved to Texas and established the New Black Panther Party and the New Black Muslims. In June of 1998, James Byrd Jr. of Jasper, Texas, reportedly took a ride with three white men, who savagely beat him and tied him to the back of a truck before dragging him to his death. The nation was shocked and appalled. Muhammad led armed members of both of his groups in Jasper, Texas, to protest the murder. "We are here to say that violence and racism and hatred of the white man in America is just as American as apple and cherry pie," Muhammad told *The Associated Press,* reprinted at ABCNews.com.

Tried to Incite Riot

Muhammad, along with Malik Zulu Shabazz and Erica Ford, began organizing a Million Youth March in Harlem in 1998. Many other local Black leaders denounced the march, including former U.S representative Floyd Flake and Congressman Charles Rangel. Mayor Rudolph Giulani called it a "hate march" and refused to grant a permit. Muhammad sued in federal court and won. An appeals court limited the march to six blocks and to four hours.

Muhammad's speech, which used his usual fiery rhetoric, also included an invitation to riot. According to *Insight on the News,* Muhammad told the marchers "[a]nd if you don't have a gun, every one of them [New York City cops] has one gun, two guns, three guns….In self-defense, if they attack you, take their guns from them and use their guns on them….Don't let nobody be arrested." A few of the 6,000 in attendance attacked police with steel railings, and some pelted the police with stones and bottles. There were two arrests and 15 policeman were injured. Another march was held in 1999, but only a couple hundred people attended.

After giving the keynote speech at the Tubman School in Harlem, Muhammad reportedly had a stroke. It was later confirmed that he had a brain aneurysm. He died in an Atlanta hospital on February 19, 2001.

Muhammad considered himself a man with a mission, a "pit bull dog in your white behind," to quote him in the *Chicago Tribune.* He saw no possibility of rapprochement between races as long as society continued to see whites as inherently superior. He felt blacks would be better served in an independent nation of their own. If his views offend people, he stated in the *Los Angeles Times,* so be it. "If you're at war, you're supposed to attack your enemies," he concluded. "It's arrogant to tell the aggrieved, to tell the victim, to tell the survivor of the African holocaust how to suffer or how to talk." Muhammad never compromised his philosophy.

Sources

Periodicals

Chicago Tribune, June 1, 1994, p. 1.
Chronicle of Higher Education, January 19, 1994, p. A33–34.
Emerge, September 1994, p. 42–46.
Insight on the News, October 12, 1998.
Jet, September 27, 1999.
Los Angeles Times, May 27, 1994, p. 1B.
Maclean's, February 28, 1994, p. 13.
Newsday, February 28, 1994, p. 3.
Philadelphia Daily News, February 28, 1994, p. 9.
Philadelphia Inquirer, March 1, 1994, p. 1A.
The Associated Press, June 14, 1998.
The Source, June 1995, pp. 48–51.
Time, February 7, 1994, p. 37.
Washington Post, May 30, 1994, p. 1A.

Online

ABCNews Online, http://www.abcnews.com
CBS News, http://www.cbsnews.com
The Black World Today, http://www.tbwt.com

—Ashyia N. Henderson

Frank E. Petersen

1932–

Marine officer

Despite enduring racism in the Marines, Frank E. Petersen, Jr. became the first black aviator in the United States Marine Corps, and the first African American to reach the level of general in the Marines. He rose through the ranks, finally becoming a lieutenant general, the first African American Marine to become a three-star ranked general. He proved that one man could make a difference.

Frank E. Petersen, Jr., was born in Topeka, Kansas on March 2, 1932. He was born to Edythe Southard and Frank Petersen, Sr., and was the second of four children. He was an active, intelligent child who played football in middle school and graduated from Topeka High School in 1949. When he went to sign up for the Navy—something he was very excited to do—he did so well on the exam, according to *Into the Tiger's Jaw: America's First Black Marine Aviator,* that the recruiter made him take the test again. This would be just the first incident of racism that Petersen would have to undergo in the Navy.

The military had been desegregated by this point, but racism was rampant, and it would be something that Petersen would have to fight again and again during his entire military career. Blacks in the military in the middle of the twentieth century faced the same biases that females did at the end of it. It wasn't until the Korean War, in fact, that African Americans served in all the different operations of the military and were involved in all major military actions. "[Petersen] spent most of his time, it seems, fighting genteel and not-so-genteel opposition from whites who, in words like those we hear now about women in the military, claimed that the armed forces were being sacrificed for the sake of the 'social experiment' of fully incorporating someone besides white males," said *Booklist.* After a few insulting suggestions that he would make a fantastic "steward" in the Navy—something that almost stopped him from joining up—Petersen's father had a small talk with the recruiting officer. After a short wait, Petersen was admitted into the Navy on June 6, 1950 with the promise that he would be sent to the El Toro electronics technician school after boot camp.

First African-American Marine Aviator

Just two short years later, on October 22, 1952, Petersen was commissioned as a Marine aviation officer—the first African American to become a Marine aviator. Petersen

At a Glance . . .

Born on March 2, 1932 in Topeka, KS; parents: Frank Petersen, Sr., and Edythe Southard Petersen; married: Eleanor, 1955-1973; Alicia Joyce Downes, 1975-; children: Frank Emmanuel Petersen III, Gayle Marie Petersen, Dana Charlette Petersen, Lindsey Monique Downes Petersen (adopted).

Career: U. S. Marine Corps officer. U.S. Marine Corps, 1950-88; U.S. Marine Aviator, 1952-72; U.S. Marine Corps Lieutenant General, 1972-85; U.S. Marine Corps Lieutenant General, 1986-88.

Awards: Distinguished Flying Cross; the Meritorious Service Medal; the Purple Heart; Robert M. Hanson award for the Most Outstanding Fighter Squadron while assigned in Vietnam, 1968; Man of the Year, NAACP, 1979; Honorary doctorate, Virginia Union University, 1987; Gray Eagle Trophy, August 21, 1987-June 15, 1988.

Addresses: *Home*—Minneapolis, Minnesota. *Publisher*—c/o Presidio Press, 505-B San Marin Drive, Suite 160, Novato, CA, 94945-1340.

joined the conflict in Korea in 1953, and from the beginning he showed himself to be a fine officer and a great aviator. According to the *African Americans in the Korean War* web site, Petersen flew 64 combat missions during the Korean War and was even awarded the Distinguished Flying Cross and six other air medals before the Korean War finally came to an end. Flying missions bent on protecting the U.S. troops from the Chinese communists, he was indispensable to the Marines on the ground.

Petersen also fought in the Vietnam War. There he commanded a squadron of attack fighters. For this role, he was awarded the Legion of Merit and the Meritorious Service Medal. During his stint in Vietnam he was also awarded the Purple Heart because he was wounded in action. In 1968 he won the Robert M. Hanson award for the Most Outstanding Fighter Squadron of 1968 while assigned in Vietnam. And on February 23, 1979 Frank E. Petersen, Jr., finally saw the culmination of his hard work when he was named brigadier general by President Jimmy Carter, making him the first African-American general in United States Marine Corps history. The same year saw him named NAACP Man of the Year. In 1986, Petersen became the Marine Corps's first African-American three-star general, with a rank of lieutenant general.

From August 21, 1987 to June 15, 1988 Petersen was awarded the Gray Eagle Trophy. The Gray Eagle Trophy

was first seen at a celebration for the 50th Anniversary of Naval Aviation. The trophy itself, according to the *Navy Military History* website, is "a silver eagle landing into the arresting gear of the Navy's first aircraft carrier, *Langley*. The inscription reads: 'The Venerable Order of the Gray Eagle. The Most Ancient Naval Aviator on Active Duty. In recognition of a clear eye, a stout heart, a steady hand, and a daring defiance of gravity and the law of averages'." The award is given to the most senior aviator in point of service in flying and is passed down through the years. Receiving this award was the perfect ending to a strong and honorable military career.

The End of a Brilliant Career

Petersen retired in 1988, as a three-star lieutenant general. After his retirement from the Marine Corps, Petersen went on into civilian life with the same fervor he had shown in his military career. He became a vice president of the Du Pont Company and was a guest speaker during his reign at several prestigious institutions, including the University of Delaware's conference on "Partnership Opportunities for Success: Across Races, Generations, and Organizations" in 1992. In 1998, Petersen also tried his hand at writing. With help from biographer J. Alfred Phelps, Petersen published his own autobiography. The book discusses the hardships he faced, not only because of war, but because of the racism of his fellow soldiers. It is an intimate look at what kind of perseverance and dedication it takes to make large changes in the world—for Petersen certainly helped to do just that. *Into the Tiger's Jaw: America's First Black Marine Aviator* is said by the *Powells.com* web site to offer "valuable insight into the evolution of both the military and the society at large through the experience of one man and his family." J. Alfred Phelps, who worked with Petersen on the book, noted on the *Amazon.com* web site, "Working with Lt. Gen. Frank E. Petersen, USMC (Retired), was an uplifting experience. . . . [T]his is the story of a true American patriot . . . This is a gentleman who helped the United States Marine Corps to stand up and be counted in the arenas of race relations and social conscience in America." Frank E. Petersen, Jr., is one of those rare men who fight for what they want, what they believe in, and manage not only to succeed beyond all expectations but also to help others along the way. Those who have interacted with him will not soon forget him, and his influence and change will be felt in the military for a very long time.

Sources

Books

Petersen, Jr., Lt. Gen. Frank E. with J. Alfred Phelps. *Into the Tiger's Jaw: America's First Black Marine Aviator*, Presidio Press, 1998.

Periodicals

Booklist, October 15, 1998, p. 377.

Online

http://www.udel.edu/PR/UpDate/92/36/10.html.
http://www.orau.gov/eeo/bhm/99bhm/bhmfacts.htm.
http://korea50.army.mil/history/factsheets/afroamer.html.
http://www.history.navy.mil/download/app32.pdf. http://www.kshs.org.

http://members.aol.com/nubiansong/montford.html.
http://www.code316.com/clean/Mainframe/mainframe.htm.
http://www/powells.com/biblio/120000©120200/0891416757.html.
http://gb.gopbi.com/servlets/siteServlet/kstate/Famous" Kansans N©R.html.
http://www.amazon.com.

—Catherine Donaldson

Homer Adolph Plessy

1862-1925

Civil Rights activist

The late nineteenth and early twentieth centuries are widely considered an especially dismal period in African-American history. For a dozen years after the Civil War the Washington-controlled Reconstruction program oversaw the former Confederate states and made a strong effort to provide free Blacks with the full rights of citizenship. During Reconstruction hundreds of Black men sat in southern state legislatures, and several Blacks were sent to the United States Congress. However, the progress made during this era soon came undone. The end of Reconstruction in 1877 unleashed virulently anti-Black forces that eventually pushed African Americans into a kind of semi-servitude that lasted for decades. In 1896, racism was given legitimacy by the Supreme Court in the Plessy v. Ferguson case which determined that a Louisiana state law requiring Black railroad passengers to sit in a separate car did not violate the United States Constitution. "By its decision the Supreme Court constitutionalized the state enactment of race prejudice," wrote Barton J. Bernstein in the *Journal of Negro History.*

Although Homer Adolph Plessy's name is prominent in American history, little is known about Plessy himself other than basic facts taken from public records. Plessy was born a free Black in New Orleans on March 17, 1862. His parents were Adolphe Plessy and Rosa Debergue. A French-speaking Roman Catholic of mostly European ancestry (the name Plessy is probably a corruption of the French name Plessis), he was considered Black because one of his great-grandparents had been Black.

Plessy, whose father died when he was five, began work as a shoemaker in 1879 (in some accounts he is listed as a carpenter), and in 1888 he married Louise Bordenave. The couple lived on North Claiborne Avenue in the Treme section of New Orleans, a racially mixed, middle-class neighborhood where whites and Blacks mingled with relative ease. Plessy served as vice president of a local benevolent organization, the Societe des Francs Amis, which provided medical and funeral expenses for dues-paying members.

Activism Began Early

It is possible that Plessy's connection to the Societe des Francs Amis led to his involvement with the Citizens' Committee to Test the Constitutionality of the Separate Car Law. In 1887, Florida became the first state to require railroads to provide separate cars for Black passengers. Several states soon followed suit, including Louisiana in 1890. Individuals disobeying the Louisiana Separate Car Law faced a $25 fine or twenty days in jail. Railroads were fined $500 if a separate car was not provided.

Almost immediately after the Separate Car Law was passed in Louisiana, New Orleans Blacks began organized protests against it. According to historian C. Vann Woodward writing in *American Counterpoint* Blacks in Louisiana were better able than Blacks in other states to voice their objections to discriminatory measures. "One source of leadership and strength that Louisiana Negroes enjoyed that Blacks in no other states shared was a well-established upper class of mixed racial origin in New Orleans with a strong infusion of French and other Latin intermixtures," Woodward wrote. "Among these people were descendants of the 'Free People of Color,' some of them men of culture, education, and wealth, often with a heritage of several generations of freedom. Unlike the great majority of Negroes, they were city people with an established professional class and a high degree of literacy. . . . By ancestry as well as by residence, they were associated with Latin cultures that were in some way at variance with Anglo-American ideas of race relations."

The Citizens' Committee to Test the Constitutionality of the Separate Car Law was established in 1891 by a group of leading Black New Orleanians, including Louis A. Martinet, founder of the *Crusader,* a newspaper advocating Black civil rights, and Rodolphe L. Desdunes, a poet and journalist. The Committee intended to challenge the Separate Car Law by way of a "test case." Albion W. Tourgee, a white Northerner who had been a Reconstruction official in North Carolina, offered his services as the committee's legal counsel free of charge. To assist Tourgee, the committee raised money to hire James C. Walker, a local white attorney and member of the Republican party. Although a Republican president, Rutherford B. Hayes, had ended Reconstruction, most white Southerners still considered the G.O.P. a Northern organization hostile to Southern attitudes.

Constitutionality Test Case

The committee's "test case" called for a Black man to deliberately break the Louisiana Separate Car Law so that his case might then be tried in federal court. It was hoped the court would find that the Louisiana law was not in accord with the thirteenth and fourteenth amendments to the United States Constitution which had abolished slavery and guaranteed the rights of citizenship and equal protection under the law for Blacks. Tourgee believed that the test case would be strengthened if the Black man arrested was someone whose race was not easy to categorize. The light-skinned Homer Plessy was given the job.

On June 7, 1892, Plessy went to the Press Street Station in New Orleans and bought a ticket on the East Louisiana Railroad to Covington, a city about forty miles north. The railroad, which did not support the Separate Car Law because of the expense and trouble involved in having to add an extra car, even if only a single Black passenger happened to be on board, had agreed to cooperate with the test case. Soon after the train pulled out of Press Street Station, the conductor informed Plessy he had to move to the "colored car." When Plessy refused to move, the conductor asked the engineer to stop the train. At this point a private detective hired by the committee boarded the train and made it clear to Plessy that he was disobeying state law by sitting in the "whites only" carriage. Plessy again refused and was consequently arrested by the detective and taken to a local police station. Committee members were waiting at the police station and provided a $500 bond allowing Plessy freedom until his court trial.

Appearing before Judge John Howard Ferguson of the Criminal District Court for the Parish of New Orleans, Plessy's attorneys Tourgee and Walker argued that the Separate Car Law was in conflict with the United States Constitution. Separate accommodations were a symbol of servitude, they maintained, and denied Blacks equal treatment under the law. Judge Ferguson ruled against Plessy, claiming that a state law requiring separate accommodations was not unfair as long as the accommodations were equal. Equal accommodations, Ferguson noted, did not have to be identical with those provided for whites. Keith Weldon Medley of *Smithsonian* quoted Ferguson as saying the Separate Car Law had not deprived Plessy of his liberty as a citizen, but only of his "'liberty of doing as he pleased, and of violating a penal statute with impunity.'" Tourgee and Walker appealed Plessy's case, now called Plessy v. Ferguson, to the Louisiana State Supreme Court which also ruled against Plessy.

Paul Oberst in the *Arizona Law Review* quoted the Louisiana Supreme Court as maintaining that the Separate Car Law "'applies to the two races with such perfect fairness and equality that the record brought up for our inspection does not disclose whether the person prosecuted is a white or a colored man. The charge is simply that he did 'then and there, unlawfully, insist on going into a coach to which, by race, he did not belong."

A Three-Year Wait for Federal Trial

Denied a rehearing before the state court, Plessy's legal representatives managed to obtain a writ of error which allowed the case to be sent to the United States Supreme Court. A backlog of cases resulted in a wait of over three years before Plessy v. Ferguson was heard by the highest court in the nation. Tourgee was pleased by the delay, hoping that during the extra time public support might be gathered for Plessy's cause and that the public support might sway the opinion of some of the justices. Oberst quoted an 1893 letter from Tourgee to committee leader Louis A. Martinet in which Tourgee advises that committee to "'bend every possible energy to secure the discussion of the principle in such a way as to reach and awaken public sentiment . . . . If we can get the ear of the Country, and argue the matter fully before the people first, we may incline the wavering to fall on our side when the matter comes up.'"

Tourgee's efforts to gain public support largely fell upon deaf ears. Influential northern white progressives of the type who had pushed for the abolition of slavery earlier in the century were mostly disinterested in the plight of free Blacks. There was a widespread notion, based on ignorance of actual conditions in the south, that free Blacks could easily fend for themselves. Also, the problems of European immigrants crowding into northern cities seemed a more immediate and compelling issue to most social reformers of the period.

Plessy v. Ferguson was finally heard by the Supreme Court in April of 1896. In addition to attacking the constitutionality of the Louisiana Separate Car Law under both the thirteenth and fourteenth amendments, Tourgee and Walker's argument also questioned the validity of allowing train conductors to assign passengers to racial categories on the basis of casual scrutiny. Plessy's status as a "colored" man had never been stated in any court and part of Tourgee and Walker's argument was that if Plessy looked white he was entitled to the privileges enjoyed by white people. Being treated like a white man was a property right which the East Louisiana Railroad had denied to Plessy.

Racism Made Legal

On May 18, 1896, the court handed down a seven-justice majority decision against Plessy. Justice John Marshall Harlan dissented and Justice David Brewer did not participate. The majority opinion quickly dismissed all aspects of Tourgee and Walker's arguments except the issue of whether state law had the power to demand racial separation. Speaking for the majority, Justice Henry Billings Brown, as quoted by Woodward, maintained that the validity of any segregation law depends upon its "'reasonableness'" and that reasonableness must be determined by "'reference to established usages, customs, and traditions of the people, and with a view to the promotion of their comfort, and the preservation of the public peace and good order.'" Brown went on to declare that "'We consider the underlying fallacy of the plantiff's argument to consist in the assumption that the enforced separation of the two races stamps the colored race with the badge of inferiority. If this is so, it is not by reason of anything found in the act, but solely because the colored race chooses to put that construction upon it.'"

The majority opinion in the Plessy v. Ferguson case is considered one of the most fatuous decisions in Supreme Court history. The court's assertion that race separation was a traditional and established custom in the South was clearly false. Under the slave-system there had been constant interaction between whites and Blacks. Even after the end of slavery rigid separation practices (a system commonly referred to as "Jim Crow," taking its name from a dim-witted Black character in minstrel shows), were not widespread. As Bernstein wrote: "Racial segregation in the Old South had been unknown. The system of slavery would have been virtually inoperative had Jim Crow prevailed. Nor did Jim Crow spontaneously arise after the war. Negroes and whites frequently shared the same coaches; although sometimes freedmen were barred from the first-class cars, the races did share the same second-class coaches."

The legal precedents cited by Brown in the majority opinion were a weak assortment of lower court rulings mostly having to do with segregated schools, chiefly Roberts v. the City of Boston, an 1850 case brought before Supreme Judicial Court of Massachusetts which established that separate schools for children of different races were no less valid than separate school for children of different sexes or ages. That Roberts v. the City of Boston had been decided before the thirteenth and fourteenth amendments had been adopted and was thus irrelevant was a fact the court simply ignored.

In his dissenting opinion Justice Harlan said that "Our constitution is color-blind, and neither knows nor tolerates classes among citizens. In respect of civil rights, all citizens are equal before the law . . . We boast of the freedom enjoyed by our people above all other peoples. But it is difficult to reconcile that boast with a state of law which, practically, puts the brand of servitude and degradation upon a large class of our fellow citizens—our equals before the law. The thin disguise of 'equal' accommodations for passengers in railroad coaches will not mislead any one, nor atone for the wrong this day done."

Historians Evaluate the Racist Judgment

Historians cite a variety of reasons why the court ruled against Plessy. Among these reasons is a desire by late-nineteenth century Americans to narrow the divide between North and South by giving in to what seemed to be the wishes of the majority of white southerners. Race separation was especially attractive to working class and poor southern whites who feared competition for jobs from Black workers. "Thirty years after the Civil War, the country wanted to put that conflict behind it. In the process, the issue of civil rights for African Americans took a back seat. Economic growth was the national preoccupation," wrote Harvey Fireside in Plessy V. Ferguson: Separate But Equal?.

Another reason often cited is the writings of certain social theorists who, using distorted Darwinian ideas, insisted that there was scientific evidence proving that whites were naturally superior to Blacks and that whites of northern European ancestry were superior to other whites. The popularity of "Social Darwinism" caused many educated Americans to believe that racism was justified by science and beneficial to society since it allowed the supposedly better element to be firmly in control. The significance of the Plessy decision was not apparent at the time of its occurrence. The *New York Times* ran only a brief factual article about the ruling along with other railroad related news on page three.

After the Supreme Court ruling against Plessy, the Committee to Test the Separate Car Law disbanded. In January of 1897, Homer Plessy stood before a Louisiana court, pleaded guilty to violating the Separate Car Law, and paid the required $25 fine. Plessy lived the remainder of his life in obscurity, later becoming a life insurance collector for the People's Life Insurance Company, and died in New Orleans on March 1, 1925. He was buried in the city's St. Louis Cemetery, no 1. His vindication had to wait another 29 years. In the meantime, the Plessy v. Ferguson decision allowed extremist racial attitudes to prevail in the South and led to an almost complete separation of southern whites and Blacks during the first half of the twentieth century. In 1954, the Brown vs. The Board of Education decision by the Supreme Court, which outlawed segregated schools, effectively overtured Plessy v. Ferguson and resulted in a vigorous resurgence of the Black civil rights movement.

Sources

Books

Encyclopedia of the American Constitution. New York: Macmillan, 2000.

Fireside, Harvey. *Plessy v. Ferguson: Separate But Equal?* Springfield, NJ: Enslow Publishers, 1997.

Garraty, John A.(ed.) *Quarrels That Have Shaped the Constitution.* New York: Harper and Row, 1987.

Woodward, C. Vann. *American Counterpoint: Slavery and Racism in the North-South Dialogue.* Boston: Little Brown, 1971.

Periodicals

Arizona Law Review, V. 15, pp. 389–418.

Journal of Negro History, July 1962, pp. 192–98, July 1963, pp. 196–205, April 1977, pp. 125–33.

New York Times, May 19, 1896, p. 3.

Smithsonian, February 1994, pp. 105–17.

Online

Afro-American Almanac, http://www.toptags.com/aama.

—Mary Kalfatovic

Kevin Powell

1966—

Political activist, writer

Kevin Powell was a poet and journalist before he got international—if sometimes negative—exposure on MTV's first *Real World* series. His by-line appeared often in *Rolling Stone, Essence,* and *The Source* before he worked as a staff writer at the urban-music and culture magazine, *Vibe.* Powell has developed a keen perspective into hot-button issues that affect blacks and Americans. After he left *Vibe* in 1996 to pursue his writing Powell produced two respectable anthologies of black writers: *In the Tradition: An Anthology of Young Black Writers,* and *Step Into a World: A Global Anthology of the New Black Literature.*

Powell was born on April 24, 1966, in Jersey City, New Jersey, "a year after Malcolm was blown away and two years before a rifle stifled MLK," he noted in *Step Into a World,* recalling the assassinations of black leaders Malcolm X and Martin Luther King, Jr. He was raised by his mother, Shirley Mae Powell, who had migrated from the south to raise her son in a Jersey City tenement. Though his maternal parents could not read, Powell wanted to be writer since he was eleven years old. Powell's childhood was "one long misery session," he said in *Step Into a World,* "complete with hunger, violence, and rage." He escaped by spending Saturdays in Jersey City's Green-

ville Public Library, where, as he described in *Step Into a World,* he "overdosed on music, TV, sports, Hemingway, Poe, Shakespeare." Powell attended Rutgers University on a financial aid package and once he got there, he remembered in *Keepin' It Real,* he "wore my newfound black pride like a medal on my pumped-out chest." After graduation, Powell spent the early 1990s teaching English at New York University.

In 1992 Powell got his first taste of life in the public eye as a cast member on the original season of MTV's the *Real World,* which became one of MTV's biggest hits. Seven disparate twentysomethings were chosen to live rent-free for three months in a lavish Manhattan loft and to have every detail of their lives and interactions taped, edited, broadcast, and re-broadcast on MTV. Powell was shown having many fallings-out with his roommates, often about issues of race.

Powell was portrayed as an "antagonistic jerk," according to the *Boston Globe* and, after all was said and done, was bitter about the MTV experience. "The people were selfish, inconsiderate, and had no respect for people's differences," Powell said in the *Globe.* "I would never, never, under any circumstances, do it again." He claimed,

At a Glance . . .

Born on April 24, 1966, in Jersey City, NJ; son of Shirley Mae Powell. *Education:* Rutgers University; State University of New Jersey, 1984–88.

Career: New York University, English instructor, 1990–92; MTV's *Real World,* writer, host, cast member, 1992; *Vibe* magazine, staff writer, 1993–96; author: *Recognize: Poems,* 1995; *Keepin' It Real: Post-MTV Reflections on Race, Sex, and Politics,* 1997; editor, *In the Tradition: An Anthology of Young Black Writers,* 1993; *Step Into a World: A Global Anthology of the New Black Literature,* 2000.

Addresses: *Publisher*—John Wiley & Sons, 605 Third Ave., New York, NY 10158.

as did other cast members, that events were artfully edited to appear more dramatic and controversial, and key moments were left out. Highly intense exchanges between Powell and his roommates were often taken out of context. His big fight with roommate Becky about race was broadcast, while Becky thanking Powell later for opening her eyes to African-American culture was not. Powell was accused of throwing a candlestick at roommate Julie in a fit of rage, but the fact that the incident happened the day the Rodney King verdict was delivered was left out.

The "angry young poet," as writer Traci Grant described him in the *Globe,* benefitted minimally, he claimed, from his appearance on the show. He considered the exposure a "Catch-22," he said in the *Atlanta Journal-Constitution*—while he was thankful as a young writer to get the attention, he also learned some of the down sides of notoriety. He found that people are "very competitive and insecure and jealous," he said in the *Atlanta Journal-Constitution*, and that the attention he received "was just a lot of hype." After the show ended, he continued writing for *Rolling Stone, Essence,* and *The Source,* all magazines he had been working for before the show. He received much flack for his honest essay that appeared in *Essence* in 1992, called "The Sexist in Me." He eventually was hired as a staff writer at *Vibe,* where he worked until 1996. He also published a book of poetry, called *Recognize: Poems,* in 1995.

For his first effort as an editor, Powell co-edited a collection of poetry and fiction called *In the Tradition: An Anthology of Young Black Writers,* which was published in 1993. Critic Angela Kinamore wrote in *Essence,* "It's a well-crafted collection … that should be read by all who want to know what's on the minds of young people." Kinamore felt that the anthology, which contained works

about politics, hip-hop, and black ancestry, was an indication that there was a "new literary movement coming forth."

By 1997 the bad memories of the *Real World* may have faded a bit, and Powell hoped to "put some distance between me and *Vibe* and MTV" he told the *Atlanta Journal-Constitution.* He published collection of essays titled *Keepin' It Real: Post-MTV Reflections on Race, Sex, and Politics.* In the book's introduction, Powell states that the book is his way of exploring black and American issues. According to critic Deborah Gregory in *Essence,* the writer put "many of his 'issues' under a microscope to magnify the larger isms that plague America." Critic Mary Carroll, in a *Booklist* review, wrote, "Powell's lucid essays give abstract social and cultural issues a human face."

In 2000 Powell edited his second collection of black writers called *Step Into a World: A Global Anthology of the New Black Literature.* The book features a diverse group of 104 contemporary writers—famous and obscure, aged 23 to 43, and from nine countries and three continents. Inclusion in the book, rather than requiring a certain criteria, was based mostly on Powell's taste. His picks include "previously published writing he has read and liked," according to critic Bakari Kitwana in the *Progressive,* and that selection provides "interesting writing . . . that covers an adequate range of issues that speak to this generation." However, Kitwana deemed the collection "hardly comprehensive."

Step Into a World, organized under the headings of essays, hip-hop journalism, criticism, fiction, poetry, and dialogue, reflects "the diversity of talent" among a group of writers who are "generally lumped together under the heading of black writers," wrote critic Vanessa Bush in the *Booklist.* With the collection, Bush continued, Powell "celebrates the enduring artistry and worth" among black writers. *Library Journal* critic Roger A. Berger wrote that the collection "maintains a precarious balance between authentic discovery and promotional marketing," with the "quality and relevance" of the writing varying widely. Kitwana praised Powell's collection in the *Progressive:* "If Black America's divided generations are going to understand each other better," reading the book would be "a good place to start."

Powell's own contribution to the anthology, an essay titled "The Word Movement," explores a contemporary turn in black communication—he celebrates hip-hop journalism, spoken word, and the works of such New York writers as Greg Tate and Lisa Jones, among others he sees as pioneers of this new literary movement. Powell labels all young black writers part of this renaissance. "I wanted this anthology to be regarded as a definitive text of this era, as the mouthpiece for the Word Movement, much in the same way that *The New Negro* and *Black Fire* represented their times," he wrote in the introduction to *Step Into a World.* "If I was going to do this, I thought, I would like to cast a wide net in search of some of the best and brightest writers of the Word Movement."

Powell has accomplished a great deal in his life. In *Keepin' It Real: Post-MTV Reflections on Race, Sex, and Politics,* Powell wrote: "Over the course of the last decade I've been a flag-waving patriot, a Christian, an atheist, a Muslim, a student leader, a homeless person, a pauper, a loner, a social worker, a poet, a misogynist, an English instructor, an MTV 'star,' a full-time journalist, an egomaniac, a manic-depressive, a bully, a punk, an optimist, a pessimist" But above all, Powell continued, he remained "someone who is always trying to find and tell the truth as I see it."

Selected writings

(Editor) *In the Tradition: An Anthology of Young Black Writers,* Harlem Writers Press, 1993.
Recognize: Poems, Harlem River Press, 1995.
Keepin' It Real: Post-MTV Reflections on Race, Sex, and Politics, One World/Ballantine, 1997.
(Editor) *Step Into a World: A Global Anthology of the New Black Literature,* John Wiley & Sons, 2000.

Sources

Books

Henderson, Ashyia, editor, *Who's Who Among African Americans,* 13th edition, The Gale Group, 2000.
Powell, Kevin, *Keepin' It Real: Post-MTV Reflections on Race, Sex, and Politics,* One World/Ballantine, 1997.
Powell, Kevin, editor, *Step Into a World: A Global Anthology of the New Black Literature,* John Wiley & Sons, 2000.

Periodicals

Atlanta Journal-Constitution, September 17, 1997, p. D2.
Booklist, September 1, 1997, p. 40; November 15, 2000, p. 604.
Boston Globe, August 15, 1992, p. 27.
Essence, July 1993, p. 46; October 1997, p. 60.
Library Journal, November 15, 2000, p. 69.
Progressive, July 2001, p. 41.

—Brenna Sanchez

Awadagin Pratt

1966–

Pianist

Pianist Awadagin Pratt has amazed and astounded both critics and audiences with his diverse and engaging interpretations of classical music. He won the Naumburg International Piano Competition and hasn't slowed down since. He has performed and conducted numerous concerts as well as released several albums displaying a unique style that set him apart from most of his contemporaries.

Pratt is an engaging and exciting new presence in the world of classical music, where his passionate playing and unique interpretations have invigorated works by such composers as Brahms, Beethoven, Franck, and Liszt. Pratt, however, has garnered as much attention for superficialities that set him apart on the classical concert stage as he has for his musical prowess. First of all, he is young—in his early 30s—and he is black. He wears his shoulder-length hair in dreadlocks. Pratt—whose first name is pronounced ah-wah-DODGE-in—told *Newsweek's* Yahlin Chang that people who learn he is a musician often assume he is part of a rock band. That is something, however, he finds uninteresting. "I don't have an interest in pop music," he said. "By and large, I find it to be boring. Rhythmically boring, harmonically boring, and melodically possibly interesting but for a very short time."

Robin P. Robinson , writing in *Emerge* magazine, said Pratt "challenges the establishment and fans alike, forcing them to rethink the way music is perceived and heard." In the *New York Times,* James Barron called Pratt "a hot young pianist with a big sound and a knack for tackling fast, risky passages." And Robert Mann, president of the Naumburg Foundation, said the young pianist "has a rare gift. Very few artists create a sense that the music is theirs."

Awadagin Pratt was born in Pittsburgh, Pennsylvania, on March 6, 1966, and began studying piano when he was six years old. In 1975 his family moved to Normal, Illinois, where his parents, Mildred and Theodore Pratt, were professors of social work and nuclear physics, respectively. For Awadagin—who began playing the piano at age six—and his younger sister, Menah, the home environment included a strict regimen of piano and violin lessons, tennis lessons, and regular practice sessions. Attending public schools in Normal, he was active in athletics, and was on the tennis team at Normal Community High School, played doubles tennis with his sister, played on basketball teams, and competed in local sports tournaments. "I was aware that I showed some reasonable level of proficiency (as a musician), but it was never a prodigy-type thing," he told Robinson. "I was much more involved in tennis. My sister and I were both ranked regionally." Pratt, in fact, appropriated his dreadlock hairstyle from tennis star Yannick Noah.

Pratt's interest in music soon deepened, and upon graduation from high school, he enrolled at the age of 16 at the University of Illinois, majoring in music and studying piano, violin, and conducting. At age 18, he declared himself financially independent from his parents because they disapproved of his plans to be a performer rather than a music instructor. After three years at Illinois, he

At a Glance . . .

Born in on March 6, 1966 in Pittsburgh, Pennsylvania; parents, Mildred (a college professor) and Theodore (a college professor) Pratt. *Education:* Studied piano and violin at the University of Illinois and went on to graduate from the Peabody Institute of Music in Baltimore.

Career: Classical pianist. Albums include: two recital albums; *A Long Way From Normal,* 1994; *Beethoven Piano Sonatas,* 1996; *Live From South Africa,* 1997; *Transformations,* 1999. Also founded the Pratt Music Foundation.

Awards: Naumburg International Piano Competition, 1992; awarded Avery Fisher Career Grant, 1994.

Addresses: IMG Artists, 420 West 45th St., New York, NY 10036.

prepared to transfer to another institution. The New England Conservatory accepted him as a violinist but not as a pianist, while the Cleveland Institute accepted him as a pianist, but not as a violinist. Pratt elected to attend the Peabody Institute of Music in Baltimore, where he became the first person in the school's 137-year history to graduate with three areas of concentration: piano, violin and conducting. In 1990, he decided to focus on the piano and conducting—and let the violin go.

Won The Naumburg Competition

Pratt burst onto the scene in 1992, when he won the prestigious Naumburg International Piano Competition at Lincoln Center in New York City. He was the first African American to win an international instrumental competition. He is described as an independent and strong-willed man who has brought a challenging style and a sensual, intellectual virtuosity to classical music. "Pratt plays with a full-bodied intensity that can be at turns intimate and grandly heart-wrenching," Chang wrote. "He has a story to tell, and you can hear him agonizing over every twist. . . . Pratt commands your unfailing attention—without ever getting ostentatious."

Pratt's victory in the Naumburg Competition in May of 1992—and the $5,000 prize, lucrative 40-city concert tour, and recording contract it brought him—came just in time. He had passed up another competition the previous month because he couldn't scrape together the $60 entrance fee. Even so, he never lost sight of his purpose. After winning Naumburg, Pratt told *People* magazine: "The audience—the people—you want them to be moved

by your music. I always figured if I had that going for me, everything else would work out—regardless of whether someone thought I should cut my hair."

After several major concert successes, Pratt was awarded the Avery Fisher Career Grant in 1994, and his full-time concert career continued at a rapid pace. He signed a recording contract with Angel/EMI in 1993. He was the first black instrumentalist since Andre Watts to get a recording contract with a major label. His first two releases were recital albums, with the initial album, *A Long Way from Normal,* released in 1994, featuring works by Brahms, Bach, Franck, and Liszt. Reviewers raved about his ability to bring fire and freshness to familiar works, including Franck's *Prelude, Chorale and Fugue.* "Pratt has plenty of taste, artistry, and insight, all of which are immediately apparent in his comparatively light- textured, deftly colored rendition of Liszt's Funerailles," *Stereo Review* magazine opined. "(He) seems to be a rare bird among competition winners: He's at home in the virtuoso repertory but comes across best in more introspective works that require genuine artistry . . . . (T)his is a wonderfully satisfying and promising debut album."

Pratt's repertoire puts a new spin on classic compositions. "He leans toward . . . . probing, dense pieces by composers such as Brahms, Franck, and Liszt, rather than the more commercially popular Mozart or Vivaldi," Robinson wrote in *Emerge.* "Some critics have found Pratt's style and interpretation of the music a bit disconcerting because it doesn't always sound the way they're accustomed to hearing it. The criticism didn't faze him. As far as he was concerned, no two musicians should be able to play the same piece of music exactly the same way. 'If one does completely play, internalizes the music, and comes to terms with it, without concern for how it will be perceived, it's bound to sound different,'" Pratt told Robinson. " 'I want to leave an audience with a sense of what these pieces of music are all about, why the composers were so moved they had to write it down on paper.'" In his interview with *Newsweek's* Chang, Pratt said, "I'll listen to five or six recordings (of a composition), and all the musicians are doing the same thing. And the interpretation will make no sense."

Performed At Many Concerts and Recitals

Initially featured in recitals and concerto performances as a Beethoven interpreter, his concert career took him to New York, Washington, D.C., Chicago, and Los Angeles. He appeared on the September of 1994 PBS television concert honoring Mystislav Rostropovitch, broadcast live from the Kennedy Center in Washington, D.C. A concert appearance at the White House, at the invitation of President and Mrs. Bill Clinton, followed. He would perform again at the White House in 2000. He also began conducting during this time. Concert appearances with major symphony orchestras during the 1994–95 season included performances with the New York and Los Angeles Philharmonic orchestras, the National Symphony Orchestra in Washington D.C., and the Minnesota Orchestra. He also performed with the Atlanta, St. Louis, and Cincinnati Symphony orchestras. Pratt made his debuts at Chicago's Ravinia Festival, Cleveland's Blossom Music Festival, and the Caramoor Music Festival in the summer of 1995.

Pratt had a full and demanding schedule as well during the 1995–96 concert season, including debut appearances as soloist with the Pittsburgh, Detroit, and New Jersey Symphony orchestras and the Buffalo Philharmonic, and return engagements with the Atlanta, St. Louis, and Seattle symphony orchestras. In addition to recital appearances at New York's Lincoln Center and the Kennedy Center, he also made his recital debut in Capetown, South Africa, in December of 1995. On February 23–24, 1996, his tour schedule brought him to Nashville, Tennessee, where he performed the Saint-Saens 4th Piano Concerto with the Nashville Symphony Orchestra.

Following a debut appearance at the Aspen Festival in the summer of 1996, Pratt traveled to Japan for recital and concert appearances in Osaka and Tokyo in September of 1996. His demanding schedule resumed during the 1996–97 season, with engagements with the New York Philharmonic and National Symphony Orchestras and recitals at Orchestra Hall in Chicago, the Dorothy Chandler Pavilion in Los Angeles, and the Tonhalle in Zurich.

Continued to Release Albums

Pratt released another album in 1996. It was an all-Beethoven album of sonatas. His next album, *Live from South Africa,* featured works for piano, was released in January of 1997. He also released *Transformations* in 1999.

Pratt has presented a challenging persona in his visage, his appearance on stage, his manner of addressing his instrument, and in the general aura he projects. He made full use of the tonal nuances and sound spectrum available from his instrument to interpret his varied repertoire. His is a forceful presence; in dreadlocks, he evokes something of the free spirit of one of his favorite composers, Ludwig van Beethoven. He evinces controlled energy, dressing comfortably, often in turtle-neck and slacks and seldom in tuxedo, leaving himself free to marshal and direct his considerable technical abilities for interpreting the music. He sat low, on a specially designed bench, for greater control, directing his energies forward towards his instrument. He offers his audiences fresh approaches and is often rewarded with their enthusiastic praise. As for the music critics, for the most part he has had excellent reviews, with many writers commenting on his stage presence, command of pianistic technique, and his ability to convey both breadth and depth in his interpretations.

Pratt's repertoire has been wide. Centered initially in the German classicists—Beethoven, Mozart, and Bach—he also featured the Romantics and French nineteenth century composers. Principally presented in concert and on records as a piano soloist with orchestra as well as in solo recitals, he has conducted both from the piano and before the orchestra in symphonic works. He has also performed in chamber music programs. His concerts have taken him to four continents to audiences in the major cities of the United States, Europe, South Africa, and Asia. Pratt shows great promise of standing in the forefront of our interpreters of the classical repertoire for the piano.

An unavoidable subtext to Pratt's story is his race. "The number of African-American pianists can be counted on one hand," Robinson pointed out. "Until recently, the best-known black soloists have been Leon Bates and Andre Watts, both of whom had established their careers by the time Pratt was born." Pratt's agent, Linda Marder, told one interviewer it was important for Pratt to be "taken seriously as a concert pianist—not qualified as an 'African-American concert pianist.'" On the other hand, Pratt's race carries with it special opportunities and responsibilities. His audiences, for example, are more racially integrated than most that attend classical concerts. And Pratt regularly plays for and talks about music with minority school children. He also started the Pratt Music Foundation that provides instruments, classes and awards scholarships to students. His goal, Barron wrote in *New York Times,* is "to be a role model for black teenagers, to demystify classical music, and to prove that professional sports are not are only paths to fame." Pratt, meanwhile, sees a day when his race and the superficial differences that set him apart will stop garnering notice—and the attention will focus where it belongs, on his music. "I sort of expect that, in time, all the excess stuff won't be news: the bench, the dreadlocks, the blackness," he told *Barron.* "Not new news. When I wear t-shirts at a performance, that's what makes me comfortable. A tux, that creates barriers."

Selected works

A Long Way from Normal, EMI Classics, 1994.
Beethoven Piano Sonatas, EMI Classics, 1996.
Transformations, EMI Classics, 1999.

Sources

Books

Contemporary Musicians, volume 19, Gale Research, 1997.
Notable Black American Men, volume 19, Gale Research, 1998.

Periodicals

Amsterdam News, September 21, 1996.
American Record Guide 57, September-October 1994.
American Visions, October/November 1994, pp. 48.
Bermuda Royal Gazette, January 24, 1997.
Charlotte Observer, October 1, 1995.
Chicago Sun Times, March 31, 1996.
Crisis 101, July 1994, pp. 49–51.
Detroit Journal, December 12, 1996.
Emerge, February 1995, p. 72.
Nashville Banner, February 26, 1996.
Nashville Tennessean, February 23, 1996; May 28, 1997.

Newsweek, Nov. 25, 1996, p. 79C.
New York Times, February 1995, pp. 244–245.
People, August 17, 1992.
Stereo Review, September 1994, pp. 111–112.

Online

Awadagin Pratt Website, http://www.awadaginpratt.com

Other

IMG Artists Presskit, and 1997 update.

—Darius L. Thieme and Ashyia N. Henderson

Gina Prince-Bythewood

1968–

Director, writer

Though minorities have made footprints in the world of filmmaking, the trails they have blazed are often distorted by the winds of sexism and racism. Women, especially, bear the brunt of this reality. While the filmmaking business is booming, the number of women breaking through in the market is bleak; the pool of African-American women may be even shallower. According to www.sundance.org, while African-American women directed nearly 30 feature films in the 1990s, most of these films were in the independent market, an indication of Hollywood's rejection.

Hollywood has only in recent years begun to accept black films, but it has not yet opened its doors to varied genres. While African-American men like Spike Lee, John Singleton, and the Hughes Brothers have caught the eye and fattened the pockets of big-name studios through their urban stories, Hollywood has all but shunned the scripts written by African-American women. According to www.sundance.org, of the 450 feature films released in 1991, African Americans directed 12; none of them were directed by a woman.

While so many African-American women continue to watch doors slam in their faces, Gina Prince-Bythewood

is doing a stellar job of pushing doors open. With her first feature movie, *Love and Basketball,* Prince-Bythewood managed to become the second African-American woman to have her work produced by a studio; her work also became the top-grossing film ever directed by an African-American woman. Her efforts and recognition led to a path of additional opportunity and made it apparent that Hollywood may be taking a second look.

Prince-Bythewood grew up in Los Angeles and spent much of her time reading. According to *Time,* she was reading 20 books a week at the age of seven—a habit she developed after her family's television broke, only to be replaced eight years later. She attended UCLA and was on the track team but realized she had a desire to direct as a student in UCLA's School of Theater. "[W]hen I was crewing on a student film, I had an epiphany—I wanted to direct. From that moment on, I knew I had to direct. But the first job I got out of school was writing," she was quoted as saying on www.dga.org.

Began Writing for Television

Prince-Bythewood began her career in television, writing

At a Glance . . .

Born Gina Prince on February 16, 1968; married Reggie Rock Bythewood, 1998; one child, 2001. *Education:* UCLA School of Theater, 1991.

Career: Writer/Director. Wrote for *A Different World,* 1987; wrote for *Sweet Justice,* 1994; wrote for *South Central,* 1994; directed *Stitches,* 1991; directed *What About Your Friends,* 1995; wrote for *Courthouse,* 1995; directed *Progress,* 1997; directed *Bowl of Pork,* 1997; directed *Damn Whitey,* 1997; *Felicity;* *Love and Basketball,* 2000; *Disappearing Acts,* 2000.

Awards: Emmy Award nominee *What About Your Friends;* NAACP Image Award recipient, *What About Your Friends;* Humanitas Prize, *Love and Basketball.*

Addresses: c/o Jeanne Williams, ICM, 8942 Wilshire Blvd., Beverly Hills, CA 90211.

for shows including *A Different World, South Central, Sweet Justice* and *Courthouse.* "I would be selected to write from a black woman's perspective on these TV shows; after I got in there I'd prove that I could write for all of the characters," she was quoted as saying on www.uclalumni.net.

Prince-Bythewood spent five years writing for television. During that time she directed the NAACP Image Award winning and Emmy nominated CBS Schoolbreak Special, "What About Your Friends." She also wrote for and co-produced *Felicity* and directed the short film, *Bowl of Pork,* which was dubbed the black Forest Gump, for Def Comedy Jam/HBO.

Despite her accomplishment, Prince-Bythewood found that television limited her creativity, as she had no control over the scripts. "The whole time I was working in television, I kept waiting for someone to hand me a screenplay. I soon realized that I would have to write my first screenplay and get myself my shot," she was quoted as saying on www.dga.org.

Broke Mold with Love and Basketball

After five years of television writing, the self-proclaimed control freak decided to dedicate a year to writing her first full-length film. Her film was a story that captured the relationship of an African-American boy and girl from upper middle-class families who share the dream of playing professional basketball and eventually fall in love. For Prince-Bythewood, getting her script in the door of a studio was a task in itself. "That year turned into

two and everywhere we sent the script, it got turned down," she was quoted as saying on www.dga.org. "...The biggest obstacle I've faced is the marketing of black films. In general, people and film companies look at them as if they're all the same. There's so little diversity in black film," she was quoted as saying on www.uclalumni.net.

Eventually, *Love and Basketball* was accepted into the Sundance Institute Writer's Lab and Director's Lab and released in 2000. Spike Lee produced the film, which starred Omar Epps as Quincy and Sanaa Lathan as Monica. *Love and Basketball,* a $15 million project, grossed $22.5 million, more money than any film produced by an African-American woman.

Prince-Bythewood's success with *Love and Basketball* placed her name on the mantle with other leading women in filmmaking like Julie Dash, who directed *Daughters of the Dust* (1992) and was the first African-American woman to receive national theater distribution, as well as Kasi Lemmons, who directed *Eve's Bayou* (1997).

Recognized for Portrayal of Positive Characters

Prince-Bythewood has made it clear that her goal is to do more than just make movies. "I want the viewer to feel uplifted and hopeful at the end. If it's not a brilliant movie with this sort of message, I don't want to make it," she was quoted as saying on www.dga.org. Critics noted her zest for the extraordinary.

A writer for *Entertainment Weekly* evaluated the movie this way: "The story of Quincy and Monica, their personal clashes and their athletic dreams, breaks away from other sports-themed dramas, thanks to the clarity and dash of Prince-Bythewood's agile directorial style and the exciting originality of the subject. We just haven't seen characters like these before." "Prince-Bythewood gives us a view of a different Los Angeles and characters we don't often see on a screen. Her game is fresh and entertaining on and off the court," a Los Angeles Magazine article stated.

In 2000, the Humanitas Prize Foundation, which presents awards to television and motion picture writers who not only entertain, but enrich their viewing audience, rewarded Bythewood's *Love and Basketball* with a Humanitas Prize. The prestigious award has various categories and is a cash prize that ranges from $10,000 to $25,000. The accomplishments of *Love and Basketball* brought with them another great reality. As quoted on www.sundance.org, film director Bridgett Davis (*Naked Acts,* 1995) said, "the most revolutionary thing an African-American female director can do is to make a second feature, because unfortunately it happens so rarely."

Directed Second Full-Length Film

Almost immediately after her breakthrough success with *Love and Basketball,* Prince-Bythewood beat the odds when she began filming *Disappearing Acts,* an adaptation for HBO of Terry McMillan's novel which tells a love story between a construction worker and an aspiring singer. Ironically, Prince-Bythewood had previously been turned down for the project, but Wesley Snipes production company, Amen Ra, decided to revisit her as a possible director. Prince-Bythewood became the fist African-American woman to direct a McMillan novel, and according to www.dga.org, she prepared for the project by reading the novel version of *Disappearing Acts,* cover to cover, more than 10 times. "I knew the characters, but it was still really hard because this book is many people's bible. When we would hit a snag, we would go back to the book. It was really important to me that the film remained true to the book."

She did, however, deviate from the true character of Franklin Swift, the novel's leading man, played by Wesley Snipes. "I didn't want this to turn into a male-bashing film. I wanted the audience to see both sides," she was quoted as saying on www.dga.org. In order to achieve a balance, Prince-Bythewood deleted some emotional as well as physical violence to make Snipes' character "more sympathetic and less self-destructive," according to *Los Angeles Times.*

Her decision to alter the book slightly did not bother McMillan, who was one of the movie's executive directors. "I was crying like a baby," she told *Los Angeles Times.* "I had to run to the bathroom and compose myself. I finally told everyone, 'I like this better than the book.' It took me back to the memories I had 20 years ago, and made me look at where I am now and what you're willing to go through when you're younger. It's elegant, sexy, gritty and honest. They didn't sugarcoat this the way they usually do in Hollywood."

Prince-Bythewood shares her passion for film with her husband Reggie Rock Bythewood, whom she met while writing for *A Different World* and married in 1998. His television credits include *New York Undercover* and his movie credits include *Get on the Bus.* The Bythewoods recently expanded their union with the birth of a baby, and have hopes of owning a production company that will specialize in promoting black films. According to *Essence,* Prince-Bythewood's next movies include directing an action film.

It is evident that Prince-Bythewood is making her mark as a director of a different breed. On one account, her attitude about actors sets her apart. "On my set, people have to respect the actor's process. I totally respect what actors do. I give them whatever time they need and I never scream out directions from the camera. I take the time to walk up to them personally," she was quoted as saying on www.dga.org.

On another account, her attitude regarding her own work may be a true reflection of what she has in store. "There's a comfort in continually working. But I don't want to end up just being a director for hire. I think my career would suffer," she was quoted as saying on www.dga.org. "I want a career like Carl Franklin's. He hasn't done a lot of films, but all of them have been great films. Like him, I want to do great work." If her track record indicates what is to come, the public is just beginning to see what Gina Prince-Bythewood has to offer.

Sources

Periodicals

Entertainment Weekly, April 28, 2000, p. 76.
Essence, April 2001, p. 26.
Los Angeles Magazine, May 2000, p. 50.
Los Angeles Times, December 3, 2000.
Time, January 24, 2000, p. 68.
UCLA Magazine, November 2000.

Online

www.dailybruin.ucla.com.
www.dga.org.
www.humanitasprize.org.
www.slamdance.com.
www.sundance.org.
www.uclalumni.net.

—Shellie M. Saunders

Busta Rhymes

1972–

Rapper, actor

Elektra executive Sylvia Rhone said of Busta Rhymes in *Billboard*, "You can never underestimate Busta; just when you think you've figured him out, he will surprise you even more." The unpredictable rapper first achieved success as a teenager in the group Leaders of the New School. But it was his 1996 solo debut, *The Coming*, and its lead single, "Woo hah!! Got You All in Check" that catapulted him to stardom. Rhymes has since released three more albums, commenced an acting career, and launched his own record and fashion companies.

Rhymes—born Trevor Smith to a Jamaican mother and U.S.-born father in Brooklyn, New York—moved with his family to the suburbs of Long Island during his adolescence. While his deep, booming voice came from his father, the rapper reported to the *Los Angeles Times*, "when it came down to discipline in my family, the true barker was Moms. That's where my real energetic side comes from." Only after he arrived in "Strong Island," as fellow natives and rap revolutionaries Public Enemy called the borough, did Rhymes began to dream of rhyming. "I was mad small," he recollected in Elektra Records press materials, "but I would start entering rap contests, lip synch contests, anything to show my skills." Fortunately, he claimed, hailing from Brooklyn stood him in good stead, since "Bronx, Brooklyn and Queens was where all the good hip hop was coming from at that time."

Found Mentor in Chuck D.

Rhymes was still in junior high school when he hooked up with another rapper, Charlie Brown. The pair eventually caught the attention of Public Enemy leader Chuck D. as well as the group's producers, Eric Sadler and Hank Shocklee. Sadler and Shocklee—known in the rap world as The Bomb Squad—helped the young Rhymes and his friends to refine their approach. As Rhymes noted in his Elektra Records biography, "Eric used to repeat this phrase to remind us what to concentrate on: C.L.A.M.P., which stood for Concept-Lyrics-Attitude-Music and Performance. He used to say when you get that down to a science, then you'll be there."

Refining this blend took some time, but Rhymes, Charlie, and their friend Dinco D. worked hard on their unison raps and choreography. After adding Rhymes's cousin, Custmaster Milo, as a DJ, they found their identity as Leaders of the New School. With the assistance of Chuck D., the quartet landed a deal with Elektra in 1989. The group's debut album, *A Future Without a Past...*, appeared in 1991 and was hailed by *Spin* as "high-energy hip hop" that "recaptures some of the giddy joys of rap." Their 1993 follow-up, *T.I.M.E.*, also enjoyed critical raves. *The Source* deemed it "a rarity in hip- hop: a sophomore album that's better than the debut," and singled out Rhymes's work for special praise. "Busta get[s] buttnaked and wild," the magazine proclaimed; "he growls, grunts, chants and basically continues to break all musical rules." According to *Los Angeles Times* writer Cheo Hodari Coker, "the group brought a lively energy to its shows and recordings by performing sing-song routines in unison rather than the normal rap pattern of just one or two main voices. The music was accompanied by lively choreographed stomps." The group also appeared as guests on an album by "Godfather of Soul" James Brown.

Rhymes has cited as influences not only old-school funk master George Clinton and rock guitar icon Jimi Hendrix, but some other figures that are, if anything, even more animated. "Secret Squirrel, Tom and Jerry, Courageous Cat," he enumerated in *Spin,* adding some other cartoon favorites: "A lot of the old s—t, too—Popeye, Mighty Mouse. That s—t just stays on at my crib 24 hours [a day]." He was able to demonstrate the range of his own cartoonish funkateer persona after Leaders took a hiatus in 1993. He put in guest appearances with R&B hitmakers Boyz II Men, hip hop explorers A Tribe Called Quest, and many others. "The rapper has proved virtual nitroglycerin as a guest star," noted *Spin* writer Chris Norris.

Rhymes also lent his presence to several films, including the 1993 rap comedy *Who's the Man* and John Singleton's university drama *Higher Learning* (1995). "He was such a scene stealer, " Singleton told *Newsweek* of Rhymes's *Higher Learning* performance. "Busta could be standing there, doing nothing, and when he turns around it's pure energy."

Released Solo Album

Shortly after Leaders of the New School took a break,

Rhymes—a member of the Five Percent sect of Islam—saw the birth of his son, T'ziah. He dedicated his album to the memory of another, now deceased, son, Tahiem, but has not discussed this loss in the press. He spent the next few years in Brooklyn experiencing what he described to *Spin* as "normal, middle-class, standard-living s—t like how I came up." By the time he'd completed his solo album, *The Coming,* T'ziah was three years old and—according to his proud papa—a delight. "That's the coolest age to be around kids," he told *Spin.* "They don't bicker, they're not looking for their moms, they just want to chill." It was the arrival of T'ziah, he insisted in the *Los Angeles Times,* that made the solo effort a necessity "I would never have done a solo record voluntarily," he claimed. "I love the group, and we're still gonna record albums. But now that I've had the chance to flourish and to blossom, I'm gonna capitalize on the best of both worlds."

Working with a variety of producers, Rhymes was able to expand his range on *The Coming.* "Usually when I'm rhyming," reads a quote from his Elektra biography, "I only get to rhyme 16 bars. Here I get to show other things. The record is energized on many different levels, including the Rhymes wild [s—t]." In addition to the massive "Woo hah!!," which was complemented by a frenetic, stylized video that earned heavy rotation on MTV, the album also features "It's a Party," a duet with female soul divas Zhane. Reviews of the album were mixed from a musical standpoint, but tended to celebrate Rhymes's vocal skills. *Rolling Stone* complained that "the mixes are simple, droopy and slow," but added that the rapper's "quavering rips and verbal acrobatics liven up the joint. He hurdles beats and measures in a single bound." Reviewer Eric Berman concluded, "Despite his musical shortcomings, Rhymes is a master MC and one of hip-hop's most jovial and vivid personalities, whose creativity on the mike may give rap a much needed shot in the arm." Coker, reviewing the disc for the *Los Angeles Times,* found it "short on deep themes but long on dazzling displays of rhyme skill." He cited the recording as proof "that there are still compelling hip-hop records to be made without dramatic narratives or weighty social politics."

Rhymes toured behind *The Coming* in an omnibus rap show that also boasted the Fugees, Cypress Hill, and A Tribe Called Quest. He promised a reunion with his LONS mates before long, but in the short time expressed nothing but gratitude. "Every time my voice is recorded," he told the *Los Angeles Times,* "I'm extremely happy. Hip-hop is paying my bills and feeding my family." Rather than cop an "arrogant attitude and mad face," he added, he wanted to emphasize his accessibility: "I want the whole world to feel like they can approach and embrace me."

Rhymes released his second solo album, *When Disaster Strikes,* in 1997. *People Weekly* called his sophomore effort "seriously great" and praised the single, "Put Your

Hands Where My Eyes Could See," for its "tightly controlled and surprisingly subdued stream of unconsciousness." The album earned multi-platinum sales status.

Headed Own Record Label

Rhymes stated his won record label, FlipMode Entertainment, in May of 1998. The FlipMode Squad, a group of which Rhymes was a member, released the label's first album, *Imperial*. Rhymes told *Billboard* that, although "being an artist is my first love," FlipMode Entertainment would allow him "to do things with music that I don't do myself, from alternative to the hottest R&B."

When *Rugrats the Movie* hit the big screen in November of 1998, Rhymes not only contributed to the animated film's soundtrack, but he also took on the role of Reptar Wagon. A month later, Rhymes's third album, *Extinction Level Event (The Final World Front)*, was released. He told *Billboard*, "I had a lot of intense emotional experiences during the recording process, so I recorded it with those emotions in detail." One of Rhymes's chief concerns while making the record was the upcoming millennium. "In every holy scripture," Rhymes told *Entertainment Weekly*, "you find [references] to the significance of this time frame." In particular, Rhymes was worried about the Y2K computer bug. In preparation for possible disaster, Rhymes told *Entertainment Weekly*, "I'm gonna store up on some food, some land, some loot—in particular, gold and silver, because it's probably gonna go back to some trade [s—t]. I'm gonna be ready."

However, Rhymes's fascination with the possibility of armageddon in 2000 was nothing new to fans of his music. "I've always been thinking about time and the end of the century," Rhymes told *Newsweek*. "The first album was called *The Coming*. The second album was called *When Disaster Strikes*. Now afer disaster strikes, it's an extreme level. An extinction level."

Two of the albums highlights—for both Rhymes and his listeners—stemmed from collaborations with Janet Jackson and Ozzy Osbourne. Jackson joined Rhymes on "What's It Gonna Be," and the video for the song received heavy air play on MTV. Rhymes worked with Osbourne on a remake of Osbourne's "Iron Man," which Rhymes called "This Means War." Rhymes had always admired the Osbourne's powerful vocals on that song. "The intensity, the effect," Rhymes told Imusic.com, "it's the same way I approach my [s—t]."

Overall, the album received positive reviews. *Newsweek*'s Veronica Chambers noted, "He heralds doomsday with a danceable beat." *Entertainment Weekly* called it "a characteristically bombastic tour de force." Imusic.com noted that Rhymes "commands the listener's attention . . . unleashing thought provoking verses one minute, and spitting out euphoric hailstones of hectic, teeth clenching rhymes the next."

Also in December of 1998, Rhymes found himself embroiled in legal problems when police discovered a loaded and unregistered gun in his Mercedes. The rapper was charged with criminal possession of a weapon. Rhymes's manager, Gerald Odom, who was also in the car at the time, was arrested for marijuana possession.

Launched Clothing Line

Joining the ranks of other hip-hop stars who have ventured into the fashion industry, Rhymes launched Bushi Designs in 1999. The company's name was derived from the Japanese for warrior—"bushido." Initially, the company produced a line of footwear, but this was soon followed by a line of men's clothes. A women's clothing line was added a year later. Rhymes, along with partner Rashib Boothe, designed all the clothing himself. "Hip-hop is a culture like .. .. any other," Rhymes told *Billboard*. "There's a dress code that goes with the spirit and cultural significance."

In the summer of 2000 Rhymes released *Anarchy*. "This album feels a little more extreme from a personal standpoint," Rhymes told *Billboard*. ". . . because I'm in a place now where I'm comfortable enough to express that level of my creative ability." The personal nature of *Anarchy* was evident in "How Much We Grew." This song chronicles Rhymes's life. "It looks back at the struggle that was so worth going through because of how rewarding it is today," Rhymes explained in *Billboard*. The album also featured a collaboration with Lenny Kravitz entitled "Make Noise."

Rhymes also returned to movie theaters in the summer of 2000, appearing alongside Samuel L. Jackson in *Shaft*. Rhymes played Rasaan, a character who helps Shaft. "I'm pretty much the guy Shaft can't be because he's a cop," he explained in *Jet*. "Shaft has to . . . follow the legal procedure to solve crimes and deal with thugs. Rasaan can assist him in a very unorthodox street way." Also in 2000, Rhymes was featured in *Finding Forrester*, starring Sean Connery. The following year, Rhymes was busy filming *Narc*, an action-packed thriller which starred Jason Patrick and Ray Liotta. Rhymes also signed on to play the Cowardly Lion in a remake of *The Wizard of Oz* for Fox television. In addition, he competed several television commercials for Mountain Dew.

When Rhymes's contract with Elektra Records ended in 2001, he decided to sign with Clive Davis at J Records. "In every area of your life, you grow to a certain level," Rhymes told *Billboard*. "The bottom line is, I don't want to people to just be in Busta Rhymes' business. I want people to be in business with Busta Rhymes. I think J Records will be the machine that can do that." Rhymes's record label became an imprint of J Records.

A man of numerous talents, Busta Rhymes has set himself up to conquer the worlds of music, film, and fashion. Yet, despite his varied interests and abilities, one thing remained constant. Rhymes told *Essence*, "As long as I can represent what I am, which is hip-hop, in whatever genre of entertainment I'm doing, then that's as real as it's going to get with Busta Rhymes. Fake isn't even an option."

Selected discography

(With Leaders of the New School)
A Future Without a Past..., Elektra, 1991.
James Brown, *Universal James* (appears on "Can't Get Any Harder"), Scotti Brothers, 1992.
T.I.M.E., Elektra, 1993.
(Solo)
The Coming, Elektra, 1996.
When Disaster Strikes, Elektra, 1997.
Extinction Level Event (The Final World Front), Elektra, 1998.
Anarchy, Elektra, 2000.

Selected filmography

Who's the Man, 1993.
Higher Learning, 1995.
The Rugrats Movie, 1998.
Shaft, 2000.
Finding Forrester, 2000.
Narc, 2001.
Halloween: The Homecoming, 2002.

Sources

Books

Contemporary Musicians, Vol. 18, Gale, 1997.

Contemporary Theatre, Film, and Television, Vol. 29, Gale, 2000.

Periodicals

Billboard, November 7, 1998; October 2, 1999; May 27, 2000; July 8, 2000; February 24, 2001.
Business Wire, September 7, 2001.
Entertainment Weekly, December 18, 1998.
Essence, November 2000.
Hollywood Reporter, January 29, 2001.
Jet, June 12, 2000.
Los Angeles Times, April 21, 1996; May 26, 1996; July 25, 1996.
Newsweek, November 23, 1998; December 14, 1998.
People Weekly, November 10, 1997; January 18, 1999.
Rolling Stone, May 2, 1996.
Source, November 1993.
Spin, July 1991; August 1996.
Vibe, September 1996.

Online

All Music Guide, http://www.allmusic.com.
IMusic, http://imusic.artistdirect.com/showcase/urban/busta.htm (September 20, 2001).
Internet Movie Database, http://us.imdb.com.

Other

Additional information was provided by Elektra Records publicity materials, 1996.

—Simon Glickman and Jennifer M. York

Run-DMC

Rap group

Widely known as one of the most innovative rap groups to emerge in the 1980s, Run-DMC helped to create a genre that has gained momentum since its inception. Run-DMC's music has been an ongoing influence on most, if not all, of rap and hip-hop. The group has helped to make rap music a profitable and influential part of society.

The middle class New York City borough of Hollis, Queens, was the birthplace of Run, DMC, and their turntable-spinning friend, Jam Master Jay. In the early 1980s, Run started to rap over breakbeats with his school friend DMC. On the advice of Run's brother, Russell Simmons, who had recently co-founded the burgeoning record label Def Jam, Run and DMC began to practice their raps and rhymes in earnest. After they graduated from high school in 1982, Run and DMC invited their friend Jam Master Jay to scratch records on the turntables over which both Run and DMC would trade rhymes. Run's father, however, wanted his son to get a college education, so he enrolled at LaGuardia Community College to study mortuary science. DMC, had also enrolled in college at St. John's University.

In 1983, Run DMC signed a recording contract with Profile Records and released their first single "It's Like That Sucker MCs." They were also managed by Russell Simmons as part of his management company, Rush Management. According to one of their many web sites, "the single sounded like no other rap at the time—it was spare, blunt, and skillful, with hard beats and powerful, literate, and daring vocals, where Run and DMC's vocals overlapped as they finished each other's lines. It was the first new school hip hop recording." "It's Like That" eventually lodged itself in the top 20 of the American rhythm and blues (R&B) chart and sold more than 250,000 copies. This was also where Run DMC's follow up single, "Hard Times/Jam Master Jay," found a home. DMC told *Entertainment Weekly,* "When we made the record, I didn't even tell my parents. . . . But then it got so big, I had to take a leave of absence from school—and I've been absent ever since."

Early 1984 saw the release of two more Run-DMC singles, "Rock Box" and "30 Days." Both of these singles were also R&B hits. The sound of "Rock Box" indicated things to come as the group sought to incorporate the rock sound of the electric guitar in the song. Run-DMC eventually released their self-titled debut album later that same year.

Always striving to break new ground by using different structural elements in their songs, Run-DMC aspired to be the kings of rock music. By 1985, their vision of cross-genre domination was not far from being realized. With the release of their follow up album, *King of Rock,* Run-DMC became the most celebrated, acclaimed, and successful rap group in the United States.

Run-DMC's tremendous success was due, in no small part, to the beats they rhymed over. The once solid divisions between rock and rap music were now starting to break down. The sound of the group was an eclectic mix of solid thumping loops of funky drum beats combined with thunderous heavy metal guitar riffs. The album *King of Rock* spawned a trio of R&B hits which included the title track, "You Talk Too Much," and "Can You Rock It Like This." Also during 1985, Run-DMC made their film debut in the rap movie "Krush Groove."

Made Innovative Song

Run-DMC entered mainstream American music in 1986. Their next single, the top ten R&B smash hit "My Adidas," elevated the shoes in question to hip hop cult status. They also signed a deal with Adidas to promote their sneakers. This was another first the group can claim.

Their third album, *Raising Hell,* unified both rockers and rappers with their cover of the old Aerosmith song, "Walk This Way," with the legendary rock group. Though Run-DMC had to be convinced to include Aerosmith, the release of the song turned out to be one of the most important events in both rap and rock's history. Russell Simmons, one of the song's producers, told *Newsweek,* "To us it wasn't a big deal as the media made it. . . . We made what we thought was a great record." The genre-busting success of the song was clear when it peaked at number four on the pop charts. The success of the single catapulted *Raising Hell* to the number one spot on the R&B album charts, which, at the time, was a first for a rap group. On the pop charts it made it into the top ten and helped to push sales of the album to over a million copies, earning Run-DMC the distinction of having the first rap album to have ever achieved platinum certification. Run-DMC was also the first rap group to have a video aired on MTV. Other hit singles culled from the album included "You Be Illin" and "It's Tricky."

Tougher Than Leather was the 1988 platinum successor to *Raising Hell.* That same year Run-DMC also starred in a movie by the same name. By this time, the climate in rap music had begun to change as the socially savvy raps and rhymes of the street-wise gangsta subgenre and the pop-friendly music of M.C. Hammer and Vanilla Ice started to erode the popularity of Run-DMC.

With the 1990 release of *Back From Hell,* Run-DMC began to incorporate some of the politics of gangsta rappers, but the change of pace failed to ignite album sales. The following year their greatest hits package, *Together Forever,* was released. Run-DMC managed a bit of a comeback with the gold selling 1993 album, *Down With the King.* The title track made it into the top ten of the R&B singles charts. The album also included Run-DMC's first large number of collaborations with some of the most popular and talented artists at the time including Fred Durst, Erick Sermon, Naughty By Nature and Jermaine Dupri.

Beginning of the End?

The group released another album eight years later. *Crown Royal* received mixed reviews from critics. According to *Music Week,* "It's not a masterpiece, but these old masters can show their younger peers a trick or two." While *Rough Guides* stated that the many collaborations wasn't "a pretty sight." The album was plagued with many problems and its release date had been changed numerous times. The album followed the same format as its predecessor, *Down With the King,* but it lacked one thing: DMC. One-third of the group wasn't on most of the tracks. During the making of *Crown Royal* and the promoting of the album, DMC was readying his solo release. His voice also changed and according to *Entertainment Weekly,* "he doesn't identify with much current hip-hop, either sonically or attitudinally." Many have speculated that *Crown Royal* may be the group's last album.

During the 1990s, the group went through many changes personally. Each member began a family, and both Run and DMC had spiritual transformations. Run was ordained as a minister and DMC was ordained as a deacon. Both were active in their churches. Run, who also goes by Rev. Run, published an autobiography, *It's Like That: A Spiritual Memoir,* in 2000. He wrote about how he turned his life around and his special connection to God. *Booklist* said of Run's autobiography, "it captures the innocence of youth and the pain of chaos, and the joy that one can only find through righteous living. This is an epic and absorbing tale from one of the most popular and complex performers of our times."

DMC published his autobiography, *King of Rock: Respect, Responsibility and My Life With Run-DMC,* in 2001. *Booklist* described *King of Rock* as "sharply observed" and "unpretentious." In it he spoke of rap reaching beyond the bling-bling age, which is viewed as destructive by many, and coming to a place of responsibility. The book's introduction was written by another pioneer of rap, Will Smith.

The group is viewed as elder statesman of the rap genre. They have parlayed their success into producing others— Jay has produced a number of other rap groups—and many began using their popularity to sell ads, from the Gap to sports channel, ESPN2. They were also featured on European deejay Jason Nevins' cover of their hit, "It's Like That." The group still perform to sold out concert halls and arenas 15 years after their debut. Fred Durst of rap-metal group Limp Bizkit, told *Entertainment Weekly,* "You can't begin to make hip-hop or hip-hop and rock & roll without feeling everything they've done."

According to Ira Robbins in the *Trouser Press Guide to 90s Rock,* Run-DMC wasn't the first (or even the best) rap group around, but superb rhyming skills, diverse subject matter, artistic integrity, and unprecedented imagination made the Hollis crew early leaders of 1980s rap. The group's use of electric guitar leads and reggae music added to their distinctive sound and helped establish them as pioneers of the rap music genre. Run-DMC was the first rap group to perform on *American Bandstand,* and the first rap group whose video was aired on MTV. They were the first to snag a major product-endorsement deal and they were the first to headline at Madison Square Garden. Many rap, hip-hop and rap-metal artists owe a lot to Run-DMC, who have taken what appeared to be a fad into a part of mainstream society.

Selected works

Singles, albums

"It's Like That/Sucker MCs," Profile, 1983.

"Hard Times/Jam Master Jay," Profile, 1983.
"Rock Box," Profile, 1984.
"30 Days," Profile, 1984.
Run DMC, Profile, 1984.
King of Rock, Profile, 1985.
Raising Hell, Profile, 1986.
Tougher Than Leather, Profile, 1988.
Back From Hell, Profile, 1990.
Together Forever, Profile, 1991.
Down With the King, Profile, 1993.
Crown Royal, Arista, 1999.

Books

(Run)

It's Like That: A Spiritual Memoir, St. Martin's Press, 2000.

(DMC)

King of Rock: Respect, Responsibility and My Life With Run-DMC, St. Martin's Press, 2001.

Sources

Books

American Decades CD-Rom, Gale Research, 1998.
Contemporary Musicians, volume 25, Gale Group, 1999.
Robbins, Ira, ed., *Trouser Press Guide to 90s Rock,* Fireside, 1997.

Periodicals

Booklist, March 15, 2001, p. 1431.
Entertainment Weekly, January 30, 1998, p. 64; July 31, 1998, p. 14; November 1, 1999, p. 129; April 13, 2001, p. 42.
Music Week, March 21, 1998, p. 3; March 31, 2001, p. 24.
Newsweek, June 28, 1999, p. 78.
Publishers Weekly, February 26, 2001, p. 70.

Online

Amazon.com, http://amazon.com
http://home.earthlink.net/tgmoren/rundmc/bio.html (January 24, 1999).
http://sonicnet.com/news/archive/ sto...ZLAACGITUIDIAKCFEQ?id502833 & pid=503778 (January 24, 1999).

—Mary Alice Adams and Ashyia N. Henderson

Deion Sanders

1967–

Professional football and baseball player

Deion Sanders has been a top-ranked athlete since the day he entered high school. Sanders has carried the nickname "Prime Time" with him from his high school days. The name summed up his goal: to be a prime time player—a famous, wealthy, and admired athlete. Playing both football and baseball, Sanders achieved his goal and became the only man to play in both a Super Bowl and a World Series.

Ever since Sanders left Florida State University as the fifth player selected in the 1989 football draft, he has cut a controversial swath across two sports. "Hey, all my life I be the man," he announced in *Sports Illustrated*. "I mean, I've been in the spotlight at *every* level. It's just a bigger spotlight. I learned the system in college. How do you think defensive backs get attention?… They don't pay nobody to be humble. Some people will come out to *see* me do well. Some people will come out to *see* me get run over. But love me or hate me, they're going to come out. I'm a businessman now, and the product is me. Prime Time. I'm the first defensive back to make a million dollars a year. Set a record for a bonus. Cash up front."

Sanders's uninhibited drive for fame led him to adorn himself with gold and bright clothes, drive a fleet of expensive cars, and occasionally quarrel with those who make an issue of his flashy attire. Sanders—the first athlete *ever* to hit a home run in a professional baseball game and score a touchdown in a professional football game in the same week—was not about to apologize for his mode of dress or his opinions.

Deion Luwynn Sanders was born and raised in Fort Myers, Florida. His name was suggested by a cousin, but his mother, Connie Knight, added the extra letters to dress it up a bit. Sanders had little to say about his upbringing in a poor section of Fort Myers, except that athletics saved him from a life of crime. "It would've been easy for me to sell drugs," he remarked in *Esquire*. "But I had practice. My friends who didn't have practice, they went straight to the streets and never left."

Sanders, on the other hand, began scoring touchdowns for the Pop Warner youth league team at the age of eight. He played football, basketball, and baseball in high school, and he liked basketball best. "Let me tell you something," Sanders was quoted as saying in *Esquire*. "The best athletes in the world end up at home on the corner. Oh you bet they do. I call them Idas." He elaborated: "'If I'da done this, I'd be here today.' 'If I'da practiced a little harder, damn, I'd be a superstar.' They'll be standing on that corner till they die telling you all the things they woulda done. I see 'em all the time. Guys who were as fast as me when we were kids."

A Cocky Freshman

Sanders's mother must have had some tense moments worrying about her son despite his athletic ability. When Deion was a teenager he came under the spell of a man he called an "uncle" from "the other side," who was a drug dealer. This glamorous, jewelry-laden man convinced Sanders to stay away from drugs entirely. Sanders

At a Glance . . .

Born Deion Luwynn Sanders on August 9, 1967, in Fort Myers, FL; son of Constance Knight; married Carolyn Chambers (divorced); married Pilar Biggers, 1999; children: (with Chambers) Diondra and Deion, Jr., (with Biggers) one child. *Education*: Attended Florida State University, 1985–88.

Career: Professional football and baseball player. Picked fifth in first round of 1989 National Football League (NFL) draft by Atlanta Falcons; cornerback and punt returner for Falcons, 1989–94; San Francisco 49ers, 1994; Dallas Cowboys, 1995–00; Washington Redskins, 2000–01. Signed with New York Yankees baseball club, 1988; played in minor leagues in Fort Lauderdale and Sarasota, FL, and Columbus, OH; promoted to major leagues in June of 1989; played in less than 20 games with parent team, 1989–90, Atlanta Braves, left-handed hitter and outfielder, 1991–94; Cincinnati Reds, 1994-.

Selected Awards: Jim Thorpe Award for best defensive back, 1988; named Pro Bowl cornerback, 1992.

Addresses: c/o Cincinnati Reds, 100 Riverfront Stadium, Cincinnati, OH 45202.

did not smoke or drink. "See, in my hometown, [drug dealing] was the community job," Sanders recalled in *Sports Illustrated*. "You graduated from high school to the streets and became a drug dealer." Sanders added that he was trying to show youngsters that one can earn the flashy jewelry and trappings of wealth without breaking the law. "Kids from the streets … look up to drug dealers," he said. "But I'm showing them something else…. I'm proving you can do it on the right side."

Sanders was heavily recruited out of high school, and he finally chose to attend Florida State University. In high school he had been a left-handed option quarterback, but in college he switched to defense and special teams. "Anybody can play wide receiver," Sanders explained in *Sports Illustrated*. "I wanted to be special." He wanted to be so special, in fact, that he arrived in Tallahassee, the site of Florida State, in a car with "Prime Time" on the front license plate. He also demanded that his own poster be sold at games.

Such cockiness in a freshman was almost beyond belief, but Sanders began to make his presence felt almost immediately. At six feet and 185 pounds, he proved to be a quick and deadly opponent. During his years at Florida State he scored six career touchdowns on punt or interception returns and was named an All-American two

times. In his last year he led the country in yardage for punt returns with a 15.2 yard average and earned the Jim Thorpe Award as the best defensive back in the nation.

Proved Baseball and Football Prowess in College

Sanders also set records for audacity, both on and off the field. Once, during the halftime show at a game against South Carolina University, he shouted to the fans of the SCU team, which was losing by a wide margin, that they ought to ask for their money back. Another time—in a move reminiscent of baseball legend Babe Ruth—he prepared for a punt return by announcing to the Clemson Tiger bench: "This one's going back!" He proceeded to run 76 yards for a touchdown, then struck a long pose in the end zone. All of this was accomplished at Clemson's field, in front of a hostile crowd.

Sanders's ability was not lost on the professional scouts nor on the sportswriters who cover football. *Sports Illustrated* reporter Albert Kim called the cocky cornerback "one of the best defensive back prospects pro scouts have ever seen." Football, however, was not the only sport Sanders conquered in college. He also played baseball, helping Florida State to advance to the 1987 college World Series—where they finished fifth—and ran the 400 meter for the track team. He was best remembered, though, for his participation in the 1987 Fiesta Bowl, in which Florida State beat Nebraska 31–28. That year, Florida State finished the season ranked second in the nation behind the perennial power, Miami University.

Small wonder, then, that Sanders was picked high in the first round of the 1989 draft by the Atlanta Falcons. The team's management soon discovered, however, that they had more than they bargained for in Deion Sanders. They offered the player $400,000. He asked for $11 million. Needless to say, contract negotiations were lengthy and at times venomous, but Sanders could afford to be patient. In 1988 he had signed with the New York Yankees organization to play professional baseball. By the time he was drafted as a football player he was already being touted as a major league prospect. Indeed, the paperwork with Atlanta was still being revised—in Sanders's favor—when he was called to Yankee Stadium to fill in for an injured outfielder.

Sanders had played in less than 100 professional baseball games when he joined the Yankees in June of 1989. His jump to the big leagues was extraordinary—many top-quality stars spend as many as five years in the minors, and Sanders was there less than a year. Even more remarkable was the attitude Sanders brought with him to Yankee Stadium. He told the media that baseball was, for him, a relief from the hard knocks of football. He played it as a rest from the real work, which he saw as his eventual move to the Falcons. "I've always said I love football and that baseball is my girlfriend," he told *Sports Illustrated* in 1989.

Offered Highest Salary for a Defensive Player

Late in the summer of 1989, the Falcons offered Sanders a $4.4 million contract—salary and bonuses—for five years, the highest sum of money ever offered to a defensive player. Only 24 hours after slugging a home run for the Yankees against the Seattle Mariners, Sanders bid his baseball pals goodbye and headed to Atlanta for his first game as a football pro. His plain-spoken attitude and high salary demands had not endeared him to the Falcons fans, but he soon changed many minds. Five minutes into his first professional game, he ran back a punt for a 68-yard touchdown. No other player—even the much-ballyhooed Bo Jackson—had ever hit a home run and scored a touchdown in professional games in the same week.

By the end of the 1991–92 season Sanders was All-Pro at his cornerback position, appreciated for his ability to defend against the league's surest receivers and for his capacity to intercept and run with the ball. He even saw a few downs in the position of wide receiver, but defense remained his strong suit. With his much-maligned "Prime Time" antics now overshadowed somewhat by the manic behavior of new Falcons coach Jerry Glanville, Sanders helped the Falcons to advance to the NFL playoffs early in 1992 for the first time since 1983.

With the onset of the 1990s, that old "girlfriend," baseball, was calling Sanders to a more serious relationship. Released by the New York Yankees in 1990—he played in less than twenty games with the parent team—Sanders signed a contract with the Atlanta Braves that allowed him to pursue both baseball and football. As a left-handed hitter who could possibly become a switch-hitter, Sanders had real potential on the diamond. He was greatly disappointed to have to sit in the stands and watch the Braves go to the World Series in 1991.

Despite his continued quality play with the Falcons, Sanders expressed a desire to seek a way out of his football contract so he can concentrate on baseball. He expressed in *Sports Illustrated* that the turning point for him was seeing a banner flying from the upper deck of Atlanta's Fulton County Stadium during a Braves game. It read: "Deion, this is your brain," followed by a drawing of a baseball, and "This is your brain on drugs," followed by a drawing of a football. Sanders said: "Best banner I've ever seen. I took it to heart."

During a lengthy negotiation process with the Atlanta Falcons during the late summer and early fall of 1992, Sanders outlined in *Sports Illustrated* what he felt were his choices: "A, play baseball full-time through the World Series and go to football on November 1; B, play baseball during the week, football on the weekends; C, play football only; D, the hell with 'em both, and just go fishing. Well, it looks like B and D are out." In a compromise, Sanders and the Falcons came to an agreement that he would stay with the squad. He missed three football games because of postseason play with the Braves, who eventually lost the World Series to the Toronto Blue Jays.

In baseball and football, Sanders continued to strut on the field, his gold chains flying. His vanity prompted a shaky relationship with the media. After the Braves won the pennant in October of 1992, the player doused CBS reporter Tim McCarver with water three times because the correspondent had criticized Sanders for planning to play for the Falcons and the Braves on the same day. Commenting on his reputation for being an egomaniac, Sanders noted in *Sports Illustrated*, "On the field, I can't help getting excited about what I do. In a white man, that's called confidence. In a black man, that's called cockiness, trash-talking. You can say one thing and be labeled a trash-talker, and a black man can't shake that image. I can't shake that image."

That image, however, slowly began to alter as Sanders became known throughout Atlanta for his charitable donations to children's hospitals and his dream of building an after-school sports program to keep youngsters away from drugs. Sanders and his fiancee, Carolyn Chambers, had a daughter, Diondra. The couple were later married, and had a son, Deion, Jr. When not on the field pursuing one or the other of his professional sports, he lived quietly with his family in Alpharetta, Georgia. "People seem to take the way I perform on my job for the way I am in life," Sanders was quoted as saying in *Sports Illustrated*. "The truth is, I'm a very family- and home-oriented person."

Left Atlanta to Pursue Super Bowl Dream

1994 brought Sanders two career changes. That spring, he left the Atlanta Braves baseball team for the Cincinnati Reds. The change was a positive one. "This is not like a military-run team," Sanders commented to the *Knight-Ridder/Tribune News Service*. "We have a great time. It reminds me of the Falcons. The reporters have been good, the fans are good, the teammates are good. Everything's all good."

In the fall, he signed to play football with the San Francisco 49ers. Turning down more lucrative offers, Sanders agreed to a year-long contract at $1.25 million. For Sanders, the decision was not so much about money, as about his desire to play in a Super Bowl. "I don't think I could have fulfilled that dream in Atlanta," he told *Knight-Ridder*.

Sanders's style and ability were a welcome addition in San Francisco. As *Knight-Ridder* writer S.A. Paolantonio observed, his "sparkling smile and dazzling talent have put the 49ers back at center stage." Paolantonio continued, "He's the Wilt Chamberlain of his time—a performer so complete and dominating that he makes the other players look like they're playing at a lower level."

At the end of the 1994 season, Sanders's dream came true. The 49ers made it to the Super Bowl. But, not only did Sanders get to play in a Super Bowl, he helped the team win.

The following year, Sanders signed a $35 million contract with the Dallas Cowboys. In addition, Sanders decided to take a year off from baseball, in order to concentrate on becoming football's only full-time player to play both offense and defense. "Now we'll see how good I can be," he told *Jet*. "I want to have an impact on both sides of the ball." The close of the 1995 season saw the Cowboys winning the Super Bowl—Sanders had now won two back-to-back Super Bowls.

In 1996 Sanders's wife filed for divorce on the grounds of adultery and, according to *Jet*, "cruel treatment." Several weeks later, though, the couple reconciled and asked the court to dismiss Carolyn's petition. However, their reconciliation did not last, and the couple divorced in 1998.

Returned to Baseball

Sanders returned to baseball and the Cincinnati Reds in 1997. Sanders told the *Sporting News*, "I honestly believe I was born to play football. It's natural for me. Baseball is tougher." And more challenging. He continued, "I know I've never played as well as I wish I could, and I'd like to have a breakthrough year. That means being more patient, getting on base more consistently so I can use my speed. I want to prove some things." Although football was his strength, Sanders was determined to improve his baseball game. He told the *Sporting News*, "I know in football they better not throw it in my zone or I'm going to get it. I want to get that confidence in baseball, too."

Even though his talent as a football player exceeded his ability as a baseball player, his fellow Reds were happy to have Sanders on the team. "We really like the guy," team captain Barry Larkin told the *Sporting News*, "because he is a legitimate good guy and because he brings an energy to a team every day that few players ever have." And Sanders was just as happy with Cincinnati. "This is the only place I want to play," he told the *Sporting News*.

Sanders's hard work and determination paid off. With his 56 stolen bases, he finished the 1997 season ranking 2nd in the National League. Sanders then decided he needed another break from baseball.

As his marriage crumbled, divorce becoming an inevitability, Sanders plunged into a spiritual and emotional darkness. Ready to end the pain, he considered (and attempted, according to some sources) suicide. One night he was awakened by a bright light illuminating his Cincinnati apartment. In that moment, Sanders found God. He turned to Bishop T.D. Jakes, who had counseled Sanders and his wife, for spiritual guidance, and Jakes became Sanders's mentor. Sanders chronicled his conversion in the 1998 book *Power, Money, & Sex: How Success Almost Ruined My Life*.

With his new-found religious conviction, Sanders began attending weekly Bible study meetings with the Dallas Cowboys, becoming, according to the *Knight-Ridder/Tribune News Service*, "a sort of spiritual ringleader for these weekly gatherings." Utilizing his trademark charm and flamboyance, Sanders sent out a weekly call over the loudspeaker, asking the team to attend the lunch-time meetings. Usually 15 or 20 teammates gathered each week. Sanders explained the importance of the weekly meetings to *Knight-Ridder*: "Some guys are bleeding inside. . . . Some are on the brink of suicide, who are hurting, in pain, don't even want to go home after practice. You don't know what they're dealing with. A lot of people don't even care. They just see them as a commodity. You (the media) see them as an interview. I see them as something different than that."

New Wife, New Life

In 1999 Sanders married Pilar Biggers, a model and actress. The wedding was held on Nassau's Paradise Island, with Bishop T.D. Jakes officiating. "Pilar is a good woman with Christian values and has helped me rebuild the shattered pieces of my life," Sanders told *Jet*. "Miracle of miracles, I am alive and in love again!" The couple's first child was born in 2000.

Sanders was cut from the Dallas Cowboys in 2000 for salary cap reasons. Days later, he signed as a free agent with the Washington Redskins. The seven-year contact provided a $56 million paycheck. "It's wonderful to be a Redskin," Sanders told *Jet*. "They've always had something special. There's nothing like these fans, this tradition." A year later, however, Sanders decided to retire from football altogether.

Many could not believe Sanders's decision. Darren Hambrick, linebacker for the Cowboys, told the *Dallas Morning News*, "How could the godfather of all corners just walk away?" Darren Woodson agreed, telling the *Dallas Morning News*, "He has a lot more game in him. I know that." But Sanders's decision was final. However, he had not spent much time thinking about what he would do now that he had retired. Sanders told the *Dallas Morning News*, "The only thing I know for sure that I'm going to do is fish until there are no more fish in the lake."

Sources

Books

The Complete Marquis Who's Who, Marquis, 2001.

Periodicals

Associated Press (wire reports), October 10, 1992; October 12, 1992; October 17, 1992; October 18, 1992.

Atlanta Constitution, September 15, 1989; October 19, 1989.

Dallas Morning News, July 28, 2001; July 29, 2001.

Esquire, June 1992; October 2000.

Jet, March 11, 1996; October 7, 1996; October 14, 1996; August 3, 1998; June 14, 1999; June 26, 2000.

Knight-Ridder/Tribune News Service, June 20, 1994; September 14, 1994; October 1, 1994; November 26, 1994; December 3, 1998;

Oakland Press (Oakland County, MI), August 1, 1992; September 20, 1992; October 10, 1992; October 12, 1992; October 17, 1992; October 18, 1992.

Publisher's Weekly, October 26, 1998.

Sports Illustrated, June 12, 1989; November 13, 1989; April 27, 1992; August 24, 1992.

Washington Post, June 4, 1989.

Other

Additional information obtained from *Atlanta Braves 1992 Media Guide*.

—Mark Kram and Jennifer M. York

Shaggy

1968–

Reggae singer

Characterized historically by political and spiritual lyrics and a serious attitude, the Jamaican musical tradition of reggae has been difficult to bring to widespread popularity with fun-loving American audiences. Yet Shaggy, with two huge hits and several successful album releases in the 1990s and early 2000s, accomplished just that. A quick and talented writer, he created a style that was rooted in Jamaican dance traditions but displayed a pop sensibility and a sense of humor that endeared him to ordinary music fans in the United States and beyond.

Shaggy was born Orville Richard Burrell in Kingston, Jamaica, on October 22, 1968. His nickname referred to his long hair and came from the hippie-like character by that name on the children's cartoon *Scooby Doo*. After growing up in Jamaica's violent central city, Shaggy left at age 18 for the Flatbush neighborhood in Brooklyn, New York, where his mother was already living and working as a medical secretary. Attending high school just as rap music was exploding in popularity, he found that his skills at Jamaican-style "toasting," a style that in fact was one of rap's forerunners, put him in high demand.

After graduating from high school Shaggy grew dis-

couraged with his prospects in Brooklyn and joined the U.S. Marine Corps in 1988. Trying to keep a hand in the reggae recording scene, he drove long hours into the night between New York and his Marine base in North Carolina. With the outbreak of the Gulf War in 1991 he was sent to Iraq. The experience sharpened his ambitions, and he made profitable use of the long waiting periods required of the U.S. forces by writing a stock of new songs. But he was also a keen observer of the war's slightly surreal aspect. "It was wild," he told *Time*. "The atmosphere was kind of like *Three Kings*," a 1999 film that starred actor George Clooney.

Back in New York at the war's end, Shaggy released several singles on small independent labels that did well in New York's numerous reggae clubs. The most successful of them, "Oh Carolina," was a remake of a pre-reggae classic of Jamaican pop, by a group called the Folkes Brothers, which in turn drew on U.S. soul music sources. Shaggy's version inventively incorporated samples of the original song. "Oh Carolina," recorded while Shaggy was still in the Marines, was released in Great Britain by the larger Greensleeves label, topped pop charts there and in several other countries, and was in turn picked up

At a Glance . . .

Born Orville Richard Burrell on October 22, 1968 in Kingston, Jamaica; grew up in Kingston; moved at age 18 to New York City, where his mother worked as a medical secretary. Took nickname "Shaggy" from *Scooby Doo* television cartoon program. *MilitaryService*: U.S. Marine Corps.

Career: Reggae/hip-hop/pop vocalist. Recorded singles that gained exposure in New York reggae dance clubs, late 1980s and early 1990s; "Oh Carolina" topped reggae dance charts; signed to Virgin International label and released debut album, *Pure Pleasure,* 1993; released second album, *Boombastic,* 1995; released third album, *Midnite Lover,* 1997; appeared on soundtrack of film *How Stella Got Her Groove Back* in duet with Janet Jackson, 1998; signed to MCA label; released *Hot Shot,* 2000; became first reggae artist since 1991 to top U.S. pop charts with single "It Wasn't Me," 2001.

Awards: Grammy award for Best Reggae Album, for *Boombastic,* 1995.

Addresses: *Agent*–The Agency Group., Ltd., 1775 Broadway, Suite 433, New York, NY 10019.

by the major Virgin International label. That led to the release of Shaggy's debut album, *Pure Pleasure*, in 1993.

Shaggy kept his momentum with his sophomore release. *Boombastic,* released in 1995, reunited him with the New York reggae DJ Shaun "Sting" Pizzonia, who had produced his earliest dancehall efforts. The title track of *Boombastic* became another international hit and also cracked open the doors of the U.S. market for the artist; the album received a gold record for sales of 500,000 copies, appeared on pop, rap, and R&B charts in the United States, and remained atop *Billboard* magazine's U.S. sales chart for a record 30 weeks. *Boombastic* earned Shaggy a 1996 Grammy award for Best Reggae Album.

Shaggy's third album, *Midnite Lover,* was released in 1997. An ambitious outing, it attempted to cover perhaps too many bases. The album contained various single-ready tracks tailored for U.S. urban radio play, but the artist also felt the need to reestablish his credibility with the dancehall reggae hard core. "We showed on this album that I can do whatever Beenie Man or Buju Banton are doing," Shaggy told *Billboard.* Despite strong initial support from the Virgin label the album went nowhere, and Shaggy was dropped from Virgin's roster. "They saw me as a guy bringing them a couple of hits, not

somebody building a career," Shaggy lamented in conversation with *Time.*

Without a record label and losing the spotlight to younger artists, Shaggy seemed to be on a downward slide. However, as he told *Ebony,* "the lesson that I have learned from my mother that has stayed with me through today is perseverance. Absolutely. That has played into my music, my career—not giving up." Shaggy kept on composing new material and making new contacts, and before long he landed a spot on the soundtrack of the film *How Stella Got Her Groove Back,* with a soundtrack helmed by the durably successful urban pop producers, Jimmy Jam and Terry Lewis. Quickly writing a song ("Luv Me Luv Me") to their specifications, Shaggy ended up recording the tune with megastar Janet Jackson on chorus vocals.

That song reached upper chart levels, and as a result the MCA label, which had released the soundtrack, signed Shaggy to a new contract and released his album *Hot Shot* in 2000. On that album Shaggy discarded all pretensions to reggae authenticity. "My album might be disputed by purists as not reggae enough, but I want it to be eclectic and crossover," he told *Time.* "To hell with categories." Co-writing all but one of the tracks on the CD, Shaggy succeeded brilliantly in his aims, crafting a radio-friendly urban-American sound with a perfect hint of Jamaican inflection that set it apart from a crowd of hip-hop-oriented competitors. *Hot Shot* contained a new version of "Luv Me Luv Me" and an energetic club number, "Dance and Shout," that sampled Michael Jackson's music.

But the album's most successful composition was "It Wasn't Me," which dominated the listening selections of Americans (and others) of all backgrounds through much of late 2000 and early 2001. In the song, Shaggy gives advice to a friend who has been caught by his girlfriend "red handed creeping with the girl next door." Though the friend has been seen in a variety of compromising positions throughout his living space (including the bathroom floor), Shaggy tells him to maintain steadfastly that "it wasn't me." Naughty but not mean-spirited, the song fit perfectly with Shaggy's genial sense of humor. With "It Wasn't Me," Shaggy became the first reggae artist to top the U.S. pop singles charts since Shabba Ranks in 1991.

Time speculated that the song's success might even be enough to kick off a new U.S. reggae craze: "So when you hear Madonna and Britney Spears singing to a reggae beat a year from now, remember, it all started with Shaggy," instructed writer David E. Thigpen. As for Shaggy himself, he began to reap rewards from his long years of creative persistence. Spending much of his free time with his two young sons, he maintained a home in Kingston, Jamaica, as well as one in New York. "There's nothing more I want to accomplish," he told *Ebony.* "I just want to create and make great music."

Selected discography

Pure Pleasure, Virgin International, 1993.
Boombastic, Virgin International, 1995.
Midnite Lover, Virgin International, 1997.
Hot Shot (contains "It Wasn't Me"), MCA, 2000

Sources

Books

Chang, Kevin O'Brien, and Wayne Chen, *Reggae Routes: The Story of Jamaican Music,* Temple University Press, 1998.

Contemporary Musicians, volume 19, Gale, 1997.
Larkin, Colin, ed., *The Virgin Encyclopedia of Reggae,* Virgin, 1998.

Periodicals

Billboard, April 29, 1995, p. 16; August 2, 1997, p. 9.
Ebony, May 2001, p. 116.
Jet, February 26, 2001, p. 64.
Time, February 19, 2001, p. 75.

Online

All Music Guide, http://allmusic.com/.

—James M. Manheim

Cheryl Shavers

19(?)(?)–

Scientist

Cheryl Shavers discovered what she wanted out of life from a young prostitute she knew only as "Miss Ann." Shocked by Miss Ann's murder, Shavers resolved to break out of her poor neighborhood and pursue a career in science. Her drive led her higher and higher on the corporate ladder, through a series of savvy career moves, until she was the highest-ranking black woman at Intel Corp. and one of Silicon Valley's most prominent female leaders. In 1999, she was named Under Secretary of Commerce for Technology at the Department of Commerce under the Clinton administration.

Cheryl Shavers was raised by her mother in a two-room apartment in a predominantly black neighborhood in South Phoenix, Arizona. Shavers's mother, who never completed high school, worked as a maid and picked cantaloupes to support Shavers and her older sister. Her dream for her daughters was that they graduate from high school and grow up to work in air-conditioned offices.

When she was a girl, Shavers sewed her own clothes and knew to hide with her family when the rent collector came looking for the rent. She learned both what she did and did not want her life to be through "Miss Ann," a young neighborhood prostitute in an abusive relationship. Shavers and her friends befriended Miss Ann. They recycled bottles for her and gave her the money every Friday. One Friday, Miss Ann did not show up. After promising her mother she wouldn't look, 13-year-old Shavers peeked from behind the curtains of the family's apartment and watched, fascinated, as forensic techni-

cians in white lab coats investigated the scene of Miss Ann's murder. "I got into science from that," she recalled in an interview with the *Arizona Republic*. "I was hooked, I knew that was what I wanted to do," she was quoted as saying in *Rocky Mountain News*. "And, today, I'm grateful to Miss Ann, for showing me a direction I didn't want to take."

Miss Ann's death prompted Shavers to seriously consider her future, and she decided she had to escape her impoverished neighborhood. "I knew how to get out because I could read and I had to get out because the environment was dangerous," Shavers told the *Knight-Ridder/Tribune Business News*. After graduating from South Mountain High School, Shavers studied chemistry on a scholarship at Arizona State University.

As a student, Shavers got a chance to fulfill the curiosity she developed while watching the crime-scene forensic scientists as a girl. She secured an internship at Phoenix's crime lab. There, she helped develop a procedure to separate blood enzymes from cloth. Soon after, the technique provided proof in a murder conviction. She also got what she considers her first dose of discrimination. For no reason, the lab director ordered Shavers to don a janitor's uniform and wash police cars. She walked away from the internship—and forensic chemistry—after that. "That experience taught me about making decisions and to just keep going but to always maintain your dignity," she told the *Arizona Republic*.

At a Glance . . .

Baised in Phoenix, AZ; married: Joe Agu, 1984; daughter: Cecily. *Education:* Arizona State University, B.S., Chemistry, 1976; Arizona State University, Ph.D. in solid state chemistry, 1981.

Career: Chemist, technical and business expert. Product engineer, Motorola c. 1976; registered patent agent, Library of Congress, U.S. Patent & Trademark Office of the Department of Commerce, Washington, D. C., 1984-; process engineer, Hewlett-Packard; microelectronics section manager, Wiltron Company; thin films applications manager, Varian Associates; general manager of advanced technology operation in the Technology and Manufacturing Group, Intel Corp.; Under Secretary of Commerce for Technology, U.S. Department of Commerce, c. 1999; chairperson, BitArts, 2001-; chairman and CEO, Global Smarts, Inc., 2001-.

Memberships: U.S.-Israel Science and Technology Commission (USISTC); Board of Directors, U.S.-Israel Science and Technology Foundation; Co-chair, Technology Subcommittee under the U.S.-Egypt Partnership for Economic Growth; Technology Committee, U.S.-China Joint Management Committee, and the U.S.-Japan Joint High Level Committee.

Awards: inducted, International Network of Women in Technology Hall of Fame, June 1996; awarded honorary master's degree in engineering management, California Polytechnic State University, 1996; selected, Arizona State University College of Liberal Arts & Sciences (CLAS) Leader, 1996; inducted, College of Liberal Arts and Sciences Hall of Fame, Arizona State University, 1997; Presenter of the Year, San Francisco Bay Area Chapter of the National Black MBA Association, 1998; Henry Crown Fellow, Aspen Institute, 1998.

Addresses: *Office*—c/o Global Smarts, Inc., 3333 Bowers Avenue, Suite 130, Santa Clara, CA 95051.

Shavers was recruited on campus at Arizona State by Motorola, Inc. for a program that exposed recent graduates to the semiconductor industry. She took the job after earning her bachelor's degree in chemistry in 1976 and worked at Motorola as a product engineer, specializing in discrete device applications. After she earned her Ph.D. in solid state chemistry from Arizona State in 1981, Shavers worked at Hewlett-Packard Co., which turned out to be a "turning point in her career," according to *Knight-Ridder/Tribune Business News.*

At Hewlett-Packard, Shavers worked as a process engineer. Her supervisor there was an extremely traditional man who chose customary methods over the innovative, production-increasing ones Shavers suggested. Frustrated, she transferred to Hewlett-Packard's legal department as a patent agent, where she was bored by the monotony. It was at this point that Shavers considered leaving the semiconductor business altogether. She began to feel that she wasn't being allowed to grow by old-fashioned bosses who were uncomfortable with women in technology. "I decided then that this was my career and I needed to own it," she told the *Knight-Ridder/Tribune Business News.*

Inspired, she strove to educate herself about every aspect of the semiconductor manufacturing business, and she left Hewlett-Packard. She went on to work for the Wiltron Company, a start-up, as a manager of its microelectronics section, and for Varian Associates, where she was thin films application manager. Finally, Shavers landed at Intel Corp., a major manufacturer of computer microprocessors. She moved swiftly up through the company. By knowing when to compete and when to collaborate with coworkers, she worked her way up to managing her own division. Working 55 hours a week probably didn't hurt. She became the highest-ranking black woman at Intel Corp. and one of Silicon Valley's most prominent female leaders. "Cheryl is smart, articulate, and driven," Charlene Ellis, a vice president at Intel told the *Arizona Republic.* "If she walks into a closed door, she will figure out how to get another one open."

Shavers shared the lessons she learned about successfully climbing the corporate ladder in a weekly column in the *San Jose Mercury-News.* In it, she gave career advice and answered such questions as how to deal with a younger boss and when to go back to school or change jobs. During the two-and-a-half years she wrote the column, Shaver formed her own five-point personal work code: 1.) no one owes her a living, 2.) she is realistic about her work environment and co-workers ("a bunch of nerds," she told the *Arizona Republic*), 3.) she does not allow her insecurities to influence her actions; she creates a plan to win, 4.) she values people for their accomplishments, and 5.) she takes risks. Shavers also is a valued speaker and is the author of several articles and other publications.

In 1999 President Bill Clinton named Shavers Under Secretary of Commerce for Technology at the U.S. Department of Commerce. In the position, Shavers was responsible for helping create federal science and technology policy and programs. She oversaw the Commerce Department's Technology Administration and the Office of Technology Policy, as well as the National Institute of Standards and Technology (NIST), the National Technical Information Service, and the Office of Space Commercialization. She served as senior advisor to the Secretary of Commerce in forming new policies and program initiatives in the areas of science and technology. She also was the Department of Commerce's representative to the National Science and Technology Council's Committee on National Security, the Committee on International Science, Engineering and Technology and the Committee on Technology, and helped coordinate the Clinton Administration's Partnership for a New Generation of Vehicles program. While at the Department of Commerce, Shavers was a member of the U.S.-Israel Science and Technology Commission (USISTC) and Technology Subcommittee under the U.S.-Egypt Partnership for Economic Growth (co-chaired by Vice President Gore and President Mubarak). She also participated on the U.S.-South Africa Science and Technology Committee, U.S.-Russia Science and Technology Committee, U.S.-China Joint Management Committee, and the U.S.-Japan Joint High Level Committee.

In 2001, BitArts, a UK-based digital-security start-up company, hired Shavers as its chairperson. The company develops programs to protect software from piracy. Shavers believed the company would set new standards in the industry. Shavers is chairperson and CEO of Global Smarts, Inc. a "technology globalization enterprise that specializes in integration of capital, technology, and information across national borders," according to her Website. She also hosts a radio show that addresses technological and societal issues.

Sources

Periodicals

Arizona Republic, May 30, 1999, p. D1.
Financial Times, February 28, 2001, p. 14.
Government Computer News, December 13, 1999, p. 6.
Knight-Ridder/Tribune Business News, July 8, 1996.
Rocky Mountain News, May 11, 2001, p. 3B.

Online

Cheryl Shavers Homepage, http://www.cshavers.com (May 30, 2001).
Technology Administration Homepage, http://www.ta.gov (May 30, 2001).
Women in Technology International Homepage, http://www.witi.com (May 30, 2001).
CLAS Alumni Newsletter, http://clasdean.la.asu.edu/CLASNews/Fall97/Pg14.jpg (July 19, 2001).
Dr. Shavers on the Radio, http://www.drshavers.com (August 3, 2001).

Other

Additional information was provided by Dr. Shavers, 2001.

—Brenna Sanchez

Norman "Turkey" Stearnes

1901-1979

Negro League baseball player

One of the brightest stars in the Negro Leagues for more than twenty years, outfielder Norman "Turkey" Stearnes turned a unique playing style into a tool for greatness. Complementing his dynamic skill at the plate and finesse in the field, Stearnes led by example with a dignified, almost regal model of behavior. By successfully bridging those elements, Stearnes' induction into the Major League Baseball Hall of Fame in 2000 finally put the formal and official stamp of respect on his career that Stearnes so richly deserved.

Stearnes was born on May 8, 1901 in Nashville, Tennessee. He joined his first professional team, the Montgomery Grey Sox of the Negro Southern League, in 1921, when he was twenty years old. According to the Negro League Baseball website, Stearnes was a "fleet-footed power hitter with an unusual batting style." On the website, former teammate Jimmie Crutchfield described Stearnes as a "quirky-jerky sort of guy who could hit the ball a mile. Turkey had a batting stance that you'd swear couldn't let anybody hit a baseball at all. He'd stand up there looking like he was off balance. But, it was natural for him to stand that way, and you couldn't criticize him for it when he was hitting everything they threw at him." Equally as odd was the way Stearnes circled the bases, allegedly with his arms flailing, earning him the nickname "Turkey."

The lefthander parlayed such an unusual style into an outstanding ability. Unfortunately, it was during an American era where the success of African-American baseball players lived in the shadow of white culture. Stearnes

played professional baseball from 1921 to 1942. For half of that career, he roamed centerfield for the Detroit Stars. Stearnes hit 140 home runs and had a .352 batting average in his time with the Stars. He also led the league in home runs six times during his tenure. His statistics in the 1920s and 1930s clearly rivaled, if not surpassed, those of white big leaguers. In the 1920s, he hit better than .360, winning the league batting title four times.

Following his stint with Detroit, Stearnes joined the Chicago American Giants in 1932, where he played for several seasons. There, he earned four appearances in the East-West All-Star fame, not to mention the inaugural All-Star game in 1933. Stearnes later moved to Philadelphia where, he hit higher than..360 again. He returned to Detroit for the 1937 season, where he had a ..383 batting average and added yet another All-Star appearance.

Stearnes traveled from team to team throughout his twenty-year career. In addition to Detroit, Chicago, and Philadelphia, Stearnes also played for the Nashville Elite Giants, the Memphis Red Sox, the New York Lincoln Giants, the Kansas City Monarchs, Cole's American Giants, the Detroit Black Sox, and the Toledo Cubs.

Quick of foot in the field and relentless at the plate, Stearnes not only impressed audiences, but earned the respect and adulation of Negro League teammates and opponents. Fellow league players remembered Stearnes as a great player, but one with a certain amount of quirks. "He was a peculiar guy," former teammate Ray Sheppard told the *New York Times*. "He was a loner. He didn't run

At a Glance . . .

Born Norman Stearnes on May 8, 1901, in Nashville, TN; died September 4, 1979, in Detroit, MI; married Nettie; children: Rosalyn Stearnes Brown.

Career: Baseball player. Signed with the Montgomery Grey Sox, 1921; played outfield for the Detroit Stars, 1923–31; signed with the Chicago American Giants, 1932; signed with the Philadelphia Stars, 1933; returned to Detroit Stars, 1937; also played for the Nashville Elite Giants, Memphis Red Sox, New York Lincoln Giants, Kansas City Monarchs, Cole's American Giants, Detroit Black Sox and the Toledo Cubs.

Awards: Three-time Negro League All-Star; four batting titles; led the Negro League in home runs six different times; inducted into Baseball Hall of Fame, 2000.

with anybody or fool around or drink. You couldn't use his bat or glove. Sometimes he didn't want a locker by you." Negro League Hall of Famer William Johnson said in the *New York Times*, "Stearnes was very particular about his bat. If he made out, he'd sit there holding it and talking 'I hit that good,' he'd say." Johnson added, "I believe sometimes he carried that bat to bed.'"

If his unusual demeanor with fellow ballplayers branded him "peculiar," his on-field prowess impressed some of the Negro League's best players. Batting for .340 or better throughout a career will do that. In the *New York Times* Negro League legend and Hall of Famer Satchel Paige described Stearnes as "one of the greatest hitters...as good as anybody." At pitchblackbaseball.com, Negro League Star Ted "Double Duty" Radcliffe compared Stearnes to James "Cool Papa" Bell: "Everyone knows that Cool Papa Bell was the fastest man. But Cool Papa Bell couldn't field with Turkey Stearnes. He was faster, but Turkey Stearnes was one of the best fly ball men." And even Bell himself had high praise for the left-handed hitting Stearnes. "If they don't put him in the Hall of Fame, they probably shouldn't put anyone in," Bell was quoted as saying in the *New York Times*.

Not only was Stearnes a talented baseball player, but he also possessed limitless patience. Stearnes was a star athlete in a time when the white-only major leagues enjoyed the nation's love and admiration. White professional players did so in large and lush baseball parks, before thousands of adoring fans and for, at that time, a handsome salary. Negro Leaguers played on dirt fields, traveling from city to city, sometimes as part of a circus-like show, just to get an audience. And while their play was equal, if not superior to the white players, their efforts were often lost on the general public. For some,

this might be grounds to harbor a grudge, to become bitter or angry at the powers that would stunt the impressive abilities of the equally capable black players. But not Stearnes. "He wasn't bitter," Jerry Green wrote in the *Detroit News*. "There were a lot of things he didn't like, but he wasn't bitter ... He loved baseball. He talked about baseball all the time. He was quiet and reserved. Whenever we had a conversation, it became baseball."

And while he loved to talk baseball, Stearnes, despite his on-field success and the ability to hit the home run, was a humble creature. "I never counted my home runs," Stearnes was quoted as saying on the UAW website. "If they didn't win a ball game, they didn't amount to anything. . . . That's what I wanted, to win the game."

Stearnes took his love for baseball well into his retirement. Stearnes left the game in 1942—after batting 181 home runs in 903 games and earning a batting average of .352—and took a job at a Ford plant that same year, at the age of 41. Stearnes become a fixture in the outfield bleachers at Tiger Stadium, often sitting with fans and doing what he loved the most: talking baseball. "I sit in the bleachers," Stearnes told the *New York Times*. "I know a lot of boys and I have fun out there with them. We talk. We discuss things without fighting." And of the game itself? Stearnes told the *New York Times*, "It's a good game. It's the best game known. You go to see it, you'll like it." Stearnes died on September 4, 1979, in Detroit.

Twenty years after his death, the Michigan State Senate petitioned the Hall of Fame to consider Stearnes for induction. State Senator Joe Young Jr., as quoted on the Michigan State Senate website, said, "He was a spectacular athlete." In the spring of 2000 baseball's Hall of Fame Induction Committee announced that Stearnes' plaque would go into the Hall, alongside the game's greatest players.

Sources

Periodicals

The Detroit News, July 20, 2000
The New York Times, July 23, 2000, pg. 27.

Online

www.negroleaguebaseball.com/1999/September/
    turkey_stearnes/html.
www.pitchblackbaseball.com/nlomturkeystearnes.html.
www.uaw.org/solidarity/00/0600/front07.html.
www.senate.state.mi.us/dem/PR/12–01-99.html.

—John Horn

Angie Stone

1965–

Vocalist

Though the era of classic soul vocals reached its peak in the 1970s, it lived on into the twenty-first century in the voice of Angie Stone. Around the year 2000 a group of vocalists, predominantly female, turned to older soul and R&B styles in order to express various musical ideas, but it was Stone who evoked the pure vocal sounds of the pre-hip hop era. Releasing her debut solo album at the age of 35, Stone outsold many of the artists half her age who had begun to dominate the U.S. musical scene.

Stone was born in Columbia, South Carolina, around 1965. A strong gospel influence in her mature vocal style resulted from her singing gospel music at the city's First Nazareth Baptist Church and by attending gospel concerts with her father, a member of a local gospel quartet. In high school Stone was a standout basketball player (her father was also a fine football player). She received several offers of college basketball scholarships. But Stone, who had written poetry since she was a girl, hoped for a musical career; standing in front of her bedroom mirror she would lip-synch whole concerts to recordings of soul vocalists such as Aretha Franklin and Marvin Gaye.

Stone broke into the music business as a rap artist—which

was ironic since her music would later be seen as offering an alternative to a hip-hop-dominated urban radio mainstream. In New York in the early 1980s, she joined with two other women to form the Sequence. That group landed on the roster of the pioneering rap label Sugarhill, and they are generally regarded as the first female act in the rap genre. Stone, who was known as "Angie B," delivered raps in such Sequence dance-club hits as a remake of Parliament's "Tear the Roof Off."

Statuesque and strong, with a large Afro hairstyle that she has retained throughout her career, Stone had a look that was little influenced by the high-fashion inclination of many urban artists. "I loved Pam Grier. Cleopatra Jones," she told *Rolling Stone*. "Strong, beautiful, dark-skinned women. Pam had the Afro, the strong 'I'm beautiful, but I'm bad and I'll take it there.'" But as with many of the other acts of rap's first generation, the popularity of the Sequence did not last. For a time, Stone supported herself by singing commercial jingles.

Recorded Budweiser Jingles

"I did Afro Sheen," she told *Rolling Stone*. "Budweiser,

too. Budweiser ran for eight years, and I'm gonna tell you something: That stuff really pays well, because it really helped me survive when I was in transition with my career." But Stone's creative side didn't take long to reassert itself. A prolific songwriter, she began to work with other rap acts, such as the group Mantronix and the innovative rocker Lenny Kravitz. By 1988 Stone had formed an R&B trio, Vertical Hold, that incorporated more of her own affinity for the classic style of soul vocals and enabled her to emulate such models as Aretha Franklin, Marvin Gaye, and Donny Hathaway.

Vertical Hold's records bubbled around the lower end of *Billboard* magazine's urban music charts for several years, and in 1993 the group released a self-titled CD. One dance number from the album, "Seems You're Much Too Busy," rose into the top 20, and several other singles made an impression, but that wasn't enough to propel the group to an ongoing recording career. Stone's family began to doubt her chances for success. "My mom used to say, 'If God had meant you to make it, then you'd have made it by now,'" she told the London *Daily Telegraph.* But Stone continued with her songwriting, numbering among her collaborations those with soul veteran Al Green and modern R&B hitmaker Mary J. Blige.

One collaboration in particular proved both personally and professionally fruitful. Stone contributed songs to the recordings of D'Angelo, whose 1995 debut album *Brown Sugar* is often credited with kicking off the neo-soul musical phenomenon, and who remains the most significant male representative of the style. Stone placed four

tracks on D'Angelo's critically acclaimed 2000 release, *Voodoo,* which incorporated a host of modern influences into a basic soul context, and she and D'Angelo became romantically involved. The relationship resulted in a child, Michael, but after three years Stone and D'Angelo called it quits.

As Stone assembled material for her own debut release, *Black Diamond,* she was sometimes dogged by publicity connected to her relationship with D'Angelo, who remains a strong draw for female crowds. In conversation with the *St. Louis Post-Dispatch* she imitated the question she often faced: "Isn't that the lady that had D'Angelo's baby?" Nevertheless, she and D'Angelo remained friends; he contributed guest vocals on *Black Diamond* (as did Lenny Kravitz), and he continued to influence Stone musically.

Stone offers her own explanation for the preponderance of female vocalists in the neo-soul movement. "Our men are frustrated," she told the *Daily Telegraph.* "That's why you hear all that anger [in hip-hop music]. They feel it's the only way they can make themselves heard. We are able to tolerate more, and in any culture women will always take on that motherly role. We caress and comfort our men through song, because we understand how bruised they are."

Released Solo Debut

In her mid-thirties in late 1999, an age when the careers of many urban contemporary vocalists are on a downward trajectory, Stone released her solo debut on the Arista label. *Black Diamond* was a creative triumph. Gaining momentum over several months, the album, and its lead single, "No More Rain (In This Cloud" (co-written by Stone and based on a phrase she had often heard her father say), stayed on the charts for more than 30 weeks. The album spawned a successful tour which, unlike those of Stone's neo-soul rivals Macy Gray and Jill Scott, attracted predominantly African- American crowds. *Billboard* named *Black Diamond* its 2000 album of the year.

Part of the reason for the album's success was that it intelligently updated classic soul with samples and other manifestations of hip-hop techniques. Paying homage to such vocalists as Gladys Knight through samples (Knight's "Neither One of Us" is heard in "No More Rain (In This Cloud)", Stone also drew on the 1970s funk styles of Rufus and other bands (the hard-edged vocals of Rufus frontwoman Chaka Khan are another influence on Stone's style). Yet it was Stone's voice that made the greatest impression. Clearly reflecting her gospel origins, it exuded a raw power of a kind not often heard in the increasingly electronics-dominated world of urban music.

"Real soul singers have used hip-hop beats as a crutch for too long now," Stone told the London *Daily Telegraph.*

"My music stems from the church, and in church there are no limits to where music can take you." Stone emphasized a religious message in her concerts and in the liner notes to *Black Diamond.* Those notes said that the album represented "a woman's life, all the ups and downs, the trials and tribulations, and the joys." After 20 years of trials in the music business, Angie Stone had earned the right to a few joys.

Selected discography

(with The Sequence) *The Sequence,* Sugarhill, 1982.
(with Vertical Hold) *Vertical Hold,* A&M, 1993.
Black Diamond, Arista, 2000.

Sources

Periodicals

Billboard, April 8, 2000, p. 27.
Daily News (New York), April 24, 2000, p. 46.
Daily Telegraph (London, England), April 6, 2000, p. 27.
The Observer (London, England), February 27, 2000, p. 10.
Rolling Stone, March 16, 2000, p. 31.
St. Louis Post-Dispatch, February 21, 2000, p. C2.
Washington Post, May 5, 2000, p. C3.

Online

All Music Guide, http://www.allmusic.com

—James M. Manheim

Billy Strayhorn

1915-1967

Jazz composer

Called "a nearly invisible genius" by Scott Yanow of the *All Music Guide* but an immensely important figure in jazz history, Billy Strayhorn spent much of his career as an associate of jazz composer and bandleader Duke Ellington. Strayhorn was the composer of several vocal numbers performed and recorded by Ellington's band, including "Take the 'A' Train" and "Lush Life," that went on to become familiar jazz standards widely known to pop fans as well; he was also a classically trained musician who was a crucial contributor to the large concert compositions that Ellington undertook later in his career.

Ellington, for his part, wrote in his autobiography *Music Is My Mistress* that Strayhorn was "my right arm, my left arm, and the eyes in the back of my head." Strayhorn further enjoyed a career apart from Ellington's group, and on top of all this he might be viewed as a pioneer in the emergence of gay culture in the United States. Among the most important of the many behind-the-scenes figures who have lubricated the musical interactions of the intensely collaborative jazz genre, Billy Strayhorn was one of jazz's most sophisticated musical thinkers.

Born William Strayhorn in Dayton, Ohio, on November 29, 1915, Billy Strayhorn was known simply as Bill during his years as a serious student of classical music in school. His father was an industrial worker and sometime janitor, and his family bounced around under difficult circumstances for much of Strayhorn's early childhood. In 1920 they landed outside Pittsburgh, attracted by the employment possibilities of the steel mills there. Strayhorn was often sent to Hillsborough, North Carolina, to visit his maternal grandmother, a church pianist who introduced him to music.

But it was in high school in Pittsburgh that Strayhorn's musical talents really began to blossom. Attending Westinghouse High School, Strayhorn at first studied classical music exclusively. "Billy was about as serious as they get," recalled Westinghouse music teacher Carl McVicker (who later taught jazz keyboardist Ahmad Jamal) to Strayhorn biographer David Hadju. "Earnest, hardworking, wanted to get ahead in music . . . He was an intellectual. . . . He was a serious pianist and concentrated strictly on the concert repertoire."

Toward the end of his high school years, Strayhorn performed two piano concertos with full symphony orchestra, and his classical training perhaps shows through

At a Glance . . .

Born William Strayhorn November 19, 1915, in Dayton, OH; died of esophageal cancer May 31, 1967, in New York; son of James Strayhorn, a factory worker, and Lillian Young Strayhorn. *Education:* Westinghouse High School, Pittsburgh; attended Pittsburgh Musical Institute.

Career: Jazz composer, arranger, and pianist. Composer and small-group jazz player, Pittsburgh, mid-1930s; composed song "Lush Life," 1936; hired as arranger, lyricist, and pianist, Duke Ellington Orchestra, 1939; composed numerous songs for Ellington Orchestra during ASCAP strike, early 1940s; compositions include "Take the 'A' Train," "Rain Check," and "Passion Flower"; collaborated with Ellington on orchestral compositions including *Far East Suite,* 1950s and 1960s.

in the complex harmonies found in some of his compositions. In the 1930s, however, the doors of the classical music world were largely closed to black musicians. Strayhorn persisted, taking courses at the Pittsburgh Musical Institute, but soon it became clear that more promise lay in a different direction. He composed a musical revue called *Fantastic Rhythm,* which had its beginnings in a high school senior-class presentation but expanded into a full-fledged professional show, and around the same time friends introduced him to the serious-minded jazz of pianist Art Tatum and other artists who saw jazz as a complex art music, rather than simply as accompaniment for dancers.

Hired by Ellington

Strayhorn's talents as a jazz composer and arranger grew quickly, and one of his most famous songs, "Lush Life," was completed in 1936. Although the song is generally identified with Duke Ellington, that was well before Strayhorn joined Ellington's organization. By December of 1938, when Ellington visited Pittsburgh, Strayhorn was ready to make the most of the opportunity of meeting him. Impressing the bandleader with letter-perfect renditions of (and even suggestions for improvement upon) some of his piano solos, Strayhorn was hired at first, early in 1939, as a lyricist and arranger. Ellington accurately predicted that the partnership would last a lifetime.

A 1941 power struggle between U.S. radio broadcasters and the American Society of Composers, Authors, and Publishers (ASCAP) had the side effect of inaugurating one of Strayhorn's most fertile periods as a songwriter; the songs of Ellington himself, an ASCAP member, were withheld from radio, so Ellington turned to the non-member Strayhorn for new vocal compositions. Several of the pieces Strayhorn produced in 1941 and 1942 became pop standards, including "Rain Check, "Chelsea Bridge," and "Passion Flower," but the most famous of all, "Take the 'A' Train," was initially discarded by Strayhorn as too similar to the style of rival bandleader Fletcher Henderson. Ellington's brother Mercer retrieved the song from a trash can, and it went on, in both vocal and instrumental arrangements, to become the Ellington Orchestra's signature. Many of Strayhorn's more than 100 songs were extremely sophisticated and complex, well suited to the treatment they later received from avant-garde jazz artists such as John Coltrane.

Collaborated on Orchestral Works

In the years after World War II, as the interests of young American dancers shifted from big-band swing toward rhythm-and-blues and rock and roll, Ellington aimed more often to create large concert works of a semi-classical nature—an enterprise that was of course very comfortable for the classically oriented Strayhorn. The two composers worked together on adaptations for the Ellington Orchestra of such classical works as Tchaikovsky's *Nutcracker Suite* and on original compositions in the same vein, such as the acclaimed *Far East Suite.* Part of the impetus for the interest in Strayhorn's work that grew in the decades after his death was the realization that Ellington was more than just a jazz artist; he was one of the most significant American composers for orchestra, and Strayhorn contributed a great deal to what Ellington accomplished.

Despite his long association with Ellington, Strayhorn maintained an independent career. He recorded several albums as a jazz pianist, composed a series of musical shows for a benevolent association in New York's Harlem neighborhood that were major events in the uptown social season, and wrote songs for vocalist Lena Horne. Horne had a romantic interest in Strayhorn, but got nowhere owing to Strayhorn's homosexuality—which was, unlike that of almost every other creative artist of his day, openly practiced. Some have speculated that Strayhorn was willing to stay largely behind the scenes with Ellington because his secure place in Ellington's organization gave him the chance to be honest about his sexual orientation. Late in life Strayhorn contributed music to a never-realized theatrical presentation based on the works of the gay Spanish playwright, Federico Garcia Lorca.

Stricken with cancer of the esophagus, Strayhorn died on May 31, 1967. A deeply shaken Ellington wrote (as quoted by Strayhorn biographer David Hadju) that "the legacy he leaves, his *oeuvre,* will never be less than the ultimate, on the highest plateau of culture." Although at the time Strayhorn was rarely numbered among the pantheon of jazz greats, fellow musicians were well aware of his importance and had paid tributes to him by recording albums of his compositions even before his death. Ellington's own tribute, entitled *And His Mother Called Him Bill,* was released as a memorial to Strayhorn's career and is considered one of his finest pieces of work by jazz critics.

Selected discography

Historically Speaking: The Duke, Bethlehem, 1956.
The Billy Strayhorn Septet, Felsted, 1958.
Live!, Roulette, 1958.
Billy Strayhorn/Johnny Dankworth, Roulette, 1958.
Cue for Saxophone, Verve, 1959.
The Peaceful Side, United Artists, 1961.
Lush Life, Red Baron, 1964.
The Billy Strayhorn Songbook, Concord Jazz, 1997

Sources

Books

Collier, James Lincoln, *Duke Ellington,* Oxford University Press, 1997.
Contemporary Musicians, volume 13, Gale, 1995.
Hadju, David, *Lush Life: A Biography of Billy Strayhorn,* Farrar Straus Giroux, 1996.
Tucker, Mark, ed., *The Duke Ellington Reader,* Oxford University Press, 1993.

Periodicals

Down Beat, September 1996, p. 10.

Online

All Music Guide, http://www.allmusic.com.

—James M. Manheim

Guy Torry

19(?)(?)—

Actor, comedian

Born in St. Louis, Missouri, Guy Torry has become famous not only as a stand-up comedian, but also as an actor playing parts in movies such as *American History X* and *Pearl Harbor.* But with all the success Torry has seen since his entry into the entertainment world, he never planned on becoming an actor. Attending first the Visual and Performing Arts High School and then Southeast Missouri State University, Torry majored in Marketing. He planned on staying in Missouri and settling down to work there, but before doing that Torry decided to travel and eventually move west to see another part of the world before he got so embroiled in everyday life that he didn't have the time.

When he moved to Los Angeles, Torry followed in his older brother's footsteps, fellow actor Joe Torry, and tried his hand at entertaining. He landed a job on the television show *Martin* where he so impressed the show's executives that he eventually ended up writing a few episodes for the series. He next appeared in roles on *NYPD Blue, The X-Files,* and *Sparks.* From there he went on to became part of the stand-up comedy team in Russell Simmons's *Def Comedy Jam,* on HBO, even touring with the group when they performed across the country. Later he was brought in to write for three seasons of the show. Torry has also written for television shows like *Minor Adjustments* and *Moesha.*

In 1994, after the Los Angeles riots, according to the Break TV website, Torry "created a weekly showcase for upcoming comedians known as *Phat Comedy Tuesdays* at L.A.'s Comedy Store." The show became so popular that not long after the show commenced famous comedians were continually contacting Torry to ask to be part of the show. Torry spent a lot of time getting the *Phat Comedy Tuesdays* up and running, finally putting his Marketing degree to good use. About all the work he put into the comedy show Torry told the *St. Louis Post-Dispatch,* "I do it because I want it to be done right. I want to give an opportunity for comics to show their talent. It's a blessing for me to be here and I want to help others."

Torry returned to acting in 1996, appearing in such films as *Don't Be a Menace to South Central While Drinking Your Juice in the Hood* and *Sunset Park.* He then won roles in *Back in Business,* (1997), *One Eight Seven* (1997), and 1998's *Ride.* He caught Hollywood's eye, however, with his role of the gentle laundryman Lamont in *American History X,* starring opposite Edward Norton.

At a Glance . . .

Born in St. Louis, Missouri. *Education*: Visual and Performing Arts High School; Southeast Missouri State University, B.S., Marketing.

Career: Actor. Television guest appearances: *Martin*, 1992; *NYPD Blue*, 1993; *The X Files*, 1993; *Sparks*, 1996; tv mini-series: *The 70s*, 2000; tv movies: *Introducing Dorothy Dandridge*, 1999; film appearances: *Sunset Park*, 1996; *Don't Be a Menace to South Central While Drinking Your Juice in the Hood*, 1996; *The Good News*, 1997; *One Eight Seven*, 1997; *Back in Business*, 1997; *American History X*, 1998; *Ride*, 1998; *The Strip*, 1999; *Trippin'*, 1999; *Life*, 1999; *Pearl Harbor*, 2001; *The Animal*, 2001; *Don't Say a Word*, 2001; *Tara*, 2001; writer: *Martin*; *Def Comedy Jam*, HBO; *Minor Adjustments*; *Moesha*.

Addresses: *Agent*—William Morris Agency, 1325 Ave Of The Americas Fl 15, New York, NY, (212) 586–5100.

In this 1998 film Torry played an inmate in a jail who becomes friends with a neo-Nazi skinhead, played by Norton, and helps him change his racist views. With real-life skinheads on the set, however, Torry found his working environment rather tense. "Some of those skinheads couldn't wait to say the N-word," Torry told E Online. "Even before they called action, they were saying *Nnnn*. I said, 'Quit saying it now.' And they said, 'We're just warming up.'" But the tension didn't affect Torry's performance. According to a biography on the William Morris Agency website, "Torry received rave reviews for his work in the film, being singled out by publications such as *Daily Variety, Entertainment Weekly,* and *New York Magazine,* who referred to him as 'marvelous,' 'scene-stealing,' and 'superb.'"

In 1997 he was seen in the half-hour comedy show *Good News,* a show centering on a gospel church. Here he played Little T, a choir member and church porter. In 1998 Torry was the host of the successful comedy tour *The Kings of Comedy*. The troupe was seen in 52 cities and featured comedians like Steve Harvey, Bernie Mac, and Cedric the Entertainer. *The Kings of Comedy* was so popular that it actually sold out at the Radio City Music Hall in New York City. From there he was also seen on the television action drama series *The Strip,* which was produced by Joel Silver, the same man who produced *Die Hard* and *Lethal Weapon*. He played opposite Sean Patrick Flannery as a policeman. He also had a part in the television movie *Introducing Dorothy Dandridge,* in 1999.

Also in 1999 Torry appeared in two movies: *Life,* alongside Eddie Murphy and Martin Lawrence, and *Trippin',* a comedy about a high school senior who is constantly getting swept up in amusing fantasies. He was next seen in the NBC mini-series *The '70s*. His co-stars included Brad Rowe, Vinessa Shaw, and Amy Smart; the four played friends who attended Kent State University together and spend the next ten years exploring the world and discovering their places in it. *Variety* said of the mini-series, "[T]hese are four realistic lives played out by adept actors…each actor is supremely suited to play each role."

In 2001 Torry was seen in the movie *The Animal,* produced by Adam Sandler. He played alongside Rob Schneider as a man who complains that, he thinks, he gets preferential treatment because he's black. "It was fun to learn from cats like Rob and Adam," Torry told E Online. "The biggest thing I learned," Torry continued," is to trust in smart writing. If it's there on the page, just go with it. A lot of times as comedians and actors, we try to bring in our own flavor—which is cool—but you got to learn to mix it with what's already on the page." E Online called Torry's performance charming and said of him, "[I]f you haven't heard of this Guy yet, you probably will soon."

Also in 2001 Torry portrayed a Navy pilot alongside Cuba Gooding, Jr. in the movie *Pearl Harbor*. He got a little more out of this role than he expected, he told E Online, "I was supposed to jump out of the way as this missile comes through the ship, but it brought the whole set with it. I got out of the way just in the nick of time. I knew something was wrong, so the expression they got on my face was real." Also in 2001, Torry appeared alongside Michael Douglas in suspense thriller *Don't Say a Word*. He also supplied the voice for Will in Nickelodeon's animated series *As Told By Ginger,* and Hugo in HBO's animated *The Steadfast Tin Soldier*. Torry has also devoted much time building his own production company, Phat Lyke Dat Productions.

But even with his busy schedule Torry has still found time to perform at comedy clubs around the country, including The Comedy Store, The Improv, The Comedy Act Theater, The Fun House, The Punchline, The Laugh Factory, and others. A multi-talented performer, the entertainment world can definitely expect great things of Torry in the future.

Sources

Periodicals

Daily Herald (Arlington Heights, IL), May 12, 1999, p. 19.
Dallas Morning News, October 12, 1999, p. 1C; April 30, 2000, p. 3.
Entertainment Weekly, November 6, 1998, p. 51; April 9, 1999, p. 78.
The Florida Times Union, April 3, 1998, p. D-12; June 29, 1999, p. C-6.
The Fresno Bee (Fresno, CA), March 24, 2000, p. E3.

The Seattle Times (Seattle, WA), May 12, 1999, p. C3; June 1, 2001, p. H30.
Variety, April 24, 2000, p. 36.

Online

Break TV, http://www.breaktv.com/nbc/70s_guy.html.

E Online, http://www.eonline.com/Celebs/Who/gt.tml.
Just Call Ivan, http://www.justcallivan.com/events.html.
http://mrvideo.vidiot.com/UPN/GN/.
William Morris Agency, http://www.wma.com/Music/ adult_contemporary/Guy_Torry.htm.

—Catherine Victoria Donaldson

Gabrielle Union

1973–

Actress

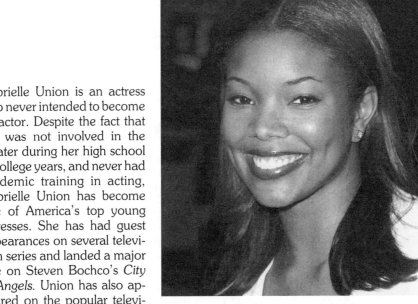

Gabrielle Union is an actress who never intended to become an actor. Despite the fact that she was not involved in the theater during her high school or college years, and never had academic training in acting, Gabrielle Union has become one of America's top young actresses. She has had guest appearances on several television series and landed a major role on Steven Bochco's *City of Angels.* Union has also appeared on the popular television show *Friends*, portraying an African-American character involved in a romantic relationship-a first for that particular show. After appearing on several television shows, Union tried her hand at acting for the big screen. After playing some minor roles in several well-received movies including *Ten Things I Hate About You* and *She's All That,* Union was cast as a major character in movies such as *Bring It On* and *The Brothers.* Since the beginning of her acting career, in 1996, she has had a steady stream of acting jobs that have revealed her integrity and talent.

Disillusioned in College

Union was born on October 29, 1973 in Omaha, Nebraska, but was raised in Pleasanton, California.

Though the small town was populated by mostly white people, Union's mother made sure that Union and her siblings learned about their Black heritage. As a high school student Union was a member of several sports teams, including basketball, soccer, and track.

After finishing high school, Union attended the University of Nebraska, where she was a member of the soccer team. However, her Pleasanton background caused friction between her and other African-American students. She endured harassing phone calls because other students felt "she was too friendly with white students," according to *Savoy* magazine.

After one semester, Union transferred to Cuesta College in southern California. She only lasted a semester before returning home. Disillusioned and full of self doubt, Union found work at the local Payless Shoe Source. Though most of her friends worked there, this store would be the place where Union would go through one of her most painful moments.

One night, while Union was closing the store with another woman, a man entered and pulled out a gun. He cleaned out the register and forced Union into a storage

At a Glance . . .

Born on October 29, 1973, in Omaha, Nebraska. *Education*: Attended University of Nebraska; Cuesta College; UCLA, sociology.

Career: Began as model; actress. TV: *Moesha,* 1996; *Malibu Shores,* 1996; *Saved By The Bell,* 1996; *7th Heaven,* 1996-99; *Goode Behavior,* 1996; *Sister, Sister,* 1997; *Star Trek: Deep Space Nine,* 1997; *Guys Like Us,* 1998; *Clueless,* 1999; *Grown Ups,* 1999; *ER,* 2000; *The Others,* 2000; *Zoe, Duncan, Jack & Jane,* 2000; *City of Angels,* 2000; *Friends,* 2001; TV movies: *H-E Double Hockey Sticks,* ABC, 1999; Films: *She's All That,* 1999; *10 Things I Hate About You,* 1999; *Switch,* 1999; *Love & Basketball,* 2000; *Bring It On,* 2000; *The Brothers,* 2001;*Two Can Play That Game,* 2001.

Awards: Black Reel Award for Best Supporting Actress (Bring It On), 2001.

Addresses: c/o Sutton, Barth, and Venari, 145 S. Fairfax Avenue, suite 310, Los Angeles, CA, 90036

area where he raped her. He laid the gun down next to her and once he was done, asked her to hand the gun to him. Union grabbed it and tried to shoot him but the gun jammed. Her rapist then beat her into a bloody mess. Police later discovered that Union's attacker had been employed at another Payless and had actually robbed other Payless stores and raped another woman. Union sued Payless for not informing its employees of the robberies and won. She then began the long road to recovery. She also encourages other rape victims to overcome their experience and move on with their lives.

Began Modeling for Money

She later transferred to UCLA, where she graduated with honors, earning a degree in sociology. In her junior year, Union, who at that time was contemplating law school, took a modeling internship to cover some of her college expenses. Modeling naturally led to acting. Union explained to Jeffrey Epstein of *E! Online*: "I didn't want to act. I thought is was a cheesy profession-but when I was a junior, I got an internship at a modeling agency. When my internship ended, they said, 'We'd be interested in representing you. I was like, 'If you think someone will pay me to be cheesy, sure, whatever'!" Her first modeling job was for *Teen Magazine* and her first television roles were on *Saved By The Bell* and *Moesha*, both in 1996. She has also appeared on such shows as *Dave's World*

and the *Steve Harvey Show,* and also had a recurring role on *7th Heaven.*

Although Union initially regarded acting as "cheesy," she eventually ended up taking the profession very seriously. Union, who uses the set as her "acting class," admitted to *Venice* magazine's B. Jade Landry, "I used to feel like a fraud, and I would have this urge to act, but it just looked so forced." However, professionals did not view her as a fraud. For example, actress Jenifer Lewis told Gabrielle, "Whatever it is that you're doing is so completely honest, don't change a thing," she recalled to *Venice.* Furthermore, Union is known for paying attention to detail and is not afraid to ask questions of other actors. Before filming *Bring It On,* where Union plays the captain of an inner-city cheerleading squad, she and her "team mates" went off to cheerleading camp. Although Union was a cheerleader in eighth grade and an active athlete during high school, she finished the cheer camp smelling of Ben-Gay and with a new respect for the young men and women who are on cheerleading teams. Before playing surgical resident, Courtney Ellis, on *City of Angels,* Union made attempts to visit some hospitals. However, after the entire cast witnessed a death in a South Central L. A. hospital, she instead studied other medical shows on television and also talked with the medical consultant hired by the *City of Angels.*

Union modeled herself after veteran actors that she admired. Interviewer B. Jade Landry wrote, "One thing about Gabrielle—she doesn't find soul in the hoopla of stardom. She wishes to make her mark as a lady of authority and independence, worthy of carrying herself in the manner of her mentor, screen goddess Diahann Carroll." As a young girl, Union loved to watch Carroll on the dramatic television series, *Dynasty.* A fan of Carroll's, Union studied other parts that Carroll has played, including her role as a Vietnam widow and single mother who worked as a nurse in the television series, *Julia,* that aired before Union was born. Discussing Carroll with *Essence* magazine, Union said, "She has never compromised herself on screen—ever. From *Julia* to *Dynasty.*" In a review of *The Brothers* in the *Los Angeles Times,* Union's style was compared to the "pluck, gravitas, and beauty of actress Alfre Woodard."

The Hollywood environment is extremely competitive, with numerous actors vying for the few available roles. Although there are even fewer roles for minority actors, Union does not accept any offers without careful consideration. When Union was asked to play the role of a "love interest" on *Friends,* she hesitated, but her peers urged her to accept take the role, arguing that her participation in this popular show would lead to opportunities for other minorities. Union accepted the offer and had a very positive professional experience. She was particularly impressed by the professionalism of *Friends* cast members David Schwimmer and Matt LeBlanc. Union told *Venice* magazine, ". . . it was a huge deal for minorities because if felt as if we finally got asked to the dance—and we were able to dance."

Union, whose favorite past-time is an impromptu game of flag football with some friends in an empty lot rather than an athletic field, is engaged to Chris Howard, a running back for the Jacksonville Jaguars. Describing Howard as the down-to-earth type, she remarked that what really attracted her to him was the fact that he has his own Scrabble board and Boggle game. In 2000, E!Online's Epstein asked Union what she wanted to do next—"I want to be Miss USA or Miss America. I would bring the trophy back to Nebraska. My interests are agriculture and corn. Hey, I'm just riding this train as long as I can. As long as I am having fun I'll do it. When it stops being fun, I'll try something else. Maybe I'll open up a chain of Popeye's Chicken."

Selected filmography

Films

She's All That, 1998.
10 Things I Hate About You, 1999.
Love and Basketball, 2000.
Bring It On, 2000.
The Brothers, 2001.

Made For Television Movies

H-E-Double Hockey Sticks, ABC, 1999.

Television Series

Moesha, 1996.
7th Heaven, 1996–99.
Saved By The Bell, 1996.
Star Trek: Deep Space Nine, 1997.
ER, 2000.
City of Angels, 2000.
Friends, 2001.

Sources

Periodicals

Essence, April 2001.
Savoy, February 2001.

Online

E!Online, www.eonline.com/Celebs/Who/gu.html
Venice Magazine, www.angelfire.com/celeb/unionfan/articles/Venice.htm
http://celebs.absolutenow.com/gabrielle_union/Biography.html
http://www.reelimages.com/txt_features/conversations/conversation_with_gabrielle_union/html

—Christine Miner Minderovic

Hosea Lorenzo Williams

1926–

Civil rights activist, politician

Hosea Williams—research chemist, ordained minister, and politician—is best known for his activities during the Civil Rights Movement of the 1960s, when he worked closely with Martin Luther King, Jr. Williams, whom King called "my [Cuban strategist Fidel] Castro," supervised voter registration in hostile areas, led many dangerous marches, and was arrested more than 100 times. His wife and two of his children were also arrested during civil rights campaigns. On March 7, 1965, Williams led the infamous "Bloody Sunday" march in Alabama, when the demonstrators were brutally beaten by state troopers. A 1965 issue of *Ebony* magazine recognized Williams as "always on hand when the going is rough."

After King was assassinated, Williams became involved in mainstream politics, as a state representative for Georgia (1974–85), Atlanta city councillor (1985–90), and DeKalb [Georgia] county commissioner (1990–94). Throughout his political career, he continued to fight for civil rights, using King's method of direct action. In 1987, Williams led a march to all-white Forsyth County, Georgia, where counter-demonstrators threw rocks and bottles while shouting racial slurs. In 1996, Williams organized a march to the state capitol to protest the current Georgia flag, which incorporates the Confederate flag.

Williams, a controversial figure, has always maintained a high public profile, though not all the publicity has been positive. He has been arrested more than 30 times for traffic offenses, and twice has been sentenced to jail terms for leaving the scene of an accident. "Largely because of his discipleship under Dr. King, and partly because of his knack for being outrageous, Mr. Williams has remained in the flash and glow of the news media for 30 years," Bert Roughton, Jr. wrote in the *Atlanta Journal-Constitution (AJC)*. The same publication quoted David J. Garrow, who wrote a Pulitzer Prize-winning history of the Civil Rights movement, as saying, "The problem is, Hosea's post-1968 credibility has not developed well."

Hosea Williams was born on January 5, 1926, in Attapulgus, Georgia. His mother, a blind woman, died giving birth to Williams's sister, leaving the children to be raised by Turner Williams, their grandfather. As a child, Williams never knew his father, who was also blind; the two met for the first time once Williams was fully grown.

At the age of 14, Williams left the farm where he had been raised, walking with a friend to Tallahassee, where

At a Glance . . .

Born on January 5, 1926, in Attapulgus, Georgia; died on November 16, 2000 in Atlanta; married Juanita Terry; children: Barbara, Elizabeth, Hosea II, Andre, Yolanda, and four adopted children. *Education:* Morris Brown College, B.A.; Atlanta University, M.S. *Religion:* Protestant.

Career: Ordained clergyman; science teacher, 1951–52; U.S. Dept. of Agriculture, research chemist, 1952–63; *Chatham County Crusader,* publisher, 1961–63; SCLC, special projects director, 1963–70, national program dir., 1967–69, regional vice president, 1970–71; natl. executive dir., 1969–71, 1977–79; Poor People's Union of America, organizer, 1973; Martin Luther King Jr. People's Church of Love, leader, 1973-; Southeast Chemical Manufacturing and Distributing Co., founder, 1976. Georgia State representative, 1974–85; Atlanta City councillor, 1985–90; De Kalb County commissioner, 1990–94.

Memberships: Phi Beta Sigma, National Order of Elks and Free and Accepted Masons, SCLC, NAACP, Disabled American Veterans, Veterans of Foreign Wars, American Legion, Natl. Science Society, Georgia's Voter League, Amer. Chemistry Soc., Natl. Committee of Black Churchmen, Natl. Democratic Party.

Awards: Most Courageous Leadership in the Freedom Movement Award, NAACP, 1960–61; Ten Years of Satisfactory Service Award, U.S. Dept. of Agriculture, 1961; Cause of Freedom in the Tradition of True Democracy, GA State-wide Registration Committee and SCLC, 1963; SCLC National Affiliate of the Year Award, National SCLC Conf., 1963; Chapter of the Year Award, Atlanta Chapter SCLC, 1973; Civil Rights Leader of the Year Award, Black Media Inc., 1975; Community Action Agency Award, Tuskegee, Ala., 1976; Essence Award, *Essence* Magazine, 2000.

he got a job washing dishes in a bus station. Three years later, he returned to his grandparents' farm and unsuccessfully tried running it, but the farm failed. When World War II began, he enlisted in the U.S. Army, eventually becoming staff sergeant. He was wounded by shrapnel in Germany and spent 13 months recuperating in a hospital in England.

While racism was less blatant in the United States military and in Europe, Williams was forcibly reminded of the color line once he returned to the South. On his way back to Georgia, he was beaten up after he drank from a "white" water fountain in a bus station. In Georgia,

Williams returned to school, earning his high school diploma when he was 23. He went on to study chemistry at Morris Brown College in Atlanta. After graduating with a B.A. at the age of 27, he taught science at a segregated high school in Douglasville, Georgia. In 1952, he took a job as a research chemist at the U.S. Department of Agriculture in Savannah, Georgia, a job he held until 1963. During that time, he also became an ordained minister. In the early 1950s, Williams married Juanita Terry. The couple would have five children of their own—Barbara Jean, Elizabeth LaCenia, Hosea Lorenzo Williams II, Andre Jerome, and Yolanda Felicia—as well as four adopted children.

Joined Civil Rights Movement

In 1952, Williams attended his first meeting of the National Association for the Advancement of Colored People (NAACP). Though Savannah had a large population of educated, middle-class blacks, it was as segregated as any other city in the South. Williams later recalled the day he took his two young sons to a drugstore and had to explain that they could not sit at the soda fountain and have a Coke. According to Williams, this incident inspired him to join the struggle for civil rights.

As a member of Savannah's NAACP, Williams became known for his skill in grass-roots organization. Later, he became an active member of Martin Luther King's Southern Christian Leadership Conference (SCLC), which stressed nonviolent protest. According to *Civil Rights: A Current Guide,* the SCLC's first major civil rights campaign began in 1960, when King called on blacks to begin "mass violation of immoral laws." That year, Williams organized an economic boycott by blacks in Savannah, after training his volunteers in non-violent tactics. He also served his first jail term—35 days.

The civil rights struggle was more violent in Savannah than in other Georgia cities, such as Atlanta or Albany. According to Donald L. Grant, author of *The Way It Was in the South,* "one reason for the militant civil rights movement in Savannah was its leader, Hosea Williams." Grant also quoted Andrew Young, one of the more conservative members of the SCLC, as once having said about him, "Hosea could scare the sheet off a Klansman." In 1962, at the Atlanta convention of the NAACP, Williams's candidacy for the national board of directors was vetoed because he was too militant. As a result, Williams left the NAACP, becoming active in the SCLC.

While lunch counters in Savannah were desegregated in the 1961, hotels, motels, theaters, and restaurants were not. In the summer of 1963, Williams led the Chatham County Crusade for Voters—which was affiliated with the SCLC—to push for total desegregation. That summer, he was arrested again after a white woman complained that the demonstrations made her fear for her life and kept her awake at night. Other whites stepped forward to press charges, so that Williams's bond came to $35,000. Williams remained in jail for 65 days—at that time, the longest continuous stretch of any movement leader—until bailed out by the president of a local bank.

Influential whites then formed a "Committee of 100" and began accompanying blacks to segregated establishments, which soon changed their policies. Savannah began integrating its schools that fall. The next year, when King visited Savannah, he declared it to be the most desegregated city in the South. Williams finally returned to the drugstore and bought his sons their Cokes. According to *The Way It Was in the South*, Williams later recalled, "That was one of the happiest days of my life."

In 1963, Williams moved to Atlanta to join the SCLC, holding the position of special projects director until 1970. He led marches, supervised voter registration, and was arrested more than 100 times. Among the SCLC leaders, Williams was one of the strongest supporters of direct action. He was known as King's "field general;" Williams was quoted in *The Way It Was in the South* as saying that his job was "to go out among black people who were too scared to death and get them jumping up, marching around, and filling up the jails."

On March 7, 1965, Williams and 600 followers began a trek from Selma to Montgomery, Alabama, to protest segregation—an event that would later be called the "Bloody Sunday" march. The demonstrators got no further than the Edmund Pettus Bridge outside Selma. There, Alabama state troopers set upon them, beating the marchers with clubs and firing tear gas canisters into the crowd. Two weeks later, King led thousands of marchers to Montgomery, and President Lyndon B. Johnson appeared on national television to support them. "That was one of the greatest triumphs of the civil rights movement," Williams later told the *AJC*. "That's when we crushed the mightiest of the mighty forces of racism." He would make the "Bloody Sunday" march again, 35 years later, with President Bill Clinton to commemorate the anniversary.

In April of 1968, Williams was with a group of activists staying at the Lorraine Motel in Memphis. As he recalled, he was turning the key to his room just as he heard a gunshot ring out. The shot had killed King, who was standing on a balcony just above him. "One of King's feet was sticking through the railing above my head….When I saw all the policemen come running a few minutes later, I was trying to take molecules from the sky to make a gun. Wanted to kill [the world]," he was quoted as saying in the *AJC*.

After King's death, Williams led the SCLC to consider the problems of poverty as well as race. He organized soup lines, clothing centers, and a legal clinic. In 1971, Williams represented the SCLC on a "Worldwide Brother-hood Tour," visiting Africa, India, Vietnam, Hong Kong, and China. He held a number of positions in the SCLC over the years, including national program director (1967–69) regional vice president (1970–71), and executive director (1969–71, 1977–79).

Ran for Political Office

Williams was one of the first civil rights leaders to try to enter politics. In 1968, he ran unsuccessfully for the Georgia House of Representatives as a Democrat. In 1970, he switched parties, running for secretary of state of Georgia as a Republican, but lost again. Changing back to the Democratic party, Williams lost the primary for the U.S. Senator from Georgia in 1972 and the primary for mayor of Atlanta in 1973. Williams finally succeeded in politics in 1974, when he was elected to the Georgia General Assembly, serving southeast Atlanta. Williams would hold the position of senator until 1985, when his wife, Juanita, succeeded him in the state legislature.

Meanwhile, Williams continued to agitate for civil rights. In 1970, Williams led a 110-mile "march against repression" from Perry, Georgia to Atlanta, as a protest against President Nixon and his administration. During the march, Williams called for "black power," a phrase that had been attacked by King, who wanted the civil rights movement to remain nonviolent. Williams later qualified his statement, saying that black power meant self-respect, not violence.

Also in 1970, Williams helped organize a church program to feed 200 homeless men on Thanksgiving. By the late 1990s, Williams's "Feed the Hungry" program had grown so that each year up to 45,000 were fed on Thanksgiving, Christmas, and Martin Luther King's birthday. In 2000, *Essence* magazine would honor Williams with the Essence Award for continuing the "Feed the Hungry" program for 30 years. After his death, record company executive and rapper, Sean "P. Diddy" Combs would be tapped to continue the tradition for Thanksgiving 2000. Popeye's Chicken also helped by donating 600 turkeys.

In 1972, Williams established the Martin Luther King, Jr. People's Church of Love, Inc., as well as the Poor People's Union of America. In 1976, Williams founded Southeast Chemical Manufacturing and Distributing Company, which he built into a substantial business as he pursued a political career in Atlanta. By 1991, Williams had founded three more chemical companies: A-1 Sanitary Chemicals and Supplies, Kingwell Chemical Corp., and Terry Enterprises.

In 1977, Williams was chosen as executive director of the SCLC. Two years later, the board fired him, claiming that he was spending too much time on Atlanta's problems, rather than national issues. Williams remained head of the Metro Atlanta SCLC chapter and formed a short-lived "Martin Luther King Jr. National Coalition to Save the SCLC." According to *The Way It Was in the South,* "Williams kept a high public persona but was considered an embarrassment by much of Atlanta's civil rights establishment."

In politics, as in the civil rights movement, Williams was not afraid to hold controversial positions. He publicly endorsed Ronald Reagan for president in 1980, faulting Jimmy Carter's civil rights record, and claiming that Reagan would help black enterprise. Once Reagan was elected, however, Williams found the White House was no longer interested in the input of black leaders. In response, Williams backed Jesse Jackson for president in 1984. That year Williams entered the primary for his U.S. congressional seat, but won only 29 percent of the vote. In 1985, he was sentenced to one year in jail after leaving the scene of a traffic accident in which another person was injured. The same year, he was elected to the Atlanta City Council, a post he held until 1990.

In January of 1987, Williams led 75 marchers to all-white Forsyth County, just north of Atlanta. The demonstrators were met by 500 Ku Klux Klan members and sympathizers—some in robes, some in military fatigues—who overwhelmed police lines, throwing rocks and bottles while shouting racial slurs. "In 30 years in the civil rights movement, I haven't seen racism any more sick than here today," Williams was quoted as saying in *The Way It Was in the South.*

Another march was scheduled for the following weekend. This time, 20,000 people came, including King's widow, Coretta Scott King; Mayor Andrew Young of Atlanta; former Colorado Senator Gary Hart; and Reverend Jesse Jackson. More than 1,700 National Guard members and 500 other law officers were present to protect the marchers from 1,000 white counter-demonstrators. It was the largest civil rights demonstration in Georgia's history, and received international media coverage. Afterward, Williams and other marchers filed a class-action suit against the Klan members who had attacked them. Williams later withdrew from the suit, claiming that it was "un-Christian" to punish the attackers with financial damages. "Even though white racists may extend only hate to us, we must extend only love to them," he wrote in an article published in the *AJC.*

In 1989, Williams ran for mayor of Atlanta against Democratic candidate Maynard Jackson. Lacking the money to buy television or newspaper advertisements, Williams based his campaign on personal appearances and guest slots on radio and television shows. He was eventually defeated. Meanwhile, Williams continued to be interested in bringing blacks and the Republican Party together. "Blacks are sick and tired of being hostages of

the Democratic Party," he told a group of Atlanta Republicans in 1989, according to the *AJC.* "Please open your mind and your hearts and make the Republican party a multiracial party….Not for the good of the party, but for the good of the country."

Retired from Politics

In 1990, Williams was elected as a De Kalb County Commissioner, with 82 percent of the vote. However, his tenure was marred by controversy. He came under fire in 1991, when he voted to give a grant to a small business development corporation, without disclosing that he had founded the agency or that his daughter was among its officers. Later that year, the *AJC* ran a front-page expose on the Martin Luther King Jr. Poor People's Church of Love, charging that the tax-exempt organization held no worship services, and its main activity seemed to be hosting bingo games.

Williams also continued to make headlines for his driving offenses—convictions which he claimed were politically motivated. In 1992, Williams avoided going to trial on felony hit and run charges by pleading guilty. He spent 30 days in jail before spending time in an alcohol treatment center. In 1994, Williams, who was in the middle of a campaign for re-election to the County Commission, announced that he was retiring from politics in order to work with the poor. He told the *AJC* that he planned to rejuvenate his cash-strapped Feed the Hungry program, write an autobiography, and complete a "true history" of the civil rights movement. Williams, who was 68 at the time, had recently undergone back and neck surgery, but said his health did not influence his decision.

In 1995, Williams participated in the Million Man March, organized by Louis Farrakhan, in Washington, DC. Later that year, he tried to organize a similar march in the Atlanta area. Though he had hoped for 100,000, only about 400 turned up. In 1996, Williams led a march to the state capitol to protest the current Georgia flag, which incorporates the Confederate flag.

Williams, whom *The Atlanta Journal-Constitution* has described as "the Energizer bunny of the civil rights movement," continues to advocate direct action as the best way of achieving social change. As Williams himself told that paper, "When I get too old to march, I'll go get me a rolling chair—one of those wheelchairs with batteries….Marching is the way you keep black folk nonviolent, focused, and progressive."

In 1999 Williams had surgery to remove a cancerous kidney, though it was successful, he died of cancer on November 16, 2000. Atlanta mayor Bill Campbell told *Jet,* "Rev. Hosea Williams was a true American hero, freedom fighter, and dedicated public servant."

Sources

Books

Adams, A. John and Burke, Joan Martin, *Civil Rights: A Current Guide to the People, Organizations, and Events,* Bowker, 1970, pp. 92–9, 104.

Contemporary Authors, Gale Research, 1975.

Facts on File World News Digest, January 30, 1987; November 4, 1988; October 6, 1989.

Grant, Donald L., *The Way It Was in the South,* 1993, pp. 416–18, 550–57.

Grossman, Mark, *The Civil Rights Movement,* 1993, p. 179.

Hawkins, Walter L., *African-American Biographies, 2: Profiles of 332 Current Men and Women,* 1994, pp. 316–17.

Lichtenstein, Nelson, *Political Parties and Elections in the United States,* Facts on File, 1976.

Lowery, Charles D. and John F. Marszalek (editors), *Encyclopedia of African-American Civil Rights,* Greenwood Press, 1992.

Periodicals

Atlanta Journal-Constitution, November 16, 1988, p. A11; March 9, 1989, p. H1; September 24, 1989, p. B1; February 4, 1990, p. D1; November 7, 1990, p. A9; July 21, 1991, p. A1; March 3, 1994, p. A3; July 24, 1994, p. D2; February 26, 1995, p. A11; November 12, 1995, p. H4; July 18, 1996, p. S16; July 20, 1996, p. A14; November 16, 1996, p. D1.

The Christian Century, December 6, 2000.

Ebony, June 1965, p. 170.

Essence, May 2000.

Jet, October 25, 1999, p. 9; December 4, 2000, p. 16.

Nation's Restaurant News, December 11, 2000, p. 22.

PR Newswire, November 20, 2000.

—Carrie Golus and Ashyia N. Henderson

Natalie Williams

1970–

Professional basketball player

The list of athletes who have reached top competitive levels in more than one sport is a short one indeed. One name that appears on that list is that of Natalie Williams, who was named to the Women's National Basketball Association (WNBA) all-league First Team 1999, 2000, and 2001 after consistent standout seasons with the Utah Starzz team. A gifted natural athlete who impresses observers with sheer power, Williams was also a world-class volleyball player during and after her college years at the University of California at Los Angeles in the early 1990s. In addition, she is a superior golfer, weightlifter, surfer, downhill skier, long jumper, tennis player, and softball player. And she plays keyboards, too.

Williams was born in Long Beach, California, on November 30, 1970, but grew up in Taylorsville, Utah, outside Salt Lake City. Her father Nate Williams played for nine seasons in the National Basketball Association (NBA), but Natalie did not meet him until she was 16 years old. Nate Williams signed a legal agreement to refrain from contact with her after his Utah State University romance with his white, Mormon girlfriend Robyn Barker resulted in Barker's pregnancy. Natalie Williams was raised by her mother, who struggled along on a $75-a-week secre-tary's salary but made sure that her daughter had the chance to develop her athletic abilities.

Noticed Father's Style in Own Playing

Later, Williams would reflect on the unique combination of nature and nurture that formed her skills. She noticed that certain traits of her basketball playing, such as her instinctive drives to the basket, resembled her father's style. After the Williams family reconciled father and daughter grew closer, but Nate Williams was never really Natalie's basketball instructor; she credits her mother with having supported her athletic development. "I love my father, but I don't think he had a lot to do with who I am," she told *Sports Illustrated.*

"I don't think I've had a summer to myself since I was 8," Williams told *Women's Sports and Fitness;* she attended sports camps and played in basketball, volleyball, and softball tournaments all through her high school years, many of them paid for by her mother's overtime work hours. In her senior year, 1989, she led Taylorsville High School to state championships in both basketball and volleyball, and took the state long jump championship as an individual. That triple play got the attention of the

At a Glance . . .

Born November 30, 1970, in Long Beach, CA; raised in Taylorsville, UT, near Salt Lake City; parents: Nate Williams, later a professional basketball player, and Robyn; adopted twins, 2001. *Education:* Taylorsville High School; University of California at Los Angeles, B.A.,1992.

Career: Professional basketball player; also played volleyball at top competitive levels. Led UCLA to national volleyball championship in her sophomore year; played volleyball on U.S. team at World University Games, 1991 and 1993; signed to Portland Power of Women's American Basketball League, 1996; signed to Utah Starzz of Women's National Basketball Association, 1999.

Awards: Pac-10 Athlete of the Decade, 1996; Utah Woman Athlete of the Century, 1996; named to All-ABL First Team and ABL All-Star Team, 1997–98; ABL Most Valuable Player, 1998; played for U.S. Olympic basketball team, 2000; named to All-WNBA First Team, 2001.

Addresses: *Team office*—Utah Starzz, 301 W. South Temple, Salt Lake City, UT 84101.

women's athletics program at the University of California at Los Angeles. Focused intensely on athletics, Williams never had much time to think about her biracial background, unusual in homogeneous Utah. "I guess I knew I was black, but I didn't feel like I was," she told *Sports Illustrated.* "I didn't know how to act black. I don't talk black. I have a Utah twang."

Williams's multiple talents became evident early on in her collegiate career; in basketball she averaged 14.2 points per game as a freshman, and she led the UCLA volleyball team to a national championship as a sophomore (winning an Asics/Volleyball Monthly player of the year honor in the process). She played both basketball and volleyball for all four years of her attendance at UCLA and was named the Pac-10 conference Athlete of the Decade in both sports. Once she even played in both a basketball game (an exhibition contest) and a volleyball game on the same day—a feat thought to be unique in college sports history.

Focused on Volleyball

"Sometimes I just want to be a student," Williams told *Women's Sports and Fitness* at the time. A woman gifted with a knack for putting animals at ease, Williams hoped to become a veterinarian after graduating from UCLA in

1992 (her college major was sociology). But it became clear that she had the talent to continue with sports past the college level. Despite her size and her sheer aggressive enthusiasm as a basketball rebounder, she focused on volleyball at first.

Representing the United States on a volleyball team that played in the 1991 and 1993 World University Games, Williams set her sights on the highest prize in the still predominantly amateur sport of volleyball: an appearance in the 1996 Olympic Games. Despite several seasons of training with the nation's elite players, Williams was cut from the squad. "I was extremely disappointed," she told *Sports Illustrated for Kids.* "The hardest thing for me was watching the team walk into the stadium for the opening ceremony. I started crying. I wanted to be there so much."

Signed to Utah Starzz

Fortunately, however, Williams had her second career to fall back upon. Signed to the Portland Power of the Women's American Basketball League, she played two strong seasons before the league disbanded in 1998. In both 1997 and 1998 she was named to the All-ABL All-Star Team, and in her second year she was honored as the league's Most Valuable Player. After the breakup of the ABL, Williams was an object of keen attention in the 1999 WNBA draft. She was picked third by a team that was a perfect fit for her—the Utah Starzz. An enthused Williams pointed out that she had some 150 family members in the Salt Lake City area.

Williams flourished from the start with the Utah team, averaging nearly 17 points per game over the 1999, 2000, and 2001 seasons and finishing among the league's top scorers. She also pulled down over 10 rebounds per game and led the league in rebounds in 2000, provoking comparisons with another Utah power forward, Karl Malone of the Utah Jazz. Malone, whom Williams had always admired, encouraged her after she lost her Portland slot. "He said he hoped that Utah got me because they needed a powerful player in the post [the area at the basket end of the court's key-shaped "lane"]," Williams told the *Washington Post.* "That really made me feel good; it was a big compliment, coming from 'The Man.' I like to be very aggressive in the post area; he's the same way."

In the year 2000, Williams finally fulfilled her Olympic dreams, playing for the U.S. team at the summer games in Sydney, Australia, that year. By that time, with her shoulder-length blonde hair and her spectacular combination of power and grace, she had emerged as a real star in Utah; fans voted her Utah's female Athlete of the Century. Named to the all-WNBA first team in 2001, she was one of only two players who had made the team during each year they had played in the WNBA. She also adopted twins. If Natalie Williams continues this pace, she will be regarded as one of the great basketball players in history.

Sources

Periodicals

Salt Lake Tribune, August 31, 2001.
Sports Illustrated, December 24, 1990, p. 79; February 22, 1993, p. 36.
Washington Post, June 10, 1999, p. H7.
Women's Sports and Fitness, September 1991, p. 56.

Online

Lifetime Online,
http://www.lifetimetv.com/shows/sports/players/williams.html
Women's National Basketball Association, http://www.wnba.com

—James M. Manheim

Saul Williams

1972-

Poet, actor, musician

In an oft-quoted remark, Saul Williams recounted his birth: "My mother was rushed from a James Brown concert to give birth to me." It was 1972 and Brown's song "Say It Loud, I'm Black and I'm Proud," was becoming an anthem for a new generation of African Americans. As he told *Time Out*, "I didn't have to go through what my parents did to 'say it loud' because it's implicit in my nature." Indeed, as a poet, rapper, actor, and musician, Williams has made a career of speaking up, shouting out, and saying it loud. What has he been saying? Nothing less than the truth. "That's the most invigorating feeling," he told *Time Out*, "Speaking truth into a microphone."

Influenced by Hip-Hop and the Bard

Williams was born in 1972 to a schoolteacher mother and a preacher father. The family enjoyed a middle class lifestyle in Newburgh, New York. From both parents Williams inherited a desire to feed his mind. "Reading was compulsory," Williams told *The Independent*. He tackled Shakespeare in third grade and first stepped on stage in his elementary school's performance of *Julius Caesar*.

Of his father Williams told *Interview*, "My father's influence was just realizing the importance of having a calling." The 1980's hip-hop group T La Rock put Williams on the path to his own calling. He was in fourth grade and upon hearing the group's song "It's Yours," Williams wrote his first poem. After that he led a dual life as student

of literature and self-taught student of the spoken word. "It was always important to me to be that kid who could rock the party as well as rock the English professor's mind," Williams told *Interview*.

Following high school, Williams followed his cerebral bent with a bachelor's degree in philosophy from Atlanta's Morehouse College, a liberal arts college for African-American men. Next, he was off to study acting at New York University's Tisch School of the Arts in New York City. He soon earned a Master's of Fine Arts, but instead of heading for the theater, Williams found himself center stage in a poetry revival based in coffeehouses and the culture of "slam."

From the Café Scene to Cannes

Williams first made a name for himself on New York's poetry scene at the infamous Nu-yorican Poets Café. Of that time, he told annonline.com, "It was a great moment in my life. It felt like a calling." As a breeding ground for up and coming word artists, Nu-yorican had developed a reputation for cut-throat "poetry slams." In a "slam" poets are given a few minutes to mesmerize the audience with their verbal wizardry. Would-be poets not up to the challenge suffer the vicious jeers of the crowd and are booed, often in tears, offstage. Of the often cruel nature of the slams, Williams told *Interview*, "I'm not into the competitive aspects, but I am all for getting people to become poets or poetry critics." Yet his dislike of the battle didn't stop him from slamming his competition and

At a Glance . . .

Born in 1972; son of a schoolteacher mother and a preacher father, raised in Newburgh, New York; children: Saturn. *Education:* Morehouse College, BA in philosophy; Tisch School of the Arts, New York University, MFA in drama.

Career: Poet, Actor, Musician. Since 1995 has performed poetry readings; published books of poetry include: *Sorcery of Self,* 2001, *She,* 1999, *The Seventh Octave,* 1998. Film work includes: *K-Pax,* 2001; voice over for lead character, *Origin of Cotton,* 2000; *Kings of L.A.,* 2000; star and co-author, *Slam,* 1998; recordings include: *Amethyst Rock Star,* 2001; appeared on several poetry/hip-hop compilation albums, including: *Eargasms: Urban Hip-Hop; Lyricist Lounge; Black Whole Styles.*

Awards: "Breakout Performance"Award, New York's Independent Film Project, for *Slam;* Grand Slam Champion, Nu-yorican Poet Café, 1996.

Addresses: *Home*–Los Angeles, CA.

in 1996 he scored the esteemed title of Nu-yorican Poet Café's Grand Slam Champion.

As a result of his victory, Williams caught the attention of independent film director Marc Levin and was cast in the lead role in 1998's *Slam.* Williams played the main character, Raymond Joshua, a small-time Washington D.C. dope dealer who is imprisoned on trumped up charges. Against the harsh chaos of prison life, Joshua finds refuge in his own voice as he realizes the power of his poetry.

Williams wrote all his own lines and the film wowed audiences worldwide. *Slam* won the 1998 Grand Jury Prize at the Sundance Film Festival and both the Camera d'Or and Audience Award at Cannes. For his performance Williams received an award for "Breakout Performance" by New York's Independent Film Project. However, for Williams the reactions of the audience was far more rewarding. Veteran actress Alfre Woodard tearfully told Williams that *Slam* was the most important film to have been made in the past 25 years and a French woman in Cannes grabbed his arm to tell him she had seen the film twice because she had been a resistance fighter in WWII and *Slam* reflected her own struggle for freedom. His poetry was reaching people and making a difference in their lives. He told *Time Out,* "I realized that we have the power to change reality, because we dictate reality . . . but if we want to change how it is, then we have to make a film about how it should be."

Williams continued to evolve as an actor. In 2000 he had a role in *Kings of L.A.,* and also provided the voice for Jean-Michel Basquiat's character in *Origin of Cotton,* a movie originally made in the 1980s but whose sound was lost during a break in production. His first major motion picture, *K-Pax* with Kevin Spacey was due for release in 2001.

Turned Life and Dreams into Poetry

As his fledgling film career gained momentum, so did his work as a poet. "[My poetry] is about making things matter. Making those invisible, intangible ideas and dreams, things that you can touch, that you can feel," he told *Interview.* So far he has done that in three volumes of his work. In 1998 his first book of poetry, *The Seventh Octave,* was published by Moore Black Press. His 1999 effort, *She,* is a searingly intimate account of the demise of his relationship with the book's illustrator, performance artist Marcia Jones, with whom he bore a daughter, Saturn, in 1996. The book has enjoyed three printings and publication by MTV Pocket Books. Williams acknowledged the privilege he felt at being able to share his poetry. "To be a young poet and publish books is quite a blessing, because publishers print poetry like churches sing hymns—to maintain some sort of traditional stance," he told *Time Out.*

In the spring of 2001 his third book of poetry hit the bookshelves. Called *Sorcery of Self,* it is distilled from seven years of journal writing. Its publication reinforced the advice he gave to aspiring poets in *The Hoya,* George Washington University's student paper: "experience things and write it down." He also advised the use of poetry as therapy, saying "If you can channel [pain] into something, that's the healing."

Where No Rapper Has Gone Before

Like his role model, the African-American singer, actor, athlete, and civil rights activist Paul Robeson (1898–1976), Williams kept adding to his roster of talents causing biographers to add more commas behind his name. In 1997 he recorded his first spoken word piece on the well-received album *Eargasms: Urban Hip Hop.* He also appeared on several other poetry/hip-hop compilations in the late 1990s. He has performed live with Erykah Badu, The Roots, and The Fugees. Of his recordings *Melody Maker,* as quoted on ninjatune.net, called Williams, "A poet redefining the boundaries of the possible and the impossible in hip-hop."

After *Slam,* famed record producer Rick Rubin approached Williams to produce a full-length album. The result, *Amethyst Rock Star* was released in the United Kingdom in August of 2001 and was slated to be released in the U.S. soon after. Following the release, Williams embarked on a popular European tour with a six-piece band. On the album Williams combines his literary training, slam-cured word work, and minimal, almost surreal music to produce a rap record unlike any other. "This is not a pop release, nor will it prove popular," he told *The Observer*, "I'm taking rap somewhere it's never been before." Still, he was confident that it would find its own audience. "I do believe in the power of what I'm doing, and people's ability to thing for themselves beyond what's being sold to them," he assured *The Independent*.

And why not? Williams has successfully introduced Shakespearean form into hip-hop, has brought poetry to the rock arena, and has made his way in Hollywood—all by speaking his own brand of truth. "The most positive thing you can do when someone puts the microphone up to you is to speak truth," he told *Time Out*. His own multimedia outlet, Williams has shared that truth through books, films, and CDS. Expect to hear more from him.

Selected writings

The Seventh Octave, 1998.
She, 1999.
Sorcery of Self, 2001.

Selected filmography

Slam, 1998.
Kings of L.A., 2000.
K-Pax, 2001.

Periodicals

The Hoya, February 25, 2000.
The Independent (London), August 17, 2001, p. 18.
Interview, March 2000.
The Observer (London), August 5, 2001, p. 14.
Time, October 19, 1998, p. 106.
Time Out, New York, October 15, 1998.

Online

www.aalbc.com/poet.saul.
www.annonline.com.
www.ninjatune.net.
www.saulwilliams.com.

—Candace LaBalle

Charlie Wilson

1953–

Vocalist

With his 2000 album release *Bridging the Gap,* Charlie Wilson became one of the few leading figures of 1980s R&B to mount a successful comeback in the changed musical landscape of the turn of the century. As the lead vocalist of the trio of performing brothers that went by the name of the Gap Band, Wilson had propelled the group to a consistent string of major hits. His reemergence a decade later was due not only to musical talent, but also perhaps to spiritual rebirth.

Charlie Wilson was born in Tulsa, Oklahoma, on January 29, 1953; he was the son of the Rev. Oscar Wilson, a minister in the Church of God in Christ. With his older brother Ronnie and younger brother Robert, Wilson often sang in church before their father's Sunday sermons, accompanied on piano by their mother. Secular music was forbidden at home, but the brothers smuggled music by the likes of James Brown into the house. "When I heard Stevie Wonder's 'Fingertips,'" Wilson told *Rolling Stone,* "it was like, 'I can sing like that, Mom.' My mother said, "Go to bed! Go to bed! You're not going to sing that blues."

Took Name from Neighborhood Streets

What became the Gap Band grew out of jam sessions held in neighborhood garages in the brothers' Tulsa neighborhood. The group's original name, in its first incarnations around 1970, was the Greenwood Archer and Pine Street Band, referring to major streets in the neighborhood where the brothers grew up; that was later

shortened (at first as the result of a typographical error on a poster advertising one of the band's performances) to the acronym Gap Band. In the year 2001 a nearby street, intersecting both Greenwood and Pine, was renamed Gap Band Avenue in recognition of the band's accomplishments.

After the addition of Charlie Wilson to the Gap Band as lead vocalist in 1973, the band's fortunes began to improve beyond gigs in small Tulsa clubs. At a performance at the International Club in 1974 the band was spotted by an acquaintance of the iconoclastic country rock singer, Leon Russell, a familiar figure in Texas and Oklahoma musical circles due to his long beard and mane of silver hair. Invited to audition at Russell's studio, the band encountered a hostile attitude from the singer at first. But that attitude evaporated after two hours of playing, after which the Gap Band had been hired as Russell's backup ensemble. They toured with Russell for several years, also working with Russell's friend Willie Nelson for a time.

The Gap Band's little-known debut album was released in 1974 on Russell's own Shelter label. It barely made an impact on the charts at the time, however, and when Russell dropped the band as accompanists in the mid-1970s, the brothers found themselves without a record label. "Leon Russell got us on our feet, took us around the rock & roll world, then he kicked us out of his nest," Wilson told *Rolling Stone.* Wilson led his brothers to Los Angeles, where they recorded a gospel single, "This Place Called Heaven," for the A&M label and won

At a Glance . . .

Born Charles Kent Wilson in Tulsa, OK, January 29, 1953; parents: the Rev. Oscar Wilson, a Pentecostal minister, and Irma Wilson; married, wife Mahin, a substance abuse rehabilitation center director. *Education:* Attended high school in Tulsa. *Religion:* Church of God in Christ.

Career: Vocalist. Sang with brothers Ronnie and Robert Wilson in high school; joined with them to form the Greenwood Archer and Pine Street Band, later shortened to Gap Band; hired by rock musician Leon Russell as backup band, 1974; Gap Band released debut album, *Magician's Holiday,* on Russell's Shelter label, 1974; moved to Los Angeles, mid-1970s; Gap Band signed with Mercury label, 1979; sang lead vocals and wrote or co-wrote most Gap Band hits, 1980s; released solo debut, *You Turn My Life Around,* 1992; released *Bridging the Gap,* 2000.

Address: *Label—*Interscope Records, 2220 Coloroad Ave., Santa Monica, CA 90404.

industry notice for the album *The Gap Band,* released on the RCA label's Tattoo subsidiary.

Signed with Mercury

Finally the group struck paydirt after signing with the Mercury label and joining forces with impresario, Lonnie Simmons, a record executive and former nightclub owner who honed their sound as producer and as co-writer of several of the hits that started to come around 1980. The 1980 releases "Shake" and "I Don't Believe You Want to Get Up and Dance (Oops, Upside Your Head)," the latter inspired by a refrain chanted by fans at a Pittsburgh concert given by the band, reached the U.S. R&B top 10. In December of that year, the Gap Band had its first R&B number one single, "Burn Rubber (on Me)." The album from which "Burn Rubber" and its successor "Yearning for Your Love" were drawn, *Gap Band III,* was certified platinum for sales of over one million copies.

At the center of the band's success were the vocals of Charlie Wilson; in the words of *Rolling Stone* at the time he "looks like a young version of Wilson Pickett and sings like Stevie Wonder." In 1985 the magazine called him "the best singer in pop music today, the unacknowledged heir to the tradition of Cooke and Redding." Several of his numbers began with a unique and inimitable vocal device that lay somewhere between a yodel

and a scream, and his vocals had the rare capacity to communicate romantic passion over a hard funk beat.

The band notched several more platinum albums, enjoyed three more Number One R&B singles ("Early in the Morning" and "Outstanding," both from 1982, and 1989's "All of My Love), and crossed over to the pop Top 40. Perhaps their most enduring song, "You Dropped a Bomb on Me," reached only the Number Two position. Given 24 hours to devise a theme song for the 1989 film parody *I'm Gonna Git You Sucka,* the brothers responded with what became another Top Fifteen hit.

"We were just some country boys," Wilson later told *Essence* in recalling their reactions to their ten-year run of success. "We were like, 'Wow.'" Success took its toll on all the brothers; as younger brother Ronnie Wilson struggled with cocaine addiction (he later turned to Christianity and became a minister), Charlie's songwriting contributions helped keep the group afloat. Charlie Wilson later confessed to *Essence* that he had been a substance abuser for nearly 20 years, beginning around 1974. In the early 1990s, as the hits dried up for the Gap Band, Wilson hit bottom.

Married Rehab Center Director

In 1994, Wilson spent 28 days in a Los Angeles rehabilitation center. Known as a womanizer during his days as a vocal star, Wilson married the center's director. "With her and God, that's how I made it," he told *Essence.* "I told [other entertainers] it's a dead end down there. You got the bling-bling with all the babes and it's all a big party, but a few years from now, you won't have anything and everybody's going to be gone. They listen to me because they know Uncle Charlie has been them. And I'm still here today."

Wilson had released a solo album, *You Turn My Life Around,* in 1992, well before his rehabilitation; it failed to crack the R&B Top 40. Continuing to tour with his brothers in the 1990s, Wilson put his life back together. In 2000 he released a second album, *Bridging the Gap,* which found strong appeal even among young listeners who hadn't even owned a radio during the Gap Band's heyday but remembered Wilson's sound as one of the hardest-edged of the 1980s. Touring in support of the album, Wilson, in the words of *New York Times* critic Jon Pareles, "wooed the audience . . . . like an ex-boyfriend hoping for another chance."

Bridging the Gap took a chance by featuring a romantic ballad, a style not strongly identified with the Gap Band, as the album's lead single. But "Without You" dominated radio playlists in the fall of 2000, and the album as a whole, featuring guest appearances by such contemporary stars as Snoop Dogg, Nate Dogg, Angie Stone, and others, effectively fused hip-hop with Wilson's own style— to which numerous hip-hop acts had paid homage in the form of sampling. "A lot of rap artists wanted to blaze me," Wilson explained to the website sonicnet.com. "I didn't want to put out a CD where I had to depend on hip-hoppers . . . to try to win over somebody." Indeed, it seemed that one of the top stars of the 1980s still had a lesson or two to teach contemporary musical audiences.

Selected discography

with the Gap Band

Magician's Holiday, Shelter, 1974.
The Gap Band, Tattoo, 1977.
The Gap Band II, Mercury, 1979.
The Gap Band III, Mercury, 1980.
The Gap Band IV, Total Experience, 1982.
The Gap Band V, Total Experience, 1983.
The Gap Band VI, Total Experience, 1985.
The Gap Band VII, Mercury, 1986.
Straight from the Heart, Total Experience, 1987.
Round Trip, Capitol, 1989.
Best of the Gap Band, Mercury, 1994.
Testimony, Rhino, 1994.
Ain't Nothin' but a Party, 1995.

solo releases

You Turn My Life Around, Bon Ami, 1992.
Bridging the Gap, Interscope, 2000.

Sources

Books

Hitchcock, H. Wiley, and Stanley Sadie, eds., *The New Grove Dictionary of American Music,* Macmillan, 1985.
Larkin, Colin, ed., *The Encyclopedia of Popular Music,* Muze UK, 1998.
Romanowski, Patricia, and Holly George-Warren, *The New Rolling Stone Encyclopedia of Rock & Roll,* Fireside, 1995.

Periodicals

Essence, June 2001, p. 66.
Jet, July 23, 2001., p. 13.
New York Times, October 10, 2000, p. E5.
Rolling Stone, March 1, 1984, p. 44; March 28, 1985, p. 97.
USA Today, January 2, 2001, p. D4.

Online

All Music Guide, http://www.allmusic.com.
ArtistDirect Network, http://imusic.artistdirect.com.
http://www.sonicnet.com.

—James M. Manheim

Eldrick "Tiger" Woods

1975–

Professional golfer

Tiger Woods is a great athlete, and well on the road to becoming a hero. Before the age of 20, he'd already attracted thousands of worshippers. For example, *Sports Illustrated,* the American bible of sports coverage rarely reserves ten pages to profile a college kid. But the magazine fairly gushed with reverence over the young golfer in March of 1995, exclaiming, "Only 19, amateur sensation Tiger Woods has the golf world shaking its head in awe." Likewise, *Newsweek* heralded Woods's prodigious talent, declaring in bold print: "He can hit like [Greg] Norman, putt like [Jack] Nicklaus, and think like a Stanford freshman. He's already the best 19-year-old American golfer ever." According to the *Cincinnati Post,* on August 27, 1996, he sent a message to the tour officials at the Greater Woods that read, "This is to confirm that, as of now, I am professional golfer." Reasoned *The Source,* Woods turned pro, "because there were no challenges left for him at the amateur level...."

Writers had ample reason to employ so many superlatives. At the age of 15, Woods had become not only the first black man to win the U.S. Junior Amateur Championship, but also its youngest victor. He was also the first male to win three U.S. Junior titles—1991, 1992, 1993—and had enjoyed a few casual rounds with professional golfers Sam Snead, Greg Norman, Jack Nicklaus, and John Daly. Woods's amateur title also qualified him for a trio of prestigious professional events—the Masters, the U.S. Open, and the British Open. Perhaps more importantly, the Stanford freshman captured the latter championship by staging the greatest comeback in a game in the 99-year history of the tournament. It was a dazzling

performance that suggested Woods was a champion of the highest order.

Tom Watson, a tried and true legend himself, called Woods "the most important young golfer in the last 50 years." Another golfing great, Bryon Nelson, told *Newsweek* that compared to the youthful games of Ben Hogan, Jack Nicklaus, and Tom Watson, Woods stood alone. "I've seen 'em all," he said, adding, "This fellow has no weakness." Coach Butch Harmon, who tutored Greg Norman and later Woods, declared, "He handles pressure like a 30-year-old. And his creativity is amazing. Some of the shots I've seen him hit remind me of Norman and Arnold Palmer."

Despite the outpouring of professional praise, Woods did not abandon his college studies to join the pro tour following his historic win. *The New York Times* stated that Woods played golf with the "steadfast persistence of a man many years his senior," and the same could be said of his life off the greens. Woods was committed to his studies at Stanford, determined to maintain a 3.0 grade point average and become the top collegiate golfer in the country. Never mind that millions in endorsements and prize money was essentially his for the asking. Woods, and his parents, weren't yet ready to cash in on his talent. "Money can't buy us," Tiger's mother, Kultida (Tida), a native of Thailand, told Rick Reilly of *Sports Illustrated.* "What [does] he need money for? If you turn him pro, you take his youth away from him."

At a Glance . . .

Born Eldrick Woods, December 30, 1975, in Cypress, CA; son of Earl D. (a U.S. Army officer) and Kultida "Tida" (a U.S. Army secretary) Woods. *Education:* Attended Stanford University, 1994.

Career: Appeared on television's *Mike Douglas Show* with Bob Hope, 1978; hit first hole in one, 1981; broke score of 70 (18 holes), 1987; U.S. Golf Association, National Junior Amateur Champion, 1991–94; Insurance Youth Golf Classic Champion, 1992; youngest player to compete in PGA tournament, the 1992 Los Angeles Open (16 years and two months); Jerry Pate Intercollegiate Golf Tournament, 1994; U.S. Amateur Golf Championship, 1994; youngest player to compete in the Masters, 1995; turned professional, August 27, 1996; exempted from the 1997 Professional Golfers Association (PGA) Tour Qualifying Tournament, October, 1996; won Las Vegas Invitational, 1996; won Masters, 1997, 2001; won Buick Invitational, 1999; won PGA Championship, 1999, 2000; won U.S. Open, 2000; won British Open, 2000, won Memorial Tournament, 1999, 2000, 2001.

Awards: American Jr. Golf Association, Player of the Year, 1991–92; Rolex, First Team All American, 1991–92; Golfweek/Titleist, Jr. Golfer of the Year, 1991; PGA Player of the Year, 2000.

Addresses: *Home*—Florida. *Agent*—Hughes Norton. *Office*—PGA, PO Box 109601, 100 Avenue Of Champions, Palm Beach Gardens, FL, 33418–3665.

According to Woods, his youth was a normal one. "I did the same things every kid did," he told *Newsweek*. "I studied and went to the mall. I was addicted to TV wrestling, rap music, and The Simpsons. I got into trouble and got out of it. I loved my parents and obeyed what they told me. The only difference is I can sometimes hit a little ball into a hole in less strokes than some other people." But that was hardly the only difference. Typical childhoods, after all, are not launched on the golf course: Woods was introduced to the game at nine months. By the age of three, he'd already scored 50 for nine holes and outputted Bob Hope on the *Mike Douglas Show*. Still, if observers needed further proof that Woods was a child prodigy, they got it when he hit a hole-in-one at the age of six and broke 80 by the age of eight.

His extraordinary success, in part, stemmed from early psychological training, including a series of subliminal tapes that Woods began listening to at the age of six. The messages intended to shape an unshakable confidence with declarations like: "I focus and give it my all!," "My will moves mountain!," "I believe in me!," and "I will my own destiny!" As Reilly of *Sports Illustrated* reported, "From the beginning, the boy understood what the tape was for, and he liked it. He would pop in the tape while swinging in front of the mirror or putting on the carpet or watching videos of old Masters tournaments. In fact, he played the tape so often that it would have driven any other parents quite nuts." Hardly the stuff of a normal childhood.

Earl and Kultida Woods were not ordinary parents. Earl, a former Green Beret and U.S. Army officer, discovered golf at the age of 42, after he had served his time in Vietnam and Thailand and met and married Tida, a woman 14 years his junior. A gifted athlete, Earl had competed in collegiate baseball; a catcher, he was the first black player at Kansas State. When Tiger came along, Earl was determined that his son start golf early. Taking him to the Navy Golf Course—just five minutes from their home—Earl put a putter into Tiger's hands before he could walk and taught him the fundamentals of the game before he could barely talk. By the age of two, Tiger could offer rather advanced criticism of other people's swings. By second grade, Woods won his first international tournament. 10-year-old Tiger began taking formal lessons with golf pro legend John Anselmo and would continue to do so until he was 17. At 11, he had played some 30 junior tournaments in Southern California, winning every title.

Woods's adeptness was not limited to golf. During his teen years he participated in many sports. *Newsweek* acknowledged that Woods was "a natural switch-hitter [in baseball], loved playing shooting guard [in basketball], was a wide receiver [in football], and a 400-meter runner [in track]." But golf always seemed to be his main love, so much so that his parents often had to remind or encourage him to do other things. The pleasure he derived from doing so well on the course was always apparent. Even as a pro, *Sports Illustrated's* Gary Van Sickle noted, "He smiles on the course and looks as if he's having fun. He emotes, whether it's punching the air with an uppercut . . . or straight-arming a putt into the hole." And the tougher the challenge, the more Woods enjoyed himself. As Van Sickle remarked, "Woods . . . is a dangerous golfer. Difficult situations bring out the best in him."

If one single secret to Tiger's early success exists, it was mental toughness. Earl Woods tried to ensure that his son's swing would not unravel during the pressure of competition. When Tiger practiced, Earl made it his mission to drive his son to distraction by jingling change, dropping golf bags, tearing open the Velcro his glove, anything to unnerve the young golfer. As Reilly reported, "What his dad tried to do, whenever possible, was cheat, distract, harass, and annoy him. You spend 20 years in the military, train with the Green Berets, do two tours of

[Viet]Nam and one of Thailand, you learn a few things about psychological warfare." The concentration that the elder Woods had to maintain during combat was passed on to his son for the purpose of winning a golf game rather than a war. "The boy learned coldness, too. Eventually, nothing the father did could make him flinch. The boy who once heard subliminal messages under rippling brooks now couldn't hear a thing," Reilly concluded.

Indeed, it was Tiger's ability to focus, his almost other-worldly capacity for concentration and poise, that made all the difference during the 1994 Amateur Championship. When Woods found himself six holes down after 13 holes of the 36-hole final, he began his improbable comeback. Heading into the final nine, he had closed the gap but still held a precarious three-hole deficit. He continued to find his birdies—golf scores of one stroke less than standard on a hole—pulling even with the leader, Trip Kuehne of Oklahoma State, by the 17th hole.

It was then that Woods created some magic, hitting a "fearless tee shot," in the words of some spectators, on a par-3. The ball landed on the green, just four paces from the water's edge. "You don't see to many pros hit it right of that pin," Kuehne later recalled for the *New York Times.* "It was a great gamble that paid off." Woods dropped a 14-foot putt and played steadily on the 18th to become the youngest winner of America's oldest golf championship, as well as the event's first black champion. "When Tiger won his first U.S. Junior [in 1991]," his father told *Sports Illustrated,* "I said to him, 'Son, you have done something no black person in the United States has ever done, and you will forever be a part of history.' But this is ungodly in its ramifications."

It is possible that Tiger Woods and his family did not fully anticipate the implications of his success. For one, African Americans promptly heralded Woods as the next "Great Black Hope." Woods, in turn, sought to distance himself from the people who wanted to pigeonhole him. He did not want to assume the role of a crusader. Again and again he pointed out to the press that he was not only African American but also part Thai, part Chinese, and part Indian. On applications requesting ethnic identity, he described himself as Asian.

Tida, in particular, voiced her dismay at the racial stereotyping. "All the media try to put black in him," she told *Sports Illustrated.* "Why don't they ask who half of Tiger is from? In the United States, one little part black is all black. Nobody wants to listen to me. I been trying to explain to people, but they don't understand. To say he is 100 percent black is to deny his heritage. To deny his grandmother and grandfather. To deny me!" Some writers took offense to the Woods's racial stance. *Jet* magazine, for example, subtly voiced this retort: "Woods's description of his racial identity led one observer to wonder how he could say he is only 25 percent black, when his father is black." The public exchange was an early sign that Woods's fame was going to force him to confront issues of race.

Other pitfalls emerged in the wake of Woods's great feat. As coach Harmon confessed to Reilly of Sports Illustrated, "This young man is one of the best young players to come out of this country in a long, long time. That is the good news. The bad news is that he has to live up to it now." The question on most everyone's mind was, would Tiger succeed as a professional? It seemed unlikely that the young star would pass up so many millions to be made off his sport, "especially now," as Sports Illustrated noted, "that he has been stamped with the undeniable look of a future superstar." So eager were companies to own a piece of Woods that they called Stanford trying to negotiate deals to start lines of Tiger Woods sporting apparel and Tiger Woods clubs. "Nobody believes," Newsweek suggested, "Woods will live up to his avowed goal of staying at Stanford for four years, passing up the tour and the hundreds of millions of dollars awaiting him in the endorsement village."

Still, heading into his sophomore year, Woods remained an amateur. Tida, for one, was determined that her son earn a degree. No amount of money, in her eyes, could replace the value of a good education. Earl was inclined to leave his son's future open to other possibilities. If Tiger completely dominated college golf during his sophomore and junior years, he told *Sports Illustrated,* then perhaps his son would joined the tour, juggling tournaments around his Stanford schedule. For all the promise of glamour and gold, the family's decision to invest in education was a prudent one. As the *New York Times* pointed out, "Winners of the U.S. Amateur do not necessarily go on to become great golfers—the roll call of amateur champions who had marginal careers is a lengthy one."

Speculation about the future of Tiger Woods ended, however, in the late summer of 1996, when the 20-year-old, joined the professional ranks. He quickly won two of his first seven Professional Golf Association (PGA) starts, which *Newsweek* cheekily noted was "the most successful professional golf debut since dimples on the ball." In just seven weeks, he went from his debut at the Greater Milwaukee Open, where he finished in 60th place, to coming "within range of his stated goal of making the top 125 on the money list and earning a PGA Tour exemption [meaning he would not have to play in the 1997 PGA Tour Qualifying Tournament]," according to Gary Van Sickle in *Sports Illustrated.* Van Sickle further asserted that "By winning in [the] Las Vegas [Invitational], in only his fifth start as a pro, Tiger Woods proved beyond a doubt that his time had come."

Though some felt his initial pro games were shaky—for example, in his third professional event, the Quad City Classic, he blew the lead in the final round—Woods steadily improved. And, as Reilly assessed, Woods was "making history almost daily." Having found his rhythm,

Woods was the picture of confidence, telling Reilly, "I really haven't [even] played my best golf yet." Woods was scoring off the field as well having signed $60 million in endorsements with Nike and Titleist. Still, PGA Tour veteran and friend Davis Love III cautioned to Van Sickle, "He's not playing for the money. He's trying to win. He thinks about winning and nothing else."

Despite being driven, Love's comment was not exactly true, however. Like many young adults, Woods anticipated the many rites of passage. The same article mentioned that Woods, "was looking forward to returning to Las Vegas in a year, when he'll be 21. 'I'll be legal,' Woods said, smiling. I can actually do some stuff around here." Though he feels he had a "normal" childhood, Woods has worked harder than most of his peers in order to accomplish all that he has. "You guys don't understand," he chastised Reilly. "When I played in those [early] tournaments, I was either in high school or college. I'd get dumped into the toughest places to play, and I usually was trying to study, get papers done and everything else."

In 1997 Woods proved again he was capable of doing anything he set out to do. At 21, he became the youngest player and first African American to win the Masters. This important win had many repercussions, both positive and negative. Golfer Ron Townsend, the first African-American member of the Augusta National told the *St. Louis Post-Dispatch*, "What [Woods is] doing is great for America and great for golf. He's just an amazing talent, and it's pleasure to watch him play."

But one incident threatened to tarnish Wood's star. At the ceremony, while Woods accepted his green jacket and trophy, one of the other golfers, Fuzzy Zoeller, made a tasteless joke that many thought was racist. Woods brushed it off and Zoeller apologized.

Since winning the Masters, Woods has become Mr. Golf. Swarms of people followed him all over the golf courses watching his every move. Instead of quietly following the sport, many of the "new" crowd behaved as if it were a contact sport, not one of subdued concentration. Every time Woods played, ratings went up and when he won, they were astronomical. "He has changed the way the public looks at golf. Tiger has become one of the most prominent worldwide personalities in current times," former CBS Sports president Neal Pilson told the *St. Louis Post-Dispatch*. His face has been on the box of Wheaties and promptly turned into a collector's item. Woods has been compared to golf great Jack Nicklaus and basketball legend Michael Jordan.

Both Woods' winnings and endorsement deals, with Nike and Buick among others, has made him one of the highest paid athletes. He was ranked number two in *Forbes* magazine. He has been the subject of many books, including his own, *How I Play Golf,* published in October of 2001. His father has also been published, his

tome aptly titled, *Training A Tiger: A Father's Account of How to Raise a Winner in Both Golf and Life.* Woods has also been the topic of sports videos and he has his own video games.

In six years, Woods has 29 PGA Tour victories. He has won six majors, including the PGA Championship and U.S. Open. He even did a Grand Slam, by winning four majors consecutively. According to the *Cincinnati Post,* he played 52 consecutive rounds at par or better. During the 2000 season, Woods played under par at every tournament. He has even shattered or matched many records. He told the *St. Louis Post-Dispatch,* " My goal is to obviously be the best. It's a lofty goal, and if I do, great. If I don't, at least I tried." His father told the *Cincinnati Post,* "He finally reached maturity last year. Now, he's trying to bring under control the resources that he has."

In 2001 Wood's golf game, according to many, was below average. Many blamed everything from his swing to injury to Woods suffering from burnout. Some have even blamed love. According to *Sports Illustrated,* rumors floated that he was infatuated with a well-known volleyball star and model. But Woods shrugged it off. He told the *St. Louis Post-Dispatch,* "That's golf. It's part of playing sports. You can't play well all of the time. You can't have everything go your way . . ."

Though his play may have been off the first half of the year, Woods rallied back and won his second Masters. "This is really special. When I won [the Masters] in '97, I hadn't been pro a full year yet. I was a little young, a little naive. I didn't appreciate what I had done. I have a much better appreciation for major championships now," he was quoted as saying in *Jet*.

Fame may have many perks for Woods, but it has also come at a price. His identity was stolen, and he was bilked out of $17,000 before the perpetrator was caught and jailed. He complained in the press that the PGA was using his image to promote events he wasn't participating in. During a tour in Thailand, he met with a protest of 100 people upset over layoffs by Nike. To deal with the pressure of competition and being in the spotlight, Woods cuts loose at times. He would like to get married and raise a family, so he has begun dating. He has been known to eat McDonald's on flights and smokes an occasional cigarette. Woods dyed his hair blond in 2000 (he has since changed it back.)

To help keep himself grounded, Woods relies on "The Brothers"—basketball players, Michael Jordan, Charles Barkley and former football player and sportscaster Ahmad Rashad. These three have been mentoring Woods since he met Jordan after winning the 1997 Masters. The four keep in constant contact and have given or asked for advice from one another. Though he raised him to be a formidable force and taught him all the fundamentals of golf and helped him keep his focus, Earl Woods has given the control of his golf career to Woods since the elder Woods has taken ill. His father is still in charge of the Tiger Woods Foundation and Tiger Woods Inc. He also goes to the tournaments, but watched his son's victories from TV.

Perhaps most inspiring about Woods' accomplishments as such a young man is that he has literally, and single-handedly, transformed the image of the game, making it more attractive to a wider spectrum of people while glamorizing it. "Tiger Woods is the biggest draw of any athlete on television these days," ABC Sports president Howard Katz exclaimed to the *Dallas Morning News.* As Reilly pointed out, "Golf used to be four white guys sitting around a pinochle table talking about their shaft flexes. . . . Now golf is [supermodel] Cindy Crawford sending Woods a letter." Indeed, Woods's presence has attracted a multitude of new fans to the sport of golf—minorities and young people among them. Van Sickle reiterated Jack Nicklaus's belief that "someone would come along who could hit 30 yards past everyone else, much as he did decades ago, have a great short game, and dominate the sport." In so many ways, Woods already has. Though golf is and will be an integral part of his life for many years to come, as he has matured, he has come to appreciate his victories and his life outside of golf. He commented to *Sports Illustrated,* "No doubt about it, I have a wonderful balance in my life. I've learned what's best for me."

Sources

Periodicals

Business Wire, September 4, 2001, p.2319; September 11, 2001, p.0197.

The Cincinnati Post, August 28, 2001, p. 6C.
Dallas Morning News, July 28, 2001, p. 9B.
Entertainment Weekly, November 15, 1996, p. 16.
Jet, August 26, 1991, p. 48; September 12, 1994, p. 51; November 14, 1994, p. 49; April 24, 1995, p. 8; September 18, 2000, p. 48; November 27, 2000, p. 48; January 22, 2001, p. 33; April 23, 2001, p. 54; May 21, 2001, p. 35; July 9, 2001, p. 51.
Library Journal, July 2001, p. 145.
Nation's Restaurant, September 3, 2001, p. 36.
Newsweek, April 10, 1995, pp. 70–72; December 9, 1996, pp. 52–56; June 18, 2001.
New York Times, August 28, 1994.
People, September 23, 1991, p. 81.
PR Newswire, June 10, 2001, p. 7445.
The San Francisco Chronicle, April 22, 1997, p. B7.
The Source, November 1996, p. 121.
Sports Illustrated, September 5, 1994, pp. 14–15; March 27, 1995, pp. 62–72; October 4, 1996, pp. 37–38; October 28, 1996, pp. 47–50; April 3, 2000, p. 78+; August 27, 2001, p. 1.
St. Louis Post-Dispatch, April 14, 1997, p.1C; August 20, 2001, p. D7; September 9, 2001, p. 10; September 11, 2001, p.A1.
Time International, November 27, 2000, p.60.
USA Weekend, July 24–26, 1992, pp. 4–6.

Online

Amazon, http://amazon.com

—Ami Walsh, Lorna Mabunda and Ashyia N. Henderson

Cumulative Nationality Index

Volume numbers appear in **bold**

Cumulative Occupation Index

Volume numbers appear in **bold**

Fields, Cleo **13**
Flake, Floyd H. **18**
Flipper, Henry O. **3**
Fortune, T. Thomas **6**
Foster, Ezola **28**
Franks, Gary **2**
Fulani, Lenora **11**
Gantt, Harvey **1**
Garvey, Marcus **1**
Gibson, Johnnie Mae **23**
Gibson, Kenneth Allen **6**
Gibson, William F. **6**
Goode, W. Wilson **4**
Gravely, Samuel L., Jr. **5**
Gray, William H., III **3**
Grimké, Archibald H. **9**
Guinier, Lani **7, 30**
Haley, George Williford Boyce **21**
Hamer, Fannie Lou **6**
Harmon, Clarence **26**
Harris, Alice **7**
Harris, Patricia Roberts **2**
Harvard, Beverly **11**
Hastie, William H. **8**
Hastings, Alcee L. **16**
Hayes, James C. **10**
Henry, Aaron **19**
Herenton, Willie W. **24**
Herman, Alexis M. **15**
Hernandez, Aileen Clarke **13**
Hill, Bonnie Guiton **20**
Hilliard, Earl F. **24**
Holder, Eric H., Jr. **9**
Ifill, Gwen, **28**
Irving, Larry, Jr. **12**
Jackson, George **14**
Jackson, Jesse **1**
Jackson, Jesse, Jr. **14, 27**
Jackson Lee, Sheila **20**
Jackson, Maynard **2**
Jackson, Shirley Ann **12**
Jacob, John E. **2**
James, Sharpe **23**
Jarvis, Charlene Drew **21**
Jefferson, William J. **25**
Johnson, Eddie Bernice **8**
Johnson, Harvey Jr. **24**
Johnson, James Weldon **5**
Johnson, Norma L. Holloway **17**
Johnson, Robert T. **17**
Jones, Elaine R. **7**
Jordan, Barbara **4**
Kennard, William Earl **18**
Keyes, Alan L. **11**
Kilpatrick, Carolyn Cheeks **16**
Kincaid, Bernard **28**
King, Martin Luther, III **20**
Kirk, Ron **11**
Lafontant, Jewel Stradford **3**
Lee, Barbara **25**
Leland, Mickey **2**
Lewis, Delano **7**
Lewis, John **2**
Mallett, Conrad, Jr. **16**
Marshall, Bella **22**
Marshall, Thurgood **1**
Martin, Louis E. **16**
McCall, H. Carl **27**
McKinney, Cynthia Ann **11**

McKissick, Floyd B. **3**
Meek, Carrie **6**
Meeks, Gregory **25**
Meredith, James H. **11**
Metcalfe, Ralph **26**
Mfume, Kweisi **6**
Millender-McDonald, Juanita **21**
Morial, Ernest "Dutch" **26**
Morial, Marc **20**
Moses, Robert Parris **11**
Norton, Eleanor Holmes **7**
O'Leary, Hazel **6**
Owens, Major **6**
Page, Alan **7**
Paige, Rod **29**
Patrick, Deval **12**
Patterson, Louise **25**
Payne, Donald M. **2**
Perez, Anna **1**
Perkins, Edward **5**
Perry, Lowell **30**
Pinchback, P. B. S. **9**
Powell, Adam Clayton, Jr. **3**
Powell, Colin **1, 28**
Powell, Debra A. **23**
Raines, Franklin Delano **14**
Randolph, A. Philip **3**
Rangel, Charles **3**
Reeves, Triette Lipsey **27**
Rice, Condoleezza **3, 28**
Rice, Norm **8**
Robinson, Randall **7**
Rogers, Joe **27**
Ross, Don **27**
Rush, Bobby **26**
Rustin, Bayard **4**
Sampson, Edith S. **4**
Satcher, David **7**
Sayles Belton, Sharon **9**
Schmoke, Kurt **1**
Scott, Robert C. **23**
Sears-Collins, Leah J. **5**
Shakur, Assata **6**
Shavers, Cheryl **31**
Sharpton, Al **21**
Simpson, Carole **6, 30**
Sisulu, Sheila Violet Makate **24**
Slater, Rodney E. **15**
Stanton, Robert **20**
Staupers, Mabel K. **7**
Stokes, Carl B. **10**
Stokes, Louis **3**
Stone, Chuck **9**
Street, John F. **24**
Sullivan, Louis **8**
Thomas, Clarence **2**
Thompson, Bennie G. **26**
Towns, Edolphus **19**
Tribble, Israel, Jr. **8**
Trotter, Donne E. **28**
Tubbs Jones, Stephanie **24**
Tucker, C. DeLores **12**
Turner, Henry McNeal **5**
Usry, James L. **23**
Von Lipsey, Roderick K. **11**
Wallace, Phyllis A. **9**
Washington, Harold **6**
Washington, Val **12**
Waters, Maxine **3**

Watkins, Shirley R. **17**
Watt, Melvin **26**
Watts, J. C., Jr. **14**
Weaver, Robert C. **8**
Webb, Wellington **3**
Wharton, Clifton R., Jr. **7**
Wheat, Alan **14**
White, Jesse **22**
White, Michael R. **5**
Wilder, L. Douglas **3**
Wilkins, Roger **2**
Williams, Anthony **21**
Williams, George Washington **18**
Williams, Hosea Lorenzo **15, 31**
Williams, Maggie **7**
Wilson, Sunnie **7**
Wynn, Albert **25**
Young, Andrew **3**

Law
Alexander, Clifford **26**
Alexander, Joyce London **18**
Alexander, Sadie Tanner
  Mossell **22**
Archer, Dennis **7**
Arnwine, Barbara **28**
Banks, William **11**
Barrett, Andrew C. **12**
Barrett, Jacqueline **28**
Baugh, David **23**
Bell, Derrick **6**
Berry, Mary Frances **7**
Berry, Theodore M. **31**
Bishop Jr., Sanford D. **24**
Bolin, Jane **22**
Bolton, Terrell D. **25**
Bosley, Freeman, Jr. **7**
Boykin, Keith **14**
Bradley, Thomas **2**
Braun, Carol Moseley **4**
Brooke, Edward **8**
Brown, Joe **29**
Brown, Lee Patrick **1, 24**
Brown, Ron **5**
Brown, Willie L., Jr. **7**
Bryant, Wayne R. **6**
Burris, Roland W. **25**
Butler, Paul D. **17**
Campbell, Bill **9**
Carter, Stephen L. **4**
Chambers, Julius **3**
Cleaver, Kathleen Neal **29**
Clendenon, Donn **26**
Cochran, Johnnie L., Jr. **11**
Conyers, John, Jr. **4**
Crockett, George, Jr. **10**
Darden, Christopher **13**
Days, Drew S., III **10**
Diggs-Taylor, Anna **20**
Dinkins, David **4**
Dixon, Sharon Pratt **1**
Edelman, Marian Wright **5**
Edley, Christopher **2**
Ellington, E. David **11**
Ephriam, Mablean **29**
Espy, Mike **6**
Fields, Cleo **13**
Frazier-Lyde, Jacqui **31**
Freeman, Charles **19**
Gary, Willie E. **12**

Count Basie **23**
Cox, Deborah **28**
Craig, Carl **31**
Crawford, Randy **19**
Cray, Robert **30**
Creagh, Milton **27**
Crocker, Frankie **29**
Crothers, Scatman **19**
Crouch, Andraé **27**
Crouch, Stanley **11**
Crowder, Henry **16**
D'Angelo **27**
Dash, Damon **31**
Dash, Darien **29**
David, Craig **31**
Davis, Anthony **11**
Davis, Miles **4**
Davis, Sammy, Jr. **18**
de Passe, Suzanne **25**
Dixon, Willie **4**
DMX **28**
Donegan, Dorothy **19**
Dorsey, Thomas **15**
Downing, Will **19**
Dr. Dre **10**
Dre, Dr. **14**, **30**
Duke, George **21**
Dupri, Jermaine **13**
Eckstine, Billy **28**
Edmonds, Kenneth
    "Babyface" **10, 31**
Edmonds, Tracey **16**
Ellington, Duke **5**
Elliott, Missy "Misdemeanor" **31**
Estes, Simon **28**
Eubanks, Kevin **15**
Europe, James Reese **10**
Evans, Faith **22**
Eve **29**
Evora, Cesaria **12**
Fats Domino **20**
Fela **1**
Ferrell, Rachelle **29**
Fitzgerald, Ella **8, 18**
Flack, Roberta **19**
Foxx, Jamie **15**
Franklin, Aretha **11**
Franklin, Kirk **15**
Freeman, Yvette **27**
Gaye, Marvin **2**
Gibson, Althea **8**
Gillespie, Dizzy **1**
Gordon, Dexter **25**
Gordy, Berry, Jr. **1**
Graves, Denyce **19**
Gray, F. Gary **14**
Gray, Macy **29**
Greely, M. Gasby **27**
Green, Al **13**
Griffiths, Marcia **29**
Guy, Buddy **31**
Hailey, JoJo **22**
Hailey, K-Ci **22**
Hammer, M. C. **20**
Hammond, Fred **23**
Hampton, Lionel **17**
Hancock, Herbie **20**
Handy, W. C. **8**
Harrell, Andre **9, 30**

Hathaway, Donny **18**
Hawkins, Coleman **9**
Hawkins, Erskine **14**
Hawkins, Screamin' Jay **30**
Hawkins, Tramaine **16**
Hayes, Isaac **20**
Hayes, Roland **4**
Hendricks, Barbara **3**
Hendrix, Jimi **10**
Hill, Lauryn **20**
Hinderas, Natalie **5**
Hinton, Milt **30**
Holiday, Billie **1**
Hooker, John Lee **30**
Horne, Lena **5**
House, Son **8**
Houston, Cissy **20**
Houston, Whitney **7, 28**
Howlin' Wolf **9**
Humphrey, Bobbi **20**
Hyman, Phyllis **19**
Ice Cube **8, 30**
Ice-T **6, 31**
Isley, Ronald **25**
Jackson, Fred James **25**
Jackson, George **19**
Jackson, Isaiah **3**
Jackson, Janet **6, 30**
Jackson, Mahalia **5**
Jackson, Michael **19**
Jackson, Millie **25**
Jackson, Milt **26**
James, Etta **13**
James, Rick **17**
Jarreau, Al **21**
Jay-Z **27**
Jean-Baptiste, Marianne **17**
Jean, Wyclef **20**
Jenkins, Ella **15**
Jerkins, Rodney **31**
Jimmy Jam **13**
Johnson, Beverly **2**
Johnson, James Weldon **5**
Johnson, Robert **2**
Jones, Bobby **20**
Jones, Donell **29**
Jones, Elvin **14**
Jones, Quincy **8, 30**
Joplin, Scott **6**
Jordan, Montell **23**
Jordan, Ronny **26**
Joyner, Matilda Sissieretta **15**
Joyner, Tom **19**
Kelly, R. **18**
Kendricks, Eddie **22**
Khan, Chaka **12**
King, B. B. **7**
King, Coretta Scott **3**
Kitt, Eartha **16**
Knight, Gladys **16**
Knight, Suge **11, 30**
Kravitz, Lenny **10**
L.L. Cool J **16**
LaBelle, Patti **13, 30**
León, Tania **13**
Lester, Julius **9**
Levert, Gerald **22**
Lewis, Ananda **28**
Lewis, Terry **13**

Lil' Kim **28**
Lincoln, Abbey **3**
Little Richard **15**
Love, Darlene **23**
Lover, Ed **10**
Lymon, Frankie **22**
Madhubuti, Haki R. **7**
Makeba, Miriam **2**
Marley, Bob **5**
Marrow, Queen Esther **24**
Marsalis, Wynton **16**
Mase **24**
Masekela, Hugh **1**
Massenburg, Kedar **23**
Master P **21**
Mathis, Johnny **20**
Maxwell **20**
Mayfield, Curtis **2**
Maynor, Dorothy **19**
McClurkin, Donnie **25**
McDaniel, Hattie **5**
McKee, Lonette **12**
McKnight, Brian **18**
Mingus, Charles **15**
Monica **21**
Monk, Thelonious **1**
Moore, Chante **26**
Moore, Melba **21**
Moore, Undine Smith **28**
Morton, Jelly Roll **29**
Mos Def **30**
Moses, Gilbert **12**
Moten, Etta **18**
Mumba, Samantha **29**
Murphy, Eddie **4, 20**
Muse, Clarence Edouard **21**
N'Dour, Youssou **1**
Nascimento, Milton **2**
Ndegéocello, Me'Shell **15**
Neville, Aaron **21**
Nicholas, Fayard **20**
Nicholas, Harold **20**
Norman, Jessye **5**
Notorious B.I.G. **20**
O'Neal, Shaquille **8, 30**
Ongala, Remmy **9**
Osborne, Jeffrey **26**
Parker, Charlie **20**
Parks, Gordon **1**
Pendergrass, Teddy **22**
Peoples, Dottie **22**
Perry, Ruth **19**
Peterson, Marvin "Hannibal" **27**
Powell, Maxine **8**
Powell, Bud **24**
Pratt, Awadagin **31**
Price, Kelly **23**
Price, Leontyne **1**
Pride, Charley **26**
Prince **18**
Pritchard, Robert Starling **21**
Queen Latifah **1, 16**
Ralph, Sheryl Lee **18**
Razaf, Andy **19**
Reagon, Bernice Johnson **7**
Redman, Joshua **30**
Reid, Antonio "L.A." **28**
Reese, Della **6, 20**
Rhone, Sylvia **2**

Emeagwali, Philip **30**
Ericsson-Jackson, Aprille **28**
Fields, Evelyn J. **27**
Fisher, Rudolph **17**
Flipper, Henry O. **3**
Foster, Henry W., Jr. **26**
Freeman, Harold P. **23**
Fulani, Lenora **11**
Fuller, Arthur **27**
Fuller, Solomon Carter, Jr. **15**
Gates, Sylvester James, Jr. **15**
Gayle, Helene D. **3**
Gibson, Kenneth Allen **6**
Gibson, William F. **6**
Gregory, Frederick D. **8**
Hall, Lloyd A. **8**
Hannah, Marc **10**
Harris, Mary Styles **31**
Henderson, Cornelius Langston **26**
Henson, Matthew **2**
Hinton, William Augustus **8**
Irving, Larry, Jr. **12**
Jackson, Shirley Ann **12**
Jawara, Sir Dawda Kairaba **11**
Jemison, Mae C. **1**
Jenifer, Franklyn G. **2**
Johnson, Eddie Bernice **8**
Julian, Percy Lavon **6**
Just, Ernest Everett **3**
Kountz, Samuel L. **10**
Latimer, Lewis H. **4**
Lawless, Theodore K. **8**
Lawrence, Robert H., Jr. **16**
Leffall, LaSalle, Jr. **3**
Lewis, Delano **7**
Logan, Onnie Lee **14**
Lyttle, Hulda Margaret **14**
Manley, Audrey Forbes **16**
Massey, Walter E. **5**
Massie, Samuel P., Jr. **29**
Mboup, Souleymane **10**
McCoy, Elijah **8**
McNair, Ronald **3**
Millines Dziko, Trish **28**
Morgan, Garrett **1**
O'Leary, Hazel **6**
Person, Waverly **9**
Pitt, David Thomas **10**
Poussaint, Alvin F. **5**
Prothrow-Stith, Deborah **10**
Quarterman, Lloyd Albert **4**
Riley, Helen Caldwell Day **13**
Robeson, Eslanda Goode **13**
Robinson, Rachel **16**
Roker, Al **12**
Samara, Noah **15**
Satcher, David **7**
Shabazz, Betty **7, 26**
Shavers, Cheryl **31**
Sinkford, Jeanne C. **13**
Staples, Brent **8**
Staupers, Mabel K. **7**
Sullivan, Louis **8**
Terrell, Dorothy A. **24**
Thomas, Vivien **9**
Tyson, Neil de Grasse **15**
Washington, Patrice Clarke **12**
Watkins, Levi, Jr. **9**
Welsing, Frances Cress **5**

Williams, Daniel Hale **2**
Williams, O. S. **13**
Witt, Edwin T. **26**
Woods, Granville T. **5**
Wright, Louis Tompkins **4**
Young, Roger Arliner **29**

Social issues

Aaron, Hank **5**
Abbot, Robert Sengstacke **27**
Abbott, Diane **9**
Abdul-Jabbar, Kareem **8**
Abernathy, Ralph David **1**
Abu-Jamal, Mumia **15**
Achebe, Chinua **6**
Adams, Sheila J. **25**
Agyeman, Jaramogi Abebe **10**
Ake, Claude **30**
Al-Amin, Jamil Abdullah **6**
Alexander, Clifford **26**
Alexander, Sadie Tanner
    Mossell **22**
Ali, Muhammad, **2, 16**
Allen, Ethel D. **13**
Andrews, Benny **22**
Angelou, Maya **1**
Annan, Kofi Atta **15**
Anthony, Wendell **25**
Archer, Dennis **7**
Aristide, Jean-Bertrand **6**
Arnwine, Barbara **28**
Asante, Molefi Kete **3**
Ashe, Arthur **1, 18**
Auguste, Rose-Anne **13**
Azikiwe, Nnamdi **13**
Ba, Mariama **30**
Baisden, Michael **25**
Baker, Ella **5**
Baker, Gwendolyn Calvert **9**
Baker, Houston A., Jr. **6**
Baker, Josephine **3**
Baker, Thurbert **22**
Baldwin, James **1**
Baraka, Amiri **1**
Bates, Daisy **13**
Beals, Melba Patillo **15**
Belafonte, Harry **4**
Bell, Derrick **6**
Bell, Ralph S. **5**
Bennett, Lerone, Jr. **5**
Berry, Bertice **8**
Berry, Mary Frances **7**
Bethune, Mary McLeod **4**
Betsch, MaVynee **28**
Biko, Steven **4**
Blackwell, Unita **17**
Bolin, Jane **22**
Bond, Julian **2**
Bonga, Kuenda **13**
Bosley, Freeman, Jr. **7**
Boyd, John W., Jr. **20**
Boyd, T. B., III **6**
Boykin, Keith **14**
Braun, Carol Moseley **4**
Brooke, Edward **8**
Brown, Elaine **8**
Brown, Jesse **6**
Brown, Jim **11**
Brown, Lee P. **1**
Brown, Les **5**

Brown, Tony **3**
Brown, Zora Kramer **12**
Bryant, Wayne R. **6**
Bullock, Steve **22**
Bunche, Ralph J. **5**
Burroughs, Margaret Taylor **9**
Butler, Paul D. **17**
Butts, Calvin O., III **9**
Campbell, Bebe Moore **6, 24**
Canada, Geoffrey **23**
Carby, Hazel **27**
Carmichael, Stokely **5, 26**
Carter, Mandy **11**
Carter, Rubin **26**
Carter, Stephen L. **4**
Cary, Lorene **3**
Cary, Mary Ann Shad **30**
Cayton, Horace **26**
Chavis, Benjamin **6**
Chideya, Farai **14**
Childress, Alice **15**
Chissano, Joaquim **7**
Christophe, Henri **9**
Chuck D **9**
Clark, Joe **1**
Clark, Kenneth B. **5**
Clark, Septima **7**
Clay, William Lacy **8**
Claytor, Helen **14**
Cleaver, Eldridge **5**
Cleaver, Kathleen Neal **29**
Clements, George **2**
Cobbs, Price M. **9**
Cole, Johnnetta B. **5**
Collins, Barbara-Rose **7**
Comer, James P. **6**
Cone, James H. **3**
Connerly, Ward **14**
Conté, Lansana **7**
Conyers, John, Jr. **4**
Cook, Toni **23**
Cooke, Marvel **31**
Cooper, Anna Julia **20**
Cooper, Edward S. **6**
Cosby, Bill **7**
Cosby, Camille **14**
Cose, Ellis **5**
Creagh, Milton **27**
Crockett, George, Jr. **10**
Crouch, Stanley **11**
Cummings, Elijah E. **24**
Cunningham, Evelyn **23**
da Silva, Benedita **5**
Dash, Julie **4**
Davis, Angela **5**
Davis, Danny K. **24**
Davis, Ossie **5**
Dee, Ruby **8**
Delany, Martin R. **27**
Dellums, Ronald **2**
Diallo, Amadou **27**
Dickerson, Ernest **6**
Diop, Cheikh Anta **4**
Divine, Father **7**
Dixon, Margaret **14**
Dodson, Howard, Jr. **7**
Dove, Rita **6**
Drew, Charles Richard **7**
Du Bois, W. E. B. **3**

Thomas, Debi **26**
Thomas, Derrick **25**
Thomas, Frank **12**
Thomas, Isiah **7, 26**
Thompson, Tina **25**
Thugwane, Josia **21**
Tyson, Mike **28**
Unseld, Wes **23**
Upshaw, Gene **18**
Ussery, Terdema, II **29**
Walker, Herschel **1**
Washington, MaliVai **8**
Watson, Bob **25**
Watts, J. C., Jr. **14**
Weathers, Carl **10**
Webber, Chris **15, 30**
Westbrook, Peter **20**
Whitaker, Pernell **10**
White, Bill **1**
White, Jesse **22**
White, Reggie **6**
Whitfield, Fred **23**
Wilkens, Lenny **11**
Williams, Doug **22**
Williams, Serena **20**
Williams, Natalie **31**
Williams, Venus Ebone **17**
Wilson, Sunnie **7**
Winfield, Dave **5**
Woods, Tiger **14, 31**

Television
Allen, Byron **3**
Allen, Debbie **13**
Allen, Marcus **20**
Amos, John **8**
Anderson, Eddie "Rochester" **30**
Arkadie, Kevin **17**
Banks, William **11**
Barden, Don H. **9**
Bassett, Angela **6, 23**
Beach, Michael **26**
Beaton, Norman **14**
Beauvais, Garcelle **29**
Belafonte, Harry **4**
Bellamy, Bill **12**
Berry, Bertice **8**
Berry, Halle **4, 19**
Blake, Asha **26**
Boston, Kelvin E. **25**
Bowser, Yvette Lee **17**
Bradley, Ed **2**
Brandy **14**
Braugher, Andre **13**
Brooks, Avery **9**
Brown, James **22**
Brown, Joe **29**
Brown, Les **5**
Brown, Tony **3**
Brown, Vivian **27**
Burnett, Charles **16**
Burton, LeVar **8**
Byrd, Robert **11**
Campbell, Naomi **1, 31**
Campbell, Tisha **8**
Carroll, Diahann **9**
Carson, Lisa Nicole **21**
Cash, Rosalind **28**
Cedric the Entertainer **29**
Cheadle, Don **19**

Chestnut, Morris **31**
Chideya, Farai **14**
Christian, Spencer **15**
Clash, Kevin **14**
Clayton, Xernona **3**
Cole, Nat King **17**
Cole, Natalie Maria **17**
Cornelius, Don **4**
Cosby, Bill **7, 26**
Crothers, Scatman **19**
Curry, Mark **17**
Curtis-Hall, Vondie **17**
Davidson, Tommy **21**
Davis, Ossie **5**
de Passe, Suzanne **25**
Dee, Ruby **8**
Devine, Loretta **24**
Dickerson, Eric **27**
Dickerson, Ernest **6**
Diggs, Taye **25**
Dr. Dre **10**
Duke, Bill **3**
Dutton, Charles S. **4, 22**
Elder, Larry **25**
Ephriam, Mablean **29**
Erving, Julius **18**
Esposito, Giancarlo **9**
Eubanks, Kevin **15**
Evans, Harry **25**
Fishburne, Larry **4**
Fox, Rick **27**
Foxx, Jamie **15**
Foxx, Redd **2**
Freeman, Al, Jr. **11**
Freeman, Morgan **2**
Freeman, Yvette **27**
Gaines, Ernest J. **7**
Givens, Robin **4, 25**
Glover, Danny **3, 24**
Glover, Savion **14**
Goldberg, Whoopi **4**
Goode, Mal **13**
Gooding, Cuba, Jr. **16**
Gordon, Ed **10**
Gossett, Louis, Jr. **7**
Greely, M. Gasby **27**
Grier, David Alan **28**
Grier, Pam **9, 31**
Guillaume, Robert **3**
Gumbel, Bryant **14**
Gumbel, Greg **8**
Gunn, Moses **10**
Guy, Jasmine **2**
Haley, Alex **4**
Hampton, Henry **6**
Hardison, Kadeem **22**
Harrell, Andre **9, 30**
Harris, Robin **7**
Harvey, Steve **18**
Hayes, Isaac **20**
Hemsley, Sherman **19**
Henry, Lenny **9**
Hickman, Fred **11**
Hill, Dulé **29**
Hill, Lauryn **20**
Hinderas, Natalie **5**
Horne, Lena **5**
Hounsou, Djimon **19**
Houston, Whitney **7, 28**

Hughley, D.L. **23**
Hunter-Gault, Charlayne **6, 31**
Hyman, Earle **25**
Ice-T **6, 31**
Ifill, Gwen **28**
Iman **4**
Ingram, Rex **5**
Jackson, George **19**
Jackson, Janet **6, 30**
Jackson, Jesse **1**
Joe, Yolanda **21**
Johnson, Beverly **2**
Johnson, Dwayne "The Rock" **29**
Johnson, Robert L. **3**
Johnson, Rodney Van **28**
Jones, Bobby **20**
Jones, James Earl **3**
Jones, Orlando **30**
Jones, Quincy **8, 30**
Jones, Star **10, 27**
King, Gayle **19**
King, Regina **22**
King, Woodie, Jr. **27**
Kirby, George **14**
Kitt, Eartha **16**
Knight, Gladys **16**
Kotto, Yaphet **7**
L.L. Cool J **16**
La Salle, Eriq **12**
LaBelle, Patti **13, 30**
Langhart, Janet **19**
Lathan, Sanaa **27**
Lawrence, Martin **6, 27**
Lawson, Jennifer **1**
Lemmons, Kasi **20**
Lewis, Ananda **28**
Lewis, Byron E. **13**
Lil' Kim **28**
Lindo, Delroy **18**
LisaRaye **27**
Long, Nia **17**
Lover, Ed **10**
Mabrey, Vicki **26**
Mac, Bernie **29**
Martin, Helen **31**
Martin, Jesse L. **31**
Mathis, Greg **26**
McDaniel, Hattie **5**
McEwen, Mark **5**
McKee, Lonette **12**
McKenzie, Vashti M. **29**
McQueen, Butterfly **6**
Meadows, Tim **30**
Michele, Michael **31**
Mickelbury, Penny **28**
Miller, Cheryl **10**
Mitchell, Brian Stokes **21**
Mitchell, Russ **21**
Moore, Chante **26**
Moore, Melba **21**
Moore, Shemar **21**
Morgan, Joe Leonard **9**
Morris, Garrett **31**
Morris, Greg **28**
Morton, Joe **18**
Mos Def **30**
Moses, Gilbert **12**
Moss, Carlton **17**
Murphy, Eddie **4, 20**

Cumulative Subject Index

Volume numbers appear in **bold**

ganizations

African/African-American Summit
Sullivan, Leon H. **3**, **30**

African American Catholic Congregation
Stallings, George A., Jr. **6**

African American folklore
Bailey, Xenobia **11**
Brown, Sterling **10**
Driskell, David C. **7**
Ellison, Ralph **7**
Gaines, Ernest J. **7**
Hamilton, Virginia **10**
Hughes, Langston **4**
Hurston, Zora Neale **3**
Lester, Julius **9**
Morrison, Toni **2, 15**
Primus, Pearl **6**
Tillman, George, Jr. **20**
Williams, Bert **18**

African American folk music
Handy, W. C. **8**
House, Son **8**
Johnson, James Weldon **5**
Lester, Julius **9**

African American history
Angelou, Maya **1, 15**
Ashe, Arthur **1, 18**
Bennett, Lerone, Jr. **5**
Berry, Mary Frances **7**
Burroughs, Margaret Taylor **9**
Camp, Kimberly **19**
Chase-Riboud, Barbara **20**
Cheadle, Don **19**
Clarke, John Henrik **20**
Cooper, Anna Julia **20**
Dodson, Howard, Jr. **7**
Douglas, Aaron **7**
Du Bois, W. E. B. **3**
DuBois, Shirley Graham **21**
Dyson, Michael Eric **11**
Feelings, Tom **11**
Franklin, John Hope **5**
Gaines, Ernest J. **7**
Gates, Henry Louis, Jr. **3**
Haley, Alex **4**
Harkless, Necia Desiree **19**
Hine, Darlene Clark **24**
Hughes, Langston **4**
Johnson, James Weldon **5**
Lewis, David Levering **9**
Madhubuti, Haki R. **7**
Marable, Manning **10**
Morrison, Toni **2**
Painter, Nell Irvin **24**
Pritchard, Robert Starling **21**
Quarles, Benjamin Arthur **18**
Reagon, Bernice Johnson **7**
Ringgold, Faith **4**
Schomburg, Arthur Alfonso **9**
Wilson, August **7**
Woodson, Carter G. **2**

African American Images
Kunjufu, Jawanza **3**

African American literature
Andrews, Raymond **4**
Angelou, Maya **1, 15**
Baisden, Michael **25**
Baker, Houston A., Jr. **6**
Baldwin, James **1**
Bambara, Toni Cade **1**
Baraka, Amiri **1**
Bontemps, Arna **8**
Briscoe, Connie **15**
Brooks, Gwendolyn **1**
Brown, Wesley **23**
Burroughs, Margaret Taylor **9**
Campbell, Bebe Moore **6, 24**
Cary, Lorene **3**
Childress, Alice **15**
Cleage, Pearl **17**
Cullen, Countee **8**
Curtis, Christopher Paul **26**
Dickey, Eric Jerome **21**
Dove, Rita **6**
Du Bois, W. E. B. **3**
Dunbar, Paul Laurence **8**
Ellison, Ralph **7**
Evans, Mari **26**
Fauset, Jessie **7**
Feelings, Tom **11**
Fisher, Rudolph **17**
Fuller, Charles **8**
Gaines, Ernest J. **7**
Gates, Henry Louis, Jr. **3**
Giddings, Paula **11**
Giovanni, Nikki **9**
Goines, Donald **19**
Golden, Marita **19**
Guy, Rosa **5**
Haley, Alex **4**
Hansberry, Lorraine **6**
Harper, Frances Ellen Watkins **11**
Himes, Chester **8**
Holland, Endesha Ida Mae **3**
Hughes, Langston **4**
Hurston, Zora Neale **3**
Iceberg Slim **11**
Joe, Yolanda **21**
Johnson, Charles **1**
Johnson, James Weldon **5**
Jordan, June **7**
July, William **27**
Kitt, Sandra **23**
Larsen, Nella **10**
Lester, Julius **9**
Little, Benilde **21**
Lorde, Audre **6**
Madhubuti, Haki R. **7**
Major, Clarence **9**
Marshall, Paule **7**
McKay, Claude **6**
McKay, Nellie Yvonne **17**
McKinney-Whetstone, Diane **27**
McMillan, Terry **4, 17**
Morrison, Toni **2, 15**
Mowry, Jess **7**
Naylor, Gloria **10**
Painter, Nell Irvin **24**
Petry, Ann **19**
Pinkney, Jerry **15**
Randall, Dudley **8**
Redding, J. Saunders **26**

Redmond, Eugene **23**
Reed, Ishmael **8**
Ringgold, Faith **4**
Sanchez, Sonia **17**
Schomburg, Arthur Alfonso **9**
Shange, Ntozake **8**
Smith, Mary Carter **26**
Taylor, Mildred D. **26**
Thurman, Wallace **16**
Toomer, Jean **6**
Tyree, Omar Rashad **21**
Van Peebles, Melvin **7**
Verdelle, A. J. **26**
Walker, Alice **1**
Wesley, Valerie Wilson **18**
Wideman, John Edgar **5**
Williams, John A. **27**
Williams, Sherley Anne **25**
Wilson, August **7**
Wolfe, George C. **6**
Wright, Richard **5**

African American studies
Carby, Hazel **27**

African dance
Ailey, Alvin **8**
Fagan, Garth **18**
Primus, Pearl **6**

African folk music
Makeba, Miriam **2**
Nascimento, Milton **2**

African history
Chase-Riboud, Barbara **20**
Clarke, John Henrik **20**
Diop, Cheikh Anta **4**
Dodson, Howard, Jr. **7**
DuBois, Shirley Graham **21**
Hansberry, William Leo **11**
Harkless, Necia Desiree **19**
Jawara, Sir Dawda Kairaba **11**
Madhubuti, Haki R. **7**
Marshall, Paule **7**
van Sertima, Ivan **25**

African literature
Farah, Nuruddin **27**
Head, Bessie **28**

African Methodist Episcopal Church (AME)
Flake, Floyd H. **18**
McKenzie, Vashti M. **29**
Murray, Cecil **12**
Turner, Henry McNeal **5**
Youngblood, Johnny Ray **8**

African National Congress (ANC)
Baker, Ella **5**
Hani, Chris **6**
Ka Dinizulu, Mcwayizeni **29**
Kaunda, Kenneth **2**
Luthuli, Albert **13**
Mandela, Nelson **1, 14**
Mandela, Winnie **2**
Masekela, Barbara **18**
Mbeki, Thabo Mvuyelwa **14**
Nkomo, Joshua **4**

Webb, Wellington **3**
White, Michael R. **5**
Williams, Anthony **21**
Young, Andrew **3**
Young, Coleman **1, 20**

Civil rights
Abbott, Diane **9**
Abernathy, Ralph **1**
Agyeman, Jaramogi Abebe **10**
Al-Amin, Jamil Abdullah **6**
Alexander, Clifford **26**
Ali, Muhammad **2, 16**
Angelou, Maya **1**
Anthony, Wendell **25**
Aristide, Jean-Bertrand **6**
Arnwine, Barbara **28**
Baker, Ella **5**
Baker, Houston A., Jr. **6**
Baker, Josephine **3**
Bates, Daisy **13**
Baugh, David **23**
Beals, Melba Patillo **15**
Belafonte, Harry **4**
Bell, Derrick **6**
Bennett, Lerone, Jr. **5**
Berry, Mary Frances **7**
Berry, Theodore M. **31**
Biko, Steven **4**
Bishop Jr., Sanford D. **24**
Bond, Julian **2**
Booker, Simeon **23**
Boyd, John W., Jr. **20**
Brown, Elaine **8**
Brown, Tony **3**
Brown, Wesley **23**
Campbell, Bebe Moore **6, 24**
Carmichael, Stokely **5, 26**
Carter, Mandy **11**
Carter, Rubin **26**
Carter, Stephen L. **4**
Cary, Mary Ann Shad **30**
Cayton, Horace **26**
Chambers, Julius **3**
Chavis, Benjamin **6**
Clark, Septima **7**
Clay, William Lacy **8**
Cleaver, Eldridge **5**
Cleaver, Kathleen Neal **29**
Clyburn, James **21**
Cobbs, Price M. **9**
Cooper, Anna Julia **20**
Cosby, Bill **7, 26**
Crockett, George, Jr. **10**
Cunningham, Evelyn **23**
Davis, Angela **5**
Days, Drew S., III **10**
Dee, Ruby **8**
Diallo, Amadou **27**
Diggs, Charles C. **21**
Diggs-Taylor, Anna **20**
Divine, Father **7**
Dodson, Howard, Jr. **7**
Du Bois, W. E. B. **3**
Edelman, Marian Wright **5**
Ellison, Ralph **7**
Evers, Medgar **3**
Evers, Myrlie **8**
Farmer, James **2**
Fauntroy, Walter E. **11**

Forman, James **7**
Fortune, T. Thomas **6**
Franklin, John Hope **5**
Gaines, Ernest J. **7**
Gibson, William F. **6**
Gregory, Dick **1**
Grimké, Archibald H. **9**
Guinier, Lani **7, 30**
Haley, Alex **4**
Haley, George Williford Boyce **21**
Hall, Elliott S. **24**
Hamer, Fannie Lou **6**
Hampton, Fred **18**
Hampton, Henry **6**
Hansberry, Lorraine **6**
Harper, Frances Ellen Watkins **11**
Harris, Patricia Roberts **2**
Hastie, William H. **8**
Hawkins, Steven **14**
Hedgeman, Anna Arnold **22**
Height, Dorothy I. **2, 23**
Henderson, Wade J. **14**
Henry, Aaron **19**
Higginbotham, Jr., A. Leon **13, 25**
Hill, Jessie, Jr. **13**
Hill, Oliver W. **24**
Hilliard, David **7**
Holland, Endesha Ida Mae **3**
Hooks, Benjamin L. **2**
hooks, bell **5**
Horne, Lena **5**
Houston, Charles Hamilton **4**
Howard, M. William, Jr. **26**
Hughes, Langston **4**
Innis, Roy **5**
Jackson, Alexine Clement **22**
Jackson, Jesse **1, 27**
James, Daniel, Jr. **16**
Johnson, Eddie Bernice **8**
Johnson, James Weldon **5**
Johnson, Norma L. Holloway **17**
Jones, Elaine R. **7**
Jordan, Barbara **4**
Jordan, June **7**
Jordan, Vernon E. **3**
Julian, Percy Lavon **6**
Kennedy, Florynce **12**
Kenyatta, Jomo **5**
King, Bernice **4**
King, Coretta Scott **3**
King, Martin Luther, Jr. **1**
King, Martin Luther, III **20**
King, Preston **28**
King, Yolanda **6**
Lampkin, Daisy **19**
Lee, Spike **5, 19**
Lester, Julius **9**
Lewis, John **2**
Lorde, Audre **6**
Lowery, Joseph **2**
Makeba, Miriam **2**
Mandela, Nelson **1, 14**
Mandela, Winnie **2**
Martin, Louis E. **16**
Mays, Benjamin E. **7**
Mbeki, Thabo Mvuyelwa **14**
McDonald, Gabrielle Kirk **20**
McDougall, Gay J. **11**
McKissick, Floyd B. **3**

Meek, Carrie **6**
Meredith, James H. **11**
Metcalfe, Ralph **26**
Moore, Harry T. **29**
Morial, Ernest "Dutch" **26**
Morrison, Toni **2, 15**
Moses, Robert Parris **11**
Motley, Constance Baker **10**
Mowry, Jess **7**
Ndadaye, Melchior **7**
Nelson, Jill **6**
Newton, Huey **2**
Nkomo, Joshua **4**
Norman, Pat **10**
Norton, Eleanor Holmes **7**
Nzo, Alfred **15**
Parker, Kellis E. **30**
Parks, Rosa **1**
Patrick, Deval **12**
Patterson, Louise **25**
Patterson, Orlando **4**
Perkins, Edward **5**
Pinchback, P. B. S. **9**
Pleasant, Mary Ellen **9**
Plessy, Homer Adolph **31**
Poitier, Sidney **11**
Powell, Adam Clayton, Jr. **3**
Price, Hugh B. **9**
Ramaphosa, Cyril **3**
Randolph, A. Philip **3**
Reagon, Bernice Johnson **7**
Redding, Louis L. **26**
Riggs, Marlon **5**
Robeson, Paul **2**
Robinson, Jackie **6**
Robinson, Rachel **16**
Robinson, Randall **7**
Robinson, Sharon **22**
Robinson, Spottswood W. III **22**
Rowan, Carl T. **1, 30**
Rush, Bobby **26**
Rustin, Bayard **4**
Sané, Pierre Gabriel **21**
Seale, Bobby **3**
Shabazz, Attallah **6**
Shabazz, Betty **7, 26**
Shakur, Assata **6**
Simone, Nina **15**
Sisulu, Sheila Violet Makate **24**
Sleet, Moneta, Jr. **5**
Smith, Barbara **28**
Staupers, Mabel K. **7**
Sullivan, Leon H. **3, 30**
Thompson, Bennie G. **26**
Thurman, Howard **3**
Till, Emmett **7**
Trotter, Monroe **9**
Tsvangirai, Morgan **26**
Turner, Henry McNeal **5**
Tutu, Desmond **6**
Underwood, Blair **7**
Washington, Booker T. **4**
Washington, Fredi **10**
Watt, Melvin **26**
Weaver, Robert C. **8**
Wells-Barnett, Ida B. **8**
Wells, James Lesesne **10**
West, Cornel **5**
White, Walter F. **4**

Florida A & M University
Gaither, Alonzo Smith (Jake) **14**
Humphries, Frederick **20**

Florida Marlins baseball team
Sheffield, Gary **16**

Florida state government
Brown, Corrine **24**
Meek, Carrie **6**
Tribble, Isreal, Jr. **8**

Flouride chemistry
Quarterman, Lloyd Albert **4**

Folk music
Chapman, Tracy **26**
Charlemagne, Manno **11**
Jenkins, Ella **15**
Wilson, Cassandra **16**

Football
Allen, Marcus **20**
Amos, John **8**
Anderson, Jamal **22**
Barney, Lem **26**
Brown, James **22**
Brown, Jim **11**
Bruce, Isaac **26**
Butler, LeRoy III **17**
Carter, Cris **21**
Cunningham, Randall **23**
Davis, Terrell **20**
Dickerson, Eric **27**
Dungy, Tony **17**
Edwards, Harry **2**
Farr, Mel Sr. **24**
Gaither, Alonzo Smith (Jake) **14**
Gilliam, Frank **23**
Gilliam, Joe **31**
Green, Dennis **5**
Greene, Joe **10**
Grier, Roosevelt **13**
Hill, Calvin **19**
Lott, Ronnie **9**
McNair, Steve **22**
McNabb, Donovan **29**
Moon, Warren **8**
Moss, Randy **23**
Motley, Marion **26**
Newsome, Ozzie **26**
Pace, Orlando **21**
Page, Alan **7**
Payton, Walter **11, 25**
Perry, Lowell **30**
Rashad, Ahmad **18**
Rice, Jerry **5**
Robinson, Eddie G. **10**
Sanders, Barry **1**
Sanders, Deion **4, 31**
Sayers, Gale **28**
Shell, Art **1**
Simmons, Bob **29**
Simpson, O. J. **15**
Singletary, Mike **4**
Smith, Emmitt **7**
Stewart, Kordell **21**
Swann, Lynn **28**
Taylor, Lawrence **25**
Thomas, Derrick **25**

Upshaw, Gene **18**
Walker, Herschel **1**
Watts, J. C., Jr. **14**
Weathers, Carl **10**
White, Reggie **6**
Williams, Doug **22**

FOR
See Fellowship of Reconciliation

Forces Aemées Nationales Tchadiennes (FANT)

Forces Armées du Nord (Chad; FAN)
Déby, Idriss **30**
Habré, Hissène **6**

Ford Foundation
Thomas, Franklin A. **5**
Franklin, Robert M. **13**

Ford Motor Company
Goldsberry, Ronald **18**

Foreign policy
Bunche, Ralph J. **5**
Rice, Condoleezza **3**
Robinson, Randall **7**

Forest Club
Wilson, Sunnie **7**

40 Acres and a Mule Filmworks
Dickerson, Ernest **6, 17**
Lee, Spike **5, 19**

Foster care
Hale, Clara **16**
Hale, Lorraine **8**

Foundation for the Advancement of Inmate Rehabilitation
King, B. B. **7**

Freddie Mac Corporation
Baker, Maxine **28**

Freddie Mac Foundation
Baker, Maxine **28**

Freedom Farm Cooperative
Hamer, Fannie Lou **6**

Free Southern Theater (FST)
Borders, James **9**

FRELIMO
See Front for the Liberation of Mozambique

French West Africa
Diouf, Abdou **3**

FRODEBU
See Front for Democracy in Burundi

FROLINAT
See Front de la Libération Nationale

du Tchad (Chad)

FRONASA
See Front for National Salvation (Uganda)

Front de la Libération Nationale du Tchad (Chad;
Habré, Hissène **6**

Front for Democracy in Burundi (FRODEBU)
Ndadaye, Melchior **7**
Ntaryamira, Cyprien **8**

Front for National Salvation (Uganda; FRONASA)
Museveni, Yoweri **4**

Front for the Liberation of Mozambique (FRELIMO)
Chissano, Joaquim **7**
Machel, Graca Simbine **16**
Machel, Samora Moises **8**

FST
See Free Southern Theater

Full Gospel Baptist
Long, Eddie L. **29**

FullerMusic
Fuller, Arthur **27**

Funk music
Ayers, Roy **16**
Clinton, George **9**
Collins, Bootsy **31**
Richie, Lionel **27**
Watson, Johnny "Guitar" **18**

Fusion
Davis, Miles **4**
Jones, Quincy **8, 30**

Gangs
Williams, Stanley "Tookie" **29**

Gary, Williams, Parenti, Finney, Lewis & McManus
Gary, Willie E. **12**

Gary Enterprises
Gary, Willie E. **12**

Gary Post-Tribune
Ross, Don **27**

Gassaway, Crosson, Turner & Parsons
Parsons, James **14**

Gay Men of Color Consortium
Wilson, Phill **9**

Genealogy
Dash, Julie **4**

MPS
See Patriotic Movement of
Salvation

MRND
See Mouvement Revolutionnaire
National pour la Developpement

MTV Jams
Bellamy, Bill **12**

Multimedia art
Bailey, Xenobia **11**
Simpson, Lorna **4**

Muppets, The
Clash, Kevin **14**

Murals
Biggers, John **20**
Douglas, Aaron **7**
Lee-Smith, Hughie **5**
Walker, Kara **16**

Music Television (MTV)
Bellamy, Bill **12**
Chideya, Farai **14**
Powell, Kevin **31**

Musical composition
Ashford, Nickolas **21**
Blige, Mary J **20**
Bonga, Kuenda **13**
Braxton, Toni **15**
Burke, Solomon **31**
Caesar, Shirley **19**
Carter, Warrick L. **27**
Chapman, Tracy **26**
Charlemagne, Manno **11**
Charles, Ray **16**
Cleveland, James **19**
Cole, Natalie Maria **17**
Collins, Bootsy **31**
Combs, Sean "Puffy" **17**
Davis, Anthony **11**
Davis, Miles **4**
Davis, Sammy Jr. **18**
Ellington, Duke **5**
Elliott, Missy "Misdemeanor" **31**
Europe, James Reese **10**
Evans, Faith **22**
Fats Domino **20**
Fuller, Arthur **27**
George, Nelson **12**
Gillespie, Dizzy **1**
Gordy, Berry, Jr. **1**
Green, Al **13**
Hailey, JoJo **22**
Hailey, K-Ci **22**
Hammer, M. C. **20**
Handy, W. C. **8**
Hathaway, Donny **18**
Hayes, Isaac **20**
Hill, Lauryn **20**
Humphrey, Bobbi **20**
Isley, Ronald **25**
Jackson, Fred James **25**
Jackson, Michael **19**
James, Rick **17**
Jean-Baptiste, Marianne **17**

Jean, Wyclef **20**
Jerkins, Rodney **31**
Jones, Quincy **8**, **30**
Joplin, Scott **6**
Jordan, Montell **23**
Jordan, Ronny **26**
Kelly, R. **18**
King, B. B. **7**
León, Tania **13**
Lincoln, Abbey **3**
Marsalis, Wynton **16**
Master P **21**
Maxwell **20**
McClurkin, Donnie **25**
Mitchell, Brian Stokes **21**
Monica **21**
Moore, Chante **26**
Moore, Undine Smith **28**
Muse, Clarence Edouard **21**
Ndegéocello, Me'Shell **15**
Osborne, Jeffrey **26**
Pratt, Awadagin **31**
Prince **18**
Pritchard, Robert Starling **21**
Reagon, Bernice Johnson **7**
Redding, Otis **16**
Reid, Antonio "L.A." **28**
Roach, Max **21**
Run-DMC **31**
Rushen, Patrice **12**
Sangare, Oumou **18**
Silver, Horace **26**
Simone, Nina **15**
Simpson, Valerie **21**
Strayhorn, Billy **31**
Sweat, Keith **19**
Usher **23**
Van Peebles, Melvin **7**
Warwick, Dionne **18**
Washington, Grover, Jr. **17**

Music publishing
Combs, Sean "Puffy" **17**
Cooke, Sam **17**
Edmonds, Tracey **16**
Gordy, Berry, Jr. **1**
Handy, W. C. **8**
Humphrey, Bobbi **20**
Ice Cube **8**, **30**
Jackson, George **19**
Jackson, Michael **19**
James, Rick **17**
Knight, Suge **11**, **30**
Master P **21**
Mayfield, Curtis **2**
Prince **18**
Redding, Otis **16**
Ross, Diana **8**, **27**

Muslim Mosque, Inc.
X, Malcolm **1**

The Mystery
Delany, Martin R. **27**

Mysteries
Creagh, Milton **27**
DeLoach, Nora **30**
Himes, Chester **8**
Mickelbury, Penny **28**

Mosley, Walter **5**, **25**
Thomas-Graham **29**
Wesley, Valerie Wilson **18**

NAACP
See National Association for the
Advancement of Colored People

NAACP Image Awards
Lawrence, Martin **6**, **27**

NAACP Legal Defense Fund (LDF)
Bell, Derrick **6**
Chambers, Julius **3**
Edelman, Marian Wright **5**
Guinier, Lani **7**, **30**
Jones, Elaine R. **7**
Julian, Percy Lavon **6**
Marshall, Thurgood **1**
Motley, Constance Baker **10**

NABJ
See National Association of Black
Journalists

NAC
See Nyasaland African Congress

NACGN
See National Association of Colored
Graduate Nurses

NACW
See National Association of Colored Women

NAG
See Nonviolent Action Group

NASA
See National Aeronautics and Space
Administration

Nation
Wilkins, Roger **2**

Nation of Islam
See Lost-Found Nation of Islam

National Action Network
Sharpton, Al **21**

National Aeronautics and Space
Administration (NASA)
Bluford, Guy **2**
Bolden, Charles F., Jr. **7**
Gregory, Frederick D. **8**
Jemison, Mae C. **1**
McNair, Ronald **3**
Nichols, Nichelle **11**

National Afro-American Council
Fortune, T. Thomas **6**

National Alliance Party (NAP)
Fulani, Lenora **11**

National Association for the
Advancement of Colored
Anthony, Wendell **25**

WBC
See World Boxing Council

WCC
See World Council of Churches

Weather
Brown, Vivian **27**
Christian, Spencer **15**
McEwen, Mark **5**

Welfare reform
Bryant, Wayne R. **6**
Carson, Julia **23**
Williams, Walter E. **4**

West Indian folklore
Walcott, Derek **5**

West Indian folk songs
Belafonte, Harry **4**

West Indian literature
Guy, Rosa **5**
Kincaid, Jamaica **4**
Marshall, Paule **7**
McKay, Claude **6**
Walcott, Derek **5**

West Point
Davis, Benjamin O., Jr. **2**
Flipper, Henry O. **3**

West Side Preparatory School
Collins, Marva **3**

White House Conference on Civil Rights
Randolph, A. Philip **3**

Whitney Museum of American Art
Golden, Thelma **10**

WHO
See Women Helping Offenders

"Why Are You on This Planet?"
Yoba, Malik **11**

William Morris Talent Agency
Amos, Wally **9**

WillieWear Ltd.
Smith, Willi **8**

Wilmington 10
Chavis, Benjamin **6**

WOMAD
See World of Music, Arts, and Dance

Women Helping Offenders (WHO)
Holland, Endesha Ida Mae **3**

Women's Auxiliary Army Corps
See Women's Army Corp

Women's Army Corps (WAC)
Adams Early, Charity **13**
Cadoria, Sherian Grace **14**

Women's issues
Allen, Ethel D. **13**
Angelou, Maya **1, 15**
Ba, Mariama **30**
Baker, Ella **5**
Berry, Mary Frances **7**
Brown, Elaine **8**
Campbell, Bebe Moore **6, 24**
Cannon, Katie **10**
Cary, Mary Ann Shad **30**
Charles, Mary Eugenia **10**
Chinn, May Edward **26**
Christian-Green, Donna M. **17**
Clark, Septima **7**
Cole, Johnnetta B. **5**
Cooper, Anna Julia **20**
Cunningham, Evelyn **23**
Dash, Julie **4**
Davis, Angela **5**
Edelman, Marian Wright **5**
Elders, Joycelyn **6**
Fauset, Jessie **7**
Giddings, Paula **11**
Goldberg, Whoopi **4**
Gomez, Jewelle **30**
Grimké, Archibald H. **9**
Guy-Sheftall, Beverly **13**
Hale, Clara **16**
Hale, Lorraine **8**
Hamer, Fannie Lou **6**
Harper, Frances Ellen Watkins **11**
Harris, Alice **7**
Harris, Leslie **6**
Harris, Patricia Roberts **2**
Height, Dorothy I. **2, 23**
Hernandez, Aileen Clarke **13**
Hill, Anita **5**
Hine, Darlene Clark **24**
Holland, Endesha Ida Mae **3**
hooks, bell **5**
Jackson, Alexine Clement **22**
Joe, Yolanda **21**
Jordan, Barbara **4**
Jordan, June **7**
Lampkin, Daisy **19**
Larsen, Nella **10**
Lorde, Audre **6**
Marshall, Paule **7**
Mbaye, Mariétou **31**
McCabe, Jewell Jackson **10**
McKenzie, Vashti M. **29**
McMillan, Terry **4, 17**
Meek, Carrie **6**
Millender-McDonald, Juanita **21**
Mongella, Gertrude **11**
Morrison, Toni **2, 15**
Naylor, Gloria **10**
Nelson, Jill **6**
Nichols, Nichelle **11**
Norman, Pat **10**
Norton, Eleanor Holmes **7**
Painter, Nell Irvin **24**
Parker, Pat **19**
Rawlings, Nana Konadu Agyeman **13**
Ringgold, Faith **4**

Shange, Ntozake **8**
Simpson, Carole **6, 30**
Smith, Jane E. **24**
Terrell, Mary Church **9**
Tubman, Harriet **9**
Vanzant, Iyanla **17**
Walker, Alice **1**
Walker, Maggie Lena **17**
Wallace, Michele Faith **13**
Waters, Maxine **3**
Wattleton, Faye **9**
Williams, Fannie Barrier **27**
Winfrey, Oprah **2, 15**

Women's National Basketball Association (WNBA)
Bolton-Holifield, Ruthie **28**
Cooper, Cynthia **17**
Edwards, Teresa **14**
Griffith, Yolanda **25**
Holdsclaw, Chamique **24**
Lennox, Betty **31**
Leslie, Lisa **16**
McCray, Nikki **18**
Milton, DeLisha **31**
Peck, Carolyn **23**
Perrot, Kim **23**
Swoopes, Sheryl **12**
Thompson, Tina **25**
Williams, Natalie **31**

Women's Strike for Peace
King, Coretta Scott **3**

Worker's Party (Brazil)
da Silva, Benedita **5**

Women's United Soccer Association (WUSA)
Scurry, Briana **27**

Workplace equity
Hill, Anita **5**
Clark, Septima **7**
Nelson, Jill **6**
Simpson, Carole **6, 30**

Works Progress Administration (WPA)
Alexander, Margaret Walker **22**
Baker, Ella **5**
Blackburn, Robert **28**
Douglas, Aaron **7**
Dunham, Katherine **4**
Lawrence, Jacob **4**
Lee-Smith, Hughie **5, 22**
Wright, Richard **5**

World African Hebrew Israelite Community
Ben-Israel, Ben Ami **11**

World beat
Belafonte, Harry **4**
Fela **1**
N'Dour, Youssou **1**
Ongala, Remmy **9**

World Bank
Soglo, Nicéphore **15**

Cumulative Name Index

Volume numbers appear in **bold**

El-Hajj Malik El-Shabazz
   See X, Malcolm
El-Shabazz, El-Hajj Malik
   See X, Malcolm
Elder, (Robert) Lee 1934— **6**
Elder, Larry 1952— **25**
Elders, Joycelyn (Minnie) 1933— **6**
Ellerbe, Brian 1963— **22**
Ellington, Duke 1899-1974 **5**
Ellington, E. David 1960— **11**
Ellington, Edward Kennedy
   See Ellington, Duke
Elliott, Missy
   "Misdemeanor" 1971— **31**
Elliott, Sean 1968— **26**
Ellison, Ralph (Waldo)
   1914-1994 **7**
Elmore, Ronn 1957— **21**
Emeagwali, Dale 1954— **31**
Emeagwali, Philip 1954— **30**
Emecheta, Buchi 1944— **30**
Ephriam, Mablean 1949(?)— **29**
Epps, Omar 1973— **23**
Erving, Julius Winfield, II 1950— **18**
Ericsson-Jackson, Aprille
   19(?)(?)— **28**
Esposito, Giancarlo (Giusseppi
   Alessandro) 1958— **9**
Espy, Alphonso Michael
   See Espy, Mike
Espy, Mike 1953— **6**
Estes, Rufus 1857-19(?)(?) **29**
Estes, Simon 1938— **28**
Eubanks, Kevin 1957— **15**
Europe, (William) James Reese
   1880-1919 **10**
Evans, Darryl 1961— **22**
Evans, Ernest
   See Checker, Chubby
Evans, Faith 1973(?)(?)—**22**
Evans, Harry 1956(?)— **25**
Evans, Mari 1923— **26**
Eve 1979— **29**
Everett, Francine 1917-1999 **23**
Everett, Ronald McKinley
   See Karenga, Maulana
Evers, Medgar (Riley) 1925-1963 **3**
Evers, Myrlie 1933— **8**
Evora, Cesaria 1941— **12**
Ewing, Patrick Aloysius 1962— **17**
Eyadéma, (Étienne)
   Gnassingbé 1937— **7**
Fagan, Garth 1940—— **18**
Faison, George William 1946— **16**
Farah, Nuruddin 1945— **27**
Farmer, Forest J(ackson) 1941— **1**
Farmer, James 1920— **2**
Farr, Mel 1944— **24**
Farrakhan, Louis 1933— **2, 15**
Fats Domino 1928— **20**
Fattah, Chaka 1956— **11**
Fauntroy, Walter
   E(dward) 1933— **11**
Fauset, Jessie (Redmon)
   1882-1961 **7**
Favors, Steve 1948— **23**
Feelings, T(h)om(a)s 1933— **11**
Fela 1938— **1**
Ferguson, Roger W. 1951— **25**

Ferrell, Rachelle 1961— **29**
Fielder, Cecil (Grant) 1963— **2**
Fields, C. Virginia 1946— **25**
Fields, Cleo 1962— **13**
Fields, Evelyn J. 1949— **27**
Fishburne, Larry 1962— **4, 22**
Fishburne, Laurence, III
   See Fishburne, Larry
Fisher, Rudolph John Chauncey
   1897-1934 **17**
Fitzgerald, Ella 1918-1996 **8, 18**
Flack, Roberta 1940— **19**
Flake, Floyd H. 1945— **18**
Fletcher, Alphonse, Jr. 1965— **16**
Flipper, Henry O(ssian)
   1856-1940 **3**
Flood, Curt(is) 1963— **10**
Folks, Byron
   See Allen, Byron
Forbes, Audrey Manley 1934— **16**
Ford, Harold Eugene, Jr. 1970— **16**
Foreman, George 1948— **1, 15**
Forman, James 1928— **7**
Fortune, T(imothy) Thomas
   1856-1928 **6**
Foster, Ezola 1938— **28**
Foster, Henry W., Jr. 1933— **26**
Fox, Rick 1969— **27**
Fox, Ulrich Alexander
   See Fox, Rick
Fox, Vivica A. 1964— **15**
Foxx, Jamie 1967— **15**
Foxx, Redd 1922-1991 **2**
Franklin, Aretha 1942— **11**
Franklin, Carl 1949— **11**
Franklin, Hardy R. 1929— **9**
Franklin, John Hope 1915— **5**
Franklin, Kirk 1970— **15**
Franklin, Robert
   M(ichael) 1954— **13**
Franks, Gary 1954(?)— **2**
Frazier, Edward Franklin
   1894-1962 **10**
Frazier, Joe 1944— **19**
Frazier-Lyde, Jacqui 1961— **31**
Freeman, Al(bert Cornelius),
   Jr. 1934— **11**
Freeman, Cathy 1973— **29**
Freeman, Charles
   Eldridge 1933— **19**
Freeman, Harold P. 1933— **23**
Freeman, Leonard 1950— **27**
Freeman, Marianna 1957— **23**
Freeman, Morgan 1937— **2, 20**
Freeman, Yvette **27**
French, Albert 1943— **18**
Fresh Prince, The
   See Smith, Will
Friday, Jeff 1964(?)— **24**
Fudge, Ann (Marie) 1951(?)— **11**
Fuhr, Grant 1962— **1**
Fulani, Lenora (Branch) 1950— **11**
Fuller, Arthur 1972— **27**
Fuller, Charles (Henry) 1939— **8**
Fuller, Meta Vaux Warrick
   1877-1968 **27**
Fuller, S. B. 1895-1988 **13**
Fuller, Solomon Carter, Jr.
   1872-1953 **15**

Gaines, Ernest J(ames) 1933— **7**
Gaither, Jake 1903-1994 **14**
Gantt, Harvey (Bernard) 1943— **1**
Garnett, Kevin 1976— **14**
Garrison, Zina 1963— **2**
Garvey, Marcus 1887-1940 **1**
Gary, Willie Edward 1947— **12**
Gaston, Arthur G(eorge) 1892— **4**
Gates, Henry Louis, Jr. 1950— **3**
Gates, Sylvester James,
   Jr. 1950— **15**
Gay, Marvin Pentz, Jr.
   See Gaye, Marvin
Gaye, Marvin 1939-1984 **2**
Gayle, Helene D(oris) 1955— **3**
Gentry, Alvin 1954— **23**
George, Nelson 1957— **12**
Gibson, Althea 1927— **8**
Gibson, Johnnie Mae 1949— **23**
Gibson, Josh 1911-1947 **22**
Gibson, Kenneth Allen 1932— **6**
Gibson, Tyrese
   See Tyrese
Gibson, William F(rank) 1933— **6**
Giddings, Paula (Jane) 1947— **11**
Gillespie, Dizzy 1917-1993 **1**
Gillespie, John Birks
   See Gillespie, Dizzy
Gilliam, Frank 1934(?)— **23**
Gilliam, Joe, Jr. 1950-2000 **31**
Gilliam, Sam 1933— **16**
Giovanni, Nikki 1943— **9**
Giovanni, Yolande Cornelia, Jr.
   See Giovanni, Nikki
Gist, Carole 1970(?)— **1**
Givens, Robin 1965— **4, 25**
Glover, Danny 1948— **1, 24**
Glover, Nathaniel, Jr. 1943— **12**
Glover, Savion 1974— **14**
Goines, Donald 1937(?)-1974 **19**
Goldberg, Whoopi 1955— **4**
Golden, Marita 1950— **19**
Golden, Thelma 1965— **10**
Goldsberry, Ronald 1942— **18**
Gomes, Peter J(ohn) 1942— **15**
Gomez, Jewelle 1948— **30**
Gomez-Preston, Cheryl 1954— **9**
Goode, Mal(vin Russell)
   1908-1995 **13**
Goode, W(oodrow)
   Wilson 1938— **4**
Gooden, Dwight 1964— **20**
Gooding, Cuba, Jr. 1968— **16**
Gordon, Dexter 1923-1990 **25**
Gordon, Ed(ward Lansing,
   III) 1960— **10**
Gordon, Pamela 1955— **17**
Gordone, Charles 1925-1995 **15**
Gordy, Berry, Jr. 1929— **1**
Goreed, Joseph
   See Williams, Joe
Goss, Tom 1946— **23**
Gossett, Louis, Jr. 1936— **7**
Gourdine, Simon
   (Peter) 1940— **11**
Graham, Lawrence Otis 1962— **12**
Graham, Stedman 1951(?)— **13**
Grant, Gwendolyn Goldsby
   19(?)(?)— **28**

Smith, Will 1968— **8, 18**
Smith, Willi (Donnell) 1948-1987 **8**
Sneed, Paula A. 1947— **18**
Snipes, Wesley 1962— **3, 24**
Soglo, Nicéphore 1935— **15**
Somé, Malidoma
   Patrice 1956— **10**
Sosa, Sammy 1968— **21**
Sowell, Thomas 1930— **2**
Soyinka, (Akinwande
   Olu)Wole 1934— **4**
Spaulding, Charles Clinton
   1874-1952 **9**
Spencer, Anne 1882-1975 **27**
Spikes, Dolores Margaret
   Richard 1936— **18**
Sprewell, Latrell 1970— **23**
St. Jacques, Raymond
   1930-1990 **8**
St. John, Kristoff 1966— **25**
St. Julien, Marlon 1972— **29**
Stackhouse, Jerry 1974— **30**
Stallings, George A(ugustus),
   Jr. 1948— **6**
Stanford, John 1938— **20**
Stanton, Robert 1940— **20**
Staples, Brent 1951— **8**
Stargell, Willie "Pops"
   1940(?)-2001 **29**
Staton, Candi 1940(?)— **27**
Staupers, Mabel K(eaton)
   1890-1989 **7**
Stearnes, Norman "Turkey"
   1901-1979 **31**
Steele, Claude Mason 1946— **13**
Steele, Lawrence 1963— **28**
Steele, Shelby 1946— **13**
Steinberg, Martha Jean
   1930(?)-2000 **28**
Stephens, Charlotte Andrews
   1854-1951 **14**
Stevens, Yvette
   See Khan, Chaka
Steward, Emanuel 1944— **18**
Stewart, Alison 1966(?)— **13**
Stewart, Kordell 1972— **21**
Stewart, Paul Wilbur 1925— **12**
Stokes, Carl B(urton) 1927— **10**
Stokes, Louis 1925— **3**
Stone, Angie 1965(?)— **31**
Stone, Charles Sumner, Jr.
   See Stone, Chuck
Stone, Chuck 1924— **9**
Stone, Toni 1921-1996 **15**
Stout, Juanita Kidd 1919-1998 **24**
Strawberry, Darryl 1962— **22**
Strayhorn, Billy 1915-1967 **31**
Street, John F. 1943(?)— **24**
Stringer, C. Vivian 1948— **13**
Sudarkasa, Niara 1938— **4**
Sullivan, Leon H(oward)
   1922— **3, 30**
Sullivan, Louis (Wade) 1933— **8**
Summer, Donna 1948— **25**
Swann, Lynn 1952— **28**
Sweat, Keith 1961(?)— **19**
Swoopes, Sheryl Denise 1971— **12**
Swygert, H. Patrick 1943— **22**
Sykes, Roosevelt 1906-1984 **20**

Tafari Makonnen
   See Haile Selassie
Tamia 1975— **24**
Tanner, Henry Ossawa
   1859-1937 **1**
Tate, Eleanora E. 1948— **20**
Tate, Larenz 1975— **15**
Tatum, Art 1909-1956 **28**
Taulbert, Clifton
   Lemoure 1945— **19**
Taylor, Billy 1921— **23**
Taylor, Charles 1948— **20**
Taylor, Helen (Lavon Hollingshed)
   1942-2000 **30**
Taylor, John (David
   Beckett) 1952— **16**
Taylor, Kristin Clark 1959— **8**
Taylor, Lawrence 1959— **25**
Taylor, Meshach 1947(?)— **4**
Taylor, Mildred D. 1943— **26**
Taylor, Regina 1959— **9**
Taylor, Susan L. 1946— **10**
Taylor, Susie King 1848-1912 **13**
Terrell, Dorothy A. 1945— **24**
Terrell, Mary (Elizabeth) Church
   1863-1954 **9**
The Artist
   See Prince
The Rock
   See Johnson, Dwayne "The Rock"
Thigpen, Lynne 19(?)(?)— **17**
Thomas, Alma Woodsey
   1891-1978 **14**
Thomas, Clarence 1948— **2**
Thomas, Debi 1967— **26**
Thomas, Derrick 1967-2000 **25**
Thomas, Frank Edward,
   Jr. 1968— **12**
Thomas, Franklin
   A(ugustine) 1934— **5**
Thomas, Irma 1941— **29**
Thomas, Isiah (Lord III)
   1961— **7, 26**
Thomas, Rufus 1917— **20**
Thomas, Vivien (T.) 1910-1985 **9**
Thomas-Graham, Pamela
   1963(?)— **29**
Thompson, Bennie G. 1948— **26**
Thompson, John W. 1949— **26**
Thompson, Tazewell (Alfred,
   Jr.) 1954— **13**
Thompson, Tina 1975— **25**
Thugwane, Josia 1971— **21**
Thurman, Howard 1900-1981 **3**
Thurman, Wallace Henry
   1902-1934 **16**
Till, Emmett (Louis) 1941-1955 **7**
Tillman, George, Jr. 1968— **20**
Tolliver, William (Mack) 1951— **9**
Toomer, Jean 1894-1967 **6**
Toomer, Nathan Pinchback
   See Toomer, Jean
Torry, Guy 19(?)(?)— **31**
Tosh, Peter 1944-1987 **9**
Touré, Amadou
   Toumani 1948?— **18**
Touré, Sekou 1922-1984 **6**
Towns, Edolphus 1934— **19**
Townsend, Robert 1957— **23**

Townsend, Robert 1957— **4**
Tribble, Isreal, Jr. 1940— **8**
Trotter, Donne E. 1950— **28**
Trotter, (William) Monroe
   1872-1934 **9**
Trouillot, Ertha Pascal
   See Pascal-Trouillot, Ertha
Tsvangirai, Morgan 1952(?)— **26**
Tubbs Jones, Stephanie 1949— **24**
Tubman, Harriet 1820(?)-1913 **9**
Tucker, C. DeLores 1927— **12**
Tucker, Chris 1973(?)— **13, 23**
Tucker, Cynthia (Anne) 1955— **15**
Tucker, Rosina Budd Harvey
   Corrothers 1881-1987 **14**
Ture, Kwame
   See Carmichael, Stokely
Turnbull, Walter 1944— **13**
Turner, Henry McNeal
   1834-1915 **5**
Turner, Tina 1939— **6, 27**
Tutu, Desmond (Mpilo) 1931— **6**
Tutuola, Amos 1920-1997 **30**
Tyree, Omar Rashad 1969— **21**
Tyrese 1978— **27**
Tyson, Cicely 1933— **7**
Tyson, Mike 1966— **28**
Tyson, Neil de Grasse 1958— **15**
Uggams, Leslie 1943— **23**
Underwood, Blair 1964— **7, 27**
Union, Gabrielle 1973— **31**
Unseld, Wes 1946— **23**
Upshaw, Eugene, Jr. 1945— **18**
Usher 1978(?)— **23**
Usry, James L. 1922— **23**
Ussery, Terdema Lamar,
   II 1958— **29**
Utendahl, John 1956— **23**
van Sertima, Ivan 1935— **25**
Van Peebles, Mario (Cain)
   1957(?)— **2**
Van Peebles, Melvin 1932— **7**
Vance, Courtney B. 1960— **15**
VanDerZee, James (Augustus
   Joseph) 1886-1983 **6**
Vandross, Luther 1951— **13**
Vann, Harold Moore
   See Muhammad, Khallid Abdul
Vanzant, Iyanla 1953— **17**
Vaughan, Sarah (Lois)
   1924-1990 **13**
Vaughn, Mo 1967— **16**
Verdelle, A. J. 1960— **26**
Vereen, Ben(jamin
   Augustus) 1946— **4**
Vieira, Joao 1939— **14**
Vincent, Marjorie Judith
   1965(?)— **2**
Vincent, Mark
   See Diesel, Vin
Von Lipsey, Roderick 1959— **11**
wa Ngengi, Kamau
   See Kenyatta, Jomo
wa Thiong'o, Ngugi 1938— **29**
Waddles, Charleszetta
   (Mother) 1912— **10**
Waddles, Mother
   See Waddles, Charleszetta
   (Mother)